R. Taylor.

D0334838

PARISH PRAYERS

By the same author

YOUR CHILD'S BAPTISM
  (Christian Commitment Series)

THE GOSPELS
  (Prayer Book Commentaries)

THE CATECHISM AND THE ORDER OF CONFIRMATION
  (Prayer Book Commentaries)

TOTAL CHRISTIANITY

CHRIST'S AMBASSADORS
  (Christian Foundations Series No. 8)

LENT WITH PILGRIM'S PROGRESS (Editor)
  (Mowbrays)

CONTEMPORARY PARISH PRAYERS

He is Editor of the Prayer Book Commentaries and Joint Editor
of the Christian Foundations Series

PARISH PRAYERS

Compiled and edited
by
FRANK COLQUHOUN

With a Foreword by
THE ARCHBISHOP OF YORK

HODDER AND STOUGHTON
LONDON SYDNEY AUCKLAND TORONTO

*New Material © Frank Colquhoun 1967. First
published 1967. Sixth impression 1975. ISBN
0 340 02622 7. Printed in Great Britain for Hodder
and Stoughton Limited, St. Paul's House, Warwick
Lane, London, EC4P 4AH by Richard Clay (The
Chaucer Press), Ltd., Bungay, Suffolk.*

To
the Parochial Clergy of the
Church of England
in grateful memory of
my Father
The Reverend
ROBERT WOODS COLQUHOUN
(1857–1940)

FOREWORD

BY HIS GRACE THE ARCHBISHOP OF YORK
THE MOST REV. AND RT. HON. F. D. COGGAN, P.C., D.D.

I WELCOME this book warmly. I welcome it because I believe that it will prove an enrichment to the public worship of the Church and a help to many parish clergy on all kinds of occasions. The Editor, who has done his work against the background of long parochial experience, has produced things new and old out of the treasure-store of the Church's life of prayer—the selection of nearly 1,800 prayers is indeed a catholic one.

The pattern of the book is Anglican: about a third of the prayers are arranged under the heading *The Church's Year*. But I can well envisage the book being used by those whose church allegiance is not Anglican; indeed, it may prove another aid to union, for prayer joins Christians of varying traditions together as nothing else can.

Again, I welcome the book because I think it will help the individual at his prayers, and not only the congregation. We all know what it is to hit an arid patch in our prayer-life. At such a time it is of help to prime the pump of prayer with the aid of the prayers of other, and greater, Christians. This collection offers us just such help as we need.

May the book be widely used and greatly blessed.

DONALD EBOR.

Bishopthorpe
York

CONTENTS

x

AUTHOR'S PREFACE

THE design of this book is to make available a collection of prayers sufficiently broad and comprehensive to meet the varied needs of the parochial clergy throughout the course of their ministry. It has been my endeavour to make the work as complete as possible, so as to provide not only for the normal round of church services and meetings but also for those special and occasional needs which arise from time to time in the life of a parish.

This inclusive character is, I would claim, the particular feature of the book. Indeed, it is the only real justification for the publishing of yet another manual of prayers when so many excellent ones are already in print. The same factor also accounts for the size of the book. A work which deliberately sets out to meet all parochial needs and occasions cannot fail to assume somewhat big proportions. As will be seen, just on 1,800 prayers are here brought together, very few of which are duplicated. Whatever difficulty may be felt in the handling of so large-scale a collection will, I hope, be more than offset by the advantage of having such a wide selection of prayers compactly available in a single volume.

It may be helpful if I offer to those who are intending to use the book some words of explanation with regard to the prayers themselves and the way in which they have been arranged.

THE PRAYERS

To facilitate reference, the prayers are numbered, and also arranged under suitable headings and titles. They are derived from a variety of sources.

1. Inevitably I have drawn freely on the existing collections of prayers to which reference has already been made. In acknowledging my indebtedness to them I would at the same time express my sincere thanks to the authors and publishers in question for the permission given me to reproduce prayers of which they are the copyright owners. In certain cases it has not been easy, or even possible, to trace the authorship and origins of prayers. If inadvertently any copyrights have been infringed, I would offer my apologies to those concerned and assure them that amends will be made in any subsequent editions.

2. A good many other prayers are taken from older collections of widely varying traditions, some of them long out of print. This

has been possible as the result of a certain amount of research in the Reading Room of the British Museum, by kind permission of the Director. In this way I have gained access to some useful material which would not otherwise have come my way.

3. A third source has been the official prayer books of the Churches of the Anglican Communion. *The Book of English Collects*, edited by J. W. Suter, Jr. (Harper, New York, 1940), has been a considerable help in this connection. I have also drawn upon the Church of Scotland's *Book of Common Order* (1940) and *Prayers for the Christian Year* (1952), and from the Church of South India's more recent *Book of Common Worship* (1963). No prayers have been taken directly from the proposed Prayer Book of 1928, since this is so readily available and in such widespread use.

4. Some of the prayers are new and make their appearance here for the first time. I am most grateful to Canon Basil Naylor and Prebendary George Timms for their prayers on the Seven Last Words for use on Good Friday which they contributed at my request. Prayers have also been written for this book by Bishop Frank Houghton, Canon Gordon Hewitt, and the Rev. Leo Stephens-Hodge, and I wish to express my thanks to them; as also to the Rev. J. R. W. Stott, who has generously allowed me to make use of a number of prayers from his own personal collection.

5. Finally, the book contains a number of prayers of my own, considerably more indeed than I had originally intended. I can only say by way of explanation that most of them were written to fill certain gaps or meet specific needs, or to supplement other prayers where this seemed to be desirable.

In general, the prayers follow the traditional patterns, as regards both form and language. The attempts so far made to produce "contemporary" prayers are not, in my opinion, altogether happy and I am doubtful of their suitability for church services, except in special circumstances. On the other hand, I have studiously endeavoured to avoid prayers which have an archaic ring about them, or are couched in artificial language, or which are too long and verbose. I am convinced that prayers for use in public worship should be short, simple, and direct. For this reason some of the prayers reproduced in this collection have been deliberately altered or abbreviated (sometimes both). Where this has been done, an asterisk (*) has been attached to the name of the author or source. Prayers (mostly anonymous) which have been modified to such an extent as to be more or less rewritten have the word "Adapted" added at the end. Where no author's name is given, the origin of the prayer is unknown.

I venture to add a final word under this heading on the vexed issue of "prayers for the dead", a limited number of which find their place in this collection. The commemoration of the faithful departed in the prayers of the Church raises acute questions in the minds of some faithful churchmen; and from my own point of view I can fully appreciate this. The position is by no means simple or straightforward. On the one hand, it cannot be denied that the English reformers in the sixteenth century deliberately eliminated from the Church's common prayer any explicit petitions for the departed, due no doubt to the association of the practice with the "Romish doctrines concerning Purgatory". It is therefore a fact that since 1552 such prayers have had no place in the authorized formularies of the Church. On the other hand, it must equally be recognized that since the Reformation—and not only since the Oxford Movement—the thought of many Anglicans has undergone a change in this direction; and in any case the fact has to be faced that in one form or another prayers for the dead in Christ are now in fairly common use throughout the Church.

It therefore seemed to me that, whatever my personal opinions, it would be unrealistic to exclude this element from a collection of prayers which claims to be truly comprehensive and which seeks to meet as wide a variety of need as possible. It is scarcely necessary to add that a prayer book, like a hymn book, can do no more than offer a selection of material; those who use such books are at liberty to choose what they like and to ignore the rest.

THE ARRANGEMENT

A glance at the Contents page will show that the book is divided into six main parts.

Part I, the largest section of all, comprises prayers for the Church's Year. Not only is provision made for the Christian seasons and festivals in general; there are also prayers for each Sunday and Holy Day, based on the appointed Epistles and Gospels. The majority of the prayers in this part of the book are of a devotional character. It is hoped that they will prove suitable for use after the third collect at Mattins and Evensong, or after the sermon; or for devotional use in preparation for Holy Communion, whether personal or corporate.

Part II supplies a selection of prayers for various occasions in parish life which lie outside the Church's Year as such and for which additional prayers are required. Included in this section are those special Sundays which are set apart by authority for some particular observance, as for example Education Sunday and Remembrance Sunday; also parish festivals of one kind or another, such as a dedication festival, a missionary festival, and harvest thanksgiving. Provision is also made for such occasions as the week of prayer for Christian unity, a civic service, a gift day, and so on.

Part III is concerned with the sacraments of the gospel and other ordinances of the Church. Here, for instance, are prayers of preparation for Baptism, Confirmation, Holy Communion, marriage; a form for the renewal of baptismal vows; thanksgivings for childbirth; prayers for use in ministry to the sick; and prayers for use at a funeral service.

Part IV contains a wide selection of prayers of an intercessory nature: for the needs of the world, the work of the Church at home and overseas, and for the whole life of man. These prayers to a large extent supplement those in the second part of the book, and there is a good deal of cross reference between the two sections.

Part V is given over to devotional prayers. In some measure it supplements the prayers for the Christian Year (Part I), but its scope is wider. Thus, in addition to prayers for various Christian graces, there are opening and concluding prayers, morning and evening prayers, acts of praise and thanksgiving, and benedictions and doxologies.

Part VI contains prayers which are supplementary to the collection as a whole. Here particular provision is made for parish meetings and committees of one kind or another. There are also vestry, pulpit, and offertory prayers, as well as prayers for such occasional needs as a quiet day, a recital of music, a religious drama, and the dedication of a house.

This arrangement of the book means of necessity that the various sections overlap one another to a considerable degree. To take a simple illustration: prayers for the spread of the gospel throughout the world will be found not only in the intercessions for the Church Overseas (Part IV) but also in the prayers for Epiphanytide (Part I) and for a Missionary Festival (Part II). Likewise prayers for the home and family life occur in several parts of the book, such as in the service for Mothering Sunday (Part II), among the marriage prayers (Part III), and in the relevant section of the intercessory prayers (Part IV).

It may be thought that this arrangement is somewhat complicated and confusing; but I venture to suggest that once the general plan of the book has been clearly grasped, those who use it regularly will experience little difficulty in finding their way about it. I feel sure that there is value in having prayers conveniently grouped together for particular days and occasions; so that, for example, on any great festival or special Sunday all the needful material is found together in one place, thus avoiding the necessity of having to turn to different parts of the book for the various prayers required. In any case, the key to the matter lies in the Subject Index at the end.

Special care has been taken to ensure that this is as complete and accurate as possible, so as to facilitate simple and speedy reference.

This collection of *Parish Prayers* is the fruit of over twenty years spent in the pastoral ministry of the Church. The task of gathering the material and putting it together has occupied a good deal of my spare time during the past three or four years. It has also involved others in work and I am very grateful to Mrs. Madeline Cowan and Miss Joyce Manning for the help they have given me in the typing of the manuscript. My thanks are further due to Mr. Leonard Cutts, of Messrs. Hodder and Stoughton, for his patience and encouragement in connection with this undertaking; and not least to His Grace the Archbishop of York, who has honoured me by writing the Foreword.

I offer the work to the parochial clergy of the Church of England in the hope that it may not only meet a genuine need on their part but also make a small contribution to the enrichment of the Church's life and worship at the parish level.

FRANK COLQUHOUN

Southwark Cathedral,
London, S.E.1

I
THE CHURCH'S YEAR

ADVENT

1

WE beseech thee, O Lord, to purify our consciences by thy daily visitation; that when thy Son our Lord cometh, he may find in us a mansion prepared for himself; through the same Jesus Christ our Lord. *Gelasian Sacramentary*

2

Make us, we beseech thee, O Lord our God, watchful and heedful in awaiting the coming of thy Son Christ our Lord; that when he shall come and knock, he shall find us not sleeping in sin, but awake and rejoicing in his praises; through the same Jesus Christ our Lord.
Gelasian Sacramentary

3

Grant, O Almighty God, that as thy blessed Son Jesus Christ at his first advent came to seek and to save that which was lost, so at his second and glorious appearing he may find in us the fruits of the redemption which he wrought; who liveth and reigneth with thee and the Holy Spirit, one God world without end.
Scottish Prayer Book

4

O God, who didst send thy blessed Son into the world to be the Saviour of all men, and hast promised that he will come again to be our Judge: We beseech thee to increase in us the spirit of watchfulness and prayer, that in the day of his appearing the lamps of our spirit may be trimmed and burning, and we may enter with joy into the marriage supper of the Lamb. Hear us, O heavenly Father, of thy mercy, through the same Jesus Christ our Lord.

5

O Almighty Father, fountain of light and salvation, we adore thine infinite goodness in sending thy only begotten Son into the world that, believing in him, we may not perish but have everlasting life; and we pray thee that, through the grace of his first advent to save the world, we may be made ready to meet him at his second advent to judge the world; through the same thy Son Jesus Christ our Lord. *W. Walsham How*

6

O God, Father of mercies, who didst so love the world that thou didst give thine only begotten Son to take our nature upon him for us men and for our salvation: Grant to us who by his first coming have been called into thy kingdom of grace, that we may always abide in him, and be found watching and ready when he shall come again to call us to thy kingdom of glory; through the same Jesus Christ our Lord. *H. Stobat*

7

O Lord Jesus Christ, who at thy first coming didst warn us to prepare for the day when thou shalt come to be our judge: Mercifully grant that being awake from the sleep of sin, we may always be watching and intent upon the work thou hast given us to do; who livest and reignest with the Father and the Holy Spirit, ever one God, world without end. *W. E. Scudamore*

8

Keep us, O Lord, while we tarry on this earth, in a serious seeking after thee, and in an affectionate walking with thee, every day of our lives; that when thou comest, we may be found not hiding our talent, nor serving the flesh, nor yet asleep with our lamp unfurnished, but waiting and longing for our Lord, our glorious God for ever and ever. *Richard Baxter**

9

O Thou, who hast foretold that thou wilt return to judgment in an hour that we are not aware of, grant us grace to watch and pray always, that whether thou shalt come at even, or at midnight, or in the morning, we may be found among the number of those servants who shall be blessed in watching for their Lord, to whom be all glory now and for evermore. *Non-Jurors' Prayer Book*

10

Stir up our hearts, O Lord, we beseech thee, to prepare the way of thine only begotten Son; so that when he cometh we may be found watching, and serve thee with a pure and ready will; through the same thy Son Jesus Christ our Lord.

11

Thou who with thine own mouth hast avouched that at midnight, at an hour when we are not aware, the Bridegroom shall come: Grant that the cry, The Bridegroom cometh, may sound evermore in our ears, that so we be never unprepared to meet him, our Lord and Saviour Jesus Christ. *Lancelot Andrewes*

The "Great Os" of Advent 12

Particularly suitable for the last week of Advent.
Each may be followed by the response:

Even so, come, Lord Jesus

O Wisdom, that camest out of the mouth of the Most High, reaching from one end to another, firmly and gently ordering all things: Come and teach us the way of understanding.

O Adonai, Captain of the house of Israel, who didst appear to Moses in the flame of the burning bush, and gavest him the law on Sinai: Come and deliver us with thine outstretched arm.

O Root of Jesse, who standest for an ensign of the people, before whom kings shall shut their mouths, to whom the nations shall seek: Come and deliver us and tarry not.

O Key of David, Sceptre of the house of Israel, who openest and no man shutteth, and shuttest and no man openeth: Come and bring forth out of the prison-house him that is bound.

O Day-spring from on high, Brightness of Eternal Light, and Sun of righteousness: Come and enlighten those who sit in darkness and the shadow of death.

O King of nations, thou for whom they long, the Cornerstone that makest both one: Come and save thy creatures whom thou didst fashion from the dust of the earth.

O Emmanuel, our King and Lawgiver, the Desire of all nations and their Saviour: Come and save us, O Lord our God.

FIRST SUNDAY IN ADVENT

Preparation for the coming 13

ALMIGHTY and everlasting God, who orderest all things in heaven and on earth: We give thee thanks and praise that thou didst make all ages a preparation for the coming of thy Son, our blessed Redeemer. Prepare us for the coming of him whom thou dost send, and grant that of his fullness we may all receive; through the same Jesus Christ our Lord. *Prayers for the Christian Year*

14

Grant, O Lord, that we who once again prepare for the commemoration of the coming of thy Son, our Saviour Jesus Christ, may so direct our hearts to the fulfilment of thy law, that he may now accept our hosannas, and in the life to come receive us in the heavenly Sion; where with thee and the Holy Ghost he liveth and reigneth, ever one God, world without end.   *Richard D. Acland*

Beginning of the new Church Year   15

O Lord God, author of our salvation, who desirest that all men should live in Christ Jesus: Grant that we may begin this new year in our spiritual life knowing our need to increase our faith and to enlarge our repentance; assist us in thy mercy to live as in a state of grace, and to regard this life as part of our eternal inheritance; grant that difficulties may not overthrow us nor temptations defeat us, but that we may go forward on our journey through this life in the spirit of courage and godliness; through the same Jesus Christ our Lord.   *Euchologium Anglicanum*

Love for our neighbour   16

O God, who hast included all the commandments in the one commandment of love, so that if we love not our neighbour we cannot fulfil thy law: We humbly pray thee, create in our hearts such a sincere love of one another, that we may be children of our Father in heaven, and true disciples of thy Son, Jesus Christ our Lord.   *Henry Alford*

17

O Eternal God, who has taught us in thy holy Word that love is the fulfilling of the law: Pour into our hearts that best of all thy gifts, that loving our neighbour as ourselves we may live as children of the day and of the light; for the glory of thy Son Jesus Christ our Lord.   *Frank Colquhoun*

The night is far spent   18

O Lord, who hast taught us in thy holy Word that the night is far spent and the day is at hand: Awaken us from all sloth and slumber, that we may live as sons of light and of the day, putting on the breastplate of faith and love, and for a helmet the hope of salvation; for his sake who died for us and rose again, even our Lord Jesus Christ.
Based on Romans 13. 11, 12; 1 Thessalonians 5. 8

Behold thy King cometh   19

O Great and glorious God, holy and immortal, who searches out the policies of nations and tries the hearts of men: Come, we pray thee, in judgment, upon the nations of the world; come and bring to destruction all that is contrary to thy holy will for mankind, and cause the counsels of the wicked to perish. Come, O Lord, into our hearts, and root out from them all that thou seest, and we cannot see, to be unlike the Spirit of thy Son, Jesus Christ our Lord.

Harold Anson

SECOND SUNDAY IN ADVENT (BIBLE SUNDAY)

Christ in the Old Testament 20

ALMIGHTY God, who in many and various ways didst speak to thy chosen people by the prophets, and hast given us, in thy Son our Saviour Jesus Christ, the fulfilment of the hope of Israel: Hasten, we beseech thee, the coming of the day when all things shall be subject to him, who liveth and reigneth with thee and the Holy Spirit, ever one God, world without end.

Church of South India

The Bible 21

O Gracious God and most merciful Father, who hast vouchsafed us the rich and precious jewel of thy holy Word: Assist us with thy Spirit that it may be written in our hearts to our everlasting comfort, to reform us, to renew us according to thine own image, to build us up into the perfect building of thy Christ, and to increase us in all heavenly virtues. Grant this, O heavenly Father, for the same Jesus Christ's sake. *Geneva Bible*

22

Almighty and most merciful God, who hast given the Bible to be the revelation of thy great love to man, and of thy power and will to save him: Grant that our study of it may not be made vain by the callousness or the carelessness of our hearts, but that by it we may be confirmed in penitence, lifted to hope, made strong for service, and, above all, filled with true knowledge of thee and of thy Son Jesus Christ. *George Adam Smith*

23

Grant, O Lord, that we may love to read thy holy Word, wherein is wisdom, wherein is the royal law, wherein are the living oracles of God; and may so read therein that we may know and love and serve thee better; through Jesus Christ our Lord.

24

Almighty God, who hast revealed thyself to us in Jesus Christ thy Son, and given thy Word and Spirit to testify of him: We bless thee for the men of faith whom thou didst inspire to write the holy Scriptures; for the labours of all who have preserved, copied, and

translated them; for the wisdom given to those who have inter-
preted them; and for that measure of light and understanding thou
hast granted unto us; and we pray that, learning what is thy will, we
may ever obey thee and live to thy glory; through the same Jesus
Christ our Lord. *James M. Todd*
See also prayers before Bible study, 1731-8

Joy and peace 25

O God of hope, fill us, we beseech thee, with all joy and peace
in believing, that we may abound in hope by the power of thy Holy
Spirit, and show forth our thankfulness to thee in trustful and
courageous lives; through Jesus Christ our Lord.
The Kingdom, the Power, and the Glory

The things that cannot be shaken 26

Eternal God, who rulest the world from everlasting to everlasting:
Speak to our hearts when men faint for fear, and the love of many
grows cold, and there is distress of nations upon earth. Keep us
resolute and steadfast in the things that cannot be shaken; and
make us to lift up our eyes and behold, beyond the things that are
seen and temporal, the things that are unseen and eternal; through
Jesus Christ our Lord.

The coming of the Lord 27

O Lord God, heavenly Father, who through thy Son hast revealed
to us that heaven and earth shall pass away: We beseech thee to keep
us steadfast in thy Word and in true faith; graciously guard us from
all sin and preserve us amid all temptations, so that our hearts may
not be overcharged with the cares of this life, but at all times in
watchfulness and prayer we may await the return of thy Son and
joyfully cherish the expectation of our eternal salvation; through the
same Jesus Christ our Lord. *United Lutheran Church, U.S.A.*

28

O God, by whose command the order of time runs its course:
Forgive, we pray thee, the impatience of our hearts; make perfect
that which is lacking in our faith; and, while we tarry the fulfilment
of thy promises, grant us to have a good hope because of thy word;
through Jesus Christ our Lord. *Gregory Nazianzen*

29

O Heavenly Father, whose most dearly beloved Son has come once
to save the world, and will come again to judge the world: Help us,
we pray thee, to watch like servants who wait for the coming of

their lord. May we abound in hope through the power of the Holy
Ghost; and, having this hope, may we purify ourselves by thy grace,
even as Christ is pure. Grant this, O Father, for his sake and for the
glory of thy holy name.   *W. Walsham How**

Ministers of Christ   30

WE pray thee, Lord, for all who minister in thy name in thy
Church. Strengthen them in time of weakness, and direct
them in all their work for thee. Give to them the spirit of power,
and of love, and of sound mind, that they may diligently preach
thy Word and set forth thy glory, to the building up of thy Church
and the salvation of souls; through Jesus Christ our Lord.
                    *Prayers of the World-Wide Church**

The Lord is judge   31

O Lord Jesus Christ, before whose judgment-seat we must all
appear and give account of the things done in the body: Grant,
we beseech thee, that when the books are opened in that day, the
faces of thy servants may not be ashamed; through thy merits, O
blessed Saviour, who livest and reignest with the Father and the
Holy Spirit, one God, world without end.
                    Scottish Prayer Book

Until the Lord come   32

O Christ our God, who wilt come to judge the world in the manhood which thou hast assumed: We pray thee to sanctify us wholly,
that in the day of thy coming we may be raised up to live and reign
with thee for ever.   *Church of South India*

Prepared hearts   33

O God, who didst send thy messengers and prophets to prepare
the way of thy Son before him: Grant that our Lord when he cometh
may find in us a dwelling prepared for himself; through the same
Jesus Christ our Lord, who came to take our nature upon him that
he might bring many sons unto glory, and now with thee and the
Holy Spirit liveth and reigneth, ever one God, world without end.
                    A New Prayer Book

Faithfulness   34

O Lord our God, in whose hands is the issue of all things, and
who requirest from thy stewards not success but faithfulness: Give
us such faith in thee and in thy sure purposes, that we measure not

our lives by what we have done or failed to do, but by our obedience to thy holy will; through Jesus Christ our Lord.   *Daily Prayer*
See also prayers for the Ember Weeks, 611–41

See also prayers for the Ember Weeks, 611–41

FOURTH SUNDAY IN ADVENT

Joy and peace 35

O LORD God, who by thy holy apostle hast taught us always to rejoice in thee, and to be anxious for nothing: Grant, we beseech thee, that, making our requests known to thee, we may be partakers of the peace that passeth all understanding, which thou hast promised us in thy Son, Jesus Christ our Lord.
Based on Philippians 4. 4–7

God so loved the world 36

Lord God Almighty, King of glory and love eternal, worthy art thou at all times to receive adoration, praise, and blessing; but especially at this time do we praise thee for the sending of thy Son our Saviour Jesus Christ, for whom our hearts do wait, and to whom, with thee and the Holy Spirit, one God, be honour and dominion, now and for ever.   *Prayers for the Christian Year*

The Coming One 37

Almighty Father, whose blessed Son at his coming amongst us brought redemption unto his people, and peace to men of goodwill: Grant that, when he shall come again in glory to judge the world and to make all things new, we may be found ready to receive him, and enter into his joy; through the same our Lord Jesus Christ.
Frederick B. Macnutt

Preparation for Christmas 38

Grant, we beseech thee, Almighty God, that the solemn feast of our redemption which is now at hand, may help us both in this present life, and further us towards the attaining of thine eternal joy in that which is to come; through Jesus Christ our Lord.
Prayers for the Christian Year

39

O God, who didst promise that thy glory should be revealed, and that all flesh should see it together: Stir up our hearts, we beseech thee, to prepare the way of thine only begotten Son; and pour out upon us thy loving kindness, that we who are afflicted by reason of our sins may be refreshed by the coming of our Saviour, and may behold his glory; who with thee and the Holy Spirit liveth and reigneth one God, world without end.   *James M. Todd*

40

O God our heavenly Father, who by the birth of thy Son Jesus Christ has visited us with thy salvation: Grant that as we welcome our Redeemer his presence may be shed abroad in our hearts and homes with the light of heavenly joy and peace; and in all our preparations for this holy season help us to think more of others than of ourselves, and to show forth our gratitude to thee for thine unspeakable gift, even the same Jesus Christ our Lord.   *Adapted*

CHRISTMAS

Christmas gladness 41

ALMIGHTY God, who hast revealed the glory of thy love in the face of Jesus Christ, and called us by him to live as thy children: Fill our hearts, as we remember his nativity, with the gladness of this great redemption; that we may join in the heavenly song of glory to God in the highest, on earth peace, and goodwill towards men; through the same Jesus Christ our Lord.   *John Hunter* *

Room for Jesus 42

O Father, who hast declared thy love to men by the birth of the Holy Child at Bethlehem: Help us to welcome him with gladness and to make room for him in our common days; so that we may live at peace with one another and in goodwill with all thy family; through the same thy Son, Jesus Christ our Lord.

A New Prayer Book

Light and love 43

O Almighty God, who by the birth of thy holy Child Jesus hast given us a great light to dawn upon our darkness: Grant, we pray thee, that in his light we may see light to the end of our days; and bestow upon us, we beseech thee, that most excellent Christmas gift of charity to all men, that so the likeness of thy Son may be formed in us, and that we may have the ever brightening hope of everlasting life; through the same Jesus Christ our Lord.

William Knight

Joy to the world 44

O Gracious Father, who sent not thy Son into the world to condemn the world, but that the world through him might be saved: Fulfil the good tidings of thine angel and bring great joy to all people through the nativity of him who is the Prince of Peace; to whom with thee and the Holy Ghost be glory in the highest, now and for evermore.

God's unspeakable gift 45

O God, who as at this time didst send thy Son to be the Saviour of the world, teach us to thank thee for thine unspeakable gift.

Help us to hate the evil that he came to destroy, and to receive the eternal life that he lived and died to bestow; that so we may love thee with all our power and may serve our day and generation according to thy will; through the same Jesus Christ our Lord.

H. Bisseker

His love and ours 46

Almighty God, as we keep the festival of the divine humility of thy Son Jesus Christ, we beseech thee to bestow upon us such love and charity as were his, to whom it was more blessed to give than to receive, and who came not to be ministered unto but to minister; that in his name we may consecrate ourselves to the service of all who are in need; through the same Jesus Christ our Lord.

Adapted

Angels, shepherds, wise men 47

O Heavenly Father, as we celebrate again the nativity of thy Son our Saviour, we pray that, like the angels, we may sing his joyful praise; like the shepherds, we may go even to Bethlehem and see the Child lying in a manger; and like the wise men, we may offer to him our worship, and give him the love and loyalty of our hearts; through the same Jesus Christ our Lord.   *Frank Colquhoun*

For our sakes he became poor 48

Merciful and most loving God, by whose will and bountiful gift Jesus Christ our Lord humbled himself that he might exalt mankind; and became flesh that he might restore in us the most celestial image; and was born of the Virgin that he might uplift the lowly: Grant unto us the inheritance of the meek, perfect us in thy likeness, and bring us at last to rejoice in beholding thy beauty, and with all thy saints to glorify thy grace; through the same Jesus Christ our Lord.   *Gallican Sacramentary*

The Saviour of the world 49

O God our heavenly Father, who hast manifested thy love towards mankind in sending thine only Son into the world, that all might live through him: We pray thee to speed forth these good tidings of great joy to every nation, that the people who sit in darkness and in the shadow of death may see the great light and may come, with us, to worship him whose name is called Wonderful, even our Lord and Saviour Jesus Christ.   *Frank Colquhoun*

Children and the home 50

Blessed Lord, who by thy wonderful birth at Bethlehem hast sanctified childhood and the life of the home: Be with us, we pray thee, in our homes this Christmastide. Bless all children who are dear to us and make them glad with the knowledge of their Saviour's love. Remember in thy mercy the children who are neglected or ill-treated, and those who are unwanted and unloved; and enter thyself, dear Master, into the unhappy homes of our land, and so make all things new; for the honour of thy holy name.

Frank Colquhoun

A CHRISTMAS CAROL SERVICE

Before a carol service   51

O LORD Jesus Christ, at whose birth the praises of God were sung by a multitude of the heavenly host: Unite our voices now with theirs, and grant that in our Christmas carols we may worship thee with joyful lips and humble hearts; for the glory of thy great name. *J. R. W. Stott*

52

Almighty God, our heavenly Father, who hast given us this season of holy joy: We bow before thee with adoring reverence and lift up our hearts with thankful praise. Fill us, we beseech thee, with the gladness of thy great redemption, and enable us to join in the angels' song, Glory to God in the highest and on earth peace, good-will toward men; through Jesus Christ our Lord.

Prayers for the Christian Year

The Bidding Prayer   53

Beloved in Christ, be it this Christmastide our care and delight to prepare ourselves to hear again the message of the angels, and in heart and mind to go even unto Bethlehem and see this thing which is come to pass, and the Babe lying in a manger.

Therefore let us read and mark in Holy Scripture the tale of the loving purposes of God from the first days of our disobedience unto the glorious redemption brought us by this Holy Child: and let us make this place glad with our carols of praise.

But first let us pray for the needs of his whole world; for peace and goodwill over all the earth; for unity and brotherhood within the Church he came to build, ~~and especially in the dominions of our sovereign lady Queen Elizabeth.~~

And because this of all things would rejoice his heart, let us at this time remember in his name the poor and the helpless, the cold, the hungry, and the oppressed; the sick and them that mourn; the lonely and the unloved; the aged and the little children; all those who know not the Lord Jesus, or who love him not, or who by sin have grieved his heart of love.

Lastly, let us remember before God all those who rejoice with us, but upon another shore and in a greater light, that multitude which no man can number, whose hope was in the Word made flesh, and with whom, in this Lord Jesus, we for evermore are one.

These prayers and praises let us humbly offer up to the Throne of Heaven, in the words which Christ himself hath taught us:

Our Father, which art in heaven, Hallowed be thy Name. Thy kingdom come. Thy will be done, in earth as it is in heaven. Give us this day our daily bread. And forgive us our trespasses, As we forgive them that trespass against us. And lead us not into temptation; But deliver us from evil: For thine is the kingdom, the power, and the glory, For ever and ever. Amen.

The Almighty God bless us with his grace: Christ give us the joys of everlasting life; and unto the fellowship of the citizens above may the King of Angels bring us all. *King's College, Cambridge*

At the end of a carol service 54

O Almighty God, we beseech thee, give us grace to receive thy Son our Lord Jesus Christ, and to believe on his name, whose birth we have this day celebrated in sacred song; and grant that abiding steadfast in thy faith, we may evermore rejoice in thy salvation; through the merits of the same thy Son, who liveth and reigneth with thee and the Holy Spirit, one God, world without end.

Liturgy of the Catholic Apostolic Church★

55

O God, to whom glory is sung in the highest, while on earth peace is proclaimed to men of good will: Grant that good will to us thy servants, cleanse us from all our sins, and give perpetual peace to us and to all people; through thy mercy, O God, who art blessed, and dost govern all things, world without end.

Mozarabic Sacramentary

56

O Lord our God, who didst manifest thy love toward us by sending thine only begotten Son into the world, that we might live through him: Grant us, by thy Holy Spirit, the precious gift of faith, whereby we may know that the Son of God has come; and help us to join our praises with the song of the heavenly host: Glory to God in the highest, and on earth peace, goodwill towards men.

James M. Todd

33

THE CHRISTMAS CRIB

57

I N the faith of Christ, and in thy name, O God most holy, do we hallow this crib of Christmas, to set before the eyes of thy children the great love and humility of Jesus Christ thine only Son; who for us men, and for our salvation, came down as at this time from heaven, and was incarnate by the Holy Ghost of the Virgin Mary his mother, and was made Man; to whom with thee and the same Spirit be all honour, majesty, glory, and worship, now and world without end.   *After the Third Collect*

58

O Holy Jesus, who to deliver us from the power of darkness didst deign to be born as a child and laid in a manger: Let the light of thy love shine evermore in our hearts, and make us an offering meet for thine honour; who livest and reignest with the Father and the Holy Spirit, one God, world without end.

59

O God the Son, highest and holiest, who didst humble thyself to share our birth and our death: Bring us with the shepherds and wise men to kneel before thy lowly cradle, that we may come to sing with thine angels thy glorious praises in heaven; where with the Father and the Holy Spirit thou livest and reignest God world without end.   *After the Third Collect*

60

May the humility of the shepherds, the perseverance of the wise men, the joy of the angels, and the peace of the Christ-child be God's gifts to you this Christmas time, and always.

CHRISTMAS EVE

Redeemer and Judge   **61**

O GOD, who makest us glad with the yearly remembrance of the birth of thy only Son Jesus Christ: Grant that as we joyfully receive him for our Redeemer, so we may with sure confidence behold him when he shall come to be our Judge; who livest and reigneth with thee and the Holy Ghost, ever one God, world without end.   *Gelasian Sacramentary*

The true light   **62**

O God, who hast made this most sacred night to shine with the illumination of the true light: Grant, we beseech thee, that as we have known the mystery of that light upon earth, we may also perfectly enjoy it in heaven; through the same Jesus Christ our Lord.   *Gelasian Sacramentary*

The shepherds   63

O God, who before all others didst call shepherds to the cradle of thy Son: Grant that by the preaching of the gospel the poor, the humble, and the forgotten, may know that they are at home with thee; through Jesus Christ our Lord.   *Church of South India*

Darkness and light   64

Almighty God, who by the incarnation of thy only begotten Son hast banished the darkness of this world, and by his glorious birth didst enlighten this most holy night: Drive away from us, we beseech thee, the darkness of sin, and illuminate our hearts with the glory of thy grace; through the same our Lord Jesus Christ.

Christ in our hearts   65

We pray thee, O Lord, to purify our hearts that they may be worthy to become thy dwelling place. Let us never fail to find room for thee, but come and abide in us that we also may abide in thee, who as at this time wast born into the world for us, and dost live and reign, King of kings and Lord of lords, now and for evermore.   *William Temple*

Adoration   66

O God, who as on this night, by a glorious company of the heavenly host, didst proclaim the birth of thy Son our Saviour upon earth: With heart and voice we join in their holy song, praising thee and saying, Glory to God in the highest, and on earth peace, good-will toward men; through the same Jesus Christ our Lord.
Prayers for the Christian Year

Before the Blessing   67

May God Almighty, who by the incarnation of his only-begotten Son drove away the darkness of the world, and by his glorious birth enlightened this most holy night, drive away from us the darkness of sin, and enlighten our hearts with the light of Christian grace.
Prayers for the Christian Year

CHRISTMAS DAY

Christmas morning   68

Let us now go even unto Bethlehem and see this thing which is come to pass, which the Lord hath made known unto us.

For unto us a Child is born, unto us a Son is given, and the government shall be upon his shoulder; and his name shall be called Wonderful, Counsellor, The Mighty God, The Everlasting Father, The Prince of Peace. *Luke 2. 15; Isaiah 9. 6*

Gloria in excelsis Deo 69

Glory be to God in the highest, and on earth peace, goodwill towards men; for unto us is born this day a Saviour, who is Christ the Lord. We praise thee, we bless thee, we glorify thee, we give thanks to thee, for this greatest of thy mercies, O Lord God, heavenly King, God the Father almighty. *Thomas Ken*

The Word made flesh 70

Most merciful God, who hast so loved the world as to give thine only begotten Son, that whosoever believeth in him should not perish but have everlasting life: Vouchsafe unto us, we humbly pray thee, the precious gift of faith, whereby we may know that the Son of God is come; and, being rooted and grounded in the mystery of the Word made flesh, may have power to overcome the world, and gain the blessed immortality of heaven; through the merits of the same incarnate Christ, who liveth and reigneth with thee in the unity of the Holy Spirit, ever one God, world without end. *Book of Common Order*

Christmas Worship 71

Grant us, O God, such love and wonder that, with humble shepherds, wise men and pilgrims unknown, we may come and adore the holy Babe, the heavenly King, and with our gifts worship and serve him, our Lord and Saviour Jesus Christ.

James Ferguson

The spirit of reconciliation 72

O God our Father, who didst send thy Son to be born for us as the Prince of Peace, and whom the innumerable company of the heavenly host did praise, saying, Glory to God in the highest, on earth peace, good will towards men: Grant that the kingdoms of this world may become the kingdom of Christ and learn from him the way of peace. Send forth among all men the spirit of goodwill and reconciliation, so that all thy children may live together as one family, praising thee and blessing thee for the great redemption which thou hast wrought for us, through Jesus Christ our Lord.

*William Knight**

Peace on earth 73

O God our Father, who by the glorious birth of thy Son didst enlighten the darkness of the world: We pray that the light of his presence may shine more and more in the lives of men; that being filled with his spirit of goodwill, the nations may inherit that gift of peace which he came to bring. We ask it in his name.

Hugh Martin

For the sorrowful and afflicted 74

O Father of all, who didst give thy Son Jesus Christ to be born as on this day in the rude and bare stable of Bethlehem: We would remember before thee those for whom Christmas brings little joy. We pray for those who pass through sickness or suffering, and for all in hospital. Comfort the mourners and send thy peace into their souls. Give courage to those who suffer through oppression and persecution, and make plain the way of help. Grant to us all by acts of kindness and words of goodwill to spread the spirit of him whose birthday we keep, even thy Son, our Lord and Saviour Jesus Christ.

The divine image 75

Merciful and most loving God, by whose will and bountiful gift thine eternal Son humbled himself that he might exalt mankind, and became flesh that he might renew in us the divine image: Perfect us in thy likeness, and bring us at last to rejoice in beholding thy beauty, and, with all thy saints, to glorify thy grace; through the same Jesus Christ our Lord. *Prayers for the Christian Year*

Room for Christ 76

Most merciful God, for whose chosen handmaid and her Holy Babe there was no room in the inn at Bethlehem: Help us all by thy Spirit to make room for the Christ in our common days, that his peace and joy may fill our hearts, and his love flow through our lives to the blessing of others; for his name's sake.

Prayers for the Christian Year

SUNDAY AFTER CHRISTMAS

The adoption of sons 77

GOD of all grace, who didst in the fullness of time send Jesus Christ thy Son to be born of a woman, that he might redeem the sons of men and make them the sons of God: Accept our endless praise for this thy mercy; and grant that the Spirit of thy Son may so dwell in our hearts that we may evermore serve and worship thee with the freedom of thy children; through the same Jesus Christ our Lord. *Adapted*

78

O Almighty God, Creator and Ruler of all things, whom the heaven of heavens cannot contain, and who yet dost condescend to give us the Spirit of adoption whereby we cry Abba, Father: Grant unto us thy children that we may ever rejoice in thy fatherly protection, and be bound one to another in brotherly love; that using the freedom of sons in all holiness and purity of life, we may grow up into him who is not ashamed to call us brethren, even thy Son Jesus Christ our Lord.

Born of the Virgin Mary
79

O merciful Jesus, who when thou tookest upon thee to deliver man, didst not abhor the Virgin's womb: Vouchsafe evermore to dwell in the hearts of us thy servants. Inspire us with thy purity; strengthen us with thy might; guide us into thy truth; that we may conquer every adverse power, and be wholly devoted to thy service and conformed to thy will, to the glory of God the Father.

Thy kingdom come
80

O God, who when the fullness of the time was come didst send forth thy Son, born of a woman, to redeem mankind: Hasten the day of his dominion in all lands, and the increase of his government and of peace; to whom with thee and the Holy Ghost be all honour and glory, world without end.

Thanksgiving
81

O God, who hast given us grace at this time to celebrate the birth of our Saviour Jesus Christ: We laud and magnify thy glorious name for the countless blessings which he hath brought unto us; and we beseech thee to grant that we may ever set forth thy praise in joyful obedience to thy will; through the same Jesus Christ our Lord.

Scottish Prayer Book

THE CIRCUMCISION

The Name of Jesus
82

O ALMIGHTY God, who hast given unto thy Son Jesus Christ the name which is above every name, and hast taught us that there is none other whereby we may be saved: Mercifully grant that as thy faithful people have comfort and peace in his name, so they may ever labour to publish it unto all nations; through the same Jesus Christ our Lord.　　　　*Scottish Prayer Book*

83

O Saviour of the world, who as on this day wast called Jesus, according to the word of the angel: Fulfil unto us, we beseech thee, the gracious promise of that holy name, and, of thy great mercy, save thy people from their sins; who, with the Father and the Holy Ghost, livest and reignest one God world without end.

Irish Prayer Book

84

O God, who hast made the most glorious name of our Lord Jesus Christ, thine only-begotten Son, to be exceeding sweet and supremely lovable to thy faithful servants: Mercifully grant that all who devoutly venerate this name of Jesus on earth may in this life receive thy holy comfort, and in the life to come attain thine unending joy; through the same Jesus Christ our Lord.

Sarum Missal

85

O God, who didst ordain thine only-begotten Son to be the Saviour of mankind, and didst command that his name should be called Jesus: Mercifully grant that as we do love and honour his holy name upon earth, so we may evermore enjoy the vision of him in heaven; through the same thy Son Jesus Christ our Lord.

The inward circumcision **86**

O Heavenly Father, whose blessed Son, that he might keep the law which he came to fulfil, received as on this day the outward circumcision: Cleanse our minds by the inward circumcision from all incentives to sin, that we may worship thee in spirit and glory in the same Christ Jesus, now and for evermore.

87

O Almighty God our heavenly Father, whose blessed Son was circumcised and kept the law for us, that we might enter into the glorious liberty of the sons of God: Grant us grace to bring forth the fruits of his righteousness, and ever more to serve thee with pure hearts and holy lives; through the same Jesus Christ our Lord.

The new year **88**

Eternal God, who makest all things new, and abidest for ever the same: Grant us to begin this year in thy faith, and to continue it in thy favour; that, being guided in all our doings, and guarded all our days, we may spend our lives in thy service, and finally, by thy grace, attain the glory of everlasting life; through Jesus Christ our Lord.

W. E. Orchard

89

O Almighty God, who alone art without variableness or shadow of turning, and hast safely brought us through the changes of time to the beginning of another year: We beseech thee to pardon the sins we have committed in the year that is past, and give us grace that we may spend the remainder of our days to thy honour and glory; through Jesus Christ our Lord.   *Irish Prayer Book*

90

O Lord Christ, who art both Alpha and Omega, the beginning and the end, and whose years shall not fail: Grant us so to pass through the coming year with faithful hearts, that in all things we may please thee and glorify thy name; who livest and reignest with the Father and the Holy Ghost, ever one God, world without end.   *Mozarabic Sacramentary**

91

O Eternal Lord Christ, who art the First and the Last, and the Living One, and who in thy mercy hast brought us safely to the beginning of another year: Accept our thanksgiving for the blessings of the past, renew our strength and courage in the present, and direct all our way in the future; for thy honour and glory, who art the same yesterday, to-day, and for ever.   *Frank Colquhoun*
See also prayers for a Watchnight Service, 642–55

The worship of the wise men 92

ALMIGHTY and everlasting God, who hast made known the incarnation of thy Son by the bright shining of a star, which when the wise men beheld they adored thy majesty and presented costly gifts: Grant that the star of thy righteousness may always shine in our hearts, and that for our treasure we may give to thy service ourselves and all that we have; through the same Jesus Christ our Lord. *Gelasian Sacramentary**

93

O Blessed Jesus, who by the shining of a star didst manifest thyself to them that sought thee: Show thy heavenly light to us, and give us grace to follow until we find thee; finding, to rejoice in thee; and rejoicing, to present to thee ourselves, our souls and bodies, for thy service for evermore: for thine honour and glory.
Edward Hawkins

94

O God, who by the leadings of thy providence didst bring wise men from far to give homage to Jesus, born to be King of all: Help us, who by various ways are led to Christ, humbly and thankfully to adore him with our gifts, and as our costliest treasure to present before him ourselves for his honour and service, now and always.
James Ferguson

95

O God, who by the guidance of a star didst manifest to the Gentiles the glory of thine only begotten Son: Grant us grace that, being led by the light of thy Holy Spirit, we may, in adoring love and lowliest reverence, yield ourselves to thy service; that thy kingdom of righteousness and peace may be advanced among all nations, to the glory of thy name; through Jesus Christ our Lord.
Book of Common Order

96

Almighty Lord God, who didst give thy Son Jesus Christ to be the light of the world: We praise and magnify thy holy name that in him thou hast revealed the wonder of thy saving love to men. With those of old who brought their tribute to his feet, confessing him as King of heaven and earth, we now present the worship of our grateful hearts, beseeching thee to give us grace to give ourselves to thee; through the same Jesus Christ our Lord.   *James M. Todd*

97

O God, who by the shining of a star didst guide the wise men to behold thy Son, our Lord: Show us thy heavenly light, and give us grace to follow until we find him, and, finding him, rejoice. And grant that as they presented gold, frankincense, and myrrh, we now may bring him the offering of a loving heart, an adoring spirit, and an obedient will; for his honour, and for thy glory, O God most high.
Prayers for the Christian Year

Following the star   97

Lord Jesus, our Master, go with us while we travel to the heavenly country; that, following thy star, we may not wander in the darkness of this world's night, while thou, who art our Way, and Truth, and Life dost shine within us to our journey's end; for thy mercy's sake.
After Mozarabic Sacramentary

Christ for the world   99

Almighty and everlasting God, the brightness of faithful souls, who didst bring the Gentiles to thy light and made known unto them him who is the true light, and the bright and morning star: Fill the world, we beseech thee, with thy glory, and show thyself by the radiance of thy light unto all nations; through Jesus Christ our Lord.   *Gregorian Sacramentary**

100

O God, who by a star didst guide the wise men to the worship of thy Son: Lead, we pray thee, to thyself the wise and the great in every land, that unto thee every knee may bow, and every thought be brought into captivity; through Jesus Christ our Lord.
Church of South India

101

Lord Jesus Christ, who in the offerings of the wise men didst receive an earnest of the worship of the nations: Grant that thy Church may never cease to proclaim the good news of thy love, that all men may come to worship thee as their Saviour and King, who livest and reignest world without end.   *George Appleton*

102

O God, who didst manifest thy only begotten Son to the Gentiles, and hast commanded thy Church to preach the gospel to every creature: Bless all thy servants who are labouring for thee in distant lands. Have compassion upon the heathen and upon all who know thee not, and lead them by thy Holy Spirit to him who is the light of the world, even the same Jesus Christ our Lord.

Robert Nelson

103

We thank thee, O God, that thou didst give thy Son Jesus Christ to be the light of the world, and that in him thou hast revealed thy glory and the wonder of thy saving love. Help us to love thee who hast so loved us; strengthen us for the service of thy kingdom; and grant that the light of Christ may so shine throughout the world that men everywhere may be drawn to him who is the Saviour and Lord of all, and the whole earth be filled with thy glory; through the same Jesus Christ our Lord. *Let Us Pray*

104

Almighty God, who hast manifested thy Son Jesus Christ to be a light to mankind: Grant that we thy people, being nourished by thy word and sacraments, may be strengthened to show forth to all men the unsearchable riches of Christ, so that he may be known, adored and obeyed, to the ends of the earth; who liveth and reigneth with thee and the Holy Spirit, one God, world without end.

Church of South India

See also prayers for a Missionary Festival (753–65) and for the Church Overseas (1343–81)

The baptism of Jesus

105

Almighty God, who at the baptism of thy blessed Son Jesus Christ in the river Jordan didst manifest his glorious Godhead: Grant, we beseech thee, that the brightness of his presence may shine in our hearts, and his glory be set forth in our lives; through the same Jesus Christ our Lord. *Scottish Prayer Book*

106

Lord Jesus Christ, who didst humble thyself to take the baptism of sinful men, and wast forthwith declared to be the Son of God: Grant that we who have been baptized into thee may rejoice to be the sons of God, and servants of all; for thy name's sake, who with the Father and the Holy Spirit livest and reignest ever one God, world without end. *Church of South India*

A living sacrifice 107

ALMIGHTY God, who to wise men who sought him didst manifest the Incarnation of thy Son by the bright shining of a star: Grant that, as they presented unto him gifts, gold and frankincense and myrrh, so we also out of our treasures may offer to him ourselves, a living sacrifice acceptable in thy sight; through him who for our sakes was born on earth as a little child, Jesus Christ our Lord
Frederick B. Macnutt

108

O Thou, in whom we live and move and have our being: We offer and present unto thee ourselves, all that we are and have, our thoughts and our desires, our words and our deeds, to be a living and continual sacrifice. We are not our own; therefore we would glorify thee in our bodies and our spirits, which are thine; through Jesus Christ our Lord. *William Knight**

109

O Almighty God, who by thy holy Apostle hast taught us to present our bodies a living sacrifice, holy, acceptable unto thee, as our reasonable service: Hear us, we beseech thee, as we now come to thee in the name of Jesus Christ; and give us grace that we may dedicate ourselves wholly to thy service, and henceforth live only to thy glory; through the same Jesus Christ our Lord.
E. M. Goulburn

Jesus among the doctors 110

O Lord Jesus Christ, who didst sit lowly in the midst of the doctors, both hearing them and asking them questions: Give unto thy servants that humility of heart, and willingness to learn, without which no man can find wisdom; to the glory of thy holy name.
Daily Prayer

Our Father's business 111

O Blessed Lord, who in the days of thy earthly childhood didst earnestly desire to be about thy Father's business: Give us the grace of thy Holy Spirit early to seek thee and evermore to follow thee; that being continuously aided by thy grace, we may be exercised in thy service; who livest and reignest with the Holy Spirit, world without end. *Henry Alford*

Childhood 112

Almighty and everlasting God, whose blessed Son took upon him our manhood and increased in wisdom and stature: Grant that all Christian children may learn that fear of the Lord which is the beginning of wisdom, and as they grow in stature may also grow in love to thee; through the same Christ our Lord.

Harold Riley

SECOND SUNDAY AFTER EPIPHANY

Diversity of gifts 113

ALMIGHTY God, who hast set in thy Church some with gifts to teach and help and administer, in diversity of operation but of the same Spirit: Grant to all such, we beseech thee, grace to wait on the ministry which they have received in the body of Christ with simplicity, diligence, and cheerfulness; that none may think of himself more highly than he ought to think, and none may seek another man's calling, but rather to be found faithful in his own work; to the glory of thy name in Christ Jesus our Lord.

H. J. Wotherspoon

114

O Thou, who givest to thy children liberally and upbraidest not: Preserve us from all envy at the good of our neighbour, and from every form of jealousy. Teach us to rejoice in what others have and we have not, to delight in what they achieve and we cannot accomplish, to be glad in all that they enjoy and we do not experience; and so fill us daily more completely with love; through him in whom thou hast promised to supply all our need, our Saviour Jesus Christ.

*William Knight**

115

Lord of the Church, who hast given to thy servants a diversity of gifts, that they may share them with their brethren: Grant us the generous heart to give, the humble heart to receive; that we, with all that love thee, may know the fullness of thy grace; that thy love may be perfected in us; to the glory of thy name.

Our ministry 116

Almighty God, who has given to us gifts differing according to the measure of thy grace: Enable us each one, we beseech thee, to exercise the ministry which we have received of thee in the body of Christ with simplicity, diligence, and cheerfulness; that being bound together in brotherly affection, and showing honour one to another, we may faithfully serve thy Church and glorify thy name; through Jesus Christ our Lord. *Based on Romans 12. 6–10*

The first sign 117

Almighty God, the giver of strength and joy: Change, we beseech thee, our bondage into liberty, and the poverty of our nature into the riches of thy grace; that by the transformation of our lives thy glory may be revealed; through Jesus Christ our Lord.

Church of South India

118

O Lord Jesus, who by thy first miracle didst manifest thy glory, so that thy disciples believed on thee: Give us in our measure that faith which dwelt in them. Fill us with the riches of thy good Spirit; change thou our earthly desires into the image of thine own purity and holiness; and finally give us a place at thy heavenly feast; for the glory of thy holy name. *Henry Alford**

The holy estate of matrimony 119

O Lord Christ, who by thy presence and first miracle at Cana of Galilee adorned and beautified the holy estate of matrimony: We beseech thee to sanctify the marriage bond in the life of our people, and to bless our homes with thy abiding presence; for the honour and glory of thy name.

THIRD SUNDAY AFTER EPIPHANY

At peace with all men 120

ALMIGHTY God, we beseech thee of thy mercy to endue us with the spirit of meekness and patience; so that no evil we may suffer from others may move us to do evil to them, and that we may strive ever to live peaceably with all men; for the sake of Jesus Christ our Saviour. *J. Mountain**

121

O God, who art the God of peace, mercifully grant that, as much as lieth in us, we may live at peace with all men; and if our outward peace be broken, yet do thou preserve peace in our hearts; through him who is the Prince of peace, Jesus Christ our Lord.

Daily Prayer

A generous heart 122

Preserve us, O Lord, from the spirit of revenge. Give us, we beseech thee, the generous heart; that, if our enemy hunger, we may feed him, if he thirst, may give him drink; that we be not overcome with evil, but overcome evil with good; as servants of Jesus Christ our Lord. *Based on Romans 12. 19–21*

Jesus touched him 123

Lord Jesus, who in thy tender love didst stretch forth thy hand and touch the leper who came to thee for cleansing: Grant us a like compassion for all who claim our help, and a willingness to identify ourselves with them in their need; for thy sake who wast made sin for us, and who art our righteousness and our salvation, now and for ever. *Frank Colquhoun*

For lepers 124

Almighty Father, giver of life and health, look mercifully upon those who are stricken with leprosy, and stretch forth thy hand to cleanse and heal them, as did thy blessed Son of old. Grant wisdom to those who are seeking the cure and treatment of this disease; give tenderness and sympathy to those who minister to the sufferers; and restore to their families and friends those who have been separated from them; for the sake of the same Jesus Christ our Lord. *B. F. Westcott**
See also 482

FOURTH SUNDAY AFTER EPIPHANY

The powers that be 125

O GOD most High, who alone rulest in the kingdoms of men: Grant, we beseech thee, to all members of Parliament the light and guidance of thy Holy Spirit; that they may wisely take counsel together, and come to such decisions as shall promote thy glory, the well-being of this nation, and the peace of the world; through Jesus Christ our Lord.

126

O Lord, we pray thee to raise up leaders of the people who will fear thee, and thee alone, whose delight shall be to do thy will and forward thy work; that the heart of this people may be wise, its mind sound, and its will righteous; through Christ our Lord.

In danger's hour 127

Grant, we beseech thee, O Lord our God, that in whatever dangers we are placed we may call upon thy name, and that when deliverance is given us from on high we may never cease from thy praise; through Jesus Christ our Lord. *Leonine Sacramentary*

128

O Thou who in the days of thy humiliation didst command the winds and waves, and they obeyed thee: Do thou so dwell within us, that we may be safe from all dangers, and steadfast in all temptations; and evermore keep us in thy peace, for thy holy name's sake.

Henry Alford*

The Conqueror of evil

129

O Lord, who alone canst cast out the evil passions and desires of the soul: Come among us, we pray thee, and by thy mighty power subdue our spiritual enemies, and set us free from the tyranny of sin. We ask it in thy name and for thy glory.

Henry Alford

The voyage of life

130

O Lord, who art Master of the stormy winds and alone canst order them to be still: Be with us in all the voyage of our life; for our boat is small and the ocean is wide. When the winds are contrary, give us to know that thou rulest the raging of the sea; and when our faith is little and we cry to thee out of the midst of our fears, hear thou our prayer and grant us thy peace; for the glory of thy great name.

Adapted

FIFTH SUNDAY AFTER EPIPHANY

A forgiving spirit

131

O LORD, because being compassed with infirmities we oftentimes sin and ask for pardon: Help us to forgive as we would be forgiven; neither mentioning old offences committed against us, nor dwelling upon them in thought, nor being influenced by them in heart; but loving our brother freely, as thou freely lovest us; for Christ's sake.

Christina Rossetti

132

Deliver us, O God, from injustice, envy, hatred and malice; give us grace to pardon all who have offended us, and to bear with one another even as thou, Lord, dost bear with us, in thy patience and great loving-kindness.

Rydal School Hymnal

The seed of the Word

133

O Almighty God, we pray thee, sow the seed of thy Word in our hearts, and send down upon us thy heavenly grace; that we may bring forth the fruits of the Spirit, and at the great day of harvest may be gathered by thy holy angels into thy garner; through Jesus Christ our Lord.

Canterbury Convocation, 1862

134

O God, who hast sown in our hearts the precious seed of thy truth: Grant us to nourish it by meditation, prayer and obedience, that it may not only take root, but also bring forth fruit unto holiness; through Jesus Christ our Lord. *James Ferguson*

The tares **135**

Lord, if our hearts be hard, or choked with tares, send, we pray thee, thine angels, even if it be thine angel of sorrow, to plough and harrow and cleanse the unfruitful ground; for thy mercy's sake.
Daily Prayer

SIXTH SUNDAY AFTER EPIPHANY

The love of God **136**

ALMIGHTY and eternal God, who in thy Son Jesus Christ hast revealed thy nature as Love: We humbly pray thee to shed thy love abroad in our hearts by thy Holy Spirit; that so by thy grace we may evermore abide in thee, and thou in us, with all joyfulness, and free from fear or mistrust; through the same Jesus Christ our Lord. *Christian von Bunsen**

137

O God, fountain of love, pour thy love into our souls, that we may love those whom thou lovest with the love thou givest us, and think and speak of them tenderly, meekly, lovingly; and so loving our brethren and sisters for thy sake, may grow in thy love, and dwelling in love may dwell in thee; for Jesus Christ's sake. *E. B. Pusey*

The coming of the Son of Man **138**

O God, heavenly Father, who by thy Son hast made all things in heaven and earth, and yet desirest to draw to thyself our uncompelled love and devotion: Grant us grace to understand the manifestation of thy Son Christ the Lord and Saviour of mankind, and to engage all our affections in thy service, and labour to spread the gospel among those who know him not; that when he shall come again in great glory he may find a people gladly awaiting his kingdom; through the same Jesus Christ our Lord.
Euchologium Anglicanum

The purpose of God **139**

Almighty God, whose sovereign purpose none can make void: Give us faith to stand calm and undismayed amid the tumults of the world, knowing that thy kingdom shall come and thy will be done; to the eternal glory of thy name, through Jesus Christ our Lord.

Daily Prayer

The day of the Lord 140

O Christ our God, who wilt come to judge the world in the manhood which thou hast assumed: We pray thee to sanctify us wholly, that in the day of thy coming we may be raised to live and reign with thee for ever. *Church of South India*

SUNDAY CALLED SEPTUAGESIMA

Maker of heaven and earth   **141**

WORTHY art thou, our Lord and our God, to receive glory and honour and power, for thou didst create all things, and by thy will they existed and were created.

To him who sits upon the throne and to the Lamb be blessing and honour and glory and might for ever and ever!

Revelation 4. 11; 5. 13

142

Almighty God, whose glory the heavens are telling, the earth thy power and the sea thy might, and whose greatness all feeling and thinking creatures everywhere herald: To thee belongeth glory, honour, might, greatness, and magnificence, now and for ever, to the ages of ages.   *Liturgy of St. James*

143

O Almighty God, without beginning and without end, the Lord of thine own works: We praise and bless thee that thou gavest a beginning to time, and to the world in time, and to all mankind in the world; and we beseech thee so to dispose all men and all things that they may be gathered up in thee and thine endless heaven; through him who is the first and the last, thine everlasting Word, our Saviour Jesus Christ.   *Daily Prayer*

144

O Thou in whom we live and move and have our being, awaken us to thy presence that we may walk in thy world as thy children. Grant us reverence for all thy creation, that we may treat our fellow men with courtesy, and all living things with gentleness; through Jesus Christ our Lord.   *New Every Morning*

The race that is set before us   **145**

Grant, O Lord, we beseech thee, that we who are called to the course of the Christian life may so run the race that is set before us as to obtain the incorruptible crown which thou hast promised to them that love thee; through Jesus Christ our Lord.

J. Mountain*

Labour and its reward   146

O God, who in the beginning didst create the heavens and the earth, and didst appoint unto men their work: Grant to us that whatsoever our hand findeth to do, we may do it with our might; that when thou shalt call thy labourers to give them their reward, we may so have run that we may obtain the crown of life; through Jesus Christ our Lord.   *Henry Alford*

Fellow workers with God   147

O God, who workest all things, who hast called us to be fellow workers with thee, and dost assign to every man his separate task: Teach us, in our several callings, what thou wouldst have us do, and make us faithful to do it, in thy name and in thy strength; for Jesus Christ's sake.   *Daily Prayer*

Daily work   148

O God, who hast commanded that no man should be idle: Give us grace to employ all our talents and faculties in the service appointed to us; that whatsoever our hand findeth to do, we may do it with our whole might; through Jesus Christ our Lord.

James Martineau

SUNDAY CALLED SEXAGESIMA

The way back to God   149

O GOD of love, who in a world estranged from thee didst send forth thy Son to turn mankind from darkness to light, and from the power of Satan to thyself the living God: Overcome in us, we pray thee, all pride and self-will, and remake us a people in whom thou art well pleased; through Jesus Christ our Lord.

Triumphant in weakness   150

Almighty God, the Creator of the ends of the earth, who giveth power to the faint, and strength to them that have no might: Look mercifully, we beseech thee, on our low estate and cause thy grace to triumph in our weakness; that we may rise and follow in the way of righteousness those who by faith already inherit the promises; through Jesus Christ our Lord.

German Reformed Church, U.S.A.

The sower   151

Lord of the harvest, who dost sow good seed into the hearts of all men: Grant that our hearts may not be so hardened by the world's traffic that the seed can take no root; nor so shallow that the roots can find no depth; nor so cumbered with the cares and riches of the world that the growing shoots are choked; but that we may be good ground, bearing good fruit; to the glory of thy name.

Daily Prayer

152

Suffer not, O God, the good seed which the Son of Man hath sown to be caught away by the wicked one out of our hearts, or to be scorched by tribulation or persecution, or to be choked with cares and pleasures of this life; but grant that, being received into honest and good hearts, it may bring forth in abundance the fruits of righteousness; through our Lord and Saviour Jesus Christ.

W. Rigby Murray

153

Almighty God, who dost sow the good seed of thy Word in the lives of men: We beseech thee to make us like those who in an honest and good heart, having received the Word, keep it, and bring forth fruit with patience; through Jesus Christ our Lord.

Based on Luke 8. 15

154

O God, who sendest forth thy commandment upon earth, and whose Word runneth very swiftly: Let thy Holy Spirit so prepare our minds and wills for thy teaching, that no carelessness or shallowness or love of ease shall hinder us from bringing forth the fruits of righteousness, by which men may know that we are followers of thy blessed Son, Jesus Christ our Lord.

J. W. Suter

SUNDAY CALLED QUINQUAGESIMA

Charity **155**

O GOD, heavenly Father, whose every motion towards us springs from thine inexhaustible love: Enable us, we humbly beseech thee, cheerfully to sacrifice ourselves for the well-being of those with whom we have to do, and also to love them with the tender love which thou hast for the world; that so though now we see thee darkly through the veil of our blindness, we with them may presently see thee in the fullness of light; through Jesus Christ our Lord.

Euchologium Anglicanum

Faith, hope, and love **156**

O Lord God, perfect in us that which is lacking of thy gifts; of faith, to increase it, of hope, to establish it, of love, to kindle it; and make us to fear but one thing only, the fearing aught more than thee, our Father, our Saviour, our Lord, for ever and ever.

After Lancelot Andrewes

157

Grant us, we beseech thee, Almighty God, a steadfast faith in Jesus Christ, a cheerful hope in thy mercy, and a sincere love to thee and to all our fellow men; through the same Jesus Christ our Lord. *Lutheran Church*

The way of the cross   158

Almighty God, who hast shown us in the life and teaching of thy Son that the path of love may lead to the cross, and the reward of faithfulness may be a crown of thorns: Grant us grace to take up our cross and follow Christ in the strength of patience and the constancy of faith, and to have such fellowship with him in his sorrow that we may know the secret of his strength and peace; through the same Jesus Christ our Lord. *C. J. Vaughan**

159

O Lord Jesus Christ, who didst set thy face steadfastly to go unto Jerusalem: Deliver us from the faithless mind that shrinks from the harder paths of a dutiful life. Make us ready to meet all the counsels of thy will, and to be obedient even unto death; who, with the Father and the Holy Spirit, livest and reignest, world without end. *Book of Common Order*

The blind   160

O God, who art the Father of lights, and with whom there is no darkness at all: We thank thee for the good gift of sight which thou hast bestowed upon us, and we pray thee to fill us with thine own compassion for those who have it not. Direct and prosper the efforts that are made for their welfare. Reveal to them by thy Spirit the things which eye hath not seen, and comfort them with the hope of the light everlasting, to which, of thy great mercy, we beseech thee to bring us all; through Jesus Christ our Saviour.

Arthur W. Robinson

Spiritual sight   161

Almighty Father, whose blessed Son restored sight to the blind man who sought his mercy: Clear away, we beseech thee, the blindness of our hearts, and enlighten our minds with thy heavenly truth, that we may enter upon the approaching season of Lent with true love and spiritual understanding; through the same our Saviour Jesus Christ. *Adapted*

LENT

Lent **162**

O GOD, who by thy care and counsel for mankind hast moved thy Church to appoint this holy season wherein the hearts of those who seek thee may receive thy help and healing: We beseech thee so to purify us by thy discipline, that, abiding in thee and thou in us, we may grow in grace and in the faith and knowledge of thee; through Jesus Christ our Lord.   *After Gelasian Sacramentary*

163

O Lord and heavenly Father, who hast given unto us thy people the true bread that cometh down from heaven, even thy Son Jesus Christ: Grant that throughout this Lent our souls may so be fed by him that we may continually live in him and he in us; and that day by day we may be renewed in spirit by the power of his endless life, who gave himself for us, and now liveth and reigneth with thee and the Holy Spirit, one God, world without end.

Frederick B. Macnutt

164

O Lord Jesus Christ, who didst take upon thee the form of a servant, humbling thyself and accepting death for us, even the death of the cross: Grant that this mind may be also in us; so that we may gladly take upon ourselves the life of humility and service, and taking up our cross daily may follow thee in thy suffering and death, that with thee we may attain unto the power of thy endless life. Grant this, O Christ, our Saviour and our King.

Harold Anson

165

O Lord our God, long-suffering and full of compassion: Be present with us, we beseech thee, as we enter upon this season in which we make ready to recall our Saviour's sufferings and to celebrate his triumph. Grant us the aid of thy Holy Spirit, that as we acknowledge our sins, and implore thy pardon, we may also be enabled to deny ourselves, and be upheld in the hour of temptation; through Jesus Christ our Lord.

Adapted from Prayers for the Christian Year

Contrite hearts 166

O Lord our God, who art of purer eyes than to behold iniquity: Have mercy upon us, we beseech thee, for our sins accuse us, and we are troubled by them and put to shame. We have done wrong to ourselves in ignorance, and to our brethren in wilfulness, and by our selfish and faithless ways have grieved thy Holy Spirit. Forgive us, we humbly pray thee; through Jesus Christ our Lord.

Prayers for the Christian Year

167

Almighty God, spirit of peace and of grace, whose salvation is never far from penitent hearts: We confess the sins that have estranged us from thee, dimmed our vision of heavenly things, and brought upon us many troubles and sorrows. O merciful Father, grant unto us who humble ourselves before thee the remission of all our sins, and the assurance of thy pardon and peace; through Jesus Christ our Lord. *Prayers for the Christian Year**

Self-discipline 168

O Heavenly Father, whose blessed Son hast taught us that whosoever will be his disciple must take up his cross and follow him: Help us with willing heart to mortify our sinful affections, and depart from every selfish indulgence by which we sin against thee. Strengthen us to resist temptation, and to walk in the narrow way that leadeth unto life; through the same Jesus Christ our Lord.

Prayers for the Christian Year

The true fast 169

O God, who by thy Son dost marvellously work out the salvation of mankind: Grant, we beseech thee, that, following the example of our blessed Lord, and observing such a fast as thou dost choose, we may both be subjected to thee with all our hearts, and united to each other in holy charity; through the same Jesus Christ our Lord.

Gelasian Sacramentary

Reality in religion 170

Save us, O God, from the false piety that parades itself in the eyes of men and is not genuine in thy sight; and so sanctify us by thy Spirit that both in heart and life we may serve thee acceptably, to the honour of thy holy name; through Jesus Christ our Lord.

Frank Colquhoun

See also prayers for Penitence and Pardon, 1543–52

Temptation and trial 171

BLESSED Lord, who wast tempted in all things like as we are, have mercy upon our frailty. Out of weakness give us strength; grant to us thy fear, that we may fear thee only; support us in time of temptation; embolden us in time of danger; help us to do thy work with good courage, and to continue thy faithful soldiers and servants unto our life's end. *B. F. Westcott*

172

O Lord our God, grant us, we beseech thee, patience in troubles, humility in comforts, constancy in temptations, and victory over all our spiritual foes. Grant us sorrow for our sins, thankfulness for thy benefits, fear of thy judgment, love of thy mercies, and mindfulness of thy presence; now and for evermore. *John Cosin*

173

O Heavenly Father, subdue in us whatever is contrary to thy holy will, that we may know how to please thee. Grant, O God, that we may never run into those temptations which in our prayers we desire to avoid. Lord, never permit our trials to be above our strength; through Jesus Christ our Saviour. *Thomas Wilson*

174

O God, who willest not the death of a sinner: We beseech thee to aid and protect those who are exposed to grievous temptations; and grant that in obeying thy commandments they may be strengthened and supported by thy grace; through Jesus Christ our Lord. *Gregorian Sacramentary**

Not by bread alone 175

Almighty and eternal God, who has so made us of body, soul and spirit, that we live not by bread alone, but by every word that proceedeth from thee: Make us to hunger for the spiritual food of thy Word; and as we trust thee for our daily bread, may we also trust thee to give us day by day the inward nourishment of that living truth which thou hast revealed to us in thy Son Jesus Christ our Lord. *James Ferguson*

Self-discipline 176

Almighty and everlasting God, who for the well-being of our earthly life hast put into our hearts wholesome desires of body and spirit: Mercifully increase and establish in us, we beseech thee, the grace of holy discipline and healthy self-control; that we may fulfil our desires by the means which thou hast appointed, and for the ends thou ordainest; through Jesus Christ our Lord.

Euchologium Anglicanum

Christ our example   177

O Lord God, keep ever in our remembrance the life and death of our Saviour Jesus Christ. Make the thought of his love powerful to win us from evil. As he toiled and sorrowed and suffered for us, in fighting against sin, so may we endure constantly and labour diligently, as his soldiers and servants, looking ever unto him and counting it all joy to be partakers with him in his conflict, his cross, and his victory; through the same Jesus Christ our Lord.

C. J. Vaughan

SECOND SUNDAY IN LENT

Body and soul   178

O ETERNAL God, who has made all things for man, and man for thy glory: Sanctify our bodies and souls, our thoughts and our intentions, our words and actions. Let our body be a servant of our mind, and both body and spirit servants of Jesus Christ; that doing all things for thy glory here, we may be partakers of thy glory hereafter; through the same Jesus Christ our Lord.

Jeremy Taylor

The Spirit of purity   179

O Eternal God, who hast taught us by thy holy Word that our bodies are temples of thy Spirit: Keep us, we most humbly beseech thee, temperate and holy in thought, word and deed, that at the last we, with all the pure in heart, may see thee and be made like unto thee in thy heavenly kingdom; through Christ our Lord.

B. F. Westcott

                                          180

Write deeply upon our minds, O Lord God, the lesson of thy holy Word, that only the pure in heart can see thee. Leave us not in the bondage of any sinful inclination. May we neither deceive ourselves with the thought that we have no sin, nor acquiesce idly in aught of which our conscience accuses us. Strengthen us by thy Holy Spirit to fight the good fight of faith, and grant that no day may pass without its victory; through Jesus Christ our Lord.

C. J. Vaughan

The merciful Saviour 181

O Blessed Saviour, who art full of mercy and compassion, and wilt not cast out any that come to thee: Help us, we beseech thee, who are grievously vexed with the burden of our sins; and so increase in us the power of thy Holy Spirit that we may prevail against the enemy of our souls; for thy name's sake.

Henry Alford

The children's food 182

O God, who through thy Son Jesus Christ hast promised help to man according to his faith: Grant us the freedom of the children to taste the food of eternal life, and to share with others what we ourselves receive; through the merits of the same thy Son, our Lord.

Gordon Hewitt

THIRD SUNDAY IN LENT

Children of light 183

O ALMIGHTY Father, giver of every good and perfect gift, who hast made the light of thy truth to shine in our hearts: Make us to walk as children of light in all goodness and righteousness, that we may have no fellowship with the unfruitful works of darkness; through Jesus Christ our Lord.   *W. Walsham How**

A divided house 184

O God, who through thy Son has taught us that a house divided against itself must fall: Save us, we beseech thee, from the danger of a divided allegiance; unite our hearts to fear thy name; and grant that in all our course of life our eye may be single and our purpose one; through the same Jesus Christ our Lord.   *Henry Alford**

The Stronger than the strong 185

Lord Christ, almighty Saviour, we cry to thee for aid against our strong enemy. O thou who art the Stronger than the strong, deliver us, we pray thee, from the evil one, and take sole possession of our hearts and minds; that filled with thy Spirit we may henceforth devote our lives to thy service, and therein find our perfect freedom; for the honour of thy great name.   *Frank Colquhoun*

Truth in the inward parts 186

O Eternal God, who through thy Son our Lord hast promised a blessing upon those who hear thy Word and faithfully keep it: Open our ears, we humbly beseech thee, to hear what thou sayest, and enlighten our minds, that what we hear we may understand,

and understanding may carry into good effect by thy bounteous prompting; through the same Jesus Christ our Lord.

Euchologium Anglicanum

The soul prepared 187

O Thou who hast prepared a place for my soul, prepare my soul for that place. Prepare it with holiness; prepare it with desire; and even while it sojourneth upon earth, let it dwell in heaven with thee, beholding the beauty of thy countenance and the glory of thy saints, now and for evermore. *Joseph Hall*

FOURTH SUNDAY IN LENT: MOTHERING SUNDAY

Law and grace 188

ALMIGHTY God, who hast taught us in thy holy Word that the law was given by Moses, but that grace and truth came by Jesus Christ: Grant that we, being not under the law but under grace, may live as children of that Jerusalem which is above, and rejoice in the freedom of our heavenly citizenship; through the same Jesus Christ our Lord. *J. Mountain**

Jerusalem which is above 189

Grant us, O Lord, to rejoice in beholding the bliss of the heavenly Jerusalem; that as she is the home and mother of the multitude of the saints, we also may be counted worthy to have our portion within her; through thine only begotten Son, our Lord and Saviour Jesus Christ. *Mozarabic Sacramentary**

Refreshment Sunday 190

O Lord and Saviour Jesus Christ, who art thyself the bread of life, and hast promised that he who comes to thee shall never hunger: Grant us faith truly to partake of thee through Word and Sacrament, that we may find refreshment of spirit and be strengthened for thy service; who livest and reignest with the Father, in the unity of the Holy Spirit, ever one God, world without end.

Frank Colquhoun

191

O Lord and heavenly Father, who hast given unto us thy people the true bread that cometh down from heaven, even thy Son Jesus Christ: Grant that our souls may so be fed by him who giveth life unto the world, that we may abide in him and he in us, and thy Church be filled with the power of his unending life; through the same Jesus Christ our Lord. *Frederick B. Macnutt*

The feeding of the multitude   192

O Lord Jesus Christ, who didst feed the multitude by the lakeside, using the humble gifts of a boy's generous impulse, and a disciple's faith in thy power: Help us in thy Church to call forth such generosity in others, and strengthen our faith that the hungry millions can be fed; for thy name's sake.   *Gordon Hewitt*
See also prayers for a Mothering Sunday Service, 668–81

FIFTH SUNDAY IN LENT: PASSION SUNDAY

193

O GOD, who by the cross and passion of thy Son Jesus Christ didst save and deliver mankind: Grant that by steadfast faith in the merits of that holy sacrifice we may find help and salvation, and may triumph in the power of his victory; through the same Jesus Christ our Lord.   *Scottish Prayer Book*

194

O God, whose blessed Son did overcome death for our salvation: Mercifully grant that we, who have his glorious passion in remembrance, may take up our cross daily and follow him; through the same thy Son Jesus Christ our Lord.   *Scottish Prayer Book*

195

Holy Father, who hast redeemed us with the precious blood of thy dear Son: Keep us, we beseech thee, steadfast in faith, and enable us no longer to live unto ourselves, but unto him who died for us and rose again, even the same Jesus Christ our Lord.

196

O God, who by the example of thy Son our Saviour Jesus Christ hast taught us the greatness of true humility, and dost call us to watch with him in his passion: Give us grace to serve one another in all lowliness, and to enter into the fellowship of his sufferings; who liveth and reigneth with thee and the Holy Spirit, one God, world without end.   *W. E. Orchard*

197

Thanks be to thee, O Lord Jesus Christ, for all the benefits which thou hast given us, for all the pains and insults which thou hast borne for us. O most merciful Redeemer, Friend and Brother, may we know thee more clearly, love thee more dearly, and follow thee more nearly, now and for evermore.   *St. Richard of Chichester*

198

Grant, O Lord, that in thy wounds we may find our safety, in thy stripes our cure, in thy pain our peace, in thy cross our victory, in thy resurrection our triumph; and, at the last, a crown of righteousness in the glories of thy eternal kingdom.

Eternal redemption

199

Almighty and most merciful God, who hast given thy Son to die for our sins and to obtain eternal redemption for us through his own blood: Let the merit of his spotless sacrifice, we beseech thee, purge our consciences from dead works to serve thee, the living God, that we may receive the promise of eternal inheritance in Christ Jesus our Lord; to whom with thee and the Holy Ghost be honour and glory, world without end.

German Reformed Church, U.S.A.

200

O Lord Jesus Christ, Son of the living God, who didst devote thy life and thy death to our most plenteous redemption: Grant that what thou hast wrought for us may also be wrought in us: that, growing into thy likeness, we may serve and share thy redeeming work; who livest and reignest in the glory of the eternal Trinity now and for evermore. *A Procession of Passion Prayers*

The triumphal entry

201

O CHRIST, the King of glory, who didst enter the holy city in meekness to be made perfect through the suffering of death: Give us grace, we beseech thee, in all our life here to take up our cross daily and follow thee, that hereafter we may rejoice with thee in thy heavenly kingdom; who livest and reignest with the Father and the Holy Spirit, God, world without end.

Church of South India

202

As on this day we keep the special memory of our Redeemer's entry into the city, so grant, O Lord, that now and ever he may triumph in our hearts. Let the King of grace and glory enter in, and let us lay ourselves and all we are in full and joyful homage before him; through the same Jesus Christ our Lord.

Handley C. G. Moule

203

O Lord Jesus Christ, who as on this day didst receive the homage of those who hailed thee as their King: Accept, we beseech thee, our praise and adoration, our worship and love; and grant that we, who now confess thee with our lips, may never fail to yield thee the service of our lives; for the honour of thy holy name, who livest and reignest with the Father and the Holy Spirit, one God, world without end.

204

O Lord Jesus Christ, who as on this day didst enter the rebellious city where thou wast to die: Enter into our hearts, we beseech thee, and subdue them wholly to thyself. And, as thy faithful disciples blessed thy coming, and spread their garments in the way, covering it with palm branches, make us ready to lay at thy feet all we have and are, and to bless thee, who comest in the name of the Lord.

Prayers for the Christian Year

205

King of men, who didst set thy face steadfastly to follow to the end the stern and costly way of love: We thank thee that at the last turn of the road there were those who, though they understood but dimly, sought to honour and receive thee as their King. To their glad hosannas we would add our song of praise; and knowing our hearts to be the city thou wouldest enter now, we would fling wide the gates and pray that the King of glory will come in. For thine is the kingdom, the power and the glory, for ever and ever.

With all our Strength

The blessing of palm 206

Almighty God, who gavest thine only Son to suffer upon earth for our redemption: Send thy blessing upon us who now make our prayers unto thee, and sanctify to our use these branches of palm; that all who shall take them in thy name may enjoy the freedom of thy kingdom, and serve thee in all good works; through Jesus Christ our Lord. *Diocese of Southwark*

207

Bless, O Lord, we pray thee, these branches of palm; and grant that as thy people outwardly in their bodies do worship thee, so inwardly in their souls they may serve thee with pure devotion, that they may be victorious over the assaults of the enemy, and cleave steadfastly to all good works; through Jesus Christ our Lord.

208

Bless, O Lord, we pray thee, these branches of palm to those who receive them; that both now and in the days to come they may be a memorial of thy passion, and a pledge of thy victory over sin and death; for the glory of thy great name.

The mind of Christ 209

O God, fill us with the divine humility of Christ: that, having the same mind that was also in him, we may look not every one on his own things, but every one also on the things of others, emptying our wills of pride, and our hearts of complaining, and laying down our glories before the cross; through the same Jesus Christ our Lord. *James Martineau*

210

O Everliving God, let this mind be in us which was also in Christ Jesus; that as he from his loftiness stooped to the death of the cross, so we in our lowliness may humble ourselves, believing, obeying, living, and dying to the glory of the Father; for the same Jesus Christ's sake. *Christina Rossetti**

He emptied himself 211

O Lord Jesu Christ, pattern of humility, who didst empty thyself of thy glory and take upon thee the form of a servant: Root out of us all pride and self-seeking; that we may willingly bear contempt and reproach for thy sake, and glorying in nothing save thy cross, may esteem ourselves lowly in thy sight; who now livest and reignest with the Father and the Holy Spirit, one God, world without end. *Adapted*

212

O Lord Jesus Christ, Son of the most high God, who didst empty thyself and give thy whole life to us, even unto death, the death of the cross: Grant us to receive so immeasurable a gift penitently, gladly and thankfully; and to hold back nothing of ourselves from others and from thee; who livest and reignest in the glory of the eternal Trinity, God for ever and ever.
A Procession of Passion Prayers

The death of the cross 213

Blessed be thy name, O Jesu, Son of the most high God; blessed be the sorrow thou sufferedst when thy holy hands and feet were nailed to the tree; and blessed thy love when, the fullness of pain accomplished, thou didst give thy soul into the hands of the Father; so by thy cross and precious blood redeeming all the world, all longing souls departed and the numberless unborn; who now livest and reignest in the glory of the eternal Trinity for ever and ever.

214

Almighty God, whose Son our Saviour Jesus Christ took upon him our flesh that he might bear our sins in his own body on the tree: Mercifully grant that we may be counted worthy to have part both in the fellowship of his sufferings and in the glory of his resurrection; to whom with thee and the Holy Ghost be honour and glory, world without end. *German Reformed Church, U.S.A.*

Adoration 215

Glory be to thee, O Lord, who, having become obedient unto death, even the death of the cross, are highly exalted, and hast opened unto us the gate of everlasting life. Therefore unto thee every knee shall bow, and every tongue shall confess thee Lord, to the glory of God the Father. *Based on Philippians 2. 8–11*

The way of the cross 216

ALMIGHTY God, whose most dear Son went not up to joy but first he suffered pain, and entered not into glory before he was crucified: Mercifully grant that we, walking in the way of the cross, may find it none other than the way of life and peace; through the same thy Son Jesus Christ our Lord.   *American Prayer Book*

The barren fig tree 217

O Lord, who by thy word didst cause the barren fig tree to wither from the roots: Suffer us not by our fruitlessness to incur thy condemnation; but grant us grace to repent and obey thee while yet there is time; for thy mercy's sake.   *A. McCheane**

A bold confession 218

O Lord, who, when thine hour was near, didst go without fear among those who sought thy life: Give us such boldness to confess thee before men, and such readiness to bear thy cross, that hereafter thou mayest confess us before thy Father which is in heaven.

The cleansing of the temple 219

O God, our heavenly Father, whose blessed Son before his passion cast out from the temple those who desecrated the holy place: Cleanse our hearts and minds, we pray thee, from all evil thoughts and imaginations, from all unhallowed appetites and ambitions; that in lives made pure and strong by thy Holy Spirit we may glorify thy name and advance thy kingdom in the world, as disciples of the same thy Son, Jesus Christ our Lord.   *Frank Colquhoun*

220

O Lord Jesus Christ, who didst cleanse the temple courts, and didst teach, saying, My house shall be called a house of prayer for all nations: Cleanse thy Church, we beseech thee, of all evil, and so sanctify it by thy saving grace, that in all the world thy people may offer unto thee true and acceptable worship; for thy name's sake.   *James M. Todd*

See also 460–2

Suffering and glory 221

O LORD God, whose blessed Son, our Saviour, gave his back to the smiters, and hid not his face from shame: Grant us grace to take joyfully the sufferings of the present time, in full assurance of

the glory that shall be revealed; through the same thy Son Jesus
Christ our Lord. *American Prayer Book*

Nothing but leaves 222

Lord Jesus, who as on this day didst curse the fig tree bearing
leaves, and nothing but leaves: Grant that we, warned by this
example, may never seek to make a fair show in the flesh, but
strive to bring forth the fruit of a holy and godly life, acceptable in
thy sight; who with the Father and the Holy Ghost art one God,
world without end. *W. E. Scudamore*

Christ the teacher 223

O Lord Jesu Christ, who as on this day of the Holy Week didst
teach the people in the temple at Jerusalem, and also instruct thy
disciples on the Mount of Olives: Grant us the ready mind at all
times to learn what thou wouldest teach us, that thy word may dwell
in us richly in all wisdom; for the glory of thy holy name.

A. McCheane*

WEDNESDAY BEFORE EASTER

The mighty acts of God 224

Assist us mercifully with thy help, O Lord God of our salvation, that we may enter with joy upon the meditation of those
mighty acts whereby thou hast given us life and immortality;
through Jesus Christ our Lord. *American Prayer Book*

Preparation for the passion 225

O Lord, who didst spend this day in quiet retreat at Bethany, in
preparation for thy coming passion: Help us ever to live mindful of
our end; that when thou shalt call us to pass through the valley of
the shadow of death, we may fear no evil, for thou art with us, who
didst die that we might live with thee for ever. *A. McCheane**

The betrayal 226

O God our heavenly Father, who to redeem the world didst
deliver up thine only Son to be betrayed by one of his disciples and
sold to his enemies: Take from us, we beseech thee, all covetousness
and hypocrisy; and so strengthen us, that, loving thee above all
things, we may remain steadfast in our faith unto the end; through
him who gave his life for us, our Saviour Jesus Christ.

L. Tuttiet

The last supper 227

BLESSED Lord Jesus, who, when about to depart out of this world, having loved thine own, and loving them to the end, didst institute the holy sacrament of thy Body and Blood, the dying legacy of thy love: Vouchsafe, we earnestly pray thee, that we may never draw near thine altar, save with hearts enkindled by love for thee and for one another; for thy dear name's sake.   *W. E. Scudamore*

228

O Lord Christ, who in the days of thy flesh didst hallow bread and wine to be a perpetual memorial of thy passion, and a never-failing means of fellowship with thee: Make us so to thirst after thy righteousness that through these holy mysteries we may be filled with all the fullness of thy divine life, and be made partakers of thy heavenly treasure; for thy glory's sake.

Washing the disciples' feet 229

O Lord Jesus Christ, who on this day didst wash thy disciples' feet, leaving us an example of humble service: Grant that our souls may be washed from all defilement, and that we fail not to serve thee in the least of thy brethren; who livest and reignest for ever and ever.   *Harold Riley*

230

Lord Jesus Christ, who when thou wast about to institute thy holy Sacrament at the Last Supper didst wash the feet of the apostles, and teach us by thy example the grace of humility: Cleanse us, we beseech thee, from all stain of sin, that we may be worthy partakers of thy holy mysteries; who livest and reignest with the Father and the Holy Ghost, one God, world without end.   *The Royal Maundy*

231

O Lord Jesus Christ, enthroned in the majesty of heaven, who, when thou camest forth from God, didst make thyself as one that serveth: We adore thee because thou didst lay aside the garment of thy glory, and gird thyself with lowest humility, and minister to thy disciples, washing their feet. Teach us to know what thou hast done and to follow thine example; deliver us from pride, jealousy and ambition, and make us ready to be subject one to another, and with lowliness to serve one another for thy sake, O Jesus Christ, our Lord and Saviour.   *Prayers for the Christian Year*

Watch and pray 232

O God, who by the example of thy Son our Saviour Jesus Christ, hast taught us the greatness of true humility, and dost call us to watch with him in his passion: Give us grace to serve one another in all lowliness, and to enter into the fellowship of his sufferings; who liveth and reigneth with thee and the Holy Spirit, world without end. *W. E. Orchard*

233

O Lord Jesus Christ, who in the garden didst teach us, by word and example, to pray, that we might overcome the perils of temptation: Graciously grant that we, always continuing in prayer, may gain abundantly the fruit thereof, and be partakers of thy victory; who livest and reignest with the Father and the Holy Spirit, one God, world without end. *Adapted from Roman Breviary*

Peter's denial 234

O Lord Jesus Christ, look upon us with those eyes of thine wherewith thou didst look upon Peter in the hall; that with Peter we may repent, and by thy same love may be forgiven and restored; for thy mercy's sake. *After Lancelot Andrewes*

Gethsemane 235

O Saviour of the world, who in Gethsemane didst accept the bitter cup in submission to the Father's will: Look mercifully upon our weak and wayward lives, and arm us with such strength and courage that we may tread without fear the appointed path of duty, and evermore follow the pattern of thy costly obedience; for thy honour and glory, who now livest and reignest with the Father and the Holy Spirit, one God for ever and ever. *Frank Colquhoun*

The true vine 236

O Christ, the true vine and the source of life, ever giving thyself that the world may live; who also hast taught us that those who would follow thee must be ready to lose their lives for thy sake: Grant us so to receive within our souls the power of thine eternal sacrifice, that in sharing thy cup we may share thy glory, and at the last be made perfect in thy love. *The Kingdom, the Power, and the Glory*

GOOD FRIDAY

God commendeth his love 237

ALMIGHTY God, who of thy great love for man didst, as at this time, give thy dearly beloved Son to die for us upon the cross: Grant us a living faith in our Redeemer, and a thankful remembrance of his death. Help us to love him better for his exceeding love to us; and grant that our sins may be put away, and nailed to the cross, and buried in his grave, that they may be remembered no more against us; through the same thy Son, Jesus Christ our Lord. *W. Walsham How★*

The sacrifice of the cross 238

Almighty Father, whose blessed Son by his one perfect and sufficient sacrifice has opened for us a new and living way to thy presence: Grant that, drawing near to thee with a true heart in full assurance of faith, we may find cleansing and a quiet conscience; and give us grace, we pray thee, evermore to hold fast the confession of our hope without wavering, and to serve one another in love and good works; through the merits of the same Jesus Christ our Lord. *Based on Hebrews 10. 19–24*

239

O Lamb of God, who hast taken away the sin of the world: Look upon us and have mercy upon us, we beseech thee; and grant that those whom thou hast redeemed with thy most precious blood may evermore be defended by thy love and power; who now livest and reignest with the Father and the Holy Spirit, one God, world without end. *Old Gallican★*

240

O God, who didst send thy Son to redeem mankind by his obedience unto death: Give us grace so to remember his sacrifice for us, that we may take up our cross and follow him, dying daily unto sin and living unto righteousness; through the same Jesus Christ our Lord.

The crown of thorns 241

O Christ, who by the thorns pressed upon thy head hast drawn the thorns from the sorrows of this world, and given us a crown of joy and peace: Make us so bold as never to fear suffering, nor to suffer without cheerfulness in thy service; to the glory of thy holy name. *Daily Prayer*

Behold the Man 242

O God, the Father of mankind, who didst suffer thine only Son to be set forth as a spectacle despised, derided, and scornfully arrayed, yet in his humiliation to reveal his majesty: Draw us, we beseech thee, both to behold the Man and to worship the King, immortal, eternal, world without end. *Daily Prayer*

The appeal of the cross 243

O Lord Jesu Christ, take us to thyself, draw us with cords to the foot of thy cross: for we have no strength to come, and we know not the way. Thou art mighty to save, and none can separate us from thy love. Bring us home to thyself, for we are gone astray. We have wandered; do thou seek us. Under the shadow of thy cross let us live all the rest of our lives, and there we shall be safe.

Frederick Temple

244

Lord Jesus, who on this holy day of thy passion didst stretch out thine arms upon the hard wood of the cross, that all men might be brought within their saving embrace: Draw us to thyself with the bands of thy love; and grant that, evermore being bound to thee as thy faithful servants, we may take up our cross daily and follow thee; who livest and reignest with the Father and the Holy Spirit, world without end.

The way of the cross 245

Lord Christ, who didst enter into thy triumph by the hard and lonely way of the cross: May thy courage and steadfast loyalty, thy unswerving devotion to the Father's will, inspire and strengthen us to tread firmly and with joy the road which love bids us to take, even if it leads through suffering, misunderstanding, and darkness. We ask it for thy sake, who for the joy that was set before thee endured the cross, despising the shame, O Lord, our strength and our Redeemer.

With all our Strength

Bearing Christ's cross 246

O Holy and adorable Redeemer, by whose condemnation we are acquitted, by whose stripes we are healed, by whose death we have life, by whose cross we gain our crown: Keep us, we beseech thee, ever mindful of thy boundless love; and when thou dost call on us to bear for a while thy cross, like Simon of old, make us to rejoice that we are counted worthy to suffer for thy sake, and accept our feeble sacrifice, through the merits of thine eternal redemption.

W. E. Scudamore*

Forgiving love 247

Strong Son of God, who didst pour out thy life that we might live, and who by thy cross didst show to the uttermost the forgiving love of God: We praise thee that through death thou hast destroyed death and opened unto us the gate into life that is strong and free. Thanks be to God who giveth us the victory through Jesus Christ our Lord.

The love of Christ 248

O Holy and ever-blessed Jesus, who being the eternal Son of God and most high in the glory of the Father, didst vouchsafe in love for us sinners to be born of a pure virgin, and didst humble thyself unto death, even the death of the cross: Deepen within us, we beseech thee, a due sense of thy infinite love; that adoring and believing in thee as our Lord and Saviour, we may trust in thy infinite merits, imitate thy holy example, obey thy commands, and finally enjoy thy promises; who with the Father and the Holy Ghost livest and reignest, one God, world without end.

*John Wesley's Prayers**

The Jews 249

O God of Abraham, of Isaac and of Jacob, have mercy, we beseech thee, upon thine ancient people the Jews. Deliver them from their hardness of heart and unbelief of thy gospel; that being turned to thee in living faith, they may look upon him whom they pierced, and be brought into thy holy Church; through the same Jesus Christ our Saviour. *Adapted*

See also *1368-9*

Before meditation 250

Lord Jesus Christ, who for the redemption of mankind didst ascend the cross, that thou mightest enlighten the world that lay in darkness: Gather us this day with all thy faithful to that same holy cross; that, gazing in penitence upon thy great sacrifice for us, we may be loosed from all our sins, and entering into the mystery of thy passion, be crucified to the vain pomp and power of this passing world; and finding our glory in the cross alone, we may attain at last thy everlasting glory, where thou, the Lamb that once wast slain, reignest with the Father and the Holy Spirit, one God for ever and ever. *Adapted from Sarum Missal*

251

Almighty and eternal God, who in thy great love didst give thine only Son to die for our sins, and for the sins of the whole world: Enable us, we beseech thee, by thy Holy Spirit, to worship thee with reverence, and meditate with humility upon those mighty acts by which thou didst bring redemption to thy people; through the same Jesus Christ our Lord. *Prayers for the Christian Year*

252

O God our Father, holy and merciful, who didst give thine only Son to be a sacrifice for us: Look mercifully upon us, we beseech thee, as before his cross we meditate and pray; and give us faith so to behold him in the mystery of his passion, that we may enter into the fellowship of his sufferings; through the same Jesus Christ our Lord. *Adapted*

THE SEVEN WORDS FROM THE CROSS

Introduction 253

O GOD, who hast laid up an infinite treasure of wisdom, power, and goodness for the whole world, in the last words of thy only begotten Son, our Lord: Give us grace so to keep and ponder them in our minds, that we may be able to hear him say this last word to us: Come, ye blessed children of my Father, receive the kingdom prepared for you from the beginning of the world. Grant this, we beseech thee, O Father, through the same Jesus Christ our Lord.

A Harvest of Myrrh and Spices (trs. W. H. Draper)

254

O Lord Jesus Christ, who out of thy silence upon the cross didst bequeath to thy Church seven words: Grant that we may ponder them as the inexhaustible gospel of thy love and of the world's redemption; and learn likewise both by speech and silence to glorify our Father in heaven; who with thee and the Holy Spirit liveth and reigneth, one God, world without end.

A Procession of Passion Prayers

255

Almighty and everlasting God, grant to us, thy servants, with such deep reverence and enlightened understanding to follow the passion of thy Son our Saviour Jesus Christ, that entering into the fellowship of his sufferings we may obtain the help of his all-sufficient grace, and the pardon of our sins which were the cause of those sufferings; for his sake, who liveth and reigneth with thee and the Holy Spirit, one God, world without end.

The first word (Luke 23. 34) 256

O God and Father of us all, who heard the prayer of Jesus Christ thy Son that those who nailed him to the cross should be forgiven: We thank thee for this assurance of a love that even in our ignorance and sin always pleads on our behalf; so write this prayer of Jesus on our hearts that we may learn to love as we are forgiven, and pray for those who knowing or unknowing wrong their fellow men.

Basil Naylor

257

Blessed Lord, who in thy forgiving love didst pray for those who nailed thee to the cross, and hast taught us to forgive one another as thou hast forgiven us: Take from us all bitterness and resentment towards our fellows, and give us the spirit of mutual forgiveness and brotherly love; that so, in perfect charity, we may be partakers of thy everlasting kingdom; for thy name and mercy's sake.

*Salisbury Book of Occasional Offices**

258

Give us, O Lord, the spirit of humility, that we may never presume upon thy mercy, but live as those who have been much forgiven. Make us tender and compassionate towards others; and grant that we may show forth in our lives that enduring love which alone can triumph over all the powers of evil; after the example of thy Son Jesus Christ our Lord.   *George Timms (after C. J. Vaughan)*

259

O Lord Jesus Christ, who didst plead for those who encompassed thy death, and ever livest to make intercession for us: Show thy mercy upon us, we humbly beseech thee, and by the infinite merits of thy passion forgive us all our sins, known and unknown; that henceforth we may live as those whom thou hast redeemed with thy most precious blood; for the glory of thy holy name.

Frank Colquhoun

The second word (Luke 23. 43)   260

Lord Jesus Christ, the friend of sinners, who taught men of a Father's love that rejoiced in the return of a prodigal son, and even in the hour of death gave to a penitent thief the promise of thy continued presence: We thank thee for this word of reassurance that death cannot separate us from thy love, and pray that as we grow in understanding of thy cross, we may draw nearer to our Father's home.   *Basil Naylor*

261

Help us, dear Lord, to see ourselves as thou seest us, and in shame for what we are to cast ourselves in trust upon thy love; speak to us the word of pardon, for our trust is not in any virtue or wisdom of our own, but only in the mercy and love of God, which thou hast shown to us in thy life and in thy death, our Lord and our God.   *William Temple*

262

Blessed Saviour, who when hanging on thy cross didst welcome the penitent sinner: We beseech thee, by that same compassion, to pardon the guilty, heal the wounded, recover the fallen, restore the wandering; that casting themselves upon thy mercy they may return with penitence to the embrace of thy love, and enter at last into the joy of thy presence; for thy love's sake.

263

Blessed Saviour, who at this hour didst hang upon the cross, stretching forth thy loving arms: Grant that all mankind may look to thee and be saved; who livest and reignest with the Father and the Holy Ghost, ever one God, world without end.

264

O Saviour Christ, who on the cross, and by virtue of the cross, didst accept the faith of the penitent thief and assure him of a place with thee in paradise: Remember us too, O Lord, unworthy as we are, and open to us the kingdom of thy grace, that hereafter we may be with thee in the kingdom of thy glory, where thou livest and reignest with the Father and the Holy Spirit, one God, for ever and ever.   *Frank Colquhoun*

The third word (John 19. 26, 27)   **265**

Dear Lord, who hast blessed us with the gift of family life, that we may learn to love and care for others: We praise thee for the example of thy Son Jesus Christ, who even when deserted and betrayed by closest friends took thought for his mother and his disciple. Open our eyes to recognize in all men the claims of kinship, and stir our hearts to serve them as brethren called with us into the sonship of thy love.   *Basil Naylor*

266

O Lord Jesus Christ, who from the cross didst commend thy mother into the care of the beloved disciple: Keep, we beseech thee, under thy perpetual providence those to whom we are bound by ties of kindred and affection; and grant that the love which we know on earth may lead us onward to the love of thee; who with the Father and the eternal Spirit art one holy Trinity of love, world without end.   *George Timms*

267

O Lord Jesus Christ, who by thy holy incarnation didst enter our human family, and on the cross didst commend thy mother to the care of a beloved disciple: Purify our homes by thy abiding presence;

sanctify all our human relationships; and grant that united one with another in thee, we may together attain thy heavenly kingdom; for the honour of thy great name.

268

O Son of God, who by the travail of thy passion hast brought to birth the new family of the children of God: Grant us grace, as members of that redeemed family, to realize our kinship one with another in thee, and to love all men for thy sake, who hast loved us and given thyself for us, our Lord and Saviour Jesus Christ.

Frank Colquhoun

The fourth word (Matthew 27. 46) **269**

Our God, whose love never fails us, and from whom nothing but our self-will can finally separate us: We confess with shame the darkness of our sin that cast so deep a shadow on the cross; we thank thee for the glory of thy Son's obedience that carried him through the loneliness of his passion; and we pray that in the hour of our trial, when all is dark and there is no vision, we may be strengthened in our obedience and faith, knowing that the Spirit of him who suffered alone will never leave us to endure alone. *Basil Naylor*

270

O Lord Jesus Christ, who by thy most bitter passion hast tasted death for every man, and hast borne our sins in thine own body on the tree: Grant us, we beseech thee, a broken and a contrite heart for all thy sorrows, and the loosing from our sins in thy most precious blood; that we may live henceforth as those who have been bought with a price, and glory only in thy cross.

W. E. Orchard*

271

Lord Jesus Christ, who didst for me endure the horror of deep darkness, teach me by the depth of thine agony the vileness of my sin, and so bind me to thyself in bonds of gratitude and love that I may be united with thee in thy perfect sacrifice, my Saviour, my Lord, and my God. *William Temple*

272

O God, whose blessed Son endured the loneliness and darkness of the cross, that we might enjoy eternal fellowship with thee: Grant that amidst life's shadows we may know that we are never forsaken, but that we are ever walking in the light of thy countenance; through the same Jesus Christ our Lord. *Frank Colquhoun*

The fifth word (John 19. 28)   273

Son of Man, who entered our mortal life to be one with us in the ways of men: We bless thee for the love which stooped down to the level of our need; and though the reward of thy self-giving was the cross, we rejoice in knowing that through grief and pain and thirst the victory was won in our humanity, and the glorious hope of our salvation is in one who is both God and man.

Basil Naylor

274

Grant us, O Lord God, so to thirst after thee, that with thee we may be filled; and inspire us by thy grace to good works of compassion and love, that so we may gladden the heart of him who in his brethren cries "I thirst", even thy blessed Son, Jesus Christ our Lord.   *George Timms*

275

O Lord Jesus Christ, Son of the living God, who at the sixth hour of the day didst with great tumult ascend on Golgotha the cross of pain, whereon, thirsting for our salvation, thou didst permit gall and vinegar to be given thee to drink: We beseech thee that thou wouldest kindle and inflame our hearts with the love of thy passion, and make us continually to find our delight in thee alone, our crucified Lord; who livest and reignest with the Father and the Holy Spirit, ever one God, world without end.   *Office of Sext*

276

Blessed Lord, who on the cross didst endure the thirst both of spiritual desire and of physical anguish: Satisfy the longings of our hearts, we humbly beseech thee, and sanctify all our sufferings by thine own; who livest and reignest with the Father and the Holy Spirit, one God, for ever and ever.   *Frank Colquhoun*

The sixth word (John 19. 30)   277

Thanks be to God who gives us the victory through our Lord Jesus Christ.

We praise thee, Lord Jesus Christ, Son of God, because thou didst submit to the discipline of a son's obedience, and perfectly revealed in thy death the Father's nature as love.

We praise thee, Lord Jesus Christ, Son of Man, because as champion of men thou didst enter the battle against evil for their sakes, and won the perfect victory over its power.

We praise thee, Lord Jesus Christ, Servant of God, because thou didst accept the suffering of those who seek to be at one with those they serve, and by thy perfect sacrifice made us one with God.

Thanks be to God who gives us the victory through Jesus Christ our Lord. *Basil Naylor*

278

Grant, O Lord, unto us, and to all thy servants, the grace of perseverance unto the end; in the power of him who for the finishing of thy work laid down his life, even thy Son Jesus Christ our Lord. *George Timms*

279

O God, who by the cross and passion of thy Son Jesus Christ didst fully accomplish the redemption of mankind: Grant that by steadfast faith in the merits of that holy sacrifice we may find our whole salvation, and may triumph in the power of his victory; through the same Jesus Christ our Saviour.

280

O Lord God, Lamb of God, Son of the Father, that takest away the sins of the world: Grant that as thy sacrifice for our redemption was full, perfect, and sufficient, so nothing may be wanting in our service and sacrifice for thee as members of thy mystical body; for the honour and glory of thy holy name.

281

O Lord Christ, as we thankfully recall thy finished work for the redemption of the world, so we pray that we may ever be mindful of the unfinished task which thou hast committed to thy Church; that constrained by thy love we may labour to share thy saving gospel with all mankind, for the furtherance of thy kingdom and the glory of thy name. *Frank Colquhoun*

The seventh word (Luke 23. 46)   282

Abba, Father, in whom the Saviour trusted as in life so in death: We bless thee for this last prayer which marked the work accomplished, the end achieved; grant us so strong a faith and so ready an obedience that when our life on earth draws to its close, we may not fear to surrender it into thy hands as to an all-wise and all-loving Father; through the same Jesus Christ our Lord.

Basil Naylor

283

O Lord Jesus Christ, Son of the living God, who at the ninth hour of the day, with outstretched hands and bowed head, didst commend thy spirit to God the Father, and by thy death unlock the gates of paradise: Mercifully grant that in the hour of our death our souls may come to the true paradise, which is thyself; who livest and reignest God, world without end. *Office of None*

284

Hear us, O merciful Lord, and remember now the hour in which thou didst commend thy blessed spirit into the hands of thy heavenly Father; and so assist us by this thy most precious death, that dying unto the world, we may live unto thee; and that at the hour of our departing from this mortal life, we may be received into thine everlasting kingdom, there to reign with thee, world without end.

Office of None

285

O Heavenly Father, in whose hands are the hearts of all thy children: Grant us the faith that commits all to thee, without question and without reserve; that trusting ourselves wholly to thy love and wisdom, we may meet all that life may bring, and death itself at last, with serenity and courage; through thy Son Jesus Christ our Lord. *Frank Colquhoun*

Concluding prayer 286

Most bountiful and benign Lord God, we, thy humble servants, freely redeemed and justified by the passion, death, and resurrection of our Saviour Jesus Christ, having our full trust of salvation therein, most humbly desire thee so to strengthen our faith and illumine us with thy grace, that we may walk and live in thy favour; and after this life be partakers of thy glory in the everlasting kingdom of heaven; through our Lord Jesus Christ. *York Minster, 1547*

EASTER EVEN

The hope of the resurrection 287

O LORD Jesus Christ, Son of the living God, who as on this day didst rest in the sepulchre, and didst thereby sanctify the grave to be a bed of hope to thy people: Make us so to abound in sorrow for our sins, which were the cause of thy passion, that when our bodies rest in the dust, our souls may live with thee; who livest and reignest with the Father and the Holy Spirit, one God, world without end. *Office of Compline*

288

O God, whose loving kindness is infinite, mercifully hear our prayers; and grant that as in this life we are united in the mystical body of thy Church, and in death are laid in holy ground with the sure hope of resurrection; so at the last day we may rise to the life immortal, and be numbered with thy saints in glory everlasting; through Jesus Christ our Lord.

289

O Lord God, who didst send thy only begotten Son to redeem the world by his obedience unto death: Grant, we humbly beseech thee, that the continual remembrance of his bitter cross may teach us to crucify the flesh with the affections and lusts thereof; that in the union and merits of his death and passion we may die with him, and rest with him, and rise again with him, and live with him for ever, to whom with thee and the Holy Ghost be all honour and glory, world without end.   *W. K. Hamilton**

290

O God, who for our sakes didst give up thy well-beloved Son to endure the shameful death of the cross, that we might be delivered from the power of the devil and be cleansed from all unrighteousness: Grant unto thy servants, we beseech thee, that through his passion the body of sin may be destroyed in us, and through the power of his resurrection we may henceforth walk in newness of life; for the merits of the same Jesus Christ our Lord.

*Liturgy of the Catholic Apostolic Church**

The preaching of the gospel   **291**

Grant, O Lord, we beseech thee, that as thy Son Jesus Christ, after he had suffered in the flesh for our sins, did preach to the spirits in prison, so also thy Church may ever be ready in body and spirit to do thy will; that by the preaching of thy gospel all who shall be obedient to the faith may be gathered into thy glorious kingdom; through the same Jesus Christ our Lord.

*Liturgy of the Catholic Apostolic Church**

An act of thanksgiving **292**

THANKS be unto thee, O Christ, because thou hast broken for us the bonds of sin and brought us into fellowship with the Father.

Thanks be unto thee, O Christ, because thou hast overcome death and opened to us the gates of eternal life.

Thanks be unto thee, O Christ, because where two or three are gathered together in thy Name there art thou in the midst of them.

Thanks be unto thee, O Christ, because thou ever livest to make intercession for us.

For these and all other benefits of thy mighty resurrection, thanks be unto thee O Christ.   *New Every Morning*

Easter praise **293**

Blessed be the God and Father of our Lord Jesus Christ, who according to his abundant mercy hath begotten us again unto a living hope by the resurrection of Jesus Christ from the dead, to an inheritance incorruptible and undefiled, and that fadeth not away, reserved in heaven for all who believe in Him; to whom with thee, O Father, in the unity of the Holy Spirit, be ascribed all honour and glory, dominion and power, now and for evermore.

Based on 1 Peter 1. 3–5

294

Almighty God, who art worshipped by the heavenly host with hymns that are never silent and thanksgivings that never cease: Fill our mouths with thy praise that we may worthily magnify thy holy name for all the wonderful blessings of thy love, and chiefly on this day for the resurrection of thy Son; and grant us, with all those that fear thee and keep thy commandments, to be partakers of the inheritance of the saints in light; through the same Jesus Christ our Lord, to whom with thee and the Holy Ghost may praise from all the world be given, now and for evermore.

295

O Lord, who by triumphing over the power of darkness, didst prepare our place in the New Jerusalem: Grant us, who have this day given thanks for thy resurrection, to praise thee in that city whereof thou art the light; where with the Father and the Holy Spirit thou livest and reignest, world without end.

William Bright

296

O Almighty God, hear thy people who are met this day to celebrate the glorious resurrection of thy Son our Lord; and lead them on from this festival to eternal gladness, to the joys that have no end; through the same our Saviour Jesus Christ, who liveth and reigneth with thee and the Holy Ghost, one God, world without end. *Gothic Missal**

Christ our Passover 297

O Lord God of our fathers, who didst of old deliver thy people from the prison-house of Egypt through the paschal sacrifice: Mercifully grant that we thy new Israel, redeemed by the precious blood of Christ, may be set free from the bondage of evil and serve thee henceforth in the joy and power of the resurrection; through the same thy Son Jesus Christ, who ever liveth and reigneth with thee and the Holy Spirit, one God, world without end.

Frank Colquhoun

The risen life 298

Almighty God, whose blessed Son did as on this day rise again for us, victorious over sin and the grave: Grant that we, being risen with him, may set our affection on things above, not on things on the earth; that when he who is our life shall appear, we may also appear with him in glory; through the same our Lord and Saviour Jesus Christ. *Based on Colossians 3. 1–4*

299

Almighty God, whose blessed Son did, as at this time, burst the bonds of death, because it was not possible that he should be holden of it: Grant that we may be risen with him and walk henceforth in newness of life; and bring us at last to the joy of thy eternal kingdom. Hear us, O Father, for the sake of him who is the firstborn from the dead, and is now alive for evermore, even the same Jesus Christ our Lord. *Adapted*

300

O God, who through the mighty resurrection of thy Son Jesus Christ hast delivered us from the power of darkness and brought us into the kingdom of thy love: Grant that as he was raised from the dead by the glory of the Father, so we also may walk in newness of life and seek those things that are above, where with thee, O Father, and the Holy Spirit, he liveth and reigneth for ever and ever.

Adapted from Gelasian Sacramentary

301

O God, who for our redemption didst give thine only begotten Son to the death of the cross, and by his glorious resurrection hast delivered us from the power of the enemy: Grant us to die daily to sin, that we may evermore live with him in the joy of his resurrection; through the same Jesus Christ our Lord.

Gregorian Sacramentary

302

O God, who by the glorious resurrection of thy Son our Saviour Jesus Christ hast destroyed death, and brought life and immortality to light: Grant that we, being raised together with him, may know the comfort and strength of his presence, and rejoice in hope of thy everlasting glory; through the same Jesus Christ our Lord, to whom be dominion and praise for ever and ever.

The Resurrection and the Life 303

O Merciful God, the Father of our Lord Jesus Christ, who is the Resurrection and the Life; in whom whosoever believeth shall live, though he die; and whosoever liveth and believeth in him shall not die eternally: We bless thy holy name for all thy servants departed this life in thy faith and fear, especially those most dear to us; beseeching thee to give us grace so to follow their good examples that with them we may be partakers of thy heavenly kingdom. Grant this, O Father, for Jesus Christ's sake, our only Advocate and Redeemer.

Based on Book of Common Prayer

Easter Day evening 304

O Lord Jesus Christ, who on the evening of the first Easter Day didst appear to thy disciples when they were afraid and didst speak to them thy word of peace: Grant to us thy servants that same holy peace, that we may walk henceforth in the light of thy presence and know the power of thy risen life, until we come to the joy of thy everlasting kingdom.

Adapted from various sources

305

Lord Jesus, risen from the dead and alive for evermore: Stand in our midst to-night as in the upper room; show us thy hands and thy side; speak thy peace to our hearts and minds; and send us forth into the world as thy witnesses; for the glory of thy name.

J. R. W. Stott

Concluding prayers 306

Now the God of hope fill us with all joy and peace in believing, that we may abound in hope through the power of the Holy Spirit; through him who died for us and rose again, Jesus Christ our Lord.

Based on Romans 15. 13

307

O God of peace, who didst bring again from the dead our Lord Jesus, that great Shepherd of the sheep, by the blood of the eternal covenant: Make us perfect in every good thing to do thy will, working in us that which is well pleasing in thy sight, through Jesus Christ; to whom be glory for ever and ever. *Based on Hebrews 13. 20, 21*

MONDAY IN EASTER WEEK

The walk to Emmaus 308

GRACIOUS Lord, we remember that thou didst accompany thy two disciples as they journeyed to Emmaus. Do thou go with us O Lord, on our journey through this world. Guide us, uphold us, strengthen us; make our hearts to burn within us; and evermore manifest thyself to our souls in gracious and heavenly power. For thine own name's sake we ask it. *Adapted*

309

Make our hearts to burn within us, O Christ, as we walk with thee in the way and listen to thy words; that we may go in the strength of thy presence and thy truth all our journey through, and at its end behold thee, in the glory of the eternal Trinity, God for ever and ever. *E. Milner-White*

The breaking of bread 310

O Thou, who didst manifest thyself in the breaking of bread to thy disciples at Emmaus: Grant us ever through the same blessed sacrament of thy presence to know thee, and to love thee more and more with all our hearts. Abide with us, O Lord, that we may ever abide in thee; for thy tender mercy's sake. *E. B. Pusey*

TUESDAY IN EASTER WEEK

The risen Lord 311

O LORD God Almighty, whose blessed Son our Saviour Jesus Christ did on the third day rise triumphant over death: Raise us, we beseech thee, from the death of sin unto the life of righteousness, that we may seek those things which are above, where he sitteth on thy right hand in glory; and this we beg for the sake of the same thy Son Jesus Christ our Lord. *Scottish Prayer Book*

A living hope 312

O God, the living God, who hast given unto us a living hope by the resurrection of Jesus Christ from the dead: Grant that we, being risen with him, may seek the things which are above, and be made partakers of the life eternal; through the same Jesus Christ our Lord. *Daily Prayer*

Joys eternal 313

We give thee thanks, O heavenly Father, who hast delivered us from the power of darkness and translated us into the kingdom of thy Son; grant, we pray thee, that as by his death he has recalled us to life, so by his presence abiding in us he may raise us to joys eternal; through the same Jesus Christ our Lord. *Mozarabic Sacramentary*

FIRST SUNDAY AFTER EASTER

Overcoming faith 314

O LORD God, who hast revealed in holy Scripture what conquests faith has made both in doing, and in suffering: Grant us no smaller faith than that which overcometh the whole world, that Jesus thy Son is God, very God from the beginning, the First and the Last, who liveth and reigneth with thee and the Holy Ghost, world without end. *Daily Prayer*

Christus Victor 315

Almighty God, who broughtest again from the dead our Lord Jesus, the glorious Prince of Salvation, with everlasting victory over sin and the grave: Grant us power, we beseech thee, to rise with him to newness of life, that we may overcome the world with the victory of faith, and have part at last in the resurrection of the just; through the merits of the same risen Saviour, who liveth and reigneth with thee and the Holy Spirit, ever one God, world without end. *Book of Common Order*

The first day of the week 316

O God, who makest us glad with the weekly remembrance of the glorious resurrection of thy Son our Lord: Vouchsafe us such a blessing through our worship on the first day of the week, that the days to follow it may be hallowed by thy abiding presence; through the same Jesus Christ our Lord. *William Bright* ★

Jesus in the midst 317

O Living Lord, who on the first Easter Day didst stand in the midst of thy disciples as the conqueror of sin and death, and didst speak to them thy peace: Come to us, we pray thee, in thy risen power and make us glad with thy presence; and so breathe thy Holy Spirit into our hearts that we may be strong to serve thee and spread abroad thy good news; for the glory of thy great name.

Frank Colquhoun

Christ's last beatitude 318

O Risen Christ, who hast said, Blessed are they that have not seen, and yet have believed: Mercifully grant that this benediction may be ours; so that, walking by faith and not by sight, we may evermore rejoice in thee, and confess thee as our Saviour, our Lord, and our God.

Frank Colquhoun

319

Almighty Father, who hast given thine only Son to die for our sins, and to rise again for our justification: Grant us so perfectly, and without all doubt, to believe in his resurrection, that our faith in thy sight may never be reproved; through the same Jesus Christ our Lord.

Adapted from Book of Common Prayer

The conquest of doubt 320

O Lamb of God, Son of the Father, who hast taken away the sin of the world, and art alive for evermore: Grant us the faith that doubts not thy word, and trusts where it cannot see; that taking hold upon thy promises, we may rest in thy love and rejoice in thy mercy, now and always.

SECOND SUNDAY AFTER EASTER

Leaving us an example 321

O GOD, whose blessed Son came into the world to do thy will and went about doing good: Grant that we may ever have the pattern of his holy life before our eyes, and that it may be our meat to do thy will and to finish thy work; through the same Jesus Christ our Lord.

Harold Riley

He reviled not again 322

O God our Father, whose blessed Son, being falsely accused, answered nothing; being reviled, reviled not again: Give us faith, when men accuse us falsely, to go quietly on our way, committing ourselves to thee, who judgest righteously, after the pattern of our Lord and Saviour Jesus Christ.

Daily Prayer

The silence of Christ 323

Keep us, O Lord God, from hasty excuse when the semblance of a fault is charged upon us; that rather we may be silent with thy holy and unreprovable Son, who when he was reviled, reviled not again; and when he suffered, threatened not; but committed himself unto thee, the only righteous and true judge; with whom he liveth and reigneth in the unity of the Holy Ghost, one God, now and evermore.   *A Procession of Passion Prayers*

The good Shepherd 324

Be thou thyself, O Lord, we beseech thee, the shepherd of thy people; that we who are strengthened by thy risen presence may in our daily life walk with thee, and in humble trust seek to follow thee, as thou callest us by name and dost lead us out; for thy glory's sake.
*The Kingdom, the Power, and the Glory**

325

O Lord Jesus Christ, thou good shepherd of the sheep, who camest to seek the lost and to gather them into thy fold: Have compassion on those who have wandered from thee; feed those who hunger, cause the weary to lie down in thy pastures, bind up those who are broken in heart, and strengthen those who are weak; and lead us all, O Lord, in the paths of righteousness, for thy name's sake.

326

O Lord Jesus Christ, who art the shepherd of thy people, so that they shall not want: We pray thee to lead us peacefully to the green pastures and beside the still waters; to restore our souls when we wander from thee; and evermore to guide us in the paths of righteousness, for thy name's sake.   *Based on Psalm 23. 1–3*

THIRD SUNDAY AFTER EASTER

Pilgrims 327

O GOD our Father, who hast taught us that our citizenship is in heaven, and hast called us to tread a pilgrim's path here on earth: Guide us, we pray thee, on our journey through this world to the Celestial City; defend us from the perils that await us in the way; give us grace to endure faithfully to the end; and at the last bring us to thy eternal joy; through the mercy of thy Son, our Lord and Saviour Jesus Christ.   *Frank Colquhoun*

Christian citizenship 328

Look, we beseech thee, O Lord, upon the people of this land who are called after thy holy name, that they may ever walk worthy of their Christian profession. Grant unto us all that, laying aside our divisions, we may be united in heart and mind to bear the burdens which are laid upon us, and be enabled by patient continuance in well-doing to glorify thy name; through Jesus Christ our Lord.

Irish Prayer Book *

Sorrow turned to joy 329

O Blessed Lord, who didst promise thy disciples that through thy Easter victory their sorrow should be turned to joy, and their joy no man should take from them: Grant us, we pray thee, so to know thee in the power of thy resurrection, that we may be partakers of that joy which is unspeakable and full of glory; for thy holy name's sake. *Frank Colquhoun*

A little while and ye shall not see me 330

Help us to trust thee, O Lord Christ, when we see thee not, and our way is shadowed by sorrow or doubt; and in thy great goodness reveal thyself to us again, that our hearts may rejoice, and we may walk henceforth in the light of thy presence; for the glory of thy holy name.

FOURTH SUNDAY AFTER EASTER

The changelessness of God 331

O FATHER of lights, with whom there is no variableness, nor shadow of turning; who abidest steadfast as the stars of heaven: Give us grace to rest upon thy eternal changelessness, and in thy faithfulness find peace; through Jesus Christ our Lord.

Daily Prayer

The gifts of God 332

O God, from whom every good and perfect gift doth come: Give us grace to consecrate to thy service the talents which thou hast committed to our charge; that we may do all things as in thy sight, and to thy glory; through Jesus Christ our Lord.

The Word of truth 333

O Heavenly Father, by whose gracious will we have been born again by the Word of truth: Make us ever swift to hear that Word and responsive to its saving message, that henceforth we may live as those who are partakers of thy new creation; through Jesus Christ our Lord. *Frank Colquhoun*

The Spirit of truth   334

O Lord Jesus Christ, who hast promised in thy holy gospel that
thy disciples shall know the truth, and the truth shall make them
free: Give us, we pray thee, the Spirit of truth, sent by thee and
leading to thee, that we may find the truth in finding thee, who
art the Way, the Truth, and the Life, for ever and ever.

Daily Prayer

FIFTH SUNDAY AFTER EASTER: ROGATION SUNDAY

Doers of the Word   335

O LORD, we most humbly beseech thee to give us grace not only
to be hearers of the Word, but also doers of the same; not only
to love, but also to live thy gospel; not only to profess, but also to
practise thy blessed commandments, unto the honour of thy holy
name.   *Thomas Becon*

336

Grant unto us, O merciful God, knowledge and true understanding of thy Word, that we may know what thy will is, and also may
show forth in our lives those things that we do know: that we be
not only knowers of thy Word, but also doers of the same; by our
Lord and Saviour Jesus Christ.

The law of liberty   337

O God our Father, whose law is a law of liberty: Grant us wisdom
to use aright the freedom which thou hast given us, by surrendering
ourselves to thy service; knowing that, when we are thy willing
bondsmen, then only are we truly free; for Jesus Christ's sake.

New Every Morning

In his name   338

O Lord Jesus Christ, who didst say to thy disciples, Whatever you
shall ask in my name, that will I do, that the Father may be glorified
in the Son: Give us grace, we beseech thee, to ask aright; teach us
to bring our requests into harmony with thy mind and will; and
grant that both our prayers and our lives may be acceptable in thy
sight, to the glory of God the Father.   *Frank Colquhoun*

The hope of glory   339

O Lord Jesus Christ, who hast gone to the Father to prepare a
place for us: Grant us so to live in communion with thee here on
earth, that hereafter we may enjoy the fullness of thy presence; who
livest and reignest with the Father and the Holy Spirit, ever one
God, world without end.   *Church of South India*

I have overcome the world 340

O Lord, who hast called us to fight under the banner of thy cross against the evil of the world, the flesh and the devil: Grant us thy grace, that clothed in purity and equipped with thy heavenly armour, we may follow thee as thou goest forth conquering and to conquer, and steadfast to the last we may share in thy final triumph; who livest and reignest with the Father and the Holy Ghost, one God, world without end. *W. H. Frere**

Inward peace 341

O Lord Jesus Christ, who didst say that in thee we may have peace, and hast bidden us to be of good cheer, since thou hast overcome the world: Give us ears to hear and faith to receive thy word; that in all the confusions and tensions of this present time, with mind serene and steadfast purpose, we may continue to abide in thee, who livest and wast dead and art alive for evermore. *Frederick B. Macnutt*

For Rogation prayers, see next section

ROGATIONTIDE

FOR THE FRUITS OF THE EARTH

342

ALMIGHTY and merciful God, from whom cometh every good and perfect gift: Bless, we beseech thee, the labours of thy people, and cause the earth to bring forth her fruits abundantly in their season, that we may with grateful hearts give thanks to thee for the same; through Jesus Christ our Lord, who liveth and reigneth with thee and the Holy Ghost, one God world without end. *Canadian Prayer Book*

343

Almighty God, Lord of Heaven and earth, in whom we live and move and have our being; who doest good unto all men, making thy sun to rise on the evil and on the good, and sending rain on the just and on the unjust: Favourably behold us thy servants, who call upon thy name, and send us thy blessing from heaven, in giving us fruitful seasons, and satisfying us with food and gladness, that both our hearts and mouths may be continually filled with thy praise, and we may ever give thanks to thee in thy holy Church; through Jesus Christ our Lord. *John Cosin*

344

O Almighty God, who hast created the earth for man, and man for thy glory: Mercifully hear the supplications of thy people, and be mindful of thy covenant; that both the earth may yield her increase, and the good seed of thy Word may bring forth abundantly, to the glory of thy holy name; through Jesus Christ our Lord. *Scottish Prayer Book*

345

Almighty God, Lord of heaven and earth: We beseech thee to pour forth thy blessing upon this land, and to give us fruitful seasons; that we, constantly receiving thy bounty, may evermore give thanks unto thee in thy holy Church; through Jesus Christ our Lord. *American Prayer Book*

346

O Gracious Father, who openest thy hand and fillest all things living with plenteousness: We beseech thee to hear our supplications, to renew the face of the earth, and to multiply the harvests of the world; that our land may yield her increase and thy people may give thanks to thy name; through Jesus Christ our Lord.

*A. McCheane**

347

Almighty God, Lord of heaven and earth, in whom we live and move and have our being: We beseech thee to send thine abundant blessing upon the earth that it may bring forth its fruits in due season; and grant that we, being filled with thy bounty, may evermore give thanks unto thee, who art the giver of all good; through Jesus Christ our Lord. *B. F. Westcott*

348

Almighty Father, Lord of heaven and earth: Of thy great goodness, we beseech thee to give and preserve to our use the fruits of the earth, the treasures of the mines, and the harvest of the sea, so as in due time we may enjoy them with thanksgiving; through Jesus Christ our Lord. *E. W. Benson*

349

Almighty God, who by thy Son Jesus Christ hast bidden us to ask of thee our daily bread: Prosper the labours of the men and women working in our fields, and grant us such favourable weather that we may in due time gather in the fruits of the earth; protect the sailors who bring us food from distant lands; and give us grace day by day to deny ourselves and to remember the needs of others; through Jesus Christ our Lord. *Thomas Wilson**

350

O God, who hast blessed our ploughing and our sowing: Protect, we pray thee, from storm and blight, the young corn in our fields; and grant that, working late and early, we may enjoy a prosperous harvest; through Jesus Christ our Lord. *D. L. Couper*

351

O Lord, who alone givest seed to the sower and bread to the eater, and hast taught us to seek from thee our daily bread: Bless the sowing of the seed, and grant fertility to the soil that receives it;

and accept the labours of thy servants, for thy glory and the well-being of thy people; through Jesus Christ our Lord.

352

Vouchsafe, O Lord, we pray thee, to further with thy gracious favour these our supplications; that we, receiving thy gifts in due season, may increase in love for thee from whom they come; through Jesus Christ our Lord. *Harold Riley*

Benediction 353

May the God and Father of our Lord Jesus Christ, who is the author of all godliness and growth, pour his blessing upon all the things that he hath made, and upon us his servants, that we may use them to his glory and the well-being of all mankind; and the blessing of God Almighty . . .

FOR INDUSTRY

354

O LORD Jesus Christ, who in thy earthly life didst share man's toil, and hallow the labour of his hands: Prosper all who maintain the industries of this land, and give them pride in their work, a just reward, and joy both in supplying need and in serving thee; who with the Father and the Holy Spirit livest and reignest, ever one God, world without end. *Canadian Prayer Book*

355

O God, Father of all men, we pray for all who toil in mill or mine; for all by whose labour we are clothed and fed; for all who work in the darkness of the earth; for those who trade in shop or market; and for those who go down to the sea in ships and do business in great waters. May our service and our merchandise be holy unto the Lord; and may we do justly, love mercy, and walk humbly with thee; for the sake of Jesus Christ our Lord.

356

O God, who givest to every man his work and through his labours dost accomplish thy purposes upon earth: Grant thy blessing, we beseech thee, to those who are engaged in the industries and comerce of this land. Defend them from injustice and oppression; give them the due reward of their labours; and deepen within them the spirit of humble and unselfish service, according to the pattern of thy Son, our Saviour Jesus Christ. *Adapted*

357

O God, who hast taught us that none should be idle: Grant to all the people of this land both the desire and the opportunity to labour; that, working together with one heart and mind, they may set forward the welfare of mankind, and glorify thy holy name; through Jesus Christ our Lord.

See also prayers for Society and Industry, 1136–60, and 1674

ASCENSIONTIDE

Adoration 358

THOU art the King of glory, O Christ; thou art the everlasting Son of the Father.

When thou tookest upon thee to deliver man, thou didst not abhor the Virgin's womb.

When thou hadst overcome the sharpness of death, thou didst open the kingdom of heaven to all believers.

Thou sittest at the right hand of God, in the glory of the Father.

Te Deum

359

Glory to our ascended Lord, that he is with us always.

Glory to the Word of God, going forth with his armies, conquering and to conquer.

Glory to him who has led captivity captive, and given gifts for the perfecting of his saints.

Glory to him who has gone before to prepare a place in his Father's home for us.

Glory to the author and finisher of our faith; that God in all things may be glorified through Jesus Christ, to whom be glory and dominion now and for evermore.

360

Blessed art thou, O Lord God Almighty, the Ancient of Days, who hast set thy Son Jesus Christ our Lord upon the glorious throne of thy kingdom, exalted far above all peoples, all places, all times, eternally; that he who hath worn our flesh, and borne our manhood into the holy of holies, should henceforth pour down heavenly gifts upon his brethren, and be both our righteous judge and most merciful intercessor; to whom with thee, O Father, and thee, O Holy Spirit, one God, be ascribed all might, majesty, dominion, and praise, now and for ever.   *After the Third Collect*

The ascended High Priest 361

O Thou merciful and loving High Priest, who hast passed within the veil and art in the presence of the Father: Help us with thy mighty intercession, that, our unworthiness being clothed upon with thy perfect righteousness, we may stand accepted in the day of thy coming; who livest and reignest with the Father and the Holy Spirit, one God, world without end. *Henry Alford*

Christ the King 362

O King of men, Master of our lives, entering into thy glory by thy cross, to whom all authority is given, both in heaven and on earth: We acknowledge thy sovereignty over every realm of life. Come, O Lord, enter into thy kingdom; subdue the world by the might of thy love; for as thine is the kingdom, so thine is the power and the glory for ever and ever.

363

Almighty and everlasting God, who hast willed to restore all things in thy well-beloved Son, the King and Lord of all: Mercifully grant that all peoples and nations, divided and wounded by sin, may be brought under the gentle yoke of his most loving rule; who with thee and the Holy Spirit liveth and reigneth, ever one God, world without end. *Sarum Breviary*

The abiding presence 364

Almighty God, whose blessed Son our Saviour Jesus Christ ascended far above all heavens, that he might fill all things: Mercifully give us faith to perceive that according to his promise he abideth with his Church on earth, even unto the end of the world; through the same Jesus Christ our Lord.

Scottish Prayer Book

365

Be present, O Lord, to our supplications; that as we trust that the Saviour of mankind is seated with thee in thy majesty, so we may feel that, according to his promise, he abideth with us unto the end of the world; through the same Jesus Christ our Lord.

Leonine Sacramentary

366

O Lord Jesus Christ, who after thy resurrection from the dead didst gloriously ascend into heaven: Grant us the aid of thy loving-kindness, that according to thy promise thou mayest ever dwell with us on earth, and we with thee in heaven, where with the Father and the Holy Spirit thou livest and reignest one God for ever and ever.

Gelasian Sacramentary

The things that are above **367**

O Almighty God, who by thy holy apostle hast taught us to set our affection on things above: Grant us so to labour in this life as ever to be mindful of our citizenship in those heavenly places whither our Saviour Christ is gone before; to whom with thee, O Father, and thee, O Holy Ghost, be all honour and glory, world without end. *South African Prayer Book*

368

Christ, the King of glory, who hast gone up on high that thou mayest fill all things and bestow gifts upon thy Church: We beseech thee to dwell continually with us by thy Holy Spirit, that we may seek those things which are above, where thou sittest at the right hand of God, in the glory of the Father, for ever and ever.

Adapted

He ascended into heaven **369**

O Lord Jesus Christ, who after thy resurrection didst manifestly appear to thine apostles, and in their sight didst ascend into heaven to prepare a place for us: Grant that, being risen with thee, we may lift up our hearts continually to seek thee where thou art, and never cease to serve thee faithfully here on earth; until at last, when thou comest again, thou shalt receive us unto thyself; who livest and reignest with the Father and the Holy Spirit, one God, world without end. *Frederick B. Macnutt*

370

O Lord Jesus Christ, who hast left us for a while, giving us the promise that thou wilt come again and receive us to be with thee for ever: Grant us such communion with thyself that our souls may thirst for that time when we shall behold thee in thy glory; who livest and reignest with the Father and the Holy Spirit world without end. *Liturgy of the Catholic Apostolic Church*

Go ye into all the world **371**

O Glorious Christ, who in thy ascension didst enter into thy kingdom: Remember, we pray thee, the countless millions who have not heard of the redemption which thou hast won for them.

Grant that they may learn, through thy Church, of the new and living way which thou hast opened for them. Let them draw near in fullness of faith, to enter with thee into the holy place of the Father's presence, and receive forgiveness and peace. So may they worship, with the innumerable company of angels and with the spirits of just men made perfect, Father, Son and Holy Spirit, one God, blessed for evermore. *George Appleton*

372

Grant, O Lord Christ, that as we rejoice in thy finished work on earth, in virtue of which thou hast ascended victoriously to the throne of heaven, so we may dedicate ourselves anew to the unfinished task of preaching the gospel to every creature, that all may learn of thy redeeming grace and power, and acknowledge thee to be the Lord; who livest and reignest with the Father and the Holy Spirit, one God, world without end.

See also prayers for a Missionary Festival (753–65) and for the Church Overseas (1343–81)

SUNDAY AFTER ASCENSION DAY

Prophet, Priest and King   373

GLORY be to thee, O Christ our Prophet, who didst reveal and interpret thy Father's will and all saving truth to the world.

Glory be to thee, O Christ our Priest, who didst offer thyself a sacrifice for sin and ever livest to make intercession for us.

Glory be to thee, O Christ our King, who dost give laws to thy people, and dost govern and protect us in thy love, and who reignest with the Father and the Holy Spirit now and for evermore.

Based on Thomas Ken

Our great High Priest   374

O God, whose blessed Son, our great High Priest, has entered once for all into the holy place, and ever liveth to intercede on our behalf: Grant that we, sanctified by the offering of his body, may draw near with full assurance of faith by the way which he has dedicated for us, and evermore serve thee, the living God; through the same thy Son our Lord Jesus Christ, who liveth and reigneth with thee, O Father, and the Holy Spirit, one God, world without end.   *Church of South India*

The King of Glory   375

O Christ, the King of Glory, who through the everlasting gates didst ascend to thy Father's throne, and open the Kingdom of heaven to all believers: Grant that, whilst thou dost reign in heaven, we may not be bowed down to the things of earth, but that our hearts may be lifted up whither thou, our redemption, art gone before; who with the Father and the Holy Spirit livest and reignest, ever one God, world without end.   *Mozarabic Sacramentary*

The Forerunner 376

O God, whose dearly beloved Son was, by thy mighty power, exalted that he might prepare a place in thy kingdom of glory for them that love thee: So lead and uphold us, O merciful Lord, that we may both follow the holy steps of his life here upon earth, and may enter with him hereafter into thy everlasting rest; that where he is, we may also be; through the merits of the same Jesus Christ our Lord.   *W. E. Scudamore*

377

Almighty and merciful God, into whose gracious presence we ascend, not by the frailty of the flesh but by the activity of the soul: Make us ever by thy inspiration to seek after the courts of the heavenly city, whither our Saviour Christ hath ascended, and by thy mercy confidently to enter them, both now and hereafter; through the same Jesus Christ our Lord.   *Leonine Sacramentary*

As each has received a gift 378

Grant, O heavenly Father, that as we have each received any gift of thine entrusted to us, so we may minister the same one to another, as good stewards of thy manifold grace; that thy holy name may in all things be glorified through Jesus Christ, to whom be praise and dominion for ever and ever.

Based on I Peter 4. 10, 11

The divine purpose 379

Almighty God, who after thy Son had ascended on high didst send forth thy Spirit in the Church to draw all men unto thee: Fulfil, we beseech thee, this thy gracious purpose, and in the fullness of time gather together in one all things in Christ, both which are in heaven and which are on earth; even in him, who is the head over all things in the Church which is his body, Jesus Christ our Lord.

The Prayer Manual

Adoration 380

To thee, O Christ, O King exalted, we offer up our due praise and unfeigned hearty thanks for that thou hast sent down and dispersed abroad thine own Holy Spirit to restore and renew the spirit of men, to be the first dedication of thy Catholic Church on earth, and the first publishing of the gospel to all lands, the bond of unity, and giver of light and life; to whom with the Father and thee, one blessed Trinity, be ascribed all might, majesty, dominion, and praise, now and for ever.   *After the Third Collect*

The Church's witness 381

O God, who in the exaltation of thy Son Jesus Christ dost sanctify thy universal Church: Shed abroad in every race and nation the gift of the Holy Spirit; that the work wrought by his power at the first preaching of the gospel may now be extended throughout the whole world; through the same Jesus Christ our Lord.

*Gelasian Sacramentary**

382

O God, the Father of our Lord Jesus Christ, who after his ascension didst send upon the first disciples thy promised gift of the Holy Spirit: Regard, we pray thee, the present need of thy Church, and grant us by the same Spirit to be endued with power from on high, that we may bear effectual witness to the truth of thy holy gospel; so that they who serve thee may be strengthened and encouraged, and they who serve thee not may be convicted and converted; through the same Jesus Christ our Lord.

383

O God, we pray thee for thy Church which is set to-day amid the perplexities of a changing order, and is face to face with a new task. Fill us all afresh with the Spirit of Pentecost. Help us to proclaim boldly the coming of thy kingdom. And do thou hasten the time when the knowledge of thyself shall fill the earth as the waters cover the sea. We ask it in the name and for the sake of Christ our Lord.

384

O God, who hast made of one blood all nations of men for to dwell on the face of the earth, and didst send thy blessed Son Jesus Christ to preach peace to them that are afar off, and to them that are nigh: Grant that all the peoples of the world may feel after thee and find thee; and hasten, O Lord, the fulfilment of thy promise to pour out thy Spirit upon all flesh; through Jesus Christ our Lord.

G. E. L. Cotton

385

O Jesus Christ, who art the same yesterday, today and forever: Pour thy Spirit upon the Church that it may preach thee anew to each succeeding generation. Grant that it may interpret the eternal gospel in terms relevant to the life of each new age, and as the fulfilment of the highest hopes and the deepest needs of every nation; so that at all times and in all places men may see in thee their Lord and Saviour. *George Appleton*

The holy Guest **386**

Almighty God, who fillest all things with thy boundless presence, yet makest thy chosen dwelling-place in the soul of man: Come thou, a gracious and willing Guest, and take thine abode in our hearts; that all unholy thoughts and desires within us be cast out, and thy holy presence be to us comfort, light and love; through Jesus Christ our Lord. *James Ferguson*

387

O Almighty God, who hast fulfilled thy word of promise, and from thy heavenly throne hast poured out upon thy Church the gift of the Holy Spirit: Open our hearts, we pray thee, to receive the fullness of his grace and power; that our lives may be strengthened for the service of thy kingdom, and our souls be conformed more and more to the image of thy Son, our Lord and Saviour Jesus Christ. *Frank Colquhoun*

Some Whitsun collects **388**

O God, who didst graciously send on thy disciples the Holy Spirit in the burning fire of thy love: Grant to thy people to be fervent in the unity of faith; that abiding in thee evermore, they may be found steadfast in faith and active in service; through Jesus Christ our Lord. *Gelasian Sacramentary*

389

O Spirit of the living God, who dwellest in us; who art holy, who art good: Come thou, and fill the hearts of thy faithful people, and kindle within them the fire of thy love; through Jesus Christ our Lord. *Liturgy of the Catholic Apostolic Church*

390

O Holy Spirit of God, who didst descend upon our Lord Christ at the river Jordan, and upon the disciples at the feast of Pentecost: Have mercy upon us, we beseech thee, and by thy divine fire enlighten our minds and purify our hearts; for the sake of Jesus Christ our Lord. *Adapted from St. Nerses of Clajes*

391

O God, who according to thy promise hast given thy Holy Spirit to us thy people, that we might know the freedom of thy children and taste on earth our heavenly inheritance: Grant that we may ever hold fast the unity which he gives, and, living in his power, may be thy witnesses to all men; through Jesus Christ our Lord.
Church of South India

392

O Lord our God, who didst send thy Holy Spirit to abide with thy Church for ever: Renew the same Spirit within us, that our hearts may be cleansed from evil things, and the fruits of love and goodness may abound in our lives; to the glory of our Saviour Jesus Christ.

393

Strengthen us, we beseech thee, O Lord, with the Holy Ghost the Comforter, and daily increase in us thy manifold gifts of grace; the spirit of wisdom and understanding; the spirit of counsel and strength; the spirit of knowledge and true godliness; and fill us, O Lord, with the spirit of thy holy fear, now and for ever.
Adapted from Book of Common Prayer

394

O Lord God, heavenly Father, we beseech thee, let thy Holy Spirit dwell in us, that he may enlighten and lead us into all truth, and evermore defend us from all adversities; through Jesus Christ our Lord.

395

Almighty God, who according to promise didst pour out thy Holy Spirit on the day of Pentecost, and hast promised that he shall abide with thy Church for ever: Let that same Spirit, we pray thee, guide us into all truth, defend us from all evil, and enrich us with all grace; that henceforth we may serve thee with pure hearts and lives, to the honour of thy Son, Jesus Christ our Lord.   *Adapted*

MONDAY IN WHITSUN WEEK

396

SEND, we beseech thee, Almighty God, thy Holy Spirit into our hearts, that he may rule and direct us according to thy will, comfort us in all our afflictions, defend us from all error, and lead us into all truth; through Jesus Christ our Lord, who, with thee and the same Holy Spirit, liveth and reigneth one God world without end.
American Prayer Book

397

Almighty and everlasting God, who in days of old didst cause thy Word to grow mightily and to prevail: We praise and magnify thy holy name for the manifestation of thy presence in this our day, and we beseech thee to pour out thy Spirit upon the Church, that thy way may be known upon earth and thy saving health among all nations; through Jesus Christ our Lord.   *Scottish Prayer Book*

398

O Thou whose eye is over all the children of men, and who hast called them into a kingdom not of this world: Send forth thy Holy Spirit into all the dark places of life. Let him still the noise of our strife and the tumult of the people, carry faith to the doubting, hope to the fearful, strength to the weak, light to the mourners, and more and more increase the pure in heart who see their God; through Jesus Christ our Lord.   *James Martineau**

TUESDAY IN WHITSUN WEEK

399

GRANT, we beseech thee, merciful God, that thy Church, being gathered together in unity by thy Holy Spirit, may manifest thy power among all peoples to the glory of thy name; through Jesus Christ our Lord, who liveth and reigneth with thee and the same Spirit, one God world without end.
American Prayer Book

400

O Almighty God, who on the day of Pentecost didst send the Holy Ghost, the Comforter, to abide in thy Church unto the end: Bestow upon us, and upon all thy faithful people, his manifold gifts of grace; that with minds enlightened by his truth and hearts purified by his presence, we may day by day be strengthened with power in the inward man; through Jesus Christ our Lord, who, with thee and the same Spirit, liveth and reigneth one God world without end. *Scottish Prayer Book*

401

O Holy Spirit of God, Lord and Giver of life: Come into our hearts, we beseech thee; that enlightened by thy clear shining, and warmed by thine unselfish love, our souls may be revived to the worship of God, and our lives be dedicated anew to the service of our fellows: for Jesus Christ's sake. *H. C. Cooksey*

402

O Holy Ghost, giver of light and life, impart to us thoughts higher than our own thoughts, and prayers better than our own prayers, and powers beyond our own powers, that we may spend and be spent in the ways of love and goodness, after the perfect image of our Lord and Saviour Jesus Christ. *Daily Prayer*

THE TRINITY SEASON

TRINITY SUNDAY

Adoration 403

O LORD God Almighty, eternal, immortal, invisible, the mysteries of whose being are unsearchable: Accept, we beseech thee, our praises for the revelation which thou hast made of thyself, Father, Son, and Holy Ghost, three persons, and one God; and mercifully grant that ever holding fast this faith we may magnify thy glorious name; who livest and reignest, one God, world without end. *Scottish Prayer Book*

404

Almighty God, most blessed and most holy, before the brightness of whose presence the angels veil their faces: With lowly reverence and adoring love we acknowledge thine infinite glory, and worship thee, Father, Son, and Holy Spirit, eternal Trinity. Blessing, and honour, and glory, and power be unto our God, for ever and ever. *Book of Common Order*

405

Praise be to thee, O God the Father, who didst create all things by thy power and wisdom, and didst so love the world as to give thy Son to be our Saviour.

Praise be to thee, O God the Son, who wast made man like unto us in all things, sin except, and wast delivered for our offences and raised again for our justification.

Praise be to thee, O God the Holy Spirit, who dost lead us into all truth, and dost shed abroad the love of God in our hearts.

All praise and glory be to thee, O God, Father, Son, and Holy Spirit, for ever and ever.

Invocation 406

Bless us, O God, Father, Son, and Holy Spirit, with the vision of thy glory; that we may know thee as the Father who created us, rejoice in thee as the Son who redeemed us, and be strong in thee, the Holy Spirit who dost sanctify us; keep us steadfast in this faith, and bring us at the last into thine eternal kingdom, where thou art ever worshipped and glorified, one God, world without end.

The vision of God 407

Lord God Almighty, who hast given to us the vision of thy holiness, and therewith of our unworthiness to be thy witnesses: Touch, we pray thee, our lips with thy cleansing fire; that so cleansed and hallowed, we may go forth amongst men as those whom thou hast sent; for Jesus Christ's sake. *Daily Prayer*

408

O God, who art seeking in every age for loyal spirits ready to obey the heavenly vision: Grant that our ears may be open to thy voice, that when thou dost call us, we may answer gladly and readily, Here am I, send me; for the glory of Jesus Christ our Lord.

409

Lord, who didst bid thy seraph purge the prophet's lips with the fire from off thy altar, so that he might be free to preach thy Word unto the people: Give thy priests and people within the Catholic Church pure and wise hearts, that so they may desire to go whither thou dost send them, and do that which thou dost will, in the power of him through whom we can do all things, even thy blessed Son Jesus Christ our Lord. *Wilfred B. Hornby*

God the Three in One 410

O God, who hast made thyself known to us as Trinity in Unity and Unity in Trinity, in order that we may be informed of thy love and thy majesty: Mercifully grant that we may not be terrified by what thou hast revealed of thy majesty, nor tempted to trespass upon thy mercy by what we know of thy love for us; but that by the power of thy Spirit we may be forever drawn to thee in true adoration and worship; who livest and reignest, one God, world without end. *Euchologium Anglicanum*

411

Almighty and everlasting God, who hast revealed thyself as Father, Son, and Holy Spirit, and dost ever live and reign in the perfect unity of love: Grant that we may always hold firmly and joyfully to this faith, and, living in praise of thy divine majesty, may finally be one in thee; who art three persons in one God, world without end. *Church of South India*

Baptized into the Name 412

Keep us, O Lord, from the vain strife of words, and grant us a constant profession of our faith. Preserve us in the way of truth, so that we may ever hold fast that which we professed when we were baptized into the name of the Father, and of the Son, and of the Holy Ghost, and may give glory to thee, our Creator, Redeemer and Sanctifier, now and for evermore.   *St. Hilary of Poitiers**

Doxology   413

To God the Father, who first loved us, and made us accepted in the Beloved; to God the Son, who loved us, and washed us from our sins in his own blood; to God the Holy Ghost, who sheddeth the love of God abroad in our hearts: to the one true God be all love and all glory for time and for eternity.   *Thomas Ken*

FIRST SUNDAY AFTER TRINITY

Love for God   414

O GOD, the God of all goodness and of all grace, who art worthy of a greater love than we can either give or understand: Fill our hearts, we beseech thee, with such love toward thee that nothing may seem too hard for us to do or to suffer, in obedience to thy will; and grant that thus loving thee, we may become daily more like unto thee, and finally obtain the crown of life which thou hast promised to those that love thee; through Jesus Christ our Lord.
B. F. Westcott

415

O God, we have known and believed the love that thou hast for us. May we, by dwelling in love, dwell in thee, and thou in us. Teach us, O heavenly Father, the love wherewith thou hast loved us; fashion us, O blessed Lord, after thine own example of love; shed abroad, O thou Holy Spirit of love, the love of God and man in our hearts. For thy name's sake.   *Henry Alford*

Love for our brethren   416

O God, we know and believe in the love thou bearest towards us. May we, by dwelling in that love, dwell in thee, and thou in us. We would learn to love and to serve him whom we have not seen, by loving and serving our brethren whom we have seen; through Jesus Christ our Lord.   *William Knight*

417

O Lord, who hast taught us that whatever we do unto the least of thy brethren we do unto thee: Give us grace to see thee in all who are poor and needy, and always to be ready to serve our fellows for thy sake; who livest and reignest with the Father and the Holy Spirit, world without end.   *Adapted*

The life of service 418

Almighty God, who hast created us for thy glory and service: Give us grace, we pray thee, to hallow every gift and improve each talent thou hast committed to us; that with a cheerful and diligent spirit we may render thee our grateful service, and whatsoever we do, may do it with all our might, in the name of Jesus Christ our Lord.

Need and opportunity 419

Almighty God, our heavenly Father, who hast taught us by love to serve one another: Give us eyes of compassion for human suffering and need wherever it is found, and especially for that which lies nearest to our own doors; save us from neglecting life's opportunities; and grant that while we have time we may do good to all men, for the sake of Jesus Christ our Saviour. *Frank Colquhoun*

The last assize 420

O Lord Christ, Son of the living God, who at the last assize wilt acknowledge all deeds of mercy to others as done unto thee: Grant, in this world of sin and pain and want, that we may never pass by the poor and helpless whose cry is thine own; for the honour of thy holy name. *Daily Prayer*

SECOND SUNDAY AFTER TRINITY

The spirit of love 421

ALMIGHTY God, who thyself art love, fill us with the spirit of thy holy love; that our hearts being enkindled by thee, we may for ever love thee, and each other in thee, and all men for thee; through Jesus Christ our Lord, who liveth and reigneth with thee and the Holy Ghost, one God, world without end.

E. Milner-White

The spirit of service 422

Almighty God our heavenly Father, who hast given thy Son Jesus Christ to die for our sins, and hast commanded us to love one another as thou hast loved us: Make us, we beseech thee, so mindful of the needs and sufferings of others, that we may ever be ready to show them compassion, and according to our ability to relieve their wants; for the sake of the same Jesus Christ our Lord.

*James Mountain**

Faith and love 423

O Heavenly Father, who hast given us a commandment, that we should believe on the name of thy Son Jesus Christ, and love one another: Give us also grace to keep this commandment, that we may evermore dwell in thee, and thou in us, in the power of thy Holy Spirit; through the same Jesus Christ our Lord.

Based on I John 3. 23, 24

The great supper 424

O God, who in thy blessed Son hast prepared for us a rich feast and dost invite us day by day to partake of thy bounties: Grant that neither the distractions of business nor the allurements of pleasure may cause us to turn a deaf ear to thy call, nor to neglect thy so great salvation, which thou hast given us in the same Jesus Christ our Lord. *Henry Alford**

THIRD SUNDAY AFTER TRINITY

Be clothed with humility 425

O LORD Jesus Christ, in all the fullness of thy power so gentle, in thine exceeding greatness so humble: Bestow thy mind and spirit upon us, who have nothing whereof to boast; that clothed in true humility, we may be exalted to true greatness. Grant this, O Lord, who livest and reignest with the Father and the Holy Spirit, one God for evermore. *Daily Prayer*

Casting all your care upon him 426

Most loving Father, who willest us to give thanks for all things, to dread nothing but the loss of thee, and to cast all our care on thee who carest for us: Preserve us from faithless fears and worldly anxieties, and grant that no clouds of this mortal life may hide from us the light of that love which is immortal, and which thou hast manifested unto us in thy Son, Jesus Christ our Lord.

William Bright

The suffering Church 427

O Lord, who hast promised a blessing for all who suffer for righteousness' sake: Grant to all our brethren persecuted for the truth that they may rejoice in being counted worthy to suffer dis-honour for thy name. Strengthen their faith and renew their love, that in their patience they may possess their souls and win their persecutors to penitence and new brotherhood in thee; for the sake of him who suffered shame and reproach and remained in-vincible in his love, even thy redeeming Son, Christ our Lord.

George Appleton

The Christian conflict 428

Grant, O God, that we who have been signed with the sign of the
Cross in our baptism, may never be ashamed to confess the faith of
Christ crucified, but may manfully fight under his banner against
sin, the world, and the devil, and continue Christ's faithful soldiers
and servants unto our lives' end. *From Book of Common Prayer*

This Man receiveth sinners 429

O Saviour Christ, whose compassion embraces all men, and who
in the days of thy flesh didst welcome sinners: Graciously receive
us who now come to thee, and who have nothing to plead but our
own exceeding need, and thy exceeding love; who livest and reignest with the Father and the Holy Spirit for ever and ever.

Frank Colquhoun

The lost sheep 430

O Lord Jesus Christ, thou good shepherd of the sheep, who didst
come to seek and to save that which was lost: Inspire us and thy
whole Church, we beseech thee, with thine own compassion for
those who have wandered from thy fold and are lost; help us to be
witnesses to them of thy love; and teach us what thou wouldest
have us to do towards leading them home to thee; who livest and
reignest with the Father and the Holy Spirit, one God, world without end.

FOURTH SUNDAY AFTER TRINITY

Suffering and glory 431

O GOD, who hast taught us that in thy mysterious providence
suffering is the prelude to glory, and hast made much tribulation the entrance to thy heavenly kingdom: May we learn from
this thy will, and also from creation around us, to wait for our deliverance from the bondage of corruption into the glorious liberty
of thy children; through Jesus Christ our Lord. *Henry Alford*

432

O God, the author and fountain of hope, enable us to rely with
confident expectation on thy promises, knowing that the trials and
hindrances of the present time are not worthy to be compared with
the glory that shall be revealed, and having our faces steadfastly
set towards the light that shineth more and more to the perfect day;
through Jesus Christ our Lord. *A Devotional Diary*

Glorious liberty 433

We beseech thee, O Lord Christ, to deliver thy Church from the worship of mammon, from bondage to the world, and from all complicity in social evil and silence at wrong. Bring all mankind into the glorious liberty of the children of God, and set the whole creation free from sin and corruption; for thy holy name's sake.

Be ye merciful 434

Father of all mercies, teach us to be merciful, as thou art merciful. Father of all forgiveness, help us to forgive others, as thou hast forgiven us; knowing that, with what measure we mete, it shall be measured to us again; for Jesus Christ's sake.

Generosity 435

O God in whom all fullness dwelleth, who givest without measure to them that ask; Give us faith to ask, and faith to receive, all that thy bounty giveth; that being filled with all thy fullness we may as thy faithful stewards impart thy gifts to all thy children; for Jesus Christ's sake. *Daily Prayer*

FIFTH SUNDAY AFTER TRINITY

Called to inherit a blessing 436

O GOD, who in thy fatherly love hast called us that we should inherit a blessing: Give to us also, we pray thee, the blessing of wholesome speech and loving deed; that following always that which is good, we may do and suffer all that thou willest; in the name and strength of Jesus Christ thy Son our Lord.
L. E. H. Stephens-Hodge

The tongue 437

Set a watch, O Lord, upon our tongue, that we may never speak the cruel word which is not true; or being true, is not the whole truth; or being wholly true, is merciless; for the love of Jesus Christ our Lord. *Daily Prayer*

Launch out into the deep 438

Grant, O blessed Lord, that thy Church in this our day may hear anew thy call to launch out into the deep in the service of thy glorious gospel; that souls for whom thou hast died may be won for thee, to the increase of thy kingdom and the glory of thy holy name. *Frank Colquhoun*

Fishers of men 439

O Lord Christ, who dost call thy disciples not only to follow thee but to become fishers of men: Give to us and to thy whole Church grace to obey thy word and to engage in a bold and adventurous evangelism; and grant that, attempting great things for thee, we may also expect great things from thee; to whom be glory for ever and ever. *Frank Colquhoun*

SIXTH SUNDAY AFTER TRINITY

Baptized into Christ's death 440

O LORD Jesus Christ, into whose death we have been baptized: Grant, we beseech thee, that like as thou wast raised from the dead by the glory of the Father, even so we may walk in newness of life; that having been planted in the likeness of thy death, we may be also in the likeness of thy resurrection; for the glory of thy holy name. *Henry Alford*

Alive from the dead 441

O God, who hast called us out of the bondage of sin into the perfect freedom of thy children: Grant us grace that we may yield ourselves unto thee as alive from the dead, and our bodily members as servants of righteousness; that we may have our fruit unto holiness, and in the end everlasting life; through Jesus Christ our Lord. *Henry Alford**

Crucified and risen with Christ 442

O Lord Christ, by whose single death upon the cross the members of thy body also die to servitude and sin: Grant us so to crucify the old man, that the new may daily rise with thee in the immortal power of thy free Spirit, who liveth and reigneth with the Father and thee, one God, world without end. *E. Milner-White*

The way of reconciliation 443

Almighty God, who hast set thy law of love ever before us: Grant us thy grace that we may never harbour any resentment or ill-feeling in our hearts, but seek at all times the way of reconciliation and peace, according to the teaching of thy Son, our Lord and Saviour Jesus Christ. *L. E. H. Stephens-Hodge*

SEVENTH SUNDAY AFTER TRINITY

Servants to righteousness 444

ALMIGHTY God, who in thy Son Jesus Christ hast called us from the bondage of sin to be servants of righteousness: Give us grace to yield our lives wholly to thine obedience; that, being

made free from sin, we may have our fruit unto holiness, and hereafter may be made partakers of the life everlasting; through the
same Jesus Christ our Lord. *Frank Colquhoun*

Christ's compassion for the hungry 445

Fill us, O Christ, with thine own compassion for the hungry
multitudes of the world of our day; and use us now, as thou didst
use thy disciples of old, as thy willing instruments to minister to
their needs, through all such means as thou shalt show us; for thy
mercy's sake. *Frank Colquhoun*

446

O Lord, who seest the multitudes, and art moved with compassion
because they are an-hungered: Inspire thy Church with thy love and
pity to gather unto thee the famished souls of men, that they may
be satisfied with the living Bread; and as thou carest for the bodies
as well as for the souls of men, move us and all thy servants with
like mercy; that the needy may be fed and clothed, and that none
may be homeless or destitute; for the glory of thy holy name.

*James Ferguson**

EIGHTH SUNDAY AFTER TRINITY

Led by the Spirit 447

GRANT, O heavenly Father, that by the guidance of the Holy
Spirit we may be enabled to discern thy holy will; and that by
the grace of the same Spirit we may also be enabled to do it, gladly
and with our whole hearts; for the glory of thy Son Jesus Christ our
Lord.

The witness of the Spirit 448

O God, who hast given us not the spirit of bondage, but the
Spirit of adoption into thy family: Grant us the witness of thy
Spirit within our hearts, testifying that we are thy children; and
give us that fellowship with the sufferings of Christ which shall end
in our being glorified with him; through the same Jesus Christ our
Lord. *Henry Alford*

449

O Almighty and merciful Lord, who givest unto thy faithful people
the Holy Spirit as a sure pledge of thy heavenly kingdom: Grant
unto us this same Spirit, that he may bear witness with our spirit
that we be thy children and heirs of thy kingdom; through our Lord
and Saviour Jesus Christ. *Godly Prayers, 1559**

Beware of false prophets 450

Almighty Father, who by thy Son Jesus Christ hast taught us to beware of false prophets: Have mercy upon thy Church, we beseech thee, to deliver it from all evil; and give us faithful pastors and teachers who shall truly fulfil thy command and preach nothing contrary to thy Holy Word; that we thy people, being instructed, nurtured and comforted by thy heavenly truth, may bring forth fruit to thy glory; through the same Jesus Christ our Lord.

Adapted from a 16th c. German prayer

By their fruits 451

Grant, O Lord, we beseech thee, that as a tree is known by its fruit, so we may be recognized as thy children by our obedience to thy will. Help us to put away all hypocrisy and self-seeking, that we may truly set forth thy glory and extend thy kingdom; through Jesus Christ our Lord.   *L. E. H. Stephens-Hodge*

NINTH SUNDAY AFTER TRINITY

The temptations of life 452

MAKE us tender and compassionate towards those who are overtaken by temptation, considering ourselves, how we have fallen in times past and may fall yet again. Make us watchful and sober-minded, looking ever unto thee for grace to stand upright, and to persevere unto the end; through thy Son Jesus Christ our Lord.   *C. J. Vaughan*

453

O God, who art faithful to thy people and dost not permit them to be tempted above that they are able, but with the temptation also makest a way of escape that they may be able to bear it: We humbly entreat thee to strengthen us thy servants with thy heavenly aid and keep us with thy continual protection; that we may evermore wait on thee, and never by any temptation be drawn away from thee; through Jesus Christ our Lord.   *E. B. Pusey★*

Faithful stewards 454

Almighty God, whose loving hand hath given us all that we possess: Grant us grace that we may honour thee with our substance, and, remembering the account which we must one day give, may be faithful stewards of thy bounty; through Jesus Christ our Lord.   *American Prayer Book*

The right use of money 455

O Lord and heavenly Father, who through thy Son our Saviour hast taught us that we cannot serve both God and mammon: Deliver us, we pray thee, from the love of money; and grant us grace to use wisely and faithfully all such possessions as thou hast entrusted to us, for the furtherance of thy kingdom, the relief of those in need, and the supply of our own necessities; through the same Jesus Christ our Lord. *Frank Colquhoun*

456

Lord Christ, who for our sake didst become poor, though thou wast rich: Help us to use our money rightly, wisely, and generously, that, having used corruptible goods to thy glory, we may at last gain the inheritance incorruptible, where thou livest and reignest with the Father and the Holy Spirit, one God, world without end.

Student Prayer*

See also 808–19

TENTH SUNDAY AFTER TRINITY

Diversities of gifts 457

ALMIGHTY and everlasting God, who hast revealed thyself in all thy power through the incarnation of thy Son, Jesus Christ our Lord, and who dwellest in us by the working of thy Holy Spirit: Grant that we may, each in his several calling, profit from the operation of that one and the self-same Spirit whose gifts are manifold, to the glory of thy holy name, Father, Son, and Holy Ghost, world without end. *Euchologium Anglicanum*

The use of gifts 458

O Lord God Almighty, who dost by thy Holy Spirit endow thy servants with manifold gifts of knowledge and skill: Grant us grace to use them always for thine honour, and for the service of men; through Jesus Christ our Lord.

The things that belong to peace 459

Almighty God, whose righteous will governs all things and controls the destinies of men: Teach the nations of the world the things that belong to their peace; that they may find their freedom in obedience to thy laws, and their unity in the brotherhood of thy kingdom; through Jesus Christ our Lord. *Adapted*

Cleansing the temple 460

O Lord Christ, who in thine indignation didst cast out those who profaned thy Father's house: Enter into the temple of our hearts;

that we being cleansed from all self-contentment, all hardness and want of charity, may worship the Father in spirit and in truth; who with thee, O Saviour, in the unity of the Spirit, is glorious and adorable for ever.

461

O Lord Christ, who didst cast out them that bought and sold in the temple at Jerusalem: Cleanse and sanctify thy Church, the living temple of thy Spirit, that it may be in very truth a house of prayer for all nations; and that the kingdoms of the world, which are divided one against the other, may become one kingdom of our God, united in thy service; for thy name's sake.   *Adapted*

The house of prayer   462

O Lord Jesus Christ, who didst drive forth from the temple those who profaned the holy place, saying to them, My house shall be called the house of prayer: Make us so to love the habitation of thy house and the place where thy honour dwelleth, that with humility and godly fear we may draw near to worship thee; who livest and reignest with the Father and the Holy Spirit, one God, world without end.   *W. E. Scudamore*

ELEVENTH SUNDAY AFTER TRINITY

The gospel of the resurrection   463

O LORD our God, who hast committed to us the glorious gospel of our risen Saviour and Master: Grant that as we joyfully receive the good news for ourselves, so we may gratefully share it with others, and ever give glory to thee, by whose grace alone we are what we are: through the same Jesus Christ our Lord.
Frank Colquhoun

The resurrection hope   464

O God, who hast brought life and immortality to light by the gospel, and hast begotten us again to a living hope through the resurrection of Jesus Christ from the dead: Make us steadfast and immovable in the faith, always abounding in the work of the Lord, who died for our sins and rose again, and now liveth and reigneth with thee and the Holy Spirit, world without end.
James Mountain

The prayer of the humble   465

Almighty God, only giver of all mercies, whose Son, Jesus Christ, has taught us how to pray aright: Save us, we beseech thee, from all presumption in our prayer, and grant unto us the grace of humility and contrition; that we may, sharing the vision of thine apostle Saint Paul, know that it is by the grace of God alone that we are what we are, and that we can do nothing but through the strengthening of thy Son, Christ our Lord; who liveth and reigneth with thee in the unity of the Holy Spirit, ever one God, world without end.

Euchologium Anglicanum

Deus misereatur 466

Almighty God, who resisteth the proud and giveth grace to the humble: Deliver us when we draw near to thee from all self-sufficiency and spiritual pride; and grant us an ever deepening sense of our own unworthiness and of thy unfailing mercy; through him who is our only righteousness, thy Son Jesus Christ our Lord.

Frank Colquhoun

Against pride 467

O God, who scatterest the proud in the imagination of their hearts: Forgive our sins of pride, we beseech thee, especially our pride of race and class. May we never despise our fellow men, but in honour prefer one another; for the sake of him who humbled himself that he might exalt us, Jesus Christ our Lord.

468

Save us, we beseech thee, merciful Lord, from all pride and self-assertion, and all desire for the praise of men; that whatever we do for thy Church may be done for his sake alone who loved us and gave himself for us, Jesus Christ our Lord.

TWELFTH SUNDAY AFTER TRINITY

The new covenant 469

ALMIGHTY and everlasting God, by whose grace we have been admitted into the glory of the new covenant: Grant, we beseech thee, that being delivered from the death of sin and the bondage of the law, we may rejoice in the life and liberty of the Spirit, and evermore find our sufficiency in thee; through Jesus Christ our Lord.

Frank Colquhoun

The unveiled glory 470

O Almighty God, who hast revealed thyself in him who veiled his Godhead that he might unveil thy glory, and hast made him the eternal sacrifice and only priest of men: Grant that by the power of thy Holy Spirit the veil on our hearts may be taken away, and we may look on him who loved us and gave himself for us, and so be changed into the same image from glory to glory, until at last we shall see him with unveiled face, for evermore.   *W. M. Clow*

Opened ears and lips   471

O Gracious God, whose blessed Son set forth thy love towards mankind, in his miracles of healing and mercy, making both the deaf to hear and the dumb to speak: Grant that our ears may be opened to thy Word, and our tongues loosed to proclaim it to others, and to further the spreading of thy gospel among all nations; through the same Jesus Christ our Lord.

Euchologium Anglicanum

The deaf and dumb   472

O God, the Father of our Lord Jesus Christ, who went about doing good, and both opened the ears of the deaf and made the dumb to speak: Teach thy people, after his example, to pity and succour thy deaf children who need their help. May thy Holy Spirit bless our efforts to carry to them the knowledge of thy saving grace, and may they so serve thee in the body of their humiliation, that thereafter they may wear the body of thy glory; through the same Jesus Christ our Lord.   *Mandell Creighton*

THIRTEENTH SUNDAY AFTER TRINITY

The gospel promise   473

ALMIGHTY God, who in Christ Jesus hast fulfilled to the sons of men thy ancient word of promise: Grant us grace to lay hold upon that promise by a living faith, that we may receive thy gift of righteousness, and at the last may enter upon our eternal inheritance; through the merits of the same thy Son, Jesus Christ our Lord.   *Frank Colquhoun*

Love and service   474

O Lord our God, give us more love, more denial of self, more likeness to thee. Teach us that it is better to give than to receive, better to forget ourselves than to put ourselves forward, better to serve than to be waited on; and unto thee, the God of love, be praise and glory for ever.

475

O Blessed Lord, who by thy word and example hast shown us the meaning of neighbourliness and the way of love: Grant that we may learn to recognize as our neighbour every fellow man who needs our help, and to serve him with a love that is costly and unselfish, like thine own love for us. We ask this for thy name's sake.

Frank Colquhoun

476

Grant us, O Lord, to love thee with all our heart, with all our mind and soul and strength, and our neighbour for thy sake; that the grace of brotherly love may dwell in us, and all hatred, envy and malice may die in us, to the glory of thy name.

FOURTEENTH SUNDAY AFTER TRINITY

Faith, hope, and love 477

O OUR God, we believe in thee, we hope in thee, and we love thee, because thou hast created us, redeemed us, and dost sanctify us. Increase our faith, strengthen our hope, and deepen our love, that giving up ourselves wholly to thy will, we may serve thee faithfully all the rest of our life; through Jesus Christ our Lord. *The Narrow Way*

Walk in the Spirit 478

O Eternal Lord God, without whose aid we cannot do the things that we would: Look mercifully upon the waywardness of our hearts, and strengthen us against evil; that as citizens of thy holy kingdom we may walk henceforth in the power of the Spirit, and bring forth fruit to thy glory; through Jesus Christ our Lord.

Frank Colquhoun

The fruit of the Spirit 479

O God, who hast commanded us to walk in the Spirit and not to fulfil the lusts of the flesh: Perfect us, we pray thee, in love, that we may conquer our natural selfishness and give ourselves to others. Fill our hearts with thy joy, and garrison them with thy peace; make us longsuffering and gentle, and thus subdue our hasty and angry tempers; give us faithfulness, meekness and self-control; that so crucifying the flesh with its affections and lusts, we may bring forth the fruit of the Spirit to thy praise and glory; through Jesus Christ our Lord. *Henry Alford*

480

Enrich our lives, O Lord, with the fruit of the Spirit; that being filled with love and joy and peace, we may live together in patience and kindness, in goodness, faithfulness and gentleness, ever exercising the grace of self-control; through Jesus Christ our Lord.

Based on Galatians 5. 22, 23

Gratitude 481

Almighty God our heavenly Father, who hast bidden us to give thanks for all things and to forget not all thy benefits: Accept our praise for the great mercies we have received at thy hands; ever give us grateful hearts; and help us to magnify thee in our daily life; through Jesus Christ our Lord. *Frank Colquhoun*

Lepers 482

O Lord Jesus, who didst have compassion on lepers, and stretching forth thy hand didst touch them into health and life: Have mercy on those who suffer from the same disease to-day; prosper the efforts of all who care for them; that they may be healed in body and soul and restored to fellowship with their families and friends; for thy holy name's sake.

FIFTEENTH SUNDAY AFTER TRINITY

The glory of the cross 483

LORD Jesus Christ, who for our sake didst endure the cross, and hast bidden us to follow thee: Take away from us all fear, all coldness of heart, all unwillingness to suffer; that we, glorying in thy cross, may glory also that thou hast called us to bear it with thee; for thy name's sake. *Daily Prayer*

The marks of the Lord Jesus 484

O Lord, our Saviour and God, whom nails could not hold to the cross, but only love: Grant that we, who have received the fullness of thy love, may be ready to bear before the world the marks of thy passion; who livest and reignest with the Father and the Holy Ghost, one God, world without end.

A Procession of Passion Prayers

Freedom from anxiety 485

Almighty God, our heavenly Father, who dost feed the birds and clothe the flowers, and who carest for us as a father for his children: We beseech thee of thy tender goodness to save us from distrust and vain self-concern; that with unwavering faith we may cast our every care on thee, and live in daily obedience to thy will; through thy beloved Son, Jesus Christ our Lord.

Austrian Church Order, 1571

486

O most loving and tender Father, preserve us from all faithless cares and selfish anxieties, and help us to cast our burdens upon thee, who hast given us assurance of thy care for us, and hast promised to supply the needs of all who seek first thy kingdom; for the sake of thy Son, our Saviour Jesus Christ.

487

Almighty God, who knowest our necessities before we ask, and our ignorance in asking: Set free thy servants from all anxious thoughts for the morrow; give us contentment with thy good gifts; and confirm our faith that according as we seek thy kingdom, thou wilt not suffer us to lack any good thing; through Jesus Christ our Lord.   *St. Augustine*

Seek ye first the kingdom   **488**

Cleanse our minds, O Lord, we beseech thee, of all anxious thoughts for ourselves, that we may learn not to trust in the abundance of what we have, save as tokens of thy goodness and grace, but that we may commit ourselves in faith to thy keeping, and devote all our energy of soul, mind and body to the work of thy kingdom and the furthering of the purposes of thy divine righteousness; through Jesus Christ our Lord.   *Euchologium Anglicanum*

SIXTEENTH SUNDAY AFTER TRINITY

St. Paul's prayer   **489**

O GOD, the Father of our Lord Jesus Christ, from whom every family in heaven and on earth is named: Grant that, according to the riches of thy glory, we may be strengthened with power through thy Spirit in our inner being; that Christ may dwell in our hearts by faith; that we, being rooted and grounded in thy love, may be strong to apprehend with all the saints what is its length and breadth and height and depth, and to know the love of Christ which passeth knowledge; that we may be filled with all the fullness of God.   *Ephesians 3. 14–19*

Christ in us   **490**

Lord, who hast warned us that without thee we can do nothing; and by thy holy apostle hast taught us that in thy strength we can do all things: So take and possess us, that our weakness may be transformed by thy power; that we be no longer our own, but thine; that it be not we who live, but thou who livest in us; who now reignest with the Father and the Holy Spirit, world without end.   *Daily Prayer*

The sanctuary of the heart   491

O Thou who dwellest in every humble heart, and dost consecrate it for thy sanctuary: Hallow, we pray thee, our hearts within us, that they may be houses of prayer, the dwelling-places of thy Spirit, wherein thou dost reveal thy holy mysteries; through Jesus Christ our Lord.   *Adapted from Jeremy Taylor*

492

O Spirit of the living God, who dost sanctify the lives of thy people, and dost build them up into a holy temple for thy habitation: Grant us so to know thy indwelling presence that we may be set free from lesser desires, and by thy grace may be conformed to the likeness of Jesus Christ our Lord.   *New Every Morning**

Those who mourn   493

O Lord Jesus Christ, who hadst compassion on the widow of Nain, and didst say unto her, Weep not: Comfort, we beseech thee, the hearts of those who mourn the loss of their beloved, and when thou comest in thy kingdom, wipe away all tears from their eyes; who livest and reignest with the Father and the Holy Spirit, ever one God, world without end.

*Salisbury Book of Occasional Offices**

See also 1016–20

SEVENTEENTH SUNDAY AFTER TRINITY

The unity of the Spirit   494

O LORD Jesus Christ, who didst pray for thy disciples that they might be one, even as thou art one with the Father: Draw us to thyself, that in common love and obedience to thee we may be united to one another, in the fellowship of the one Spirit, that the world may believe that thou art Lord, to the glory of God the Father.   *William Temple*

There is one body   495

Grant, O Lord, that as there is one Spirit, one Lord, one faith, one hope of our calling; so thy Church, being one body, may draw all nations to the one baptism, as children of the one God and Father of us all, who is above all and through all and in all, now and for evermore.   *Based on Ephesians 4. 4–6*

For humility   496

Lord Jesus Christ, who by precept and example hast taught us that the greatest of all is the servant of all, and that the humble shall be exalted: Make us content to take the lowest place; and if it shall please thee to call us higher, do thou preserve within us a simple and lowly spirit; to thy great glory. *Daily Prayer*

497

Blessed Lord, who putteth down the mighty from their seat and exaltest those of low degree: Save us, we beseech thee, from pride and vainglory, from self-seeking and false ambition. Give us a humble and contrite spirit, that we may think less of ourselves, more of others, and most of all of thee, who art our mighty God and Saviour; to whom with thee and the Holy Spirit we ascribe all praise and glory, now and for evermore. *Frank Colquhoun*

498

Take from us, O Lord God, all pride and vanity, all boasting and self-assertion, and give us the true courage that shows itself in gentleness; the true wisdom that shows itself in simplicity; and the true power that shows itself in modesty; through Jesus Christ our Lord. *Charles Kingsley*

See also 1655–7

EIGHTEENTH SUNDAY AFTER TRINITY

Enriched by Christ   499

ALMIGHTY God, who hast bestowed thy grace upon thy people by thy Son Jesus Christ: Grant us, we beseech thee, to be enriched with his manifold gifts; that patiently enduring through the darkness of this world, we may be found shining like lamps in the day of our Lord Jesus Christ, when he cometh in his kingdom; to whom be praise and glory for ever and ever.

Knowledge and utterance   500

Almighty God, who art the author of all spiritual gifts: Bestow upon thy Church in this our day the grace of knowledge, to apprehend the fullness of divine truth, and of utterance to declare that truth to others; that the testimony of Christ may be confirmed among us, and in everything we may be enriched in him, even thy Son Jesus Christ our Lord. *Frank Colquhoun*

Love for God and our neighbour   501

O Heavenly Father, grant us so to love thee with all our heart and mind and strength, and our neighbour for thy sake; that the grace of charity and brotherly love may dwell in us, and all envy, harshness and ill-will may die in us; according to the perfect love of thy Son, Jesus Christ our Lord.

502

Give us grace, O God our Father, to keep this day and always the new commandment and the great commandment and all the commandments, by loving thee with all our mind and soul and strength, and one another for thy sake; in the name of Jesus Christ our Lord.

Daily Prayer

What think ye of the Christ?

503

O Lord Christ, Son of David, born for us in lowly state at Bethlehem, and now exalted to the right hand of the Majesty on high: Grant us grace to think worthily of thee both in thy humility and in thy glory; that we may ascribe to thee the honour that is thy due, now and for evermore.

Frank Colquhoun

NINETEENTH SUNDAY AFTER TRINITY

The way of holiness

504

WRITE deeply upon our minds, O Lord our God, the lessons of thy holy Word, that only the pure in heart can see thee. Leave us not in the bondage of any sinful inclination. May we neither deceive ourselves with the thought that we have no sin, nor idly acquiesce in aught of which our conscience accuses us. Strengthen us by thy Holy Spirit to fight the good fight of faith, and grant that no day may pass without its victory; through Jesus Christ our Lord.

C. J. Vaughan

Forgiving one another

505

O Lord, because we often sin and have to ask for pardon, help us to forgive as we would be forgiven; neither mentioning old offences committed against us, nor dwelling upon them in thought; but loving our brother freely as thou freely lovest us; for thy name's sake.

Christina Rossetti

506

Almighty God, renew us day by day by thy Holy Spirit, in whom thou hast sealed us for thine own: Let all bitterness be put away from us, all anger and evil-speaking and malice; may we be kind one to another, tenderhearted, forgiving one another, even as thou, O Father, hast forgiven us for the sake of thy Son, our Saviour Jesus Christ.

Based on Ephesians 4. 30–32

The forgiveness of sins

507

Blot out, we humbly beseech thee, O Lord, our past transgressions; forgive our negligence and ignorance, our mistakes and misunderstandings; and uplift our hearts to thee in new love and dedication; that unburdened from the grief and shame of past faithlessness, we may henceforth serve thee with renewed courage and devotion; through Jesus Christ our Lord.

508

Hear us, O Lord, as we come to thee burdened with our guilt, and bow in faith at thy feet. Speak to us thy word of absolution; say to our souls, Thy sins be forgiven thee; that with good courage we may rise up and go forth to serve thee, now and all our days, to the glory of thy holy name. *Frank Colquhoun*

Incurables 509

Lord Jesus, who in Capernaum didst heal the sufferer borne of four: Behold in thy mercy those whom no man can cure, and whom in prayer we lay at thy feet. O thou with whom all things are possible, grant them thy healing and help, and answer our prayer according to thy holy will; for the glory of thy great name.

Adapted

TWENTIETH SUNDAY AFTER TRINITY

Redeeming the time 510

O LORD God of time and eternity, who makest us creatures of time that, when time is over, we may attain thy blessed eternity: With time, thy gift, give us also wisdom to redeem the time, lest our day of grace be lost; for our Lord Jesus' sake.

Christina Rossetti

Be filled with the Spirit 511

O Blessed Jesus, who hast redeemed us to God by thy blood, and hast consecrated us in baptism to be temples of the Holy Ghost: Make us, we beseech thee, both in body and soul, meet for thy dwelling place; that our hearts may be houses of prayer and praise, of pure desires and holy thoughts of thee, whose we are and whom we serve, and to whom be glory, now and for evermore.

E. M. Goulburn

The spirit of praise 512

O Lord Jesus Christ, Wisdom and Word of God, fill our hearts, we beseech thee, with thy most Holy Spirit, that out of the abundance of our hearts our mouths may speak thy praise in psalms and hymns and spiritual songs; to thy everlasting glory.

After Christina Rossetti

513

O Heavenly Father, who hast taught us to show forth thy praise in psalms and hymns and spiritual songs: So fill us, we pray thee, with thy Spirit that we may make melody to thee both in our hearts and with our lives, evermore giving thee thanks for all things, in the name of Jesus Christ our Lord. *Frank Colquhoun*

Many are called, but few are chosen **514**

O Lord God, the source of all grace and the judge of all men, who hast invited us to enter thy kingdom, but dost not force our wills to obedience: Grant that we may so use thy present grace that we may not have cause to fear thy final judgment; through Jesus Christ our Lord. *Euchologium Anglicanum*

TWENTY-FIRST SUNDAY AFTER TRINITY

The armour of God **515**

GRANT us, O Lord, so to enter on the service of our Christian warfare, that, putting on the whole armour of God, we may endure hardness and fight against the spiritual powers of darkness, and be more than conquerors through him that loved us, Jesus Christ our Lord. *Leonine Sacramentary**

516

Equip us, O God, for the spiritual conflict with thine own armour: with the shield of faith, the sword of the Spirit, the helmet of salvation, the girdle of truth, the breastplate of righteousness, that we may be able to stand in the evil day; and grant that, having our feet shod with the gospel of peace, we may be able to maintain our ground unflinching to the end, through the might of Jesus Christ, the Captain of our salvation. *Based on Ephesians 6. 11–17*

The holy war **517**

O God, the Lord and leader of the hosts of the blessed: Instruct us in the spiritual warfare; arm us against all foes visible and invisible; subdue unto us our own rebellious affections; and give us daily victory in the following of him who vanquished sin and death, and now goeth forth with us conquering and to conquer, even thy Son our Saviour Jesus Christ. *After George Wither (Daily Prayer)* See also *1642–50*

Faith in Christ's word **518**

Grant us, O Lord, the faith that rests not on signs and wonders but on thy love and faithfulness; that obedient to thy word and trusting in thy promises, we may know thy peace and healing power, both in our hearts and in our homes; for the honour of thy holy name. *Frank Colquhoun*

The work of grace 519

WE give thee thanks, O God our Father, for the good work which thou hast begun in us, in that thou hast called us to the knowledge of thy grace and faith in thee; and we pray thee so to continue thy work in us that our lives may be strengthened for thy service in the fellowship of the gospel, and our love may abound yet more and more in knowledge and all discernment, to thy praise and glory; through Jesus Christ our Lord.

Love and knowledge 520

We pray thee, O God our Father, for all who profess and call themselves Christians, that their love may abound yet more and more in knowledge and in all discernment until the day of Christ; that they may be sincere and void of offence, being filled with the fruits of righteousness which are through Jesus Christ unto thy praise and glory, now and for ever. *Based on Philippians 1. 9–11*

Debtors 521

O Lord and Father, to whom alone the debtors in ten thousand talents can come with hope of mercy: Have mercy upon us, O Lord, who have aught to repay; forgive us all the debt, forgive us all our sins, and make us merciful to others; for the sake of Jesus Christ our Lord. *Adapted from Lancelot Andrewes (Daily Prayer)*

Our own shortcomings 522

O Lord, who hast taught us that we can only be forgiven, as we ourselves forgive: Help us ever to bear in mind our continued shortcomings, our manifold transgressions; that as we remember the injuries which we have suffered and never merited, we may also remember the kindnesses which we have received and never earned, the punishments which we have deserved and never suffered; and therewith may render thanks to thee for thine unfailing mercies, and the mercies of our fellowmen; for thy name's sake.

Daily Prayer

Forgiving one another 523

Grant, O Lord, that as thy Son our Saviour Jesus Christ prayed for his enemies on the cross, so we may have grace to forgive those that wrongfully or scornfully use us; that we ourselves may be able to receive thy forgiveness; though the same Jesus Christ our Lord. *Church of South India*

TWENTY-THIRD SUNDAY AFTER TRINITY

A colony of heaven 524

O HEAVENLY Father, who hast called us by thy grace to be a colony of heaven here on earth: Deepen within us, we beseech thee, a sense of our citizenship with the saints in glory; and grant that through all the days of our pilgrimage in this world we may humbly walk with thee in the way of holiness, and faithfully care for the needs of others, till we come to thy everlasting kingdom; through the mercy of thy Son Jesus Christ our Lord.

Frank Colquhoun

Citizens of heaven and earth 525

O Eternal God, our heavenly Father, who hast given to us thy children an abiding citizenship in heaven, and, in the days of our pilgrimage, a citizenship also upon earth: Give us thine aid, as we journey to that heavenly city, so faithfully to perform the duties which befall us on our way, that at the last we may be found worthy to enter into thy rest; through Jesus Christ our Lord.

Daily Prayer

526

Almighty God, whose blessed Son taught in all honesty the way of life that thou requirest: Grant that we may so live as dutiful and loyal citizens of our earthly country, that we may show ourselves to be members of that heavenly country whereof thou art sovereign Lord and King; through the same Jesus Christ our Lord.

L. E. H. Stephens-Hodge

The things that abide 527

Grant us, O Lord, not to mind earthly things, but to love things heavenly; and even now, while we are placed among things that are passing away, to cleave to those that shall abide; through Jesus Christ our Lord. *Leonine Sacramentary*

TWENTY-FOURTH SUNDAY AFTER TRINITY

The walk that pleases God 528

O GOD, the Father of our Lord Jesus Christ, give us grace, we beseech thee, to walk worthy of thee, so as to be pleasing in thy sight; that being fruitful in every good work, and increasing in the

128

knowledge of thee, we may be made meet at last to be partakers of
the inheritance of the saints in light; through the same Jesus Christ
our Lord. *Based on Colossians I. 10–12*

Increasing in the knowledge of God 529

O God, who art nigh to all them that call upon thee in truth;
who art thyself the Truth, whom to know is life eternal: Instruct
us with thy divine wisdom, and teach us thy law; that we may know
the truth and walk in it; through him in whom the truth was made
manifest, even Jesus Christ, thy Son, our Lord.

After St. Augustine

The giver of life 530

O Lord of life, who didst raise from the sleep of death the
daughter of Jairus the ruler: Extend to us, we pray thee, thy
quickening power, that we may know the life more abundant which
thou didst come to bring; for the glory of thy holy name.

Frank Colquhoun

The healing Christ 531

O Lord Jesus Christ, who still to-day dost tread the busy
thoroughfares of life in readiness to heal and save: Open our eyes
that we may recognize thy presence; open our hearts that we may
trust thy love for us; open our lips that we may joyfully confess thee
before men; we ask it for thy dear name's sake.

L. E. H. Stephens-Hodge

SUNDAY NEXT BEFORE ADVENT (TRINITY XXV)

The King of righteousness 532

O GOD, who didst wonderfully deliver thy people out of Egypt
and didst bring them into their own land: Deliver us, we beseech thee, from the tyranny of sin, and bring us into that land
where the Prince of Peace reigneth, and the lives of men proclaim
thy righteousness; through the same Jesus Christ our Lord.

L. E. H. Stephens-Hodge

The Bread from heaven 533

Almighty God, who hast given to thy people the true Bread from
heaven, even thy Son Jesus Christ: Grant that our souls may be
so fed by him who giveth life unto the world, that we may be made
strong for thy service, and share with others that which we have so
richly received; through the same Jesus Christ our Lord.

Adapted

The end of the Church's year 534

O Lord Jesus, with whom we have passed another Christian year, following thee from thy birth in our flesh to thy sufferings and triumph, and listening to the utterances and counsels of thy Spirit: Even thus would we also end this year of grace, and stand complete in thee our Righteousness; humbly beseeching thee that we may evermore continue in thy faith and abide in thy love; who liveth and reigneth with the Father and the Holy Spirit, one God, world without end. *Henry Alford**

The things eternal 535

Almighty and everlasting God, who hast put thine own eternity into our hearts, and desires which the world cannot satisfy: Lift our eyes, we pray thee, above the narrow horizons of this present world, that we may behold the things eternal in the heavens, wherein is laid up for us an inheritance that fadeth not away; through Jesus Christ our Lord. *The Daily Service*

The uncertainty of life 536

O God, whose days are without end and whose mercies cannot be numbered: Make us, we pray thee, deeply sensible of the shortness and uncertainty of life; let thy Holy Spirit lead us in the paths of righteousness all our days; that when we shall have served thee in our generation, we may have an abundant entrance into thy everlasting kingdom; through thy mercy in Jesus Christ, our only Saviour and Mediator.

537

O God, so rule and govern our hearts and minds by thy Holy Spirit, that being ever mindful of the end of all things, and the day of thy just judgment, we may be stirred up to holiness of living here, and dwell with thee forever hereafter; through Jesus Christ, thy Son, our Lord. *Lutheran Church*

St. Andrew (November 30)   538

ALMIGHTY God, who didst give such grace to thy Apostle Saint Andrew, that he counted the sharp and painful death of the cross to be an high honour, and a great joy: Grant us to take and esteem all troubles and adversities which shall come unto us for thy sake, as things profitable for us toward the obtaining of eternal life; through Jesus Christ our Lord.

Prayers for the Christian Year

539

Almighty God, at whose call thy servant Andrew left all to follow Christ, and by whose grace he was made strong for service: Help us, whom also thou hast called to be thy servants, so to persevere in the way of faith and duty, that finally we may finish our course with joy; through the same Jesus Christ our Lord.

540

O Almighty God, who hast called thy Church to bear witness for thee before all nations: Grant that as Saint Andrew brought his brother to Jesus, so we, like him, may be wise to win souls, and may labour diligently for the enlargement of thy kingdom; through the same Jesus Christ our Lord.   *Adapted*

St. Thomas (December 21)   541

Almighty God, who to thy holy Apostle Thomas didst reveal thine incarnate Son in his risen glory: Draw, we beseech thee, the people of our land to know and confess him as their Lord and God, that coming to thee by him they may believe and have life in thy name: through the same Jesus Christ our Lord and Saviour.

C.I.P.B.C. Prayer Book

542

O Lord Jesus Christ, who didst say to thy servant Thomas the Apostle, I am the Way, and the Truth, and the Life: Mercifully grant that we, looking to thee by faith, may find in thee the Way that leads to the Father, the Truth that makes us free, and the Life that is life indeed, now and always.   *Frank Colquhoun*

St. Stephen (December 26)   543

Fill us, O God, with thy Holy Spirit, the Spirit of Truth and Charity; that like the first martyr, Saint Stephen, we may contend earnestly and fearlessly for the faith of the gospel, and also may pray with hearts of love for those that despitefully use us; for the glory of Jesus Christ our Saviour.

544

Merciful God and Father, who didst give thy Son to reconcile us, thine enemies, to thee: Grant, we beseech thee, that we too may learn to pray for our enemies, as thy servant Stephen prayed for his persecutors, and, like him, be permitted to see thy glory; through Jesus Christ our Lord.

St. John the Evangelist (December 27)   545

O Almighty God, who through the holy Apostle Saint John hast revealed to us the mystery of the Word made flesh: Keep us steadfast in the faith that the Son of God has come; that believing in him we may have life through his name; to whom with thee and the Holy Spirit be glory for ever and ever.   *Frank Colquhoun*

The Innocents' Day (December 28)   546

Blessed Saviour, whose life in this world began with the slaughter of helpless infants at Bethlehem, and who knowest the sorrows of the human heart: Show thy compassion, we pray thee, on all who suffer and grieve amid the cruelty and injustice of the world; and teach both them and us that by thy grace life's bitter things can be redeemed and turned to thy praise. We ask it for thy mercy's sake.

547

O Lord, on this day when we remember how innocent children suffered death for the sake of thy holy Son: We beseech thee to slay in us everything that displeases thee and contradicts thy perfect will; that we who have been called to be thy children may glorify thee in our lives; through the same Jesus Christ our Lord.

Adapted

For the feast of the Circumcision, see 82–7

The Conversion of St. Paul (January 25)   548

O God, who didst call Saul, the persecutor of the Church, to be the Apostle Paul, and to proclaim the gospel of thy Son Jesus Christ to the Gentiles: Grant that, as thou hast called us also, we may be true to our calling, and count everything loss for the gain of knowing Christ Jesus as our Saviour; to whom with thee and the Holy Spirit be all honour and glory, world without end.

Church of South India

549

Almighty Saviour, who didst call thy servant Saint Paul to be an apostle to the Gentiles: We beseech thee to illumine the world with the radiance of the gospel of thy grace committed to his trust, that all nations may worship thee and acknowledge thee to be the Lord; who art with the Father and the Holy Spirit one God, world without end. *The Missionary Conference, 1894**

The Purification (February 2)   550

O Lord Jesus Christ, who as a child wast presented in the temple and received with joy by Simeon and Anna as the Redeemer of Israel: Mercifully grant that we, like them, may be guided by the Holy Spirit to acknowledge and love thee unto our lives' end; who with God the Father, in the unity of the Holy Spirit, livest and reignest God, world without end. *Church of South India*

551

We beseech thee, Almighty God, mercifully to endow us with thy heavenly grace, as we commemorate the holy Virgin Mary, the mother of our Lord, and to hallow thereby our bodies in chastity and our souls in humility and love; through the same thy Son Jesus Christ our Lord, who liveth and reigneth with thee and the Holy Ghost, one God, world without end.

St. Matthias (February 24)   552

Almighty God, by whose providence thy servant Matthias was chosen to be an Apostle of our Lord and a witness of his resurrection: We earnestly pray thee to raise up for the work of the ministry in this our day able and dedicated men, and to use them abundantly for the building up of thy Church and the increase of thy kingdom; through the same Jesus Christ our Lord. *Frank Colquhoun*

553

O Lord Jesus, who dost set over thy people the pastors and teachers of thy choice: Give us, we beseech thee, childlike hearts; that in humility we may receive thy Word, and in simplicity obey it; who livest and reignest with the Father and the Holy Ghost, one God, world without end. *Richard D. Acland*

The Annunciation (March 25)   554

We beseech thee, O God, pour thy grace into our hearts; that, as at the message of an angel, Mary was overshadowed by the Holy

Spirit, and became the mother of the Lord and the most blessed among women, so we, believing thy word, may receive Christ to dwell in our hearts, and by our life make manifest the mystery of his incarnation; who hath exalted our manhood into the glory of his Godhead, even Jesus Christ our Lord. *Gregorian Sacramentary*

555

O Christ our God incarnate, whose Virgin Mother was blessed in bearing thee, but still more blessed in keeping thy word: Grant us, who honour the exaltation of her lowliness, to follow the example of her devotion to thy will; who livest and reignest with the Father and the Holy Ghost, ever one God, world without end.

William Bright

556

O God, who didst choose the Blessed Virgin Mary to become the mother of the Saviour of mankind; Grant that we, having in remembrance her exceeding faith and love, may in all things seek to do thy will, and evermore rejoice in thy salvation; through the same Jesus Christ thy Son, our only Mediator and Advocate.

St. Mark (April 25) 557

Heavenly Father, by whose grace thy servant John Mark was enabled to rise above failure and to prove himself useful in thy service: Grant us that same grace, we humbly beseech thee; that abiding in Christ we may be steadfast in our faith and fruitful in every good work; through the same Jesus Christ our Lord.

Frank Colquhoun

558

O Almighty God, who for the work of the ministry and the recording of the holy gospel didst purge John Mark of youthful faults and weakness: Grant that we may abide in thy Son, the Vine, as fruitful branches, and that in love and the keeping of thy commandments we may grow up into him in all things; who with thee and the Holy Ghost liveth and reigneth, ever one God, world without end. *Richard D. Acland*

St. Philip and St. James (May 1) 559

O Lord and Master, who didst say to thine apostle Philip, He who has seen me has seen the Father: Reveal thyself to our hearts, we humbly beseech thee, and so open the eyes of our understanding that in thy face we may behold the light of the knowledge of the glory of God; for thy holy name's sake. *Frank Colquhoun*

560

O Lord Jesus Christ, who art the Way, the Truth and the Life; we pray thee suffer us not to stray from thee who art the Way, nor to distrust thee who art the Truth, nor to rest in any other thing than thee, who art the Life. Teach us by thy Holy Spirit what to believe, what to do, and wherein to take our rest. For thine own name's sake we ask it. *Erasmus*

St. Barnabas (June 11) 561

Almighty God, who through thy Son Jesus Christ hast taught us that it is more blessed to give than to receive: Grant us grace, after the example of thy servant Saint Barnabas, to know the true joy of giving, and like him to be generous in our judgments as well as in our deeds; through the same Jesus Christ our Lord.

Frank Colquhoun

562

Number us, O Lord, we beseech thee, among those whom thou hast chosen for thy friends; and grant that after the example of thy holy Apostle, the Son of Consolation, we may devote to thee all our possessions, and bring forth fruit in thy service; who with the Father and the Holy Spirit livest and reignest, one God, world without end. *Richard D. Acland*

St. John the Baptist (June 24) 563

Almighty God, who didst send thy servant John the Baptist to call men to repentance and to prepare the way of the Lord: Grant, we beseech thee, that having his teaching in mind we may turn to thee with all our hearts, and be made ready for that day when the glory of the Lord shall be revealed and all flesh shall see it together; through the same thy Son, our Saviour Jesus Christ.

Adapted

564

O God, who didst send thy servant John Baptist to be the herald of thy kingdom and the forerunner of thy Son: We pray thee to call many to serve thee in the holy ministry of thy Church, and to give them grace to be worthy of their calling; through the same Jesus Christ our Lord. *Harold Riley*

St. Peter (June 29) 565

O Almighty God, who by thy Son Jesus Christ didst give thine Apostle Saint Peter many excellent gifts, and commandedst him earnestly to feed thy flock: Grant that thy Church may be ordered by faithful and true pastors, and obediently walk according to thy will; through the same Jesus Christ our Lord.

Church of South India

566

Father of Mercies, who to thine Apostle Saint Peter didst reveal in threefold vision thy boundless compassion: Forgive we pray thee our unbelief, and so enlarge our hearts and enkindle our zeal, that we may fervently desire the salvation of all men, and with more ready diligence labour in the extension of thy kingdom; for his sake who gave himself for the life of the world, thy Son our Saviour Jesus Christ.

The Missionary Conference, 1894

St. Mary Magdalene (July 22)   567

Strong Son of God, who in thy great compassion didst deliver Mary Magdalene from the mastery of evil and didst reveal thyself to her as the living Lord: Grant us so to know thy grace and power in our lives that by word and deed we may magnify thy glorious name, now and for evermore.

Frank Colquhoun

568

Merciful and gracious God, who didst deign to make Mary Magdalene the first witness and herald of the glorious resurrection of thy Son: Grant unto those who have fallen into the torment and captivity of sin to hear that wondrous voice of Jesus, which is able to subdue and cast out all evil passions; that there may be none without hope of mercy, or beyond help of grace; through the same Jesus Christ our Saviour.

W. E. Orchard

St. James (July 25)   569

Almighty God our heavenly Father, whose servant James the Apostle was obedient to the calling of thy Son and also drank of his cup of suffering: We beseech thee to keep us faithful to thee until life shall end; and grant us grace, as those who have been baptized into Christ's death, to tread with him the path of service and sacrifice; for his holy name's sake.

Frank Colquhoun

570

Almighty God, who by the hand of the persecutor didst bestow upon the Apostle James a martyr's diadem of glory: Grant us grace to put away all vain desire of homage and dominion among men, and after the example of thy Son seek to be chief only in sacrificial ministry to others; through the same Jesus Christ our Lord.

Richard D. Acland

The Transfiguration (August 6) 571

O Almighty and everlasting God, whose blessed Son revealed himself to his chosen apostles when he was transfigured on the holy mount, and amidst the excellent glory spake with Moses and Elijah of his departure which he should accomplish at Jerusalem: Grant to us thy servants, that, beholding the brightness of his countenance, we may be strengthened to bear the cross, and be changed into his likeness from glory to glory; through the same Jesus Christ our Lord. *Scottish Prayer Book*

572

O God, who on the holy mount didst reveal to chosen witnesses thy well-beloved Son wonderfully transfigured: Mercifully grant unto us such a vision of his divine Majesty that we, being purified and strengthened by thy grace, may be transformed into his likeness from glory to glory; through the same thy Son Jesus Christ our Lord. *Canadian Prayer Book*

St. Bartholomew (August 24) 573

O Lord our heavenly Father, by the power of whose Holy Spirit thine apostles wrought many wonderful works: Fill thy Church to-day, we pray thee, with that same gracious Spirit; that believers may be added to the Lord, and those that are in sorrow, sin, and sickness may be healed; through Jesus Christ our Lord.
L. E. H. Stephens-Hodge

574

O God, who through the example and teaching of thy Son hast shown to us the royal path of service: Help us to serve others in all humility and patient love; that following in the steps of thy holy apostles we may be made worthy to inherit thy everlasting kingdom; through our Lord and Saviour Jesus Christ.
L. E. H. Stephens-Hodge

St. Matthew (September 21) 575

Almighty Father, who in the holy Gospel according to Saint Matthew hast revealed to us our blessed Lord as the promised Messiah of Israel and King of men: Mercifully grant that we, recognizing his sovereign claims, may offer him the homage and service of our lives, and ever acknowledge him to be the Lord; who livest and reignest with thee and the Holy Spirit, now and for evermore. *Frank Colquhoun*

St. Michael and All Angels (September 29) 576

We give thee thanks, Almighty Father, for the angelic hosts around thy throne who offer thee their tireless service and unending praise; and we pray that we on earth, like them, may readily fulfil thy commandments and render thee the glory that is thy due; for the worthiness of thy Son Jesus Christ our Lord.

Frank Colquhoun

577

O Christ our God, the wisdom, power and glory of the Father who didst visibly appear to all men as the Word made flesh, and having overcome the prince of darkness, didst return to thy throne on high: Grant to us thy supplicants, amid this dark world, the full outpouring of thy splendour, and appoint thy holy angels to be our defenders, to guard our going out and coming in, till we take our place at thy right hand; where thou livest and reignest with the Father and the Holy Ghost, ever one God, world without end. *Mozarabic Sacramentary**

578

We thank thee, O God, for the guardian care of thy holy Angels. Grant that being refreshed through their protection and ministry, we may serve thee on earth as they serve thee in heaven, and may rejoice in their eternal companionship hereafter; through Jesus Christ our Lord.

St. Luke (October 18) 579

Almighty God, who didst inspire thy servant Saint Luke the physician to set forth in the Gospel the love and healing power of thy Son: Manifest in thy Church the like power and love, to the healing of our bodies and our souls; through the same thy Son Jesus Christ our Lord. *American Prayer Book*

580

O Lord God, who dost look with compassion on all the needs of men: Grant thy grace to all whom thou hast called, like Luke the beloved physician, to be sharers in thine own work of healing; that they may learn their art in dependence on thee, and exercise it always under thy sanction and for thy glory; through Jesus Christ our Lord. *Adapted*

Saints Simon and Jude (October 28) 581

O Lord Christ, who didst call Simon the Zealot to be among the number of thine apostles: Deliver us, we pray thee, from all luke-warmness in thy service; and kindle within our hearts a burning love for thee and a consuming zeal for thy kingdom; for the honour and glory of thy name. *Frank Colquhoun*

All Saints' Day (November 1) 582

O Almighty God, who hast called us to faith in thee, and hast compassed us about with so great a cloud of witnesses: Grant that we, encouraged by the good examples of thy Saints, may persevere in running the race that is set before us, until at length through thy mercy we, with them, attain to thine eternal joy; through him who is the author and finisher of our faith, thy Son Jesus Christ our Lord. *American Prayer Book*

583

O Lord, who in every age dost reveal thyself to the childlike and lowly of heart, and from every race dost write names in thy book of life: Give us the simplicity and faith of thy saints, that loving thee above all things, we may be what thou wouldst have us be, and do what thou wouldst have us do. So may we be numbered with thy saints in glory everlasting; through Jesus Christ, our Saviour. *George Appleton*

584

We thank thee, O God, for the saints of all ages; for those who in times of darkness kept the lamp of faith burning; for the great souls who saw visions of larger truths and dared to declare them; for the multitude of quiet and gracious souls whose presence has purified and sanctified the world; and for those known and loved by us, who have passed from this earthly fellowship into the fuller life with thee. Accept this our thanksgiving through Jesus Christ, our Mediator and Redeemer, to whom be praise and dominion for ever. *Fellowship Litanies*

Of an Apostle 585

O Lord and Master, who didst choose twelve, that they might be with thee, and that thou mightest send them forth to preach: We give thee thanks for the glorious company of the apostles, and especially at this time for thy servant Saint *N*.; humbly beseeching thee that we, like them, may witness a good confession and fight the good fight of the faith; for thy honour and glory, now and evermore. *Frank Colquhoun*

586

O God, who by the preaching of the apostles didst cause the light of thy gospel to shine upon the nations: Grant, we beseech thee, that we, having their life and labour in remembrance, may show forth our thankfulness to thee for so great a gift, by following the example of their zeal and service; through Jesus Christ our Lord. *Prayers for the Christian Year*

Feasts of the Blessed Virgin Mary 587

O Almighty God, who didst endue with singular grace the blessed Virgin Mary, the Mother of our Lord: Vouchsafe, we beseech thee, to hallow our bodies in purity, and our souls in humility and love; through the same our Lord and Saviour Jesus Christ.

Scottish Prayer Book

588

Almighty and everlasting God, who didst stoop to raise our fallen race by the child-bearing of blessed Mary: Grant that we, who have seen thy glory manifested in our manhood, and thy love perfected in our weakness, may daily be renewed in thine image, and conformed to the likeness of thy Son; who liveth and reigneth with thee and the Holy Ghost, ever one God, world without end.

Anglican Altar Services, 1941

Of a Martyr 589

Almighty and everlasting God, who didst strengthen thy blessed martyr, *N.*, with the virtue of constancy in faith and truth: Grant us in like manner for love of thee to despise the prosperity of this world, and to fear none of its adversities; through Jesus Christ our Lord.

590

O God, who dost inspire us to confess thy holy name by the witness of thy martyrs: Grant that thy Church, encouraged by their example, may be ready to suffer fearlessly for thy cause, and to strive for the reward of thy heavenly glory; through Jesus Christ our Lord.

W. H. Frere

Missionaries and martyrs 591

O Eternal Lord God, who by the noble fortitude of missionaries and martyrs hast caused thy Word to grow mightily and to prevail: Pour thy Spirit upon thy Church in this land, that, by the service and sacrifice of our faith, thy saving health may be known among the nations; through Jesus Christ our Lord.

Anglican Altar Services, 1941

Saints of our own land 592

O God, whom the glorious companies of the redeemed adore, assembled from all times and places of thy dominion: We praise thee for the Saints of this our land who stand before the throne and serve thee day and night in thy holy temple; beseeching thee that we also may be numbered among them that work thy righteousness and see thy face; through Jesus Christ our Lord.

Anglican Altar Services, 1941

Plough Sunday (first Sunday after January 6)   **593**

O GOD, who dost give each man his work to do for thy sake: Prosper, we pray thee, throughout this year the work and workers on the fields and farms of this parish. Let the ploughman's hope be fulfilled in a plentiful harvest; let thy people be fed with the wholesome food of their countryside; and let town and country, united in gratitude to thee, be drawn nearer to the understanding and true service of each other; through Jesus Christ our Lord.

D. L. Couper

St. David (March 1)   **594**

O God, who by the preaching of thy blessed servant David didst cause the light of the gospel to shine in an age of darkness: Grant, we beseech thee, that having his life and his labours in remembrance, we may show forth our thankfulness by following the example of his zeal and patience; through Jesus Christ our Lord.

595

O God, who madest Saint David to be a victorious champion of the faith, and didst reward his rich sowing with an abundant harvest; Continue thy favour, we beseech thee, towards the people of Wales and the Church in their midst; and so bless them with spiritual gifts that the land of their fathers may be a praise in all the earth; through Jesus Christ our Lord.

St. Patrick (March 17)   **596**

O Almighty God, who in thy providence didst choose thy servant Patrick to be the apostle of the Irish people, that he might bring those who were wandering in darkness and error to the true light and knowledge of thee: Grant us so to walk in that light, that we may come at last to the light of everlasting life; through the merits of Jesus Christ thy Son our Lord.   *Irish Prayer Book*

597

O God, who didst teach thy servant Patrick to love the land of his captivity, and to spend willingly and be spent that he might bring its people unto thee: Grant that in all our troubles we may hear thy voice, and gladly learn what thou wouldest have us to do; through Jesus Christ our Lord.

St. George's Day (April 23)   598

O Lord God of hosts, who didst give grace to thy servant Saint George to lay aside the fear of man and to confess thee even unto death: Grant that all our countrymen who bear office in the world may think lightly of earthly place and honour, and seek rather to please thee, the Captain of our salvation, who hast chosen them to be thy soldiers; to whom with thee and the Holy Ghost be thanks and praise from all the armies of the saints, now and for evermore.

John Wordsworth

599

O Lord our God, who didst endue thy blessed martyr, Saint George, with grace to act and endure valiantly, so that he has become to our people an example of heroic strength: Purge us from all falsity and other weakness, we humbly beseech thee, that we too may be strong in the power of thy might; through Jesus Christ our Lord.

Labour Day (May 1)   600

O God, the Father of lights, who hast taught us by the blessed doctrine of Saint James that thou hearkenest to the cry of the oppressed, and hast chosen the poor to be rich in faith: Grant us grace, that, renouncing corruptible riches, we may so order all things in righteousness, that the precious fruits of the earth may be abundantly obtained by those who patiently labour; through Jesus Christ our Lord.   *W. E. Orchard*

Lammas Day (August 1)   601

O Lord, who by thy mercy hast brought us to the beginning of harvest and to the remembrance of Saint Peter's deliverance: Let his counsel prevail among us, we beseech thee; that girding up the loins of our minds as of our bodies, we may set our hope perfectly on the grace that is to be brought to us by the revelation of thy Son, Jesus Christ our Lord.   *W. H. Frere*

602

O God, who hast made heaven and earth and all that is in them: We humbly beseech thee to bless and hallow these first-fruits of corn, and to multiply them abundantly for us who offer them; and grant such seasonable weather that this year's harvest may be plentiful, and we, rejoicing in thy gifts, may pay our thanks to thy divine majesty; through Jesus Christ our Lord.

D. L. Couper

Festival of the Reformation (October 31) **603**

Almighty God, who through the preaching of thy servants, the blessed Reformers, hast caused the light of the gospel to shine forth: Grant, we beseech thee, that, knowing its saving power, we may faithfully guard it and defend it against all enemies, and joyfully proclaim it, to the salvation of souls and the glory of thy holy name; through Jesus Christ our Lord. *Lutheran Church*

Commemoration of All Souls (November 2) **604**

O Eternal Lord God, who holdest all souls in life: We beseech thee to shed forth upon thy whole Church in Paradise and on earth the bright beams of thy light and heavenly comfort; and grant that we, following the good example of those who have served thee here and are at rest, may at the last enter with them into the fullness of thine unending joy; through Jesus Christ our Lord.

John Wordsworth

605

Eternal Father, who art the God not of the dead but of the living: We give thee thanks and praise for all the generations of the faithful, who, having served thee here in godliness and love, are now with thee in glory; and, we beseech thee, enable us so to follow them in all godly living and faithful service, that hereafter we may with them behold thy face, and in the heavenly places be one with them for ever; through Jesus Christ our Lord.

Prayers for the Christian Year*

606

O God, before whose face the generations rise and pass away, the strength of those who labour and the repose of the holy and blessed dead: We remember all who have faithfully lived and died, especially those most dear to us. Lift us into life and love; and give us our portion at last with those who have trusted in thee, and have striven in all things to do thy will. And to thy name, with the Church on earth and in heaven, we ascribe all honour and glory, world without end. *John Hunter*

Of any Saint **607**

We beseech thee, O God, to accept our praise and thanksgiving for the lives of all thy faithful people who have served thee on earth and are now at rest [*and especially thy servant N. whom we have in remembrance today*]. Grant, O Lord, that we too may dedicate ourselves to thy service; that following their good example we, with them, may be partakers of thy heavenly kingdom; through Jesus Christ our Lord.

608

Almighty God, who dost choose thine elect out of every nation, and dost show forth thy glory in their lives: Grant, we pray thee, that following the example of thy servant Saint *N.*, we may be fruitful in good works to the praise of thy holy name; through Jesus Christ our Lord. *Scottish Prayer Book*

609

Almighty and everlasting God, who dost enkindle the flame of love in the hearts of the Saints: Grant to us, thy humble servants, the same faith and power of love; that, as we rejoice in their triumphs we may also profit by their examples; through Jesus Christ our Lord. *Gothic Missal*

Holy Women   **610**

O God, who hast built thy Church through the divers gifts and graces of thy Saints: We give thee humble thanks for all good women [*especially this day for thy servant* N.]; help us, we beseech thee, to follow their steps, and fill our hearts with love to thee, and of others for thy sake; through Jesus Christ our Lord.

Oxford Diocesan Service Book

For the increase of the ministry   **611**

O LORD, we beseech thee to raise up for the work of the ministry
faithful and able men, counting it all joy to spend and be spent
for the sake of thy dear Son, and for the souls for which he shed his
most precious blood upon the cross; and we pray thee to fit them for
their holy function by thy bountiful grace and heavenly benediction;
through Jesus Christ our Lord.   *E. W. Benson*

612

O Almighty God, look mercifully upon the world which thou
hast redeemed by the blood of thy dear Son, and incline the hearts
of many to offer themselves for the sacred ministry of thy Church;
so that by their labours thy light may shine in the darkness, and the
coming of thy kingdom may be hastened by the perfecting of thine
elect; through the same Jesus Christ our Lord.   *R. M. Benson*

613

Almighty God, who in every age hast drawn men to be ministers
in the apostolic Church: Make known thy will to those whom thou
wouldest use to-day. Grant them grace to discern, courage to respond, and firm resolve to obey, that the promise of the gospel
may be fulfilled in the lives of all people; through the power of
Jesus Christ our Lord.

614

O Lord of the harvest, raise up, we pray thee, faithful and true
men for the work of thy Church. Equip them for thy service; enrich them with thy grace; and send them forth in due time to gather
fruit unto eternal life; for the glory of our Lord and Saviour Jesus
Christ.

615

O God, who dost ever hallow and protect thy Church: Raise up
therein, through thy Spirit, good and faithful stewards of the
mysteries of Christ; that by their ministry and example thy people
may abide in thy favour, and be guided in the way of truth; through
Jesus Christ our Lord.   *American Prayer Book*

616

O God, you have told us to pray for more labourers in your harvest-field. We ask you then to call many of your sons to that work and make them ready to hear and act upon your call. Make them at all times sensitive to your guidance, willing to learn and eager to obey. We ask this in the name of him who came not to be ministered to but to minister, Jesus Christ your Son our Lord.

A.C.C.M.

617

O Almighty God, who hast committed to the hands of men the ministry of reconciliation: We humbly beseech thee by the inspiration of thy Holy Spirit to put it into the hearts of many to offer themselves for this ministry, that thereby mankind may be drawn to thy blessed kingdom; through Jesus Christ our Lord.

American Prayer Book

618

We beseech thee, Almighty God, to call many to the ministry of thy Church; and to those whom thou dost call give thy grace that they may hear and answer thy call; through Jesus Christ our Lord.

South African Prayer Book

For those in training **619**

We pray, O Lord, for thy blessing upon all who are being trained for the ministry of thy Church in every land. Take from them all pride and self-conceit, all thought of worldly advancement. May their wills be wholly surrendered unto thee; fill them with thy Spirit, that they may go forth inspired with zeal for thy glory, in the power of our Lord Jesus Christ.

Prayers of the World-wide Church

620

O Everlasting God, who art adored by the holy angels, yet dost choose men to be the stewards of thy mysteries: Bless, we beseech thee, all those who are preparing for the work of the ministry; that they who cannot do any good without thee, may by thee be illuminated with a true knowledge of thy Word, and so be made able ministers of the new covenant; through Jesus Christ our Lord.

Henry P. Liddon

621

We beseech thee, O Lord our God, to enlighten the understanding and to strengthen the wills of all who are preparing for the ministry of thy holy Church; that they may readily acknowledge thy claims, wholeheartedly believe thy truth, and cheerfully obey thy calling, for the glory of thy great name; through Jesus Christ our Lord. *Adapted*

622

Almighty God, who dost choose men to be the agents of thy purpose and the heralds of thy kingdom: We pray for thy blessing upon all who are training in our theological colleges; that they may be strengthened in faith, disciplined in loyalty, nurtured in thy Word, and, when the time is come, may go forth as ministers of the new covenant to advance thy glory and the salvation of mankind; through Jesus Christ our Lord. *Adapted*

623

Grant thy grace, O God our Father, to those who are training for the ministry of thy holy Church. Prepare them for all that thou hast prepared for them; make them what thou wouldest have them to be, that they may accomplish what thou wouldest have them to do; and so bless them that they may be made a blessing; for the sake of Jesus Christ our Lord. *Frank Colquhoun*

624

Let thy blessing, O Lord, rest upon those who are seeking to prepare themselves to be ministers of thy Word. Give them a true understanding of the needs of the human heart and a sure faith in the adequacy of Jesus Christ to fulfil those needs. Keep them steadfast in the determination to devote their lives to bringing Christ to men; and help them so to use the time of their preparation that all their studies may be made to contribute toward the fulfilment of their holy calling; through the same Jesus Christ our Lord.
Emil E. Fischer

The ministers of Christ's Church 625

O Almighty God, be pleased to remember with thy mercy and love all those who minister before thee in holy things. Prosper the great work in which they are engaged. Enable them faithfully to preach thy Word, and rightly and duly administer thy holy sacraments. May they uphold Christ, both by their words and in their lives, and in all things set forward thy glory; through Jesus Christ our Lord. *Ashton Oxenden**

626

O God, who makest thine angels spirits and thy ministers a flame of fire: Vouchsafe, we beseech thee, to stir up and confirm the sacred grace of orders in all stewards of thy mysteries; that as ministering spirits they may gather out of thy kingdom all things that offend, and may kindle in the hearts of all that fire which thou camest to send upon the earth; to the glory of thy holy name.

Henry P. Liddon

627

Almighty God, giver of all good things, who by thy one Spirit hast appointed a diversity of ministrations in thy Church: Mercifully behold thy servants who are called to the ministry, and so fill them with thy Holy Spirit, that both by word and good example they may faithfully and joyfully serve thee, to the glory of thy name and the building up of thy Church; through Jesus Christ our Lord.

Church of South India

628

O Lord Jesus Christ, the great Shepherd of thy sheep, grant to all clergy the pastoral heart, that they may tend the flocks committed to their care. May they so follow thy example that they may know their sheep and be known of them; may they go after those that are lost until they find them; that so when thou, the chief shepherd, shall appear, they may receive the crown of glory that fadeth not away. Hear us from thy throne in heaven, where with the Father and the Holy Ghost thou livest and reignest one God, world without end.

Peter Green

629

Almighty God, grant, we beseech thee, to all whom thou hast called to the sacred ministry of thy Church such a sense of their high calling that they may count no sacrifice too great to make in thy service; that so, bringing a blessing to their people, they may themselves be blessed of thee; for Jesus Christ's sake.

Peter Green

630

Remember, O gracious Lord, for good, all bishops, priests and deacons of thy Church; pour upon them evermore thy Holy Spirit, to strengthen, deepen, chasten, and purify them; that giving themselves up to thy service, they may do and suffer all that thou willest, and finally may reign with thee in life everlasting.

J. Armitage Robinson*

631

Eternal Lord Christ, thou great Shepherd and Bishop of our souls, bestow thy blessing, we beseech thee, upon the bishops and pastors of thy flock. Give them the spirit of wisdom and holiness, patience and charity, zeal and watchfulness, that they may faithfully declare thy truth, diligently administer thy sacraments, acceptably intercede for thy people, and turn many to righteousness; for thy tender mercy's sake.

632

We humbly beseech thee, O God, to illuminate all bishops, priests, and deacons with true knowledge and understanding of thy Word; that, both by their preaching and living, they may set it forth and show it accordingly; through Jesus Christ our Lord.

From the Litany

633

Grant, O God, we beseech thee, that the same mind may be in all the ministers of thy Church that was in Christ Jesus:

his self-forgetting humility;
his interest in common things;
his love for common people;
his compassion for the fallen;
his tolerance with the mistaken;
his patience with the slow;

and in all their work and converse make them continually sensitive to thy guidance and ready for thy will; through Jesus Christ our Lord. *Book of Offices, Methodist Church*

634

Almighty God, who dost choose and use men to be the agents of thy kingdom and heralds of the good news: Pour out thy Holy Spirit, we beseech thee, upon those whom thou hast called to serve in the ministry of the Word and sacraments. May they in all things seek thy glory and the good of thy Church, and set forward the salvation of those committed to their charge; through Jesus Christ our Lord.

635

Remember, O Lord, the ministers of thy Church for their labour in Word and sacrament, and in the proclamation of thy glorious gospel. Endow them with wisdom for their high task, with learning for the setting forth of thy truth, with zeal and devotion for thy glory and the salvation of souls, with humble self-surrender, lest they themselves be cast away; and grant that both by their lives and their labours they may advance thy heavenly kingdom; for the honour of thy Son our Saviour Jesus Christ.

Adapted from Liturgy of St. James

636

We commend to thee, O God, all those whom thou hast called to the sacred ministry of thy Church. Give them grace to be faithful ambassadors of Christ to the world, to feed and govern thy flock as true shepherds, and to promote love and unity among all thy people; through the same Jesus Christ our Lord. *Adapted*

Preachers of the Word · **637**

Pour out, O Lord, we beseech thee, the Spirit of power upon all those whom thou hast called to be preachers of the Word. Inflame them with the fire of thy love; grant them new tongues with which to move the hearts of men; give them utterance to meet the needs of the day and the hour; that so believers may be added to thy Church, multitudes both of men and women; through Jesus Christ our Lord. *Peter Green**

638

Almighty God, who dost send thy messengers to prepare thy way before thee: Endue with the power of the Holy Spirit all who go forth to preach and speak in thy name. Touch their hearts; enlighten their minds; cleanse and instruct their lips; give them a clear vision of thy will and purpose for the whole world; and through their voice do thou call back thy Church to simpler discipleship, readier obedience, and more loving service; through thy Son Jesus Christ our Lord. *Peter Green*

Deaconesses **639**

Almighty God, who hast committed to men and women the ministry of the gospel: Pour thy grace upon thy servants called to the order of deaconesses; that in all that they do and teach they may love and serve thee, to the glory of thy name and the benefit of thy Church; through thy Son our Saviour Jesus Christ. *Prayer of the Order*

Women workers **640**

O Lord, who wast born of a woman, and hast glorified womanhood in the sight of all people: Bless, we beseech thee, the women who have been called to the service of thy Church in the parishes of our land. Strengthen them in hours of strain and weakness, preserve in them the spirit of sympathy and love, and grant them the help of thy grace, that in all things they may be worthy of their vocation; to the glory of thy holy name.

641

Gracious Lord, who in thy earthly life didst accept the ministry of women: Bless, we beseech thee, thy servants whom thou hast called to work for thee in the parishes; that strengthened by the assurance of thy presence, they may carry the gospel of thy love into the hearts and homes of thy people, and ever advance thy glory; who with the Father and the Holy Spirit livest and reignest one God, world without end.

See also prayers for Church leaders (1340–2), for bishops (1394–5), for the clergy (1429–32), and for Church workers (1433–6)

II
VARIOUS OCCASIONS

WATCH-NIGHT SERVICE

Introduction   642

ALMIGHTY and eternal God, with whom one day is as a thousand years, and a thousand years as one day: Give us grace, as we remember the way by which thou hast led us, to offer unto thee the worship of adoring hearts, and to rest our hopes for the time to come on thine unchanging love; through Jesus Christ our Lord.

Prayers for the Christian Year

643

Most gracious God, who hast been mindful of us not only in the past year but through all the years of our life: Pardon our sins, fashion in us those virtues which are acceptable to thee, and grant that in serenity we may serve thee more faithfully in the year that is to come, for Jesus Christ's sake.

The Kingdom, the Power, and the Glory

644

O Lord our God, whose eyes are always upon us from the beginning of the year even unto the end: We bring to thee our worship and praise, remembering thy goodness to us in the days that are past, and trusting ourselves to thy mercy for the days to come; through Jesus Christ our Lord.   *James M. Todd*

The passage of time   645

Almighty and everlasting God, who makest us children of time, to the end that when time is over we may attain to thy blessed eternity: Mercifully receive our prayers, and hold up our goings in thy way; that we may apply our hearts unto wisdom, and so live all our appointed days on earth as finally to lay hold on the life everlasting; through Jesus Christ our Lord.   *Adapted*

646

O God, in whose sight a thousand years are but as yesterday when it is past, and as a watch in the night: So teach us to number our days that we may apply our hearts unto wisdom, in the faith and knowledge of him who is the same yesterday and to-day and for ever, Jesus Christ our Lord.

Penitence 647

We confess to thee, O Lord most holy, all the sins which hinder thy purpose for our lives and do harm to the lives of others. Forgive us, Lord, we humbly beseech thee, and turn our hearts to seek thee more sincerely, and to serve thee and our fellow-men more faithfully, in the coming year. We ask it through our Saviour Jesus Christ. *William Temple*

Thanksgiving 648

Almighty God, everlasting Father, as another year draws to its close we thank thee for the protection, comfort and guidance thou hast given us through its course. We thank thee for thy goodness that hath created us, for thy bounty that hath sustained us, for thy fatherly discipline that hath corrected us, for thy patience that hath borne with us. Above all, we thank thee for thine incarnate Son, sent as at this time to be our Saviour. Bless the Lord, O my soul, and all that is within me bless his holy name; through Jesus Christ our Lord. *Prayers for the Christian Year*

649

O Lord, with whom there is no variableness nor shadow of turning, and who in thy mercy hast led us in safety through all the days of our pilgrimage: Accept the sacrifice of our praise and thanksgiving, and hear our prayer as now we offer our lives afresh to thee; beseeching thee that in the time that remains to us we may devote ourselves more fully to thy service and prove ourselves more worthy of thy goodness; through Jesus Christ our Saviour. *Frank Colquhoun*

Dedication 650

Almighty God our heavenly Father, who hast called us to the knowledge of thy grace, and faith in thee: Increase our faith, we beseech thee, as thou dost increase our years; and the longer we are suffered to abide on earth, the better may our service be, the more willing our obedience, the more consistent our daily living, the more complete our devotion to thee; through our Lord and Saviour Jesus Christ.

651

Father in heaven, by whose providence we have come to the end of the year: Grant that we may meet its close with grateful hearts; and we beseech thee to confirm our resolve to amend our ways, and to walk closely with thee in the journey before us, in the faith of thy Son Jesus Christ our Lord. *Adapted*

Concluding prayers 652

Teach thy servants and pilgrims, O King of kings, to walk trustfully in thy presence and to obey thy majesty; that, while we journey to the heavenly country, thy voice may encourage, thine arm protect, and thy love transfigure us; through Jesus Christ our Lord.

653

O God of time and eternity, who makest us creatures of time, to the end that when time is over we may attain to thy blessed eternity: With time, which is thy gift, give us also wisdom to redeem the time lest our day of grace be lost; for the sake of Jesus Christ our Lord.

654

Eternal Father, who alone canst control the days that are gone and the deeds that are done: Remove from our burdened memory the weight of past years, that we may reach forth to those things that are before, and press towards the mark for the prize of the high calling of God in Christ Jesus our Lord.   *Charles H. Brent*

655

Grant, O Lord, that as the years change, we may find rest in thine eternal changelessness. May we meet this new year bravely, sure in the faith that, while men come and go, and life changes around us, thou art ever the same, guiding us with thy wisdom, and protecting us with thy love; through our Saviour Jesus Christ.

William Temple

See also prayers for the new year 88–91

The quest for unity 656

O GOD of peace, who through thy Son Jesus Christ didst set forth one faith for the salvation of mankind: Send thy grace and heavenly blessing upon all Christian people who are striving to draw nearer to thee and to each other, in the unity of the Spirit and in the bond of peace. Give us penitence for our divisions, wisdom to know thy truth, courage to do thy will, love which will break down the barriers of pride and prejudice, and an unswerving loyalty to thy holy name; that together we may seek thy glory and the advancement of thy kingdom; through Jesus Christ our Lord.

*Faith and Order Conference Manual**

657

Eternal and merciful God, who art the God of peace and not of discord: Have mercy upon thy Church, divided in thy service; and grant that we, seeking unity in Christ, and in the truth of thy holy Word, with one mind and one mouth may glorify thee, the Father of our Lord Jesus Christ.   *George Appleton*

658

O God, who by thy Son Jesus Christ dost call the children of thy Church into a great and holy unity, even as he is one with thee: Turn us again, we beseech thee, that we may redeem the years of division, and recover in thee what we have lost of ourselves; through the same Jesus Christ our Lord.

A Procession of Passion Prayers

659

O Lord, who willest that all thy children should be one in thee: We pray thee for the unity of thy Church. Pardon all our pride and our lack of faith, of understanding and of charity, which are the cause of our divisions. Deliver us from our narrow-mindedness, from our bitterness, from our prejudices. Preserve us from considering as normal that which is a scandal to the world and an offence to thy love. Teach us to recognize the gifts of thy grace amongst all those who call upon thee.   *Liturgy of the Reformed Church of France*

660

O Lord Jesus Christ, who on the eve of thy passion didst pray that all thy disciples might be one, as thou art in the Father, and the

Father in thee: Grant that we may suffer keenly on account of the infidelity of our division, and that in thee, who art perfect charity, we may find the way that leads to unity, in obedience to thy love and in loyalty to thy truth; for the honour of thy holy name.

661

O God, the Creator of the ends of the earth, with whom there is no distinction of race or habitation, but all are one in thee: Break down, we beseech thee, the barriers which divide us; that we may work together with one accord with each other and with thee; through him who is the Saviour of all, Jesus Christ thy Son our Lord.

Unity and mission
662

O Lord Jesus Christ, who didst say to thine apostles, By this shall all men know that you are my disciples, if you have love one to another: Heal our divisions, and make us one in thee; that men may know us for thy true disciples, and through us may put their trust in thee; who livest and reignest with the Father and the Holy Spirit, one God, world without end. *Adapted*

663

Spirit of Promise, Spirit of Unity, we thank thee that thou art also the Spirit of Renewal. Renew in the whole Church, we pray thee, that passionate desire for the coming of thy kingdom which will unite all Christians in one mission to the world. May we all grow up together into him, who is our Head, the Saviour of the world and our only Lord and Master. *Praying for Unity*

664

Eternal God, look mercifully upon the broken body of thy Church. Draw its members unto thee and one to another by the bands of thy love; that its restored unity may bring healing to the nations, and the life of mankind may glorify thee; through Jesus Christ our Lord. *New Every Morning*

665

O God, who didst plan the gospel for an undivided Church: Refuse not, because of the misunderstandings of its message which rend the unity of Christendom, to continue thy saving work in the broken order of our making. Prosper the labours of all churches bearing the name of Christ and striving to further righteousness and faith in him. Help us to place the truth above our conception of it, and joyfully to recognize the presence of the Holy Spirit wherever he may choose to dwell among men; through Jesus Christ our Lord.

666

O God, of whom every family in heaven and on earth is named, in whose earthly family there is neither Jew nor Greek, male nor female, bond nor free, but only children standing in equal need and equally sharing thy fatherly care: Grant that thy Church, being quickened by thy love, may manifest to the world the unity to which thou hast called it in the gospel of thy Son, and by the fellowship of his disciples may bring healing to the world; for the glory of thy name.

A prayer of dedication　　　　　**667**

Almighty God, whose will it is that brethren should dwell together in unity: Receive these our prayers, and grant us such single-mindedness, courage and patience, that in face of all difficulties and temptation to despair, we may work with confidence for the unity of thy Church, and the coming on earth of thy kingdom. And to this end, O Lord, we offer to thee our hearts and minds and strength in obedience to thy Son, Jesus Christ our Lord.
See also 1327–34

MOTHERING SUNDAY SERVICE

Introduction   668

O LORD Jesus Christ, who didst come to live among men as the child of a human mother: Bless us, we pray thee, as we gather in thy house to-day to worship thee and to thank thee for our mothers and our homes. Fill our hearts with thy love, and help us to remember thy presence with us, not only now but at all times. We ask it for thy name's sake.

Thanksgiving   669

O Heavenly Father, we thank thee for all the happiness of our life. We thank thee for our baptism and for our place in thy family, the Church. And especially to-day we thank thee for our parents, and for all those who have loved and cared for us. Give us ever thankful and happy hearts, for the sake of Jesus Christ our Lord.

670

O Lord, we thank thee for our mothers and all that they do for us. Help us to repay their love by being kind and cheerful in our homes, helping our mothers and the other members of our families; for Jesus Christ's sake.

For mothers   671

Lord Jesus Christ, who wast born of a human mother and didst care for her upon the cross: We commend to thee the mothers of our nation. May their children be nurtured in thy discipline and instruction, and their home be a haven of peace and love, made fragrant with thy presence; who with the Father and the Holy Spirit ever livest and reignest, one God, world without end.

J. R. W. Stott

For parents   672

O God, we pray thee to inspire in our hearts and in the hearts of all parents a true love for thee. Awaken us to a full sense of our responsibility, and take possession of ourselves and of our homes; through Jesus Christ our Lord.

For our homes and family life 673

Almighty God and heavenly Father, whose Son Jesus Christ shared in Nazareth the life of an earthly home: Send down thy blessing, we beseech thee, upon all Christian families, that parents by the spirit of understanding and wisdom, and children by the spirit of obedience and reverence, may be bound each to each by mutual love; through him who became a child and learned obedience to thy will, even Jesus Christ our Lord.   *Church of South India*

674

O God, our Father, bless our homes and make them thy dwelling-place. Keep us faithful to thee and helpful to one another, for the sake of him who shared an earthly home at Nazareth, Jesus Christ thy Son our Lord.   *The Daily Service*

675

O Blessed Lord Jesus, who didst grow up in an earthly home obedient to thine earthly parents: Bless all the homes in this parish. May the parents impart to their children the knowledge of thee and thy love, and may the children love, obey and succour their parents; and bring us all at last to the joy of thy heavenly home, for thy great name's sake.

676

Visit, we beseech thee, O Lord, our homes, and drive from them all the snares of the evil one; let thy holy angels dwell in them to preserve all who live there in peace; and may thy blessing be upon us evermore; through Jesus Christ our Lord.
     From the Order of Compline

For our mother the Church 677

O Heavenly Father, we thank thee that by our baptism we have been made members of thy great family the Church; and we pray that we may grow up to be faithful members of that family and learn to love and serve thee better; for Jesus Christ's sake.

For our mother-land 678

Look in thy mercy, O Lord our God, upon our mother-land of —. May we and all her people be true and upright, loyal and unselfish, fearing thee and serving one another, in the faith of Jesus Christ our Saviour.

Mary the Mother of our Lord 679

O Lord Jesus Christ, who in thy home at Nazareth didst love and honour thy blessed mother, and wast subject unto her: Grant that we may ever be mindful of her grace and virtue, and also may follow the example of her love and humility; to the glory of thy name, who livest and reignest with the Father and the Holy Spirit, one God for ever and ever.

The heavenly home 680

O Lord, who hast taught us that in thy Father's house are many mansions: We thank thee for the heavenly home which thou hast gone to prepare for us. Prepare us, we pray thee, for that home, and in thy mercy bring us all at last to be partakers of its joys, that we may dwell with thee for evermore.   *Frank Colquhoun*

The gift of flowers 681

Bless, O Lord Jesus, these small gifts of flowers, that they may be channels of thy love, imparting joy to those who give and those who receive. And we pray that all children and parents, united in thee, may ever follow thy example in loving words and deeds, to thy honour and glory, now and for evermore.

See also prayers for Home and Friends, 1214–37

Harvest collects **682**

O ALMIGHTY and everlasting God, who hast given unto us the fruits of the earth in their season: Grant us grace to use the same to thy glory, the relief of those that need, and our own comfort, through Jesus Christ, who is the living bread which cometh down from heaven and giveth life unto the world; to whom with thee and the Holy Ghost be all honour and glory, world without end.   *Canterbury Convocation, 1862*

683

O Almighty God and heavenly Father, we glorify thee that thou hast again fulfilled to us thy gracious promise, that while the earth remaineth, seed-time and harvest shall not fail. We bless thee for the kindly fruits of the earth. Teach us, we beseech thee, to remember that it is not by bread alone that man doth live; and grant us evermore to feed on him who is the true bread which cometh down from heaven, Jesus Christ our Lord, to whom with thee, O Father, and thee, O Holy Ghost, be honour and glory for ever and ever.   *Canterbury Convocation, 1862*

684

O Almighty God, we pray thee, sow the seed of thy Word in our hearts, and send down upon us thy heavenly grace; that we may bring forth the fruits of the Spirit, and at the great day of harvest may be gathered by thy holy angels into thy garner; through Jesus Christ our Lord.   *Canterbury Convocation, 1862*

685

Almighty and everlasting God, who hast given to us the fruits of the earth in their season, and hast crowned the year with thy goodness: Give us grateful hearts, that we may unfeignedly thank thee for all thy loving-kindness, and worthily magnify thy holy name; through Jesus Christ our Lord.   *John Dowden*

686

Almighty Father, who hast at this season bestowed upon us such an abundant supply for all our necessities: Grant that we may never be destitute of those better gifts which nourish and enrich the soul,

that we may bring forth abundant fruit to thy glory; through
Jesus Christ our Lord. *Canadian Prayer Book**

687

O most merciful Father, who hast blessed the labours of the
husbandman and brought us again to the season of harvest: Grant
that we may not only receive thy gifts with thankfulness, but may
also, as good stewards of thy bounty, use them to thy glory and
share with others what we have so richly received; through Jesus
Christ our Lord. *Adapted*

688

O Lord of the harvest and giver of our daily bread, we rejoice
in all thy fatherly goodness; and pray that thy loving-kindness
may so prevail in the hearts of thy children everywhere, that the
earth may be filled with gladness and peace; through Jesus Christ
our Lord. *Prayers for the Christian Year*

689

Grant us, O Lord so to bless thee with grateful hearts for the
bounty of the earthly harvest, that fulfilled with thy love we may
bring forth fruit an hundredfold in this life, and, in that harvest
where angels are the reapers, be gathered as wheat into thy garner;
through Jesus Christ our Lord.

Thanksgiving 690

O most merciful Father, who of thy gracious goodness hast heard
the devout prayers of thy Church, and hast granted us to gather in
the kindly fruits of the earth in their season: We give thee humble
thanks for this thy bounty, beseeching thee to continue thy loving-
kindness towards us, that our land may yield her increase; through
Jesus Christ our Lord. *Canterbury Convocation, 1862*

691

O God, of whose great bounty cometh the richness and use of the
seasons: We praise thee for the joy and fullness of harvest. As thou
hast given us all things richly to enjoy, grant us grateful hearts
that we may rightly use thy good gifts. Give us generous understanding of the wants of others, and a deep concern that all thy
children may have food sufficient for their need; for thy name's sake.
With all our Strength

692

O Lord God of hosts, who dwellest in the high and holy place,
and yet hast respect unto the lowly: We yield thee hearty thanks

that thou hast safely brought us to the season of harvest, visiting the earth and blessing it, and crowning the year with thy goodness. We praise thee for the fruits of the ground which thou hast bestowed upon us, filling our hearts with food and gladness. For these and all thy mercies we laud and magnify thy glorious name; beseeching thee to give us also the increase of all spiritual gifts, and the dew of thy heavenly blessing; through Jesus Christ our Lord.

*Canterbury Convocation, 1862**

693

O God, the Father Almighty, Maker of heaven and earth: We praise and magnify thy holy name for all thy goodness and loving-kindness to us and to all men; for the order and constancy of nature; for the beauty and bounty of the world; for the fruits of the earth, the harvest of the sea, and the wealth of the mines; and for all the riches of thy grace. Accept our thanksgiving, O Lord, for these thy gifts, through thy Son Jesus Christ, to whom with thee and the Holy Spirit be all honour and glory for ever and ever. *Adapted*

694

O Lord, how manifold are thy works! In wisdom hast thou made them all: the earth is full of thy riches. The eyes of all wait upon thee, and thou givest them their meat in due season. Thou openest thine hand, and satisfiest the desire of every living thing. Our mouth shall speak the praise of the Lord; and let all flesh bless his holy name for ever and ever. *Psalms 104. 24; 145. 15, 16, 21*

Intercession   695

Give, O Lord, to all who till the ground, wisdom to understand thy laws, and to co-operate with thy wise ordering of the world: and grant that the bountiful fruits of the earth may not be hoarded by the selfish or squandered by the foolish, but that all who work may share abundantly in the harvest of the soil; through Jesus Christ our Lord. *The Kingdom, the Power, and the Glory*

696

Almighty God, who fillest the earth with thy riches for the use of all thy children: Have regard, we pray thee, to the impoverishment of the nations; and on all who are in authority bestow thy gifts of wisdom and goodwill, that, being lifted above self-regard, they may establish a new order, wherein the needs of all men shall be supplied; through Jesus Christ our Lord.

697

O Almighty God, whose dearly beloved Son, after his resurrection, sent his apostles into all the world to preach the gospel to every creature: We beseech thee, O Lord, to look upon the fields now white unto harvest, and to send forth more labourers to gather fruit unto eternal life; and grant us grace to labour with them in prayers and offerings, that we, together with them, may rejoice before thee, according to the joy in harvest; through Jesus Christ our Lord.

Canterbury Convocation, 1862*

698

O God, who hast knit us together in a world family whose members live by giving and receiving the fruits of the earth according to their own and others' needs: Grant that all nations of men who share the good gifts of thy bounty may look beyond the gifts to the Giver, and increase in the knowledge and love of thee, the Father of all; through Jesus Christ our Lord. *With all our Strength*

699

O God, from whose unfailing bounty we draw our life and all that we possess, forgive our pride and self-sufficiency. Teach us to reverence the earth, which thou hast made fruitful. Help us to remember our unity with those by whose work we are fed and clothed. Touch us with compassion for all who have not enough to eat. As thou hast given us the knowledge which can produce plenty, so give us also the wisdom to bring it within the reach of all; through Jesus Christ our Lord. *J. H. Oldham*

The harvest of the sea 700

O Almighty God, who hast made the sea and all that moveth therein: We thank thee for the harvest of the waters, which thou hast made abundant in its season; and we pray thee to give us grace ever to acknowledge thee, who art the Lord of the sea and of the dry ground; through Jesus Christ our Lord.

When the harvest has been defective 701

Almighty God and heavenly Father, who hast in wisdom seen fit to withhold from us at this time thine accustomed bounty: We most humbly praise thee for still bestowing upon us far more than we deserve. Make us truly thankful for our many blessings; increase in us more and more a lively faith and love, and a humble submission to thy blessed will; through Jesus Christ our Lord.

Canadian Prayer Book

For Christian education   **702**

WE commend to thy grace, O God, all who are entrusted with
the promotion of sound education in this country. Give
wisdom to those who teach, that they may first be taught of thee;
and grant to parents so to love thee that Christian homes may be
the foundation of our common life; through Jesus Christ our Lord.
Adapted

703

Guide, O Lord, the minds of those who direct the work of
education in this district, and prosper with thy blessing our schools
and colleges; that our boys and girls and young people may be
equipped with faith and knowledge for life's journey, and go forth
strong in spirit to serve their generation by thy will; through Jesus
Christ our Lord.   *Frank Colquhoun*

704

O God, who in all ages hast called men to positions of leadership
and responsibility in thy Church: Give thy grace, we humbly
beseech thee, to all who have the duty of advancing the work of the
Church in education, that they may serve before thee as faithful
stewards in thy kingdom; through Jesus Christ our Lord.
Prayers for Education Sunday, 1956

705

O Lord, who didst found thy Church to proclaim the Faith by
preaching and teaching: Give to our leaders in religious education
undaunted courage and wisdom, and to us a new spirit of faith and
adventure, so that thy will may be done on earth as it is in heaven,
to the glory of thy name.   *Prayers for Education Sunday, 1957*

706

O Merciful Father, who hast taught us that the fear of the Lord
is the beginning of wisdom: We commend to thy care and guidance
the boys and girls in the schools of this parish [*diocese, town*];
beseeching thee that they may grow up in the faith of thy holy
Church, and so be ready to do their duty in that state of life into

which it shall please thee to call them; for the honour of thy Son Jesus Christ our Lord.

707

Almighty God, we beseech thee with thy gracious favour to behold our universities, colleges and schools, that knowledge may be increased among us, and all good learning flourish and abound. Bless all who teach and all who learn, and grant that in humility of heart they may ever look unto thee, who art the fountain of all wisdom; through Jesus Christ our Lord.   *American Prayer Book*

708

O Thou who art the God of truth and light as well as of love and righteousness: We pray for the Christian schools and colleges of all countries, that they may be such homes of fellowship and brotherhood, learning and culture, that from them shall come forth a stream of leaders to share these blessings with their fellow-countrymen and to guide their countries into the way of peace; through Jesus Christ our Lord.   *Prayers of the World-Wide Church*

For universities and colleges
709

Almighty Father, grant that our universities and colleges may be houses of faith and fruitful study; and that their students may so learn truth as to bear its light along all their ways, and so learn Christ as to be found in him; who liveth and reigneth with thee and the Holy Spirit, one God, world without end.

King's College, Cambridge

710

O God, the eternal wisdom, who wouldest that all should learn to know thee in the splendour of thy Son's life on earth: Grant that our universities and schools, first learning Christ, may impart full treasures of knowledge, truth, and faith; so that both Church and commonwealth be nobly served by lives which follow his; who liveth and reigneth with thee and the Holy Spirit, one God, world without end.

For teachers
711

O Lord God Almighty, who through thy Son Jesus Christ didst reveal thine exceeding love for children: Graciously look upon those to whom thou hast entrusted the work of teaching. Let them all be taught of thee; and so fill them with love to thee that through them thy love may be implanted in the hearts of those who are committed to their care; through the same Jesus Christ our Lord.

Salisbury Book of Occasional Offices

712

Lord Jesus Christ, who didst show on this earth thy love for children: Guide, we pray thee, with thy Spirit, those who are called to the ministry of teaching in this land; that nothing may hinder our children from growing in faith and love towards thee, and that thy name may be honoured both in our schools and in our homes.

713

Almighty and everlasting God, the giver of every good and perfect gift: Send thy blessing, we beseech thee, on all who teach in this school [*or* in the schools of this parish]; and so strengthen them by the grace of the Holy Spirit that they may build up in the faith and love of thy dear Son those committed to their care; through the same Jesus Christ our Lord.

For education in every land 714

O God, who art the goal of all knowledge and the source of all truth, who dost lead mankind towards thyself along the paths of discovery and learning: Direct with thy wise Spirit the work of education in every land. Especially we would pray for those who have the difficult task of adapting new knowledge to the mind of ancient peoples. Give them insight into the needs of those whom they teach, humility to learn from their traditions, and wisdom to combine the old and the new; through Jesus Christ, our Lord.

For children 715

O Lord Jesus Christ, Child of Bethlehem, everlasting God: Bless, we beseech thee, the boys and girls of our schools; that growing up in thy faith and fear, they may be prepared to do their duty in that state of life to which it shall please thee to call them; for thy honour and glory, who livest and reignest with the Father and the Holy Spirit, world without end. *Adapted*

716

O Lord Jesus Christ, who was thyself a child at Nazareth: We bring again to thee the children of this parish, that they may love thee above all things. Grant wisdom and faithfulness to all parents, that our Christian homes may be bulwarks of our common life, and that children may grow up to the praise of thy holy name.

Prayers for Education Sunday, 1956

For homes and parents 717

O God our Father, who hast made men to live together in families: Preserve to us the sanctities of family life; unite parents and children in true affection to one another in thy holy fear; and give wisdom to all Christian parents and teachers, that they may bring up children in true faith and in obedience to thy Word; through Jesus Christ our Lord. *Adapted*

For the National Society 718

Bless, we beseech thee, Almighty God, the work of the National Society on behalf of religious education, and grant that thy Holy Spirit may direct and rule the hearts of all who labour for the advancement of true religion. Give to them that teach the spirit of wisdom and understanding, and to those who learn grace to love the truth, that we may ever be a righteous and God-fearing people; through Jesus Christ our Lord.

For students 719

O Lord Jesus Christ, in whom are hidden all the treasures of wisdom and knowledge: Have mercy on the students of this and every land who have set themselves to seek learning. Guide them by thy Holy Spirit into all truth; grant them to realize that the fear of the Lord is the beginning of wisdom; and so spread the knowledge of thy name throughout the student world that many may turn to thee and find thee as the Way, the Truth and the Life; for thine own name's sake. *Inter-Varsity Fellowship**

720

Give thy grace, O heavenly Father, to all Christian students in the universities and colleges of this land and overseas. Deepen their devotion to thee and their commitment to thy service; and grant that both by the consistency of their lives and the faithfulness of their witness they may bring many to the knowledge of thee, and of thy Son Jesus Christ our Lord. *Adapted*
See also prayers for Education and Youth, 1161–82

Thanksgiving **721**

O LORD, thou lover of souls, who through the mouth of thy prophet of old hast declared that all souls are thine: We thank thee for the brave and faithful dead who have laid down their lives in two world wars; for the devotion and courage of the soldiers and sailors and airmen who have fallen in the cause of truth and righteousness. Grant us so to follow their good example in faithfulness and endurance, even unto death, that we may be found worthy of the crown of everlasting life; through the merits of Jesus Christ our Saviour.

722

O Almighty God, who art a strong tower of defence unto thy servants against the face of their enemies: We yield thee praise and thanksgiving for our deliverance from those great dangers wherewith we were compassed; we acknowledge it thy goodness that we were not delivered over as a prey unto them; beseeching thee still to continue thy mercies towards us, that we may always confess thee our Saviour and mighty Deliverer; through Jesus Christ our Lord.

Adapted from Book of Common Prayer

723

Almighty and everlasting God, we give thee humble thanks for the memory and good example of those who have laid down their lives in the service of our country. We bless thee for their courage and devotion, even unto death. Accept their sacrifice, we beseech thee; let it not be in vain that they have died in the cause of righteousness and honour; and in thy mercy send thy peace into the hearts of all men everywhere; through Jesus Christ our Lord.

724

We remember before thee with gratitude, O Lord our God, those who gave their lives for the cause of freedom. Grant unto all of us for whom they died that their devotion may bear fruit in us in more abundant love for others; through Jesus Christ our Lord.

For the peace of the world **725**

O Almighty God, who canst bring good out of evil and makest even the wrath of man to turn to thy praise: Teach us to live together in charity and peace; and grant, we beseech thee, that the nations of the world may henceforth be united in a firmer fellowship for the promotion of thy glory and the good of all mankind; through Jesus Christ our Lord. *A Form of Prayer, August 1914*

726

O God, whose righteous wisdom governs the heavens, and controls also the destinies of men: Teach the rulers of the nations the things that belong to their peace. Open the eyes of all men to see the sovereignty of thine eternal truth and love; that being delivered from the bondage of human vanity and corruption, they may find their freedom in obedience to thy laws and their brotherhood in the unity of thy service; through Jesus Christ our Lord. *Adapted*

727

O Lord our God, who hast reconciled us to thyself and to one another through the death of thy Son, and hast entrusted to us the ministry of reconciliation: Keep ever before our hearts and minds the price that thou hast paid for the salvation of the world, and let the cross of thy Son bear in us and in all men its fruits of righteousness and peace; for his name's sake. *Suzanne de Dietrich*

728

O God our heavenly Father, look mercifully upon the unrest of the world, and draw all men to thyself and to one another in the bonds of peace. Grant understanding to the nations, with an increase of sympathy and mutual good will; that they may be united in a true brotherhood wherein are justice and mercy, truth and freedom, so that the sacrifice of those who died may not have been in vain; for the sake of Jesus Christ our Lord.

729

Out of the darkness of our divided world we cry to thee, O God. Let not the hopes of men perish, nor the sacrifice of men be in vain. Turn to thyself the hearts of rulers and peoples, that a new world may arise where men may live as thy children in the bond of thy peace; through Jesus Christ our Lord. *New Every Morning*

For those who suffer

730

O Lord, our heavenly Father, we commend to thy mercy all who suffer as the result of war, especially the maimed, the blind, and those who are afflicted in mind. Have pity upon the homeless and friendless, and upon those who no longer have a country of their own. Fill us with compassion for them, prosper all who seek to minister to their needs, and hasten the coming of thy kingdom of justice and peace; through Jesus Christ our Lord.

For those who mourn   731

Comfort, O Lord, we pray thee, all who are mourning the loss of those who laid down their lives in war. Be with them in their sorrow, support them in their loneliness. Give them faith to look beyond the troubles of this present time, and to know that neither life nor death can separate us from thy love which is in Christ Jesus our Lord.

For the healing of the world's sorrows   732

Eternal God, the Father of all mankind: We commit to thee the needs of the whole world. Where there is hatred, give love; where there is injury, grant pardon; where there is distrust, restore faith; where there is sorrow, renew hope; where there is darkness, let there be light; through Jesus Christ our Saviour and Redeemer.

After St. Francis of Assisi

Dedication   733

On this Remembrance Day we come, O Lord, in gratitude for all who have died that we might live, for all who endured pain that we might know joy, for all who suffered imprisonment that we might know freedom. Turn our deep feeling now into determination, and our determination into deed, that as men died for peace, we may live for peace for the sake of the Prince of Peace, even Jesus Christ our Lord.   *Leslie D. Weatherhead*

734

O Lord our God, whose name only is excellent and thy praise above heaven and earth: We give thee high praise and hearty thanks for all those who counted not their lives dear unto themselves but laid them down for their friends; beseeching thee to give them a part and a lot in those good things which thou hast prepared for all those whose names are written in the Book of Life; and grant to us, that having them always in remembrance, we may imitate their faithfulness and with them inherit the new name which thou hast promised to them that overcome; through Jesus Christ our Lord.

Frank Edward Brightman

The two minutes' silence   735

They shall grow not old as we that are left grow old. Age shall not weary them, nor the years condemn. At the going down of the sun and in the morning, we will remember them.

Laurence Binyon

736

Almighty and everlasting Lord, God of the spirits of all flesh: We commend to thy mercy the souls of our brothers whom we have remembered before thee; beseeching thee that the memory of their devotion may ever be an example and inspiration to us, and that we may serve thee faithfully all the days of our life; through Jesus Christ our Lord.

737

In memory of those who made the supreme sacrifice, O God, make us better men and women, and give peace in our time; through Jesus Christ our Lord.

The blessing **738**

God grant to the living, grace; to the departed, rest; to the Church, the Queen, the Commonwealth, and all mankind, peace and concord; and to us and all his servants, life everlasting:

And the blessing of God Almighty, the Father, the Son, and the Holy Ghost, be with you and abide with you always.

Based on a 16th century prayer
See also prayers for the peace of the world, 1047–54

DEDICATION FESTIVAL

Thanksgiving and prayer   **739**

ALMIGHTY God, whom year by year we praise for the dedication of this church, and who hast preserved us in safety to worship therein: Hear, we beseech thee, the prayers of thy people, and grant that whosoever in this place shall make his supplications before thee may, by the granting of his petitions, be filled with joy, to the glory of thy holy name; through Jesus Christ our Lord.

American Prayer Book

740

Almighty and everlasting God, behold us thy servants gathered once again to give praise and thanks for the dedication of this holy house to thy service; mercifully grant, that recalling our own dedication as living temples of thy Holy Spirit, we may be enabled to rule and govern our souls and bodies according to thy commandment, and to the glory of thy holy name; through Jesus Christ our Lord.   *The Unfolding Year*

741

Blessed be thy name, O Lord, that it pleased thee to put into the hearts of thy servants in years gone by to build and adorn this house for thy honour and glory, and for the ministry of thy Word and sacraments. And we pray that we who now enjoy the benefit of their work may express our gratitude to thee for the same by showing forth thy praise from generation to generation; through Jesus Christ our Lord.

742

O Almighty God, kindle in our hearts a sense of gratitude to thee for all thy mercies to us, especially for the piety of those who have gone before, whereby we are enabled to sing thy praises, hear thy Word, and receive thy sacraments. Inspire in us the desire to give to others what we ourselves have so richly enjoyed; and this we ask through Jesus Christ our Lord.   *Guildford Diocese*

743

O holy and eternal God, who art ever to be praised in the congregation of the saints: We yield thee hearty thanks for those who in times past have given freely of their substance for the work of this parish church; and we pray thee so to continue thy mercy towards us, that we may follow in the steps of all thy faithful servants who have loved thee here on earth, and with them may enter at last into thine unending joy; through Jesus Christ, our only Mediator and Advocate. *Adapted*

744

God of our fathers, who of old didst move thy servants in this place to build an house of prayer for the offering of eternal praises to thy glorious majesty: Grant to us, and to all who herein call upon thy holy name from age to age, that, by the offering of our lives and the praises of our lips, we may ever seek the increase of thy glory and thy kingdom; through Jesus Christ our Lord.

Winchester Cathedral

For a parish church 745

O Almighty Father, who art adored by the holy angels, and yet art pleased to accept the praises of sinful men: Let thy glory fill this house of prayer, we beseech thee; and mercifully grant that all who worship thee here may be numbered at the last with those who sing the new song before thy heavenly throne; through Jesus Christ our Lord, who livest and reignest with thee and the Holy Ghost, ever one God, world without end.

746

O God our heavenly Father, make the door of our parish church wide enough to receive all who need human love and fellowship and a Father's care, and narrow enough to shut out all envy, pride, and uncharitableness. Here may the tempted find succour, and the sorrowing receive comfort; here may the careless be awakened to repentance, and the penitent be assured of thy mercy; and here may all thy children renew their strength in thee and go on their way rejoicing; through Jesus Christ our Lord.

Adapted from various sources

747

Almighty and everliving God, who, though the heaven of heavens cannot contain thee, much less a house made with hands, yet hast promised to be present wherever two or three are gathered together in thy name: Visit, we beseech thee, with thy heavenly benediction this place built for thine honour and glory; and because holiness becometh thine house for ever, sanctify with thy abiding presence the lives of all who worship thee here; through Jesus Christ our Lord.

748

O Lord, we commit to thee the work of this parish church and all those who come within its walls. May many find thee here as the Way, the Truth and the Life, and go forth joyfully to proclaim thy message and serve thee in thy world; for thy honour and glory.

St. Aldate's Church, Oxford

749

O Heavenly Father, we humbly beseech thee to make the door of this parish church a gateway to thy eternal kingdom; and grant that all who worship thee within thy house may also witness for thee in the world outside, to thy honour and glory; through Jesus Christ our Lord.

750

O God, who hast taught us to love the habitation of thy house and the place where thine honour dwelleth: Make manifest in this place the glory of thy presence, that our hearts may be uplifted to thee in true adoration, and our worship may be worthy of thy praise; through Jesus Christ our Lord.   *Frank Colquhoun*

Dedication of life
751

O Lord, our heavenly Father, renew in us, we humbly pray thee, the gifts of thy Holy Spirit; increase our faith, strengthen our hope, enlighten our understanding, enlarge our charity, and make us ever ready to serve thee in body and soul; through Jesus Christ our Lord.

752

Go thou with us, O Lord, as we enter into thy holy house; and go thou with us, as we return to take up the common duties of life. In worship and in work alike let us know thy presence near us; till work itself be worship, and our every thought be to thy praise; through Jesus Christ our Saviour.   *Daily Prayer*

Thanksgiving for missions **753**

O GOD, the Father of all mankind: We thank thee for thy servants who have gone forth to preach the gospel throughout the world. We praise thee for the witness they have borne in their lives, or by their deaths; for those who have been brought out of darkness into thy marvellous light; and for the churches planted in many dark lands. Grant, we pray thee, that we may show forth our thankfulness by greater zeal for the spread of thy kingdom and more fervent love for all those for whom Christ died; for his holy name's sake.

*Irish Prayer Book**

754

O God, mighty to save, infinite in compassion towards the nations that know thee not, and the tongues which cannot speak thy name: We humbly thank thee that thou hast made the Church of thy dear Son the chariot of the gospel, to tell it out among the nations that thou art king, and to bear thy love unto the world's end; and for all thy servants who counted not their lives dear unto them on this employment, and for all peoples newly praising thee, we praise and bless thee, Father, Son and Holy Spirit, one Lord and God for ever and ever. *After the Third Collect*

755

Thanks be unto thee, O God, for revealing thyself to man, and for sending forth thy messengers in every age.

Thanks be unto thee for the first apostles of Christ, sent forth into all the world to preach the gospel;

for those who brought the good news to our land;

for all who, in ages of darkness, kept alive the light, or in times of indifference were faithful to their Lord's command;

for all thy followers in every age who have given their lives for the faith;

for those in our own day who have gone to the ends of the earth as heralds of thy love;

for the innumerable company who now praise thee out of every kindred and nation and tongue.

With these and the whole company of heaven we worship thee; through Jesus Christ our Lord.

Missionary responsibility 756

O Lord, who hast warned us that thou wilt require much of those to whom much is given: Grant that we, whose lot is cast in so goodly a heritage, may strive together the more abundantly, by our prayers, our labours and our gifts, to extend to those who know thee not what we so richly enjoy; and as we have entered into the labours of others, so to labour that others may enter into ours, to the fulfilment of thy holy will and the salvation of all mankind; through Jesus Christ our Lord. *Fifth century*

757

Almighty and everlasting God, whose beloved Son became man for us men and for our salvation, and gave commandment to his disciples that they should go and teach all nations, and baptize them in the name of the Father and of the Son and of the Holy Ghost: Give us grace to be obedient to his command, and grant that all men may have new birth in him, and, being delivered out of the power of darkness, may be received into the kingdom of thy love: through the same Jesus Christ our Lord. *George Appleton*

758

O God, we thank thee that thou hast called us into the fellowship of thy world-wide Church. Unite us, and all its members everywhere, in love and loyalty to carry out thy purpose of love in the world to-day; and grant that we may not fail thee in this time of opportunity; through Jesus Christ our Lord.
Prayers of the World-wide Church

759

Lord of the harvest, the nations are waiting for thy message, and asking for messengers, and there are few who go, and few who give, and few who pray. O grant that we may hear thy voice, and help in whatever way we can, by prayer, by gifts, and by service, to make thy gospel known to all the world; for the sake of Jesus Christ our Saviour. *Pakenham Walsh*

760

Almighty God, who hast given to thy Son Jesus Christ the name which is above every name, and hast taught us that there is salvation in none other: Mercifully grant that as thy faithful people have comfort and peace in his name, they may ever labour to publish it to all nations; through the same Jesus Christ our Lord.

The missionary Church **761**

Almighty and everlasting God, who in days of old didst cause thy Word to grow mightily and to prevail: We praise and magnify thy holy name for the manifestation of thy Spirit's power in this our day and for all who are labouring to spread the gospel of thy salvation throughout the world; and we pray thee so to prosper and bless their endeavours that thy way may be known upon earth, thy saving health among all nations; through Jesus Christ our Lord.

762

O Thou who art the Light of the world, the Desire of all nations, and the Shepherd of our souls: Let thy light shine in the darkness, that all the ends of the earth may see the salvation of our God. By the lifting up of thy cross gather the peoples to thine obedience; let thy sheep hear thy voice and be brought home to thy fold; so that there may be one flock, one Shepherd; one holy kingdom of righteousness and peace; one God and Father of us all, to whom be glory for ever and ever. *W. E. Orchard*

763

O God of love, whose will it is that all men should be saved: Bless all who have gone forth in the fellowship of thy Church to preach, to teach and to heal; guard, guide and use them; raise up more people at home to pray and to work, to care and to understand, to give to thee and to go for thee; that thy Church may grow, thy will be done, thy kingdom come, and thy glory be revealed; through Jesus Christ our Lord. *The C.M.S. Prayer adapted*

764

O God, who willest that all men should be saved and come to the knowledge of the truth: Prosper, we pray thee, our brethren who labour in distant lands [*especially those for whom our prayers are desired*]. Protect them in all perils; support them in loneliness and in the hour of trial; give them grace to bear faithful witness to thee; and endue them with burning zeal and love, that they may turn many to righteousness; through Jesus Christ our Lord.

765

O God the Creator and Redeemer of all mankind, we praise thee for thy messengers who are telling in the dark places of the earth the story of thy love; and we pray thee to bless their labours, to protect them among all their perils bodily and spiritual, and to give them many souls for their reward; for the sake of Jesus Christ our Saviour.
See also prayers for the Epiphany (99–104), the coming of God's Kingdom (1034–46) and the Church Overseas (1343–81)

For children   **766**

ALMIGHTY God and heavenly Father, we thank thee for the
children whom thou hast given to us; give us also grace to
train them in thy faith, fear and love; that as they advance in years
they may grow in grace, and be found hereafter in the number of
thine elect children; through Jesus Christ our Lord.

John Cosin

767

O Lord Jesus Christ, who wast found in the temple listening to
the teachers and asking them questions: Be with the children who
are taught in the Sunday schools of this parish, and grant them a
right understanding of thy holy Word, and a readiness to do thy
will; who livest and reignest with the Father and the Holy Spirit,
one God, world without end.   *Canadian Prayer Book**

768

O Lord God, who didst reveal thyself to the prophet Samuel
while he was yet a child: Grant that those whom thou hast made thy
children by baptism may above all things seek to know thee, the
only true God, and Jesus Christ whom thou hast sent; for his name's
sake.   *Canadian Prayer Book**

769

O Heavenly Father, who long ago didst watch thy Son on earth
grow as in stature so in wisdom and in perfect love of thee: Teach
by the wondrous tale of Jesus and his Church the children whom
thou watchest now, that they may grow into his likeness, loving
thee, obedient to thy will, and happy in thy house; through the
same Jesus Christ our Lord.   *Book of Common Order*

770

O Lord Jesus Christ, who didst take little children into thine arms
and bless them: Bless, we beseech thee, the children of this church;
grant that they may grow up in thy fear and love; give them day by
day thy strength and guidance, that so they may continue in thy
service unto their lives' end. Grant this, O blessed Saviour, for
thine own name's sake.   *Canadian Prayer Book**

771

Merciful Father, regard with thy tender love and favour thy children. Grant that as they have been admitted by baptism into the fellowship of thy people, so they may evermore grow in grace and in the knowledge of our Lord Jesus Christ. Keep them in all temptation; teach them thy truth; and grant that they may early give their hearts to thee; through Jesus Christ our Lord.

William Bellars

772

O God, who hast commanded us to remember thee in the days of our youth, and dost promise that those who seek thee early shall find thee: Make our vision bright, our allegiance unfaltering, our service loyal; through him who as a boy was always about his Father's business, Jesus Christ thy Son our Lord. *J. R. W. Stott*

For Sunday school teachers 773

O God our heavenly Father, who art the giver of life and light: We beseech thee to help and inspire those who teach in the Sunday schools of this parish. Pour out upon them the spirit of unceasing prayer and faithful service; encourage them with good success; strengthen their faith and purpose when they are weary and disheartened; and fortify them with the assurance that they are fellow workers with thee; through Jesus Christ our Lord.

774

O Lord Jesus Christ, who art the Saviour and Friend of age and youth: Look graciously, we beseech thee, upon those who give themselves to serve and help the young. Bless their works undertaken in thy name, and so inspire them with thy Holy Spirit that old and young may be builded together as living stones into the temple of thy Church; who livest and reignest with the Father and the Holy Spirit, ever one God, world without end.

775

O God, the author of all wisdom, who hast taught us that without love we can know nothing as we ought: Pour out thy Spirit of wisdom and love on all who are called to teach in this parish; that having the mind of Christ, they may serve the needs of others and give themselves wholly to the doing of thy will; through the same Jesus Christ our Lord.

For our homes and families 776

Almighty God our heavenly Father, whose Son Jesus Christ was subject to his parents in the home of Nazareth: Grant thy blessing, we beseech thee, to all parents and their children, that every Christian family may be an image of the Holy Family, and every Christian home a school of heavenly knowledge and virtuous living; through the same Jesus Christ our Lord. *Adapted*

777
Lord Jesus, who for thirty years didst dwell in thy humble home at Nazareth: Be with us, we pray thee, in our homes. Keep from them all pride and selfishness, that they may be dwellings fit for thy presence, where we may learn to love and serve thee truly; for thy name's sake. *Fielding Ould*

778
O God our heavenly Father, we pray thee to watch in thy loving care over our homes and families; keep far from them harm and danger; may thy presence be always with them, and thy gift of peace; through Jesus Christ our Lord.

For children at school 779
O Ever-blessed Jesus, very God and very Man, who wast thyself a child, and didst submit thyself to the charge and care of earthly teachers: Bless, we beseech thee, the children who art taught in our schools. Grant that as they grow in years they may grow in knowledge of thyself; let them learn to love and serve thee truly, and daily order their lives according to thy will; for the glory of thy holy name. *Salisbury Book of Occasional Offices**

For the children of our nation 780
O Lord Jesus Christ, we beseech thee by the innocence and obedience of thy holy childhood, and by thy reverence and love for little children, to guard the children of our land, and to remove all that may hinder them from being brought up in thy faith and love; who livest and reignest with the Father and the Holy Spirit, one God, world without end. *S. Gladstone**

781
Blessed Lord, who didst welcome the children who were brought to thee, and didst lay thine hands upon them and bless them: Forgive our neglect of those who know thee not, and inspire thy Church with new zeal to guide them into the knowledge of thy love, that they may know thee as their Friend and Saviour, and serve thee unto their lives' end; for thy name's sake.
See also prayers for Home and Friends, 1214–37

Prayers for youth   **782**

G RANT to us, O Lord our God, the spirit of courage and hope-fulness. Teach us so to live that we may be enabled to help others to face life more bravely. Let no shadows oppress our spirits, lest our gloom should darken the light by which others have to live. Say to our souls, "Be of good courage; fear not, for I am with thee"; and keep us ever strong and joyful in the consciousness of thy presence; through Jesus Christ our Lord.

783

Almighty and everlasting God, by whose grace thy servants are enabled to fight the good fight of faith and ever prove victorious: We humbly beseech thee so to inspire us that we may yield our hearts to thine obedience and exercise our wills on thy behalf. Help us to think wisely, to speak rightly, to resolve bravely, to act kindly, to live purely. Let the assurance of thy presence save us from sinning, and bless us both in body and soul; for the sake of Jesus Christ our Lord.   *J. Taylor Smith**

784

O Jesus Christ, the Lord of all good life, who hast called us to build the city of God: Do thou enrich and purify our lives, and deepen in us our discipleship. Help us daily to know more of thee, and through us, by the power of thy Spirit, show forth thyself to others. Make us ready for adventure in thy cause. We do not ask that thou wilt keep us safe, but that thou wilt keep us loyal. We ask it for thy sake who for us didst face death unafraid, and dost live and reign for ever and ever.

The Kingdom, the Power, and the Glory*

785

O Blessed Jesus, who from thy childhood didst make it thy whole employment to do thy Father's will: Kindle in us a fervent zeal for thy glory, that we may consecrate our youth to thy service, and make it the great business of our lives to know and fear, to love and obey, our heavenly Father; who with thee and the Holy Spirit liveth and reigneth world without end.   *Thomas Ken*

For a youth club 786

O Lord, who didst bind thy disciples to thyself in a strong fellowship of love and service: We pray thee to bless all who are banded together in the youth club of this parish. Deepen within them a sense of purpose in life; inspire them with the spirit of service and compassion; and unite them in loyalty to one another and to thee, their Saviour Jesus Christ. *Frank Colquhoun*

[handwritten margin note: for are young people of thy Church]

[handwritten margin edit at right of line 2: w or]

For students 787

O God of truth, by whose Spirit we are taught knowledge and wisdom in all goodness: Grant thy blessing, we beseech thee, to all students in our universities and colleges. Kindle and keep alive in their hearts the holy fire of faith and love, that they may set thy will ever before them, and consecrate their lives to thy service; for the glory of thy Son Jesus Christ our Lord. *Adapted*
See also 719–20

Thanksgiving 788

We give thanks to thee, O God, for all the many blessings of this life; for health and strength and youth; for the joys of friendship and the opportunities of service; for the beauty of the world of nature; for the kindness and care of parents and for the blessings of home life. Help us to repay, through those who need our help, some of the debt we owe. We ask this for the sake of Jesus Christ our Lord.

Dedication 789

O God, take our hands and work through them; take our lips and speak through them; take our minds and think through them; take our hearts and set them on fire with love for thee; through Jesus Christ our Lord. *W. Hay Aitken*

790

O God, who wast pleased to send on thy disciples the Holy Spirit in the burning fire of thy love: Breathe into our souls the love of whatsoever is true and beautiful and good. May we fear to be unfaithful, and have no other fear. Help us to remember that we are thy children, and belong to thee. In thy service may we live, and in thy favour may we die; through Jesus Christ our Lord. *William Knight*

791

O God, from whom every good and perfect gift doth come: We thank thee for all the gifts and opportunities that are ours as young people; and we pray thee to give us grace to consecrate to thy service the talents which thou hast committed to our charge, and to use them always to thy glory; through Jesus Christ our Lord.

Before the blessing 792

Grant unto us, O God, that we may never be ashamed to confess the faith of Christ crucified, but may manfully fight under his banner against sin, the world, and the devil, and continue Christ's faithful soldiers and servants unto our lives' end.

Adapted from Book of Common Prayer
See also prayers for Education and Youth, 1161–82

Church music   793

HOLY and eternal God, whose glory cherubim and seraphim and
all the hosts of heaven proclaim: Sanctify and bless, we beseech
thee, the music of our worship and all who make it; and grant
that the service that we can only offer unworthily here we may
enjoy perfectly in thy heavenly kingdom; through Jesus Christ our
Lord.

For a church choir   794

O Lord our God, before whom the heavens do bow, who dost give
ear to the praises of thy Church on earth: Look, we beseech thee,
upon those who sing in this choir; give them reverence in worship,
sincerity of purpose, and purity of life; that what they sing with
their lips they may believe in their hearts and show forth in their
lives, to the honour and glory of thy name; through Jesus Christ our
Lord.

795

Almighty God, who hast ordained that the hearts of men shall be
kindled by music, and their minds thereby attuned to understand
thy divine mysteries: Grant, we pray thee, that all who lead thy
praises may know themselves to be thy ministers, and that the hearts
of all who hear may be lifted up to thee; through Jesus Christ our
Lord.   *Adapted*

796

Accept in thy mercy, O Lord God, the service of those who render
thee praise in the choir of this church. May they serve thee with
glad hearts and dedicated lives; and grant that by the ministry of
music thy name may be glorified and the hearts of thy people be
uplifted in worship and love; through Jesus Christ our Lord.
                                        Frank Colquhoun

797

O Lord Jesus Christ, who before thy passion didst join with thy
disciples in a hymn of praise: Grant, we beseech thee, to those who
offer the sacrifice of song in thy Church on earth that they may be

admitted hereafter to have their part in the music of thy Church in heaven, and adore thee for ever; to whom with the Father and the Holy Spirit be all honour and glory, world without end.

Salisbury Cathedral

798

O Lord God Almighty, whose glory cherubim and seraphim and all the hosts of heaven with ceaseless voice proclaim: Hear and accept, we humbly beseech thee, the praises of thy Church below; and pour down upon thy ministers in choir and sanctuary such a spirit of faith, reverence, and joy as shall lift both their hymns and their lives unto thee; through Jesus Christ our Lord.

Scottish Prayer Book

For the Royal School of Church Music 799

O Lord, bless the Royal School of Church Music and its manifold activities in every land, and grant that the grace of thy Holy Spirit may direct its labours and sanctify the lives of all its members in loyalty, zeal and purity of heart; for the sake of Jesus Christ our Saviour.

Thanksgiving 800

Lord God, Almighty and all-merciful, whom angels and archangels worship and all the host of heaven: In thy loving kindness accept the worship and praise of thy servants here gathered together, who are not worthy to praise thee but for thy mercy's sake; through Jesus Christ our Lord.

801

Great art thou, O Lord, and greatly to be praised; great is thy power, and thy wisdom is infinite. Thee would we praise without ceasing. Thou callest us to delight in thy praise, for thou hast made us for thyself, and our hearts find no rest until we rest in thee: to whom with the Father and the Holy Spirit all glory, praise and honour be ascribed, both now and for evermore.

802

O God, who didst inspire the singers of Israel to glorify thee with thanksgiving, and to praise thee upon the strings and pipes: Accept our thanks for the beauty of craftsman's art and music's measure, and grant that we may so dedicate them to thy glory that thy worship may be duly adorned, and thy name worthily magnified; through Jesus Christ our Lord.

Concluding prayers 803

O God, who in the gift of music hath given us a revelation of thy divine beauty: Teach us to love thee in all thy gifts, and so to devote ourselves in all our work to thy glory, that through music we may raise men from the sorrows of this world to the enjoyment of thy divine loveliness; through thy Son our Saviour Jesus Christ.

Harold Anson

804

O Heavenly Father, who hast filled the world with beauty, open our eyes, we beseech thee, to behold thy gracious hand in all thy works; that rejoicing in thy whole creation, we may learn to serve thee with gladness of heart; for the sake of him by whom all things were made, thy Son Jesus Christ our Lord.

GIFT DAY
OR STEWARDSHIP SUNDAY

Thanksgiving   **805**

BLESSED be thou, O Lord God, for ever and ever. Thine, O
Lord, is the greatness, and the power, and the victory, and the
majesty; for all that is in the heaven and in the earth is thine. Thine
is the kingdom, O Lord, and thou art exalted as head above all.
Both riches and honour come of thee, and of thine own do we now
give thee, for the good of thy Church and the glory of thy name;
through Jesus Christ our Lord.   *Book of Common Order*

806

Accept, O Lord God, our Father, the spiritual sacrifices which
we offer to thee; this, of praise and thanksgiving, for thy great
mercies already afforded to us; and this, of prayer, for the continuance and enlargement of them; and this, of the love of our hearts,
as the only gift thou dost ask or desire; and all these, through the
all-holy and atoning sacrifice of Jesus Christ thy Son our Saviour.
Adapted from John Donne

807

O Lord and heavenly Father, as on this day we bring our offerings
to thee, we are mindful above all things of the manifold blessings
which thou hast bestowed upon us, unworthy as we are of the least
of them. Thanks be to thee, O God, for every gift of thine, and most
of all for the gift beyond words, thy Son Jesus Christ our Lord, to
whom with thee and the Holy Spirit be glory now and for evermore.
Frank Colquhoun

Generosity   **808**

O Thou who lovest a cheerful giver, teach us by thy Spirit to be
thoughtful and prayerful in our giving. Grant us the joy of the
generous heart, and the spirit of love and self-sacrifice that was in
Jesus Christ our Lord.   *R. W. Stewart*

809

O Lord Jesus Christ, who hast taught us that it is more blessed to
give than to receive, and that to whomsoever much is given of him

shall much be required: Pour into our hearts the spirit of thine own abundant generosity, and make us ready and eager to share with others what we ourselves have so richly and freely received; for the honour of thy name, who livest and reignest with the Father and the Holy Spirit, one God, world without end. *Adapted*

810

O Almighty God, whose blessed Son, though he was rich, yet for our sakes did become poor, that we through his poverty might become rich: Grant us the spirit of generous self-giving that we may further the work of thy Church and relieve those who are in need. Help us who have received so freely from thee to give as freely in our turn, and so share the blessedness of giving as well as the happiness of receiving. We ask this in the name of him who gave himself for the life of the world, even thy Son, Jesus Christ, our Lord.

George Appleton

811

Grant, O heavenly Father, that thy love may be so shed abroad in our hearts that we may count nothing too small to do for thee, nothing too much to give, and nothing too hard to endure; for his sake who laboured and strove and gave himself for us, thy Son, Jesus Christ our Lord. *Adapted*

812

Make us ever eager, O Lord, to share the good things that thou dost give us. Grant us such a measure of thy Spirit that we may find more joy in giving than in getting. Make us ready to give cheerfully without grudging, secretly without praise, and in sincerity without looking for gratitude. For Jesus Christ's sake.

John Hunter

813

Lord Jesus, who for our sake didst become poor, that by thy poverty we might become rich: Grant to thy people so to give of their substance as to acknowledge that they belong wholly to thee; for thine own sake. *Church of South India*

814

Lord of our lives, teach us to use aright our money and all our possessions. Deliver us from meanness or extravagance; may the spirit of true generosity inspire our giving. In all our getting and our spending keep us ever mindful of thy generous love, that we may be wise and faithful stewards of the good gifts thou hast given us; for thy mercy's sake. *With all our Strength*

Christian stewardship 815

O Heavenly Father, who by thy Son Jesus Christ hast taught us that all our possessions are a trust from thee: Help us to be faithful stewards of our time, our talents, and our wealth, and gladly to consecrate to thy service all that thou hast given us; and may we have grace, O Lord, to give ourselves to thee as those who have been bought with a price; through Jesus Christ our Saviour.

Adapted

816

Almighty God, who orders all things and has called us to thy service: Enable us to use wisely the time, ability and possessions entrusted to us, that we may be good and faithful servants, and may enter at last into the joy of our Lord; through the same our Saviour Jesus Christ.

817

O God, whose blessed Son Jesus Christ earned his bread by the labours of his hands, and taught us that all things we possess are committed to us as a trust from thee: Help us to be faithful in the exercise of our stewardship; that in earning we may be just and honourable, and in spending we may seek first not our own indulgence but thy glory and the good of others; through the same Jesus Christ our Lord.

818

O Lord Jesus Christ, who by thy incarnation didst sanctify material things to be the means of thy grace: Grant us a right understanding of the nature of money and a generous heart in the use of the wealth thou hast committed to our stewardship, that by our sacrifices we may glorify thee, who with the Father and the Holy Ghost art ever to be glorified. *Central Board of Finance*

819

Almighty God, whose loving hand hath given us all that we possess: Grant us grace that we may honour thee with our substance, and remembering the account which we must one day give, may be faithful stewards of thy bounty; through Jesus Christ our Lord. *American Prayer Book*

The dedication of gifts 820

Heavenly Father, Giver of all good things, who hast taught us that it is more blessed to give than to receive: We dedicate these offerings to the service of thy Church, humbly beseeching thee that all we have and are may be used for thy glory; through Jesus Christ our Lord. *Book of Public Worship*

821

Almighty God, from whom cometh every good and perfect gift: Accept, we beseech thee, the offerings which thy people here present to thee with willing and thankful hearts; and grant us so to consecrate ourselves to thy service here, that we may glorify thee hereafter in thy heavenly kingdom; through Jesus Christ our Lord. *Book of Common Order*

822

O Lord our Governor, who art King of all the earth: Accept of thine infinite goodness the offerings of thy people which, in obedience to thy commandment, in honour of thy name, and with a free will and joyful heart, we give and dedicate to thee; and grant that the same, being devoted to thy service, may be used for thy glory, and for the welfare of thy Church and people; through Jesus Christ our Lord. *Book of Common Order*

823

Accept, we beseech thee, O Lord, these gifts which we here bring to thee as the token of our love and gratitude; and grant that they may be so wisely used that by them the work of thy Church may be prospered and thy kingdom enlarged; for the glory of Jesus Christ our Saviour.

See also Offertory Prayers, 1769–76

Self-oblation 824

O God, who desirest no sacrifice, but a humble and contrite spirit; who wilt accept no gifts, but such as come from a good and honest heart: Save us, we pray thee, lest we come before thee with hands not free from stain; and mercifully accept the offering of ourselves, who have nothing worthy to offer but what is from thee, and dare not offer what is not hallowed by thee; for Jesus Christ's sake. *Daily Prayer*

825

Teach us, good Lord, to serve thee as thou deservest; to give and not to count the cost; to fight and not to heed the wounds; to toil and not to seek for rest; to labour and not to ask for any reward, save that of knowing that we do thy will; through Jesus Christ our Lord.   *St. Ignatius Loyola*

826

Almighty God, from whom all good things do come: Grant us grace to use wisely in thy Church all thy gifts to us, and ever to show forth our gratitude by giving ourselves, our souls and bodies, to thee and to thy service; through Jesus Christ our Lord.

For the aged 827

O LORD Jesus Christ, who didst hear the prayer of thy two disciples and didst abide with them at eventide: Abide, we pray thee, with all thy people in the evening of life. Make thyself known to them, and let thy light shine upon their path; and whenever they shall pass through the valley of the shadow of death, be with them unto the end; through Jesus Christ our Lord. *George Appleton*

828

Father of mercies and God of all comfort, who hast graciously promised that at evening time it shall be light: Hear us as we commend to thee thy servants who are drawing near to the end of life's journey. Comfort them, O Lord, with the assurance of thy presence; grant them thy peace; and may their path be as the shining light, which shineth more and more unto the perfect day; through Jesus Christ our Saviour.

829

Eternal Father, whose gift is health and length of life: So teach us to number our days, that we may apply our hearts unto wisdom. Grant that failing powers of body may be matched by increase of spiritual strength; so that trusting ourselves wholly to thy mercy and care, we may rest in thy will and patiently abide thy time; through thy Son Jesus Christ our Lord.

Old and young 830

O God, who dost turn the hearts of the fathers unto the children, and hast granted unto youth to see visions and to age to dream dreams: We beseech thee to draw together the old and the young, that in fellowship with thee they may understand and help one another, and in thy service find their perfect freedom; through Jesus Christ our Lord.

The sea of life 831

Blessed are all thy saints, O God and King, who have travelled over the tempestuous sea of this life and have made the harbour of peace and felicity. Watch over us who are still on dangerous voyage. Frail is our vessel, and the ocean is wide; but as in thy mercy thou hast set our course, so pilot the vessel of our life towards the everlasting shore of peace, and bring us at last to the quiet haven of our hearts' desire; through Jesus Christ our Lord.   *St. Augustine*

The days of our pilgrimage 832

Eternal God, our heavenly Father, who hast given us thy children an abiding citizenship in heaven, and in the days of our pilgrimage a citizenship also upon earth: Give us thine aid, as we journey to that heavenly city, so faithfully to perform the duties which befall us on our way, that at the end we may enter into the joy of thy everlasting kingdom; through Jesus Christ our Lord.

For those in need 833

Grant thy help, O Lord, to all who feel ill-equipped for the demands life makes upon them, whether through age or illness, tiredness or poverty. Sustain them in overwork or anxiety. Give them friends in their need, and enable them to find thy will in changed circumstances, and to rejoice in thy love even amid hardships and difficulty; through Jesus Christ our Lord.

For those who serve the aged 834

Almighty Father, whose Son Jesus Christ came to be the servant of all: We offer to thee our praise and thanksgiving for those who have loved and served thee in the persons of the aged; and we pray for all whose lives are devoted to their welfare, that they may render their service with love and understanding, with patience and cheerfulness; for the sake of the same Jesus Christ our Lord.

Adapted

Thanksgiving 835

Father, we thank thee for all the gains that life has brought. At every stage of the journey thou hast been with us, and thy hand has guarded and guided our way. Now, as life draws on towards its earthly close, let us not miss anything thou hast for us still, or fail to learn whatever thou art seeking to teach us. O thou good and wise disposer, we are in thy hands, well contented so to be, and asking only that thy perfect will be fully done; through Jesus Christ our Lord.   *Adapted*

Concluding prayer   **836**

O Heavenly Father, we commend ourselves to thy grace and keeping. Help us always to be of good courage, and let us never be disheartened by our difficulties or doubt thy love. Give us grace to persevere patiently along life's way, with a grateful recollection of thy past goodness, and a sure confidence in thy power to keep us to the end; through Jesus Christ our Lord.

See also 1291, 1516

A CIVIC SERVICE

For the borough 837

O GOD, who has taught us to live in the towns and cities of this world as knowing our citizenship to be in heaven: Bless the people of this borough, and guide with thy heavenly wisdom the mayor, aldermen, councillors, and those who bear office in the same; that they may ever keep before their eyes the vision of that city which hath foundations, whose builder and maker is God; through Jesus Christ our Lord.

*The Kingdom, the Power, and the Glory**

838

O God, our Father, whose will is our peace: Strengthen and sustain the common life of this community. Forgive our sins and negligences; exalt our purposes: purify our aims; free us from selfish desires; and make us of one heart and mind in thy service, for the glory of thy name; through Jesus Christ our Lord.

Adapted from A Diocesan Service Book

839

Almighty God, who hast ordained that men shall dwell together for their good in the life of a community: We pray thy blessing upon all who are citizens of this borough. Give thy grace to those who occupy positions of authority, that they may fulfil their responsibilities with wisdom and equity and in the fear of God. Grant that true faith, honest dealing, and mutual service may be the standard of our common life; and make us strong to meet every challenge which the coming days may bring; through Jesus Christ our Lord.

840

Almighty God, from whom cometh every good and perfect gift: Send down, we beseech thee, upon all those who hold office in this borough the spirit of justice and integrity, of wisdom and charity; that seeking their own good in the well-being of those committed to their charge, they may ever advance thy kingdom upon earth and promote the true welfare of thy people; through Jesus Christ our Lord.

For our leaders 841

We lift up our hearts, O Lord, in intercession for all who carry civic and political responsibilities. Grant that, putting aside all merely selfish ambition, they may seek to be the instruments of thy will and carry out thy purpose for the welfare of thy people; and may they both seek and see thy glory in happier human lives; through Jesus Christ our Lord. *Leslie D. Weatherhead*

842

Almighty God, the fountain of all goodness, we humbly beseech thee to bless the county council and all who are engaged in the work of local government; that they may order all things in wisdom, righteousness, and peace, to the honour of thy holy name and the good of thy Church and people; through Jesus Christ our Lord.

843

Almighty God, who alone givest wisdom and understanding: Inspire, we pray thee, the minds of all to whom thou hast committed the responsibility of government and leadership in the nations of the world. Give to them the vision of truth and justice, that by their counsels all nations and classes may work together in true brotherhood, and serve thee in unity and peace; through Jesus Christ our Lord.

For the nation 844

Almighty God, who hast wonderfully preserved and guided our nation through the years that are past, and given us a position of responsibility in the world: Grant that we may be worthy of our high calling. Purge out from among us the sins that dishonour thee. Give us true religion; crown our faith with righteousness; and lift us up a holy people to thy praise and honour; through Jesus Christ our Lord. *Adapted*

845

Let thy blessing rest, O God, upon this our nation; upon our Queen and all in authority under her. Deliver us from all sin and corruption, from all weakness and fear; keep us faithful to the high trust thou hast laid upon us; and deepen our life in that righteousness which alone exalteth a nation; through Jesus Christ our Lord. *Adapted*

For a better order of society 846

Behold, O Lord our God, our strivings after a truer and more abiding order. Scatter every excuse of frailty and unworthiness;

consecrate us all with a heavenly mission; open to us a clearer prospect of our work; and give us strength according to our day gladly to welcome and fulfil it; through Jesus Christ our Lord.

*B. F. Westcott**

847

Stir up, O Lord, the wills of thy people and kindle our understanding; that we may discern the way to a just and ordered society, where all may work and all may find a just reward, and thy people may serve thee and one another in peace and goodwill, in the spirit of thy Son, Jesus Christ our Lord. *Harold Anson*

848

O Lord our God, prosper, we pray thee, our efforts to fashion our citizen life here on earth after the pattern of the heavenly city, whose light is thy glory, and whose builder and maker thou art; through him whom thou hast sent to deliver us from all evil and to make all things new, Jesus Christ our Lord.

A MEMORIAL SERVICE

In memoriam **849**

ALMIGHTY Father, God of the spirits of all flesh, thyself unchanged abiding: We bless thy holy name for all who have completed their earthly course in thy faith and fear, and are now at rest. We remember before thee this day thy servant *N.*, rendering thanks to thee for the gift of *his* friendship, and for *his* life of service and devotion. And we beseech thee, in thy loving wisdom and almighty power, work in *him*, as in us, all the good purpose of thy holy will; through Jesus Christ our Lord. *Adapted*

850

O God, whose days are without end, and whose mercies cannot be numbered: Make us, we beseech thee, deeply sensible of the shortness and uncertainty of human life; and let thy Holy Spirit lead us in holiness and righteousness all our days; that when we shall have served thee in our generation, we may be gathered unto our fathers, having the testimony of a good conscience; in the communion of the Catholic Church, in the confidence of a certain faith, in the comfort of an assured hope, in favour with thee our God, and in perfect charity with all men. Grant this, we beseech thee, through Jesus Christ our Lord. *Jeremy Taylor*

851

O Lord, we praise thy holy name for all thy servants departed from among us in thy faith and fear; and we humbly beseech thee so to bless us that remain on earth, that, being protected from all evil, we may ever serve and please thee with quiet minds and thankful hearts, and together with those that are gone before may have our refreshment in paradise and our portion in the resurrection of the just; through Jesus Christ our Saviour. *Frederick Temple*

852

We give thee thanks, O Lord Christ, that the life which we now live in thee is part of the life which is eternal, and the fellowship which we have with thee unites us with our brethren both on earth and in heaven. Grant that as we journey through the years we may know joys which are without end, and at the last come to that abiding city where thou livest and reignest with the Father and the Holy Spirit, one God, world without end.

853

O Almighty God, the God of the spirits of all flesh, who by a voice from heaven didst proclaim, Blessed are the dead who die in the Lord: Multiply, we beseech thee, to those who rest in Jesus, the manifold blessings of thy love, that the good work which thou didst begin in them may be perfected unto the day of Jesus Christ. And of thy mercy, O heavenly Father, grant that we, who now serve thee here on earth, may at the last, together with them, be found worthy to be partakers of the inheritance of the saints in light; for the sake of the same thy Son Jesus Christ our Lord.

American Prayer Book

854

Give rest, O Christ, to thy servant with thy saints, where sorrow and pain are no more, neither sighing, but life everlasting.

Russian Contakion of the Departed

855

O Lord, we pray thee to give us of thy strength, that we may live more bravely and faithfully for the sake of those who are no longer with us here on earth; and grant us so to serve thee day by day, that we may find eternal fellowship with them; through him who died and rose again for us all, thy Son Jesus Christ our Lord.

The communion of saints 856

O Lord our God, from whom neither life nor death can separate those who trust in thy love, and whose love holds in its embrace thy children in this world and in the next: So unite us to thyself that in fellowship with thee we may always be united to our loved ones whether here or there: give us courage, constancy and hope; through him who died and was buried and rose again for us, Jesus Christ our Lord.

William Temple

857

O Thou who art the God of all the generations of men: We thank thee for all who have walked humbly with thee, and especially those near to us and dear, in whose lives we have seen the vision of thy beauty. May we know that in the body or out of the body they are with thee. Unite us still, God of our souls, in one household of faith and love, one family in heaven and upon earth; through Jesus Christ thy Son our Lord.

John Hunter

858

Grant, we beseech thee, Almighty God, that being compassed about by so great a cloud of witnesses, we may run with patience the race that is set before us, looking unto Jesus the author and finisher of our faith; so that, this life ended, we may be gathered with those whom we have loved into the kingdom of thy glory, where there shall be no more death, neither sorrow nor crying, neither shall there be any more pain, for the former things have passed away; through him who maketh all things new, even the same Jesus Christ our Lord.

859

O God, who hast brought us near to an innumerable company of angels, and to the spirits of just men made perfect: Grant us during our pilgrimage to abide in their fellowship, and in our heavenly country to become partakers of their joy; through Jesus Christ our Lord. *William Bright*

Those who mourn 860

Comfort, O Lord, we pray thee, all who mourn for the loss of those dear to them; be with them in their sorrow; give them faith to look beyond the troubles of the present time, and to know that neither life nor death can separate us from the love of God which is in Christ Jesus our Lord.
The Kingdom, the Power, and the Glory

861

O Lord Jesus Christ, who by thy holy apostle hast bidden us not to be sorry as men without hope for them that sleep in thee: Visit, we beseech thee, with thy compassion those who mourn the loss of their beloved, and wipe away all tears from their eyes; who livest and reignest with the Father and the Holy Spirit, ever one God, world without end. *Adapted*

Concluding prayers 862

O Lord, support us all the day long of this troublous life, until the shades lengthen, and the evening comes, and the busy world is hushed, the fever of life is over, and our work is done. Then, Lord, in thy mercy grant us safe lodging, a holy rest, and peace at the last; through Jesus Christ our Lord. *After J. H. Newman*

863

Bring us, O Lord God, at our last awakening into the house and gate of heaven to enter into that gate and dwell in that house, where there shall be no darkness nor dazzling, but one equal light; no noise nor silence, but one equal music; no fears nor hopes, but one equal possession; no ends nor beginnings, but one equal eternity; in the habitations of thy glory and dominion, world without end.

John Donne

864

Almighty Father, in whose hands are our lives: We commend ourselves to the keeping of thy love. In thy will is our peace. In life or in death, in this world and the next, uphold us that we may put our trust in thee; through Jesus Christ our Lord.

William Temple

865

O Lord, who hast taught us that our citizenship is in heaven, and that here we have no continuing city: Grant that the thought of the country to which we are travelling may lighten the weariness of the journey, that so we may be enabled to endure unto the end, in the strength of Jesus Christ our Lord.

866

Grant, O Lord, that keeping in glad remembrance those who have gone before, who have stood by us and helped us, who have cheered us by their sympathy and strengthened us by their example, we may seize every opportunity of life and rejoice in the promise of a glorious resurrection with them; through Jesus Christ our Lord.

867

O God, who hast appointed unto men once to die, but hast hidden from them the time of their death: Help us so to live in this world that we may be ready to leave it; and that, being thine in death as in life, we may come to the rest that remaineth for thy people; through him who died and rose again for us, thy Son Jesus Christ our Lord.

William Bright

868

O Lord Jesus Christ, who by thy death didst take away the sting of death: Grant unto us thy servants so to follow in faith where thou hast led the way, that we may at length fall asleep peacefully in thee, and awake up after thy likeness; through thy mercy, who livest with the Father and the Holy Ghost, one God world without end.

American Prayer Book

See also prayers for the faithful departed (*1006–15*), and for the Feasts of All Saints (*582–4*) and All Souls (*604–6*)

DEDICATION OF MEMORIAL GIFTS

NOTE. The prayers below are of a purely general character. For detailed direction regarding the dedication of memorial gifts, such as a window, a lectern, or an organ, and for suitable prayers, see E. Milner-White *After the Third Collect* (Mowbrays) pp. 120–4, and Leslie S. Hunter *A Diocesan Service Book* (O.U.P.), pp. 56–76.

Sentences 869

OUR help is in the name of the Lord: who hath made heaven and earth.

Blessed be the name of the Lord: from this time forth, even for evermore.

Honour and majesty are before him: strength and beauty are in his sanctuary.

Give unto the Lord, O ye kindreds of the people: give unto the Lord glory and strength.

Give unto the Lord the glory due unto his name: bring an offering, and come into his courts.

Before the dedication 870

Blessed and glorious Lord God Almighty, by whose power, wisdom, and love all things are sanctified, enlightened and made perfect: Be merciful unto us and bless us, we beseech thee, and cause thy face to shine upon us, that what we now do may please thee, and show forth the honour of thy name. Let thy work appear unto thy servants, and thy glory unto their children. And let the beauty of the Lord our God be upon us: and establish thou the work of our hands upon us; (yea, the work of our hands, establish thou it;) through Jesus Christ our Lord.　　*Book of Common Order*

871

Almighty Father, Lord of heaven and earth, be pleased to accept these gifts of thy children for the service of this House of Prayer; for all things come of thee and of thine own do we give thee. Grant that what neither art nor costliness can make worthy for thy service may be hallowed by thy blessing; through Jesus Christ our Lord.
A Diocesan Service Book

Act of dedication 872

In the faith of Jesus Christ, and for the benefit of his holy Church, we offer and dedicate this . . . to the glory of God, (and in memory of his servant N.;) in the name of the Father, and of the Son, and of the Holy Ghost.

After the dedication 873

Almighty God, our heavenly Father, without whom no word or work of ours availeth, but who dost accept the gifts of our hands for the service and beautifying of thy sanctuary: Have respect unto the prayers of us thy servants as we dedicate this . . . to thy glory. Accept and consecrate it, we pray thee, as we set it apart from all common and unhallowed uses, ever to be employed for the service of thy Church and the honour of thy holy name; through Jesus Christ our Lord. *Adapted from Book of Common Order*

A memorial of a churchman 874

O God our Father, who hast called us into the fellowship of thy holy Church through Jesus Christ our Lord: We praise thee for those who have been lights of the world in their generation and in whose lives men have seen the likeness of thy mercy and love. Accept, we beseech thee, this memorial of thy servant, N., who by thy grace rendered unto thee in this [city and diocese] true and laudable service; and grant that it may encourage those who come after to honour thee in like manner to the benefit of thy Church and people; through the same Jesus Christ our Lord.
A Diocesan Service Book

875

O Thou who art the Creator and Lover of all men, by whom all souls do live: We bless and praise thee for all that was pure and true, beautiful and good, in the life commemorated this day; for the example *he* has left of faith and hope and duty, and of love for thy Church; and for the hope we have, through Christ, that *he* has entered into rest. *Book of Common Order*

Introductory prayers 876

O GOD, our Father, thou hast promised to hear thy children when they pray to thee. Teach us how to pray, and what to ask for. Help us to mean what we say; and give us grace to love thee more, and to love the people for whom we pray; for Jesus Christ's sake.

877

O God, our heavenly Father, we have come to thy house. Help us to remember that thou art here. Speak to us, and make us hear thy voice; and teach us to pray to thee and to sing thy praise with all our hearts; through Jesus Christ our Lord.

878

O God, our Father, we have come to thy house to sing thy praise, to pray to thee, to hear thee speaking to us. Help us to remember thy presence with us and to worship thee with reverence and love; for the Lord Jesus Christ's sake.

879

O Heavenly Father, as we meet now in thy presence, we ask thee to open our ears to hear thy voice, to open our lips to sing thy praise, and to open our hearts to love thee more and more; for Christ our Saviour's sake.

Confession 880

O Heavenly Father, we confess that we have sinned greatly against thee in thought, and word, and deed, and have done that which is wrong in thy sight. We ask thee to forgive us our sins, and to give us strength day by day to resist temptation and to do thy will; for the sake of Jesus Christ our Lord.

*Canadian Prayer Book**

Our homes 881

O Lord Jesus Christ, who didst share at Nazareth the life of an earthly home: Look in thy love upon the homes in which we live. May they be true Christian dwellings where thy name is honoured and thy peace is ever to be found; for thy tender mercy's sake.

Those we love 882

Loving Father, bless our homes and our loved ones. Help us to be grateful for all the good things we enjoy. Keep us from grumbling and ill-temper. Help us, with cheerful hearts, to be kind to one another and to do our share in making our home the abode of happiness and love; through Jesus Christ our Lord.

Service Book for the Young

883

O God, who art present in every place: Look with thy mercy on those we love, at home or wherever they may be. Defend them from all dangers; give them strength for their daily work; and grant that both they and we, drawing nearer to thee, may also draw nearer to one another, until at last we rejoice together in our heavenly home; through Jesus Christ our Lord.

Our school 884

O God, our heavenly Father, we ask for thy blessing on our school, on our work and our games, and on everything we do together. Make us loyal to each other, obedient and truthful, and ready to work hard. Help us always to do our best, so that we may all do our part to make our school successful and happy. For Jesus' sake. *Ruby E. Cleeve*

Our country 885

O Lord our God, we thank thee for our country and for the freedom and peace we enjoy. We pray thee to give wisdom to our Queen and to all who rule over us. Make us as a nation strong in faith, that we may stand firm for truth and right. So lead us and all nations in the way of peace; through Jesus Christ our Lord.

The people who govern us 886

Lord, we ask for special wisdom for the prime minister, and all his cabinet, for the members who represent us in parliament, for the leader in our town [*or* country district]. Grant that they may remember thee and make their decisions according to thy will. We ask it for Jesus' sake. *Margaret Cropper*

Missionaries 887

O God, strengthen and help those who are telling the good news of Jesus and working for thy kingdom overseas. Help them to understand the people in the far countries where they work, and to love them and teach them wisely. Comfort them when they are lonely, keep them well and strong, and grant that they may be full of the loving Spirit of Jesus. For Jesus' sake.

Margaret Cropper

888

Heavenly Father, we thank thee for loving us, and for sending thy dear Son into the world to save us from our sins. We pray to thee for all who do not know of thy love, both at home and in other lands. Grant that through the work of our missionaries they may be led to confess the faith of Christ crucified, and with us become soldiers and servants of thy holy Church; through Jesus Christ our Lord. *Canadian Prayer Book*

Children in other lands 889

O God, we bring before thee the needs of children in other lands. We pray for those who are oppressed and for those who are starving and homeless. We remember the millions who know nothing of thy love and live in want and fear. Bless our missionary doctors and teachers who go to help them, and may all children come to see in Jesus their Saviour and their Friend.

People in need 890

Loving Father, we pray for so many people who are unhappy or lonely or ill. Comfort and help them, we pray, especially those who are in hospitals, and all blind people and cripples. Help them to realize that Jesus cares for them and can bring comfort and joy into their lives. In his name we ask this. *Ruby E. Cleeve*

Those who are ill in hospital 891

O God of love, we pray for our hospitals, and for doctors and nurses in their work of mercy and healing. Bless the sick, especially those known to us whom we remember in our hearts before thee. . . . Do for them whatever is for their good, and comfort them with thy presence; through Jesus Christ our Lord.

Thanksgiving 892

O God, our heavenly Father, we thank thee for the beauty of the world around us. We thank thee for the love of our parents and our friends, for work and play, for food and clothing, and for all the happiness of life. But most of all we thank thee for the birth of Jesus Christ, thy Son, for the example of his life, and for the love which made him die for us. And we pray that we may ever serve him faithfully and fight his battles; through the same Jesus Christ our Lord.

C. S. Woodward

893

O God, our loving Father, we thank thee for all the blessings thou hast given us; for our life and health, for our homes and friends, for everything that is good and beautiful in the world; and above all for the gift of the Lord Jesus to be our Saviour and Friend. Help us to show forth our thankfulness to thee for all thy goodness by trying in everything to please thee; for Jesus Christ's sake.

A thanksgiving for the Bible   894

We thank thee, our Father, for the Bible, which teaches us about thee, and for thy servants of old who loved thy holy Word and wrote it down for us. We thank thee that we can learn there about Jesus, our Friend and Saviour. Help us to read and learn and understand, so that we may grow in the knowledge of thee. For Jesus Christ's sake.   *Ruby E. Cleeve*

Offertory prayer   895

Heavenly Father, accept these gifts which we thy children bring to thee with love and thanksgiving, and use them for the good of thy Church in all the world [*or* to help those who are in need]; through Jesus Christ our Lord.

THE CHURCH'S YEAR

Christmas   896

HEAVENLY Father, we thank thee for all thy love to us. We remember again at this Christmas time the gift of the Lord Jesus and his birth at Bethlehem. We pray that we may welcome him with gladness, and that there may always be room for him both in our hearts and in our homes. We ask it in his name, who is our Saviour and our Friend.

897

We thank thee, heavenly Father, for giving us Christmas Day, and for all the joys of Christmas time. Above all we thank thee for sending Jesus into the world on that first Christmas Day long ago. Help us to keep his birthday by being thoughtful and loving for his sake, and by offering him the love of our hearts. For his name's sake.   *Ruby E. Cleeve*

Lent   898

Teach us, O Lord, during this season of Lent, to remember thy great love to us and all that thou hast suffered for our sakes. Help us to learn more about thee, and to love thee more truly; and make us strong to overcome our temptations and to serve thee better. For thy holy name's sake.

Good Friday 899

O God our heavenly Father, help us never to forget what Jesus Christ has done for us. We remember especially at this time that he died for us to save us from sin, and that on Easter Day he rose again from the dead and is now alive for evermore. O God, we thank thee for all thy love, help us to love thee more; for Jesus Christ our Saviour's sake.

Easter 900

Blessed Jesus, we rejoice to-day in thy mighty victory over sin and death. Thou art the risen Lord, thou art the Prince of life, thou art alive for evermore. We pray that we may know thy presence with us, not only as we worship thee here, but at home and school and all the days of our life; for thy great name's sake.

Ascension 901

O Lord Jesus Christ, who didst ascend to thy heavenly home to prepare a place for us: Help us to seek the things that are above, and to be ready at all times to carry out thy commands; that at last we too may ascend to be with thee in glory and to reign with thee for evermore.

Whitsunday 902

We praise thee, O God, as we remember to-day how the Holy Spirit the Comforter was given to the first disciples, to make them strong to witness for thee in the world. Strengthen us, we pray thee, by the same Holy Spirit, that we may think rightly, speak truthfully, and live bravely, to the glory of thy Son Jesus Christ our Lord.

Harvest 903

We thank thee, O God our Father, for all thy gifts to us at this harvest time; for the ripened fruit and vegetables and the golden corn that makes our bread. We thank thee too for the harvest of the sea, and for the food that is brought to us from other lands. Give us always grateful hearts for these thy gifts to us; and may we who have plenty remember others who have little. For Jesus Christ's sake. *Ruby E. Cleeve*

904

Heavenly Father, we praise thee for all the good things of life, and especially at this time for the fruits of the earth and the blessings of the harvest. Help us to use all thy gifts carefully, thankfully, and unselfishly, for the glory of thy name; through Jesus Christ our Lord.

CONCLUDING PRAYERS

905

Be with us, O Lord, as we go forth into the world. May the lips which have sung thy praises always speak the truth. May the ears that have heard thy Word be shut to what is evil. May the feet that have brought us to thy house ever walk in thy ways; through Jesus Christ our Lord.

906

O Lord God, who didst reveal thyself to the prophet Samuel while he was yet a child: Grant unto us thy children that we may above all things seek to know thee, the only true God, and Jesus Christ whom thou hast sent; and deepen within us the love of thy holy name; through the same our Lord Jesus Christ.

Canadian Prayer Book★

III
SACRAMENTS AND ORDINANCES

Meditation 907

Lord, this is thy feast,
   prepared by thy longing,
spread at thy command,
attended at thine invitation,
blessed by thine own word,
distributed by thine own hand,
the undying memorial of thy sacrifice upon the cross,
the full gift of thine everlasting love,
and its perpetuation till the end of time.
Lord, this is Bread of heaven, Bread of life,
   that, whoso eateth, shall never hunger more.
And this, the Cup of pardon, healing, gladness, strength,
   that, whoso drinketh, thirsteth not again.
So may we come, O Lord, to thy table.
   Lord Jesu, come to us.   *A Procession of Passion Prayers*

Thanksgiving 908

Most loving God, we heartily thank thee that in the holy mystery of this blessed sacrament thou dost refresh and strengthen us with the Body and Blood of thy dear Son, our Saviour Jesus Christ. For the beauty of this worship, for the presence of Christ, for the memorial of his passion, for communion with thy saints, for this heavenly food, for Christ in us the hope of glory, we praise and bless thy holy name; beseeching thee that we may so reverently treasure and so diligently use the grace of each communion that we may grow in the knowledge and love of thee, and of thy Son Jesus Christ our Lord.

Prayers of preparation 909

Almighty and everlasting God, behold we approach the sacrament of the passion of thy only begotten Son, our Lord Jesus Christ. As sick, we come to the physician of life; as unclean, to the fountain of mercy; as blind, to the light of eternal splendour; as needy, to the Lord of heaven and earth. We pray thee of thine infinite mercy to heal our sickness, to wash our foulness, to lighten our darkness, and to enrich our poverty; that receiving the Body and Blood of thy dear Son, we may be incorporated into his mystical body, and ever be reckoned among his members; who with thee and the Holy Ghost liveth and reigneth one God, world without end.

Adapted from a prayer of St. Thomas Aquinas

910

We pray thee, O Lord, let thy Spirit purify our hearts, lest we come unworthily to the heavenly feast. Make manifest thy presence in the midst, that we may grow up into thee and become strong in spiritual growth. So grant that we may persevere in the blessed society of thy mystical body, which thou willest should be one with thee, as thou art one with the Father in the unity of the Holy Spirit; to whom be praise and thanksgiving for ever and ever.

Erasmus*

911

Most gracious God, who art at this time calling us to prepare ourselves for coming to thy holy table: Grant us the assurance of thy pardoning love, and give us grace from the heart freely to forgive one another. Accept us as we dedicate ourselves to thee; and grant that, feeding on Christ by faith, we may be strengthened by thy Holy Spirit, and enabled to live in thy fellowship, now and for evermore.

Book of Common Order

912

Grant us, O Lord, the help of thy grace, that at this holy sacrament we may bring all our thoughts and desires into subjection to thy holy will, and may offer our souls and bodies as a living sacrifice to thee, in union with the perfect sacrifice of thy Son, our Saviour Jesus Christ.

A Book of Prayers for Students

913

O God, who by the blood of thy dear Son hast consecrated unto us a new and living way into the holiest of all: Grant unto us, we beseech thee, the assurance of thy mercy, and sanctify us by thy heavenly grace; that we, drawing near to thee with pure heart and undefiled conscience, may duly celebrate these holy mysteries and offer thee a sacrifice in righteousness; through the same Jesus Christ our Lord.

Liturgy of St. James

914

Grant, O Lord, that we who shall receive the blessed sacrament of the Body and Blood of Christ may come to that holy mystery with faith, charity, and true repentance; that being filled with thy grace and heavenly benediction, we may obtain remission of our sins, and all other benefits of his passion, to our great and endless comfort; through him who died and rose again for us, thy Son Jesus Christ our Lord. *Salisbury Book of Occasional Offices*

915

Almighty Father, we beseech thee to look mercifully upon us who are about to commemorate the death of thy Son, our Saviour Jesus Christ. Grant that our whole hope and confidence may be in his merits and thy mercy. Pardon our sins; accept our imperfect repentance; and make this commemoration available to the confirmation of our faith, the establishment of our hope, and the enlargement of our love; through the same Jesus Christ our Lord. *Samuel Johnson**

916

O Lord Christ, who at the last supper didst bequeath to thy Church a perpetual memorial of the sacrifice of the cross: Help us in this holy sacrament steadfastly to contemplate thy redeeming love, that we, ever being mindful of the price wherewith thou hast bought us, may yield our lives to thine obedience; who livest and reignest with the Father and the Holy Spirit, one God, world without end. *Charles H. Brent**

917

O Lord Jesus Christ, who by the sacrifice of thyself didst break the power of sin and death and open unto us the gate of life eternal: Mercifully look upon us thy servants, and feed us with thyself, the living bread; that, established in thy grace and strengthened by thy Spirit, we may walk before thee in faith and holiness, and serve thee unto our lives' end. *Frederick B. Macnutt*

918

Grant, we pray thee, O Father, that we and all who meet at thy table may come with true repentance, steadfast purpose, living faith, and a thankful remembrance of the death and resurrection of thy dear Son; so that our bodies and souls may be preserved unto everlasting life, and we may feed on him in our hearts by faith with thanksgiving; through the same Jesus Christ our Lord. *Lionel James*

919

Lord Jesus Christ, we humbly thank thee that thou didst choose bread and wine to be the emblems of thy sacred Body and Blood, given on the cross for the sins of the world, and didst command us thus to remember thee. Deepen our repentance, strengthen our faith, and increase our love for the brethren, that, eating and drinking the sacrament of our redemption, we may truly feed on thee in our hearts with thanksgiving, for the sake of thy great and worthy name.   *J. R. W. Stott*

920

Almighty God, our heavenly Father, who hast given thy Son our Saviour Jesus Christ not only to die for us, but also to be our spiritual food and sustenance in the most comfortable sacrament of his Body and Blood: Grant that we may celebrate the memorial of his death with reverence and godly fear, and offer the sacrifice of praise and thanksgiving with holiness and joy, to the benefit of thy Church and the honour of thy name; through the same Jesus Christ our Lord.

921

Most merciful Father, who hast given thy Son, our Lord Jesus Christ, to die for us and to take away the sin of the world: Prepare us in heart and mind so worthily to commemorate his death, by partaking of the bread of life and the cup of salvation, that our lives may be made strong for thy service, and our hearts may rejoice in thee, now and for evermore.   *Adapted*

Before reception   922
O God, who feedest us thy children with the true manna, the living bread from heaven: Grant, we beseech thee, that this precious food may be our support throughout our earthly pilgrimage, until we reach that land where we neither hunger nor thirst; through Jesus Christ our Lord.   *Priest's Book of Private Devotion*

923

O Lord Jesus Christ, who hast taught us that man doth not live by bread alone: Feed us, we humbly beseech thee, with the true bread that cometh down from heaven, even thyself, O blessed Saviour; who livest and reignest with the Father and the Holy Spirit, one God, world without end.   *John Dowden*

924

Lord Christ, our living Saviour, who in thy risen power didst make thyself known to thy disciples in the breaking of bread: Grant to us, as we now approach the holy mysteries of thy Body and Blood, a fresh manifestation of thy grace and glory, that in fellowship with thee and one another we may gain refreshment of spirit and renewal of strength; for thy holy name's sake.
Frank Colquhoun

925

Blessed Lord, by whose command we now remember thee and show forth thy death: Enable us, we pray thee, to approach thy table with penitence, faith, and gratitude; and grant that our souls being fed with the bread of life, we may live as those who are not their own but are bought with a price, to the glory of thy holy name.

926

Come, Lord Jesus, in the fullness of thy grace, and dwell in the hearts of thy servants; that, adoring thee by faith, we may with joy receive thee, and with love and thankfulness abide in thee, our Saviour and our King for evermore.

After communion   **927**

Strengthen, O Lord, the hands which have been stretched out to receive thy holy things, that they may daily bring forth fruit to thy glory. Grant that the ears which have heard thy songs may be closed to the voice of clamour and dispute; that the eyes which have seen thy great love may also behold thy blessed hope; that the tongues which have uttered thy praise may speak the truth; that the feet which have trodden thy courts may walk in the region of light; that the souls and bodies which have fed upon thy living Body may be restored to newness of life.   *From the Liturgy of Malabar*

928

Almighty God, who hast given thine only Son to die for us: Grant that we who have been united in the communion of his most precious Body and Blood may be so cleansed from our past sins, and so strengthened to follow the example of his most holy life, that we may hereafter enjoy everlasting fellowship with thee in heaven, through him who loved us and gave himself for us, the same Jesus Christ our Lord.   *B. F. Westcott*

929

Visit, we beseech thee, O Lord, thy family, and guard with watchful tenderness the hearts which have been hallowed by these sacred mysteries; that as by thy mercy they receive the healing grace of thy salvation, so by thy power and protection they may evermore retain them; through Jesus Christ our Lord.
    Leonine Sacramentary

930

O Lord our God, thou Saviour of the world, through whom we have celebrated these holy mysteries: Receive our humble thanksgiving, and of thy great mercy vouchsafe to sanctify us evermore in body and soul; who livest and reignest with the Father and the Holy Spirit, one God, world without end.   *Scottish Prayer Book*

931

O God, who in these holy mysteries hast vouchsafed to feed us with the flesh and blood of thy dear Son: We beseech thee that all who faithfully partake of the same may grow up in the communion of the body of Christ, and finally attain to the glory of the resurrection; through the merits of the same Jesus Christ our Lord.
Liturgy of the Catholic Apostolic Church

See also 227–8

and we particularly
pray for Leo.

HOLY BAPTISM

Candidates for baptism
932

O LORD God, our heavenly Father, remember for good, we beseech thee, those who at this time are preparing for holy baptism. Strengthen their faith, enlighten their minds, purify their hearts; and grant that, by the washing of regeneration and renewal in the Holy Spirit, they may receive the fullness of thy grace, and ever remain in the number of thy faithful and elect children; through Jesus Christ our Lord.

933

Almighty God, thou Shepherd of Israel, who didst deliver thy chosen people Israel from the bondage of Egypt, and didst establish them with a sure covenant: Have mercy, we beseech thee, on thy flock, and grant that *these persons*, who are by baptism to be received into thy heritage, may be delivered from the bondage of sin through thy covenant of grace, and attain the promise of eternal life which thou hast given us in thy Son our Saviour Jesus Christ; who liveth and reigneth with thee and the Holy Spirit, ever one God, world without end.   *Church of South India*

The baptized
934

O God, by whose Spirit the whole body of the Church is multiplied and governed: Preserve in the new-born children of thy family the fullness of thy grace; that, being renewed in body and soul, they may be fervent in the faith, and be enabled to serve thee all the days of their life; through Jesus Christ our Lord.
Gelasian Sacramentary

935

O God, who hast united men of every nation in the confession of thy name, and dost continually multiply thy Church with new offspring: Grant that those who have been born again, of water and of the Spirit, may be one both in inward faith and in outward devotion, and with thankful hearts may show forth in their lives the grace of that sacrament which they have received; through Jesus Christ our Lord.   *Scottish Prayer Book*

936

O Lord Jesus Christ, who in thine own appointed ordinance dost accept and seal thy disciples as members of thy mystical body: Grant, we pray thee, that all who by baptism have been admitted into thy holy Church may be faithful to their vows, and may live henceforth as those who, having died to sin, are partakers of thy risen power and glory; for the honour of thy holy name.

Frank Colquhoun

937

O God of love, who in baptism hast received us into the congregation of Christ's flock, and hast sealed us as thine own: Grant that we may never be ashamed to confess the faith of Christ crucified, but may fight manfully under his banner against sin, the world, and the devil, and may continue his faithful soldiers and servants unto our lives' end. *Adapted from Book of Common Prayer*

The sign of the cross **938**

O Lord God, who by thy divine mercy hast called us to be Christians, servants of the Crucified, signed with his cross: Enable us, for the love which he bore unto us, to choose the good and refuse the evil, swerving neither to the right hand nor to the left, under the standard and in the strength of the same our Saviour Jesus Christ.

A Procession of Passion Prayers

Thanksgiving after baptism **939**

We yield thee hearty thanks, most merciful Father, that it hath pleased thee to receive us through baptism for thine own children and to incorporate us into thy holy Church; and we humbly beseech thee to grant that, as we are partakers of the death of thy Son, so we may also be partakers of his resurrection, and may finally, with thy whole Church, be inheritors of thine everlasting kingdom; through the same Jesus Christ our Lord.

Adapted from Book of Common Prayer

Renewal of baptismal vows (at Easter) **940**

The minister, standing at the font, shall say:

As we celebrate again the rising of our Lord Jesus Christ from the dead, and so join ourselves to the triumph of life over death, let us remember that in our baptism we were united to him both in his death and in his resurrection. Let us therefore again affirm the promises of the new and risen life, renouncing evil, confessing faith, and pledging our obedience.

Do you here, in the presence of God and of this congregation, renounce the devil and all his works, the pomps and vanity of this wicked world, and all the sinful lusts of the flesh, so that you will not follow nor be led by them?

Answer: We renounce them all.

Do you believe all the articles of the Christian faith as contained in the Apostles' Creed?

Answer: We do.

Will you endeavour to keep God's holy will and commandments, and to walk in the same all the days of your life?

Answer: We will.

Let us pray.

Grant, O Lord, that as we are baptized into the death of thy blessed Son our Saviour Jesus Christ, so by continual mortifying our corrupt affections we may be buried with him; and that through the grave, and gate of death, we may pass to our joyful resurrection; for his merits, who died, and was buried, and rose again for us, thy Son Jesus Christ our Lord. *Collect of Easter Even*

CONFIRMATION

Before a confirmation class 941

O LORD and heavenly Father, who art calling us at this time to seek thy grace in confirmation and to dedicate our lives to thy service: Prepare us, we pray thee, for this solemn ordinance, and make us faithful members of thy Church. Open our hearts to receive all that thou art waiting to bestow upon us. Teach us more of thy truth, more of thy love, more of thyself. And grant that in lives made strong by thy Holy Spirit we may serve thee gladly and bravely all our days; for the sake of Jesus Christ our Lord.

Frank Colquhoun

942

Lord Jesus Christ, who didst say to thy disciples of old, Follow me: Help us to hear thy call as it comes to each one of us to-day; that committing ourselves wholly to thee as our Saviour and King, we may yield our lives to thine obedience, and serve thee faithfully all our days in the fellowship of thy Church. We ask it for the glory of thy holy name.

Those preparing for confirmation 943

O Heavenly Father, look in thy mercy upon thy children who are now preparing to dedicate themselves to thee and to seek the strengthening grace of thy Holy Spirit in the laying on of hands. Give them an earnest desire to yield their lives to thy service; and so fit them, O Lord, for this holy ordinance that they may receive the fullness of thy blessing; through our only Mediator and Advocate, Jesus Christ. *W. Walsham How**

944

O Merciful Lord, we beseech thee so abundantly to strengthen these thy servants with the sevenfold gift of thy Holy Spirit, that they who are admitted by thine ordinance to the perfection of Christian graces, may grow into the perfection of Christian life, in the exercise of the power which thou hast given them; through thy Son Jesus Christ, our Mediator and Redeemer. *R. M. Benson*

945

O Lord our God, we commend to thee those who are about to seek thy grace and to renew their vows in confirmation. Let thy fatherly hand, we beseech thee, ever be over them; let thy Holy Spirit ever be with them; daily increase in them thy manifold gifts of grace; and grant that they may continue thine for ever, until they come to thy everlasting kingdom; through Jesus Christ our Lord.

Based on Confirmation Service

946

Grant, O heavenly Father, that those who are about to be admitted into the full communion of thy Church by confirmation may be so strengthened by the gift of thy Holy Spirit that they may ever be faithful to the vows which they shall make, and serve thee henceforth with singleness of purpose as true followers of thy Son, our Lord and Saviour Jesus Christ. *Adapted*

947

Strengthen, O Lord, we pray thee, by thy Holy Spirit, thy children who are now preparing to seek thy help in the sacred rite of confirmation; and grant that, boldly confessing thee before men, they may walk steadfastly in the way of life, and serve thee faithfully all their days; through Jesus Christ our Lord.

948

Grant, O Lord, that all who shall kneel before thee to receive thy blessing in the laying on of hands may be strengthened with the Holy Ghost the Comforter, and daily increase in thy Holy Spirit more and more until they come unto thy everlasting kingdom; through Jesus Christ our Lord.

A personal prayer of preparation **949**

O God my Father, I thank thee that thou hast welcomed me into thy family and made me thy child.

I thank thee for sending thy dear Son to bear my sins, and to set an example for me to follow in my daily life.

Give me courage in my confirmation to confess him as my Saviour and Lord, and not to be ashamed of him.

Fill me with thy Holy Spirit, that he may strengthen me to overcome temptation, and at all times to be a good soldier of Jesus Christ.

Make me thine for ever, and help me to grow steadily in the knowledge of thee, and in the love of thy holy Word.

Show me how to introduce my friends to thee, that together we may follow thee all our days; through Jesus Christ our Lord.

Frank Houghton

After confirmation 950

Almighty Father, whose grace is sufficient for the needs of all thy children: Hear us as we commend to thee those who in confirmation have been admitted into the full communion of thy Church. Establish them in thy faith and fear; bind them ever more closely to thee in the fellowship of thy people; and keep them steadfast to the end; through Jesus Christ our Lord.

Frank Colquhoun

951

Come, Holy Spirit, and daily increase in these thy servants thy manifold gifts of grace; the spirit of wisdom and understanding, the spirit of counsel and strength, the spirit of knowledge and true godliness; and fill them with the spirit of thy holy fear, now and evermore.

Gelasian Sacramentary

MARRIAGE

At the publication of banns 952

O ETERNAL God, we humbly beseech thee favourably to behold these thy servants about to be joined in wedlock according to thy holy ordinance; and grant that they, seeking first thy kingdom and thy righteousness, may obtain the manifold blessings of thy grace; through Jesus Christ our Lord. *American Prayer Book*

953

Most merciful Father, we beseech thee to send thy blessing upon these thy servants who are to be joined together in holy matrimony; that they may be faithful to the vows they shall make one to the other, and may ever remain in perfect love and peace together; through Jesus Christ our Lord.

954

Almighty Father, who hast hallowed the ordinance of marriage to the blessing of mankind: Give thy grace to these thy servants who are to be joined together as husband and wife, that they may be faithful in love to one another, and live in obedience to thy will; for the sake of Jesus Christ our Lord.

955

O Thou who by thy presence in Cana of Galilee didst sanctify the holy estate of matrimony: Send thy blessing upon these thy servants, that living together in perfect love and peace, they may serve and worship thee all the days of their life; for the glory of thy holy name.

956

O God our Father, bless these thy servants who are to be joined together in holy matrimony; that they obeying thy will, and always being in safety under thy protection, may abide in thy love unto their lives' end; through Jesus Christ our Lord.

Preparation for marriage 957

O Lord God, giver of life and love, let thy blessing rest upon those whom thou hast drawn together in love. Build thou their home, that it may be for all who live in it a likeness of thy kingdom.

Give them of thy wisdom and patience that they may walk together in happiness and peace, be the way rough or smooth. If to them is given the joy of children and their care, grant them grace to bring them up in the knowledge of thee and within the fellowship of thy holy Church; and in all things and at all times be thou their strength and guide; through Jesus Christ our Lord.

A Diocesan Service Book

958

Almighty and most merciful Father, without whose help we cannot do anything as we ought: We pray that, as thou hast brought these persons together by thy providence, thou wilt enrich them by thy grace, that they may enter into the marriage covenant as in thy sight, and truly keep the vows they are about to make; through Jesus Christ our Lord.   *Church of South India*

959

O Lord and Saviour Jesus Christ, who didst share at Nazareth the life of an earthly home: Reign, we beseech thee, in the home of these thy servants as Lord and King; give them grace that they may minister to others as thou didst minister to men; and grant that by deed and word they may be witnesses of thy saving love to those amongst whom they live; for thy holy name's sake, who livest and reignest with the Father and the Holy Spirit, one God, world without end.   *Church of South India*

960

Most blessed Father, from whom all pure love cometh, bless thy children *M.* and *N.* who are shortly to be joined together in marriage. Grant that the hopes and prayers in their hearts may be fulfilled through thy mercy. Draw them ever closer to one another and to thee; give them grace to bear one another's burdens and to share one another's joys; and grant that they may live together in faithful love unto their lives' end; through Jesus Christ our Lord.

Let Us Pray

Dedication of the ring   **961**

In thy name, O Lord, we hallow and dedicate this ring; that by thy blessing he who gives it and she who wears it may abide together in thy peace, continue together in thy favour, may live together in thy love, and at the last may dwell together in thy eternal kingdom.

962

Bless, O Lord, this ring which we hallow in thy name; that he who gives it and she who wears it, keeping true faith one with an-

other, may abide in the circle of thy love now and unto their lives'
end; through our Saviour Jesus Christ.

PRAYERS SUITABLE FOR USE AT A MARRIAGE
REUNION SERVICE

963

O HEAVENLY Father, we humbly thank thee for all thy blessings
to us, unworthy though we be. We thank thee for all things
that have enriched our lives, for all people who have blessed us with
their love and friendship. We thank thee for Christian marriage,
for our homes and families and friends. Give us, O Lord, this
further blessing, that as we have freely received, so we may freely
give. Confirm and strengthen our marriages, that our homes may be
to us, and to friend and stranger, places of joy and gladness. We
ask this in the name of Jesus Christ our Lord.

Brompton Parish Church

964

O God, our heavenly Father, so strengthen us by thy Holy
Spirit that by our example and witness we may uphold the sanctity
of marriage, and teach our children to be faithful members of thy
holy Church. And grant that by prayer and worship we may lead
our families in holiness and purity of life, and help others to do the
same; through Jesus Christ our Lord.

965

O Heavenly Father, who hast consecrated the state of matrimony to such an excellent mystery, that in it is signified and repre-
sented the spiritual marriage and unity betwixt Christ and his
Church: Give thy grace, we beseech thee, to all who are joined together in holy wedlock, that they may surely perform and keep the
vow and covenant betwixt them made; for his sake who adorned and
beautified with his presence, and first miracle that he wrought, the
marriage in Cana of Galilee, thy Son Jesus Christ our Lord.

Based on Book of Common Prayer

966

O Thou who settest the solitary in families and sendest thy peace
upon the households of the faithful: Grant thy blessing, we pray
thee, to us and to the members of our families; that in lives made
strong for thy service, and homes sanctified by thy presence, we
may show forth thy glory before the world; through Jesus Christ
our Lord. *Adapted*

967

Remember, O Lord, thy holy childhood, and look in love upon the children whom thou hast given us to our great comfort. May thy holy angels be their guardians, thyself their guide; and may they increase in wisdom and stature, and in favour with God and man, being daily conformed to thy likeness; who with the Father and the Holy Spirit livest and reignest one God for ever.

Mothers' Union

968

We thank thee, O God, for the children who have grown up in our homes. Keep them faithful, we pray thee, to thyself, and to us, and to one another. Let thy love protect those who are absent from us; bless those who are married, and fill their homes with peace; and make us all to be one in the joy and service of thy greater family; through Jesus Christ our Lord.

Mothers' Union

Dedication
969

O God our Father, in thy presence we give ourselves afresh to have and to hold from this day forward, for better for worse, for richer for poorer, in sickness and in health, to love and to cherish, till death us do part, according to thy holy laws; through Jesus Christ our Lord.

See also prayers for family life, 1214–22

FOR THE BLESSING OF A CIVIL MARRIAGE

970

ALMIGHTY God, our heavenly Father, source of all life and love: Bestow thy rich and effectual blessing upon these thy servants who have covenanted before thee to dwell together as husband and wife. Unite their hearts in true sympathy and love, that they may keep their vows, and live together in holy peace; bestow thy blessing upon the home in which they dwell, that it may be a place of true affection, pure religion, and consecrated joy; and bring them at the last to that heavenly home where love and joy are perfect; through Jesus Christ our Lord.

*Book of Common Order**

971

Father of mercies and giver of all grace: We commend to thee these thy servants who desire thy help and guidance for the new life which they begin together. Grant them the grace of mutual love and forbearance; bestow upon them thy pure and peaceable wisdom to enlighten them in all perplexities; and strengthen them with the power of thy Holy Spirit, to keep them constant in their trust in thee and in one another; through Jesus Christ our Lord.

*Diocese of Southwark**

972

Almighty and most merciful Father, who hast ordained the holy estate of matrimony to guard, to hallow, and to perfect the sacred gift of love: Look mercifully upon these thy servants whom we now commend to thy protection and care. Forgive them all their sins; keep them ever in thy peace; and grant them grace so to live together in true and enduring affection that the blessing which they have sought this day upon their union may never be withheld; through Jesus Christ our Lord.   *Adapted*

CHILDBIRTH

Before childbirth   973

O GOD, the creator and giver of life, we thank thee for entrusting this woman to bear a child. Help her to respond to this gift by preparation of herself in heart, and mind, and body. Strengthen her for the task and responsibility of motherhood. Grant her also the gift of faith in thy Son Jesus Christ, that she may have peace and quiet confidence in him. So may her hope be realized and her joy be full; through the same Jesus Christ our Lord.

*Guild of Health**

974

O God, who didst choose Blessed Mary to be the mother of thy Son Jesus Christ: Prepare the heart and mind and body of this woman, that she may be worthy to be the mother of the child thou wilt give her, and that she may rejoice in her motherhood, as Mary did with Jesus Christ our Lord.   *Guild of Health*

After childbirth   975

O God, our heavenly Father, who hast blessed thy servants with the gift of a child: Grant, we beseech thee, that they may show their love and thankfulness to thee in so ordering their home, that by their example and teaching they may guide their child in the way of righteousness, to thy great glory; through Jesus Christ our Lord.   *South African Prayer Book**

976

O God, our heavenly Father, by whose creative power and love this woman has been granted the gift of a child: Give to her and her husband wisdom and guidance, that they may know how to train their child in the way that leadeth to eternal life; through Jesus Christ our Lord.   *Church of South India*

977

Almighty God, we give thee hearty thanks for thy loving care during this woman's pregnancy and delivery, and for the skill and devotion of all who have guarded the health of both mother and child. Grant that she, remembering thy love for her, may serve thee faithfully in the daily care of her home and family; through Jesus Christ our Lord. *Guild of Health*

978

O Heavenly Father, we thank thee that thou hast been pleased to deliver this thy servant and to give her a healthy living child. We pray that thou wouldest keep her safe, and grant her and her husband grace to bring up their child in thy steadfast fear and love; through Jesus Christ our Lord.

British Hospital for Mothers and Babies

979

O God our heavenly Father, who hast crowned the love of these thy servants with the gift of a child: We humbly beseech thee to give them grace so to order the life of their home that they may ever rejoice in thy presence, and may lead their child in the way of righteousness; through Jesus Christ our Lord.

When a baby has died 980

O God, our heavenly Father, whose ways are hidden and thy works wonderful: Comfort, we pray thee, this woman and her husband whose hearts are heavy with sorrow. Surround them with thy protection, and grant them grace to face the future with good courage and hope. Teach them to use this pain in deeper sympathy for all who suffer, so that they may share in thy work of turning sorrow into joy; through Jesus Christ our Lord.

Guild of Health

THE SICK

Visitation of the sick

981

O LORD Jesu Christ, thou great physician: Look with thy gracious favour upon this thy servant; give wisdom and discretion to those who minister to *him* in his sickness; bless all the means used for *his* recovery; stretch forth thy hand, and, if it be thy will, restore *him* to health and strength, that *he* may live to praise thee for thy goodness and thy grace; to the glory of thy holy name.

Canadian Prayer Book

982

Sanctify, we beseech thee, O Lord, the sickness of this thy servant, that the sense of *his* weakness may add strength to *his* faith and seriousness to *his* repentance; and grant that *he* may dwell with thee in life everlasting; through Jesus Christ our Lord.

American Prayer Book

983

O God, the strength of the weak and the comfort of sufferers: Mercifully accept our prayers, and grant to thy servant the help of thy power; that *his* sickness may be turned into health, and our sorrow into joy; through Jesus Christ our Lord.

American Prayer Book

984

Almighty, everliving God, maker of all mankind: We beseech thee to have mercy upon this thy servant in *his* affliction. Give *him* grace to take *his* sickness with patience and courage; and grant that, if it be thy gracious will, *he* may recover *his* bodily health, and serve thee henceforth in newness of life; through Jesus Christ our Lord.

South African Prayer Book

A sick child

985

O Lord Jesus Christ, Good Shepherd of the sheep, who dost gather the lambs with thine arms, and carry them in thy bosom: We commit into thy loving hands this child. Relieve *his* pain, guard *him* from all danger, restore unto *him* the gifts of gladness and strength, and raise *him* up to a life of service to thee. Hear us, we beseech thee, for thy dear name's sake. *Irish Prayer Book*

The laying on of hands 986

O Almighty God, who art the giver of all health, and the aid of them that seek to thee for succour: We call upon thee for thy help and goodness mercifully to be showed upon this thy servant; that being healed of *his* infirmities *he* may give thanks unto thee in thy holy Church; through Jesus Christ our Lord.

987

Our Lord Jesus Christ, who gave authority and power to his disciples to lay hands on the sick that they might recover: Have mercy upon you; and by the authority committed unto me in his Church I now lay hands upon you, that you may be made whole, through the power and in the name of Jesus Christ.

A Diocesan Service Book

988

O Almighty God, whose blessed Son did lay his hands upon the sick and heal them: Grant, we beseech thee, to this person, upon whom we now lay our hands in his name, refreshment of spirit, and, if it be thy holy will, perfect restoration to health; through the same thy Son Jesus Christ our Lord. *Scottish Prayer Book*

989

O Lord Jesus Christ, who in the days of thy flesh didst lay thy hands upon the sick who were brought to thee, and didst heal them: Have mercy, we beseech thee, upon this thy servant; that being delivered from sickness and restored to health, *he* may serve thee with all *his* strength, and walk before thee humbly and faithfully all *his* days, to the glory of thy name.

990

In the name of God most High, may release from thy pain be given thee, and thy health be restored according to his will. In the name of Jesus Christ, the Prince of life, may new life quicken thy mortal body. In the name of the Holy Spirit mayest thou receive inward health, and the peace which passeth all understanding. And the God of peace himself sanctify you wholly; and may your spirit and soul and body be preserved entire, without blame at the coming of our Lord Jesus Christ.

The anointing of the sick 991

Almighty God, our heavenly Father, who hast taught us by thy servant Saint James to pray over the sick, and to anoint them with oil in thy holy name, that they may recover their health: Bless, we beseech thee, thy servant to be anointed with this oil, that *he* may be delivered from all infirmity of body, mind and spirit, and may be raised up to serve thee in fullness of health; through Jesus Christ our Lord.

992

N., in the faith of Jesus Christ I anoint thee with this holy oil, in the name of God, the Father, the Son, and the Holy Spirit.

993

As with this oil your body is outwardly anointed, so may your whole being [*or* mind and heart] be sanctified by the Holy Spirit of God. May the merciful Father give you release from pain and disease, and restore you to health; and may he also give you faith to offer your sufferings in communion with your crucified Lord, as a prayer for others; through the same Jesus Christ our Lord.

A Diocesan Service Book

994

O Almighty God, giver of life and health, who hast taught us in thy holy Word to pray over the sick, and to anoint them with oil in the name of the Lord: Grant, we beseech thee, to this person, whom we anoint in thy name, refreshment of spirit, and, if it be thy will, perfect restoration to health; through Jesus Christ our Lord.

Scottish Prayer Book

Prayers for a service of healing   **995**

O Lord Jesus Christ, who hast promised that where two or three are gathered together in thy name, thou art in the midst: Open our ears that we may hear thy gracious voice, and prepare our hearts that we may make intercession according to thy will; who livest and reignest with the Father and the Holy Spirit, one God, world without end.

Guild of St. Raphael

996

O Risen Christ, who makest intercession for us and in us, and who art the giver of life and health and healing: Fill us with thy life-giving love and power, that we may worthily intercede for others. May the Holy Spirit make us one with those for whom we pray, and deepen our understanding of thy great love for them and for us; and grant that we, giving ourselves to thy good purposes, may be delivered from self-concern and made fit to be channels of thy grace. To thee be all honour and glory and thanksgiving for ever.

Guild of Health

997

O God our Father, who art the source of all life and health, all strength and peace: Teach us to know thee truly; take from us all that hinders the work of thy healing power, all our sins, all our anxieties and fears, all resentment and hardness of heart; and help us to learn to enter into stillness and peace with thee, and to know that thou art our healer and redeemer; through Jesus Christ our Lord.   *Guild of Health*

998

Eternal Lord Christ, who art the strength of all that trust in thee: We bring now into thy presence thy servants . . . We know not what is best for them, but thou knowest. Lay thy healing hand upon them, we beseech thee, giving them all that is needful for health both of body and soul. Grant them patience and endurance, with a perfect dependence on thy never-failing love; and work out in them the good pleasure of thy will; who livest and reignest with the Father and the Holy Ghost, one God, world without end.

Guild of St. Raphael

999

Lord Jesus, who chose twelve disciples and sent them forth to preach the gospel and to heal the sick: Forgive the faithless disobedience of thy children, and help us to restore the healing ministry to thy Church. Grant that thy whole Church as thy body may be inspired to teach and to heal; that again signs may follow upon faith in thee, and the world may know that thou art our mighty Saviour; to whom be all praise and glory, now and for evermore.

Guild of Health

1000

O Christ our Lord, our good physician and our salvation: Look upon all thy faithful people who are sick, and who love to call upon thy name; take their souls into thy keeping, and vouchsafe to deliver them from all sickness and infirmity; who livest and reignest with the Father and the Holy Spirit, one God, world without end.

Adapted from Mozarabic Sacramentary

1001

O Lord our God, into thy hands we commend all for whom we have prayed. Thou art infinite Love, infinite Wisdom, infinite Power. Bless them according to their several necessities out of the abundance of thy grace; through Jesus Christ our Lord.

Guild of St. Raphael

A thanksgiving

1002

We praise thee, O God, for all the blessings given to the sick for whom we have prayed. We thank thee for those who have been made whole, for those who are better, and for those who have been drawn closer to thee. We bless thee for the sense of thy presence enabling those who suffer to endure with patience. And finally we thank thee for bringing good out of evil, joy out of suffering, and above all, for the cross of thy Christ and the certain hope of the redemption of body and soul to everlasting life.

Guild of St. Raphael

See also 1186–90, 1264–81

THE DEPARTED

The hope of glory   1003

GOD of all grace, who didst send thy Son our Saviour Jesus Christ to bring life and immortality to light: Most humbly and heartily we give thee thanks that by his death he destroyed the power of death, and by his glorious resurrection opened the kingdom of heaven to all believers. Grant us assuredly to know that because he lives we shall live also, and that neither death nor life, nor things present nor things to come, shall be able to separate us from thy love, which is in Christ Jesus our Lord.   *Book of Common Order*

1004

Eternal God, our heavenly Father, who lovest us with an everlasting love, and canst turn the shadow of death into the morning: We bow before thee with reverent and submissive hearts; speak to us afresh thy gracious promises; that through patience and the comfort of the Scriptures we may have hope, and be lifted above our darkness and distress into the light and peace of thy presence; through Jesus Christ our Lord.   *Book of Common Order*

1005

Most merciful Father, who hast been pleased to take unto thyself the soul of this thy servant [*child*]: Grant to us, who are still in our pilgrimage and who walk as yet by faith, that, having served thee with constancy on earth, we may be joined hereafter with thy blessed saints in glory everlasting; through Jesus Christ our Lord.   *American Prayer Book*

The faithful departed   1006

Receive, O Lord, in tranquillity and peace, the souls of thy servants who, out of this present life, have departed to be with thee. Grant them rest, and place them in the habitations of life, the abodes of blessed spirits; and give them the life that knoweth not age, the good things that pass not away; through Jesus Christ our Lord.   *St. Ignatius Loyola*

1007

O God, the maker and redeemer of all believers: Grant to the soul of thy servant *N.* all the unsearchable benefits of thy Son's passion; that in the day of his appearing *he*, and all the faithful departed, may be manifested as thy children; through the same Jesus Christ our Lord, who liveth and reigneth with thee and the Holy Ghost, one God world without end.

South African Prayer Book

1008

Remember thy servant, O Lord, according to the favour which thou bearest unto thy people; and grant that, increasing in knowledge and love of thee, *he* may go from strength to strength in the life of perfect service in thy heavenly kingdom; through Jesus Christ our Lord. *American Prayer Book*

1009

O Heavenly Father, help us to entrust our loved ones to thy care. When sorrow darkens our lives, teach us to look up to thee, remembering the cloud of witnesses by which we are compassed about. And grant that we on earth, rejoicing ever in thy presence, may share with them the rest and peace which thy presence gives; through Jesus Christ our Lord. *Canadian Prayer Book*

1010

Grant unto us, O God, to trust thee not for ourselves alone, but for those also whom we love and who are hid from us by the shadow of death; that, as we believe thy power to have raised our Lord Jesus Christ from the dead, so we may trust thy love to give eternal life to all who believe in him; through the same Jesus Christ our Lord. *New Every Morning*

1011

Remember, O Lord, thy servants and thy handmaidens who have departed hence in the Lord, especially *N.*, and all others to whom our remembrance is due. Give them eternal rest and peace in thy heavenly kingdom, and to us such a measure of communion with them as thou knowest to be best for us; through Jesus Christ our Lord. *E. B. Pusey*

1012

O Thou Lord of all worlds, we bless thy name for all those who have entered into their rest, and reached the promised land where thou art seen face to face. Give us grace to follow in their footsteps, as they followed in the footsteps of thy holy Son. Keep alive in us the memory of those dear to ourselves whom thou hast called to thyself, and grant that every remembrance which turns our hearts from things seen to things unseen may lead us always upwards to thee, till we too come to the eternal rest which thou hast prepared for thy people; through Jesus Christ our Lord.

F. J. A. Hort*

1013

O God, before whose face the generations rise and pass away, the strength of those who labour, and the repose of the holy and blessed dead: We remember all who have faithfully lived and died, especially N. Lift us into light and love, and give us at last our portion with those who have trusted in thee and striven to do thy will. And unto thy name, with the Church on earth and the Church in heaven, we ascribe honour and glory, world without end. *John Hunter*

1014

Almighty God, whose love is over all thy works in this and every world: Into thy hands we commit the souls of those whom thou hast taken out of our sight; beseeching thee to grant to them the unutterable joys of thine eternal kingdom, and to those who mourn them grace to abide thy will in fortitude of spirit and in patient faith; through Jesus Christ our Lord.

1015

Into thy hands, O Lord, we commend the souls of thy servants, as unto a faithful Creator and most loving Redeemer; beseeching thee of thy great mercy to fulfil in them the purpose of thy love, and to bring us with them to the joy of thy heavenly kingdom; through the merits of thy Son our Saviour Jesus Christ.

Those who mourn
1016

Grant, O Lord, to all who are bereaved, the spirit of faith and courage, that they may have the strength to meet the days to come with steadfastness and patience; not sorrowing as those without hope, but in thankful remembrance of thy great goodness in past years, and in the sure expectation of a joyful reunion in the heavenly places; and this we ask in the name of Jesus Christ our Lord.

Irish Prayer Book

1017

O Heavenly Father, whose blessed Son Jesus Christ did weep at the grave of Lazarus: Look, we beseech thee, with compassion upon those who are now in sorrow and affliction; comfort them, O Lord, with thy gracious consolations; make them to know that all things

work together for good to them that love thee; and grant them evermore sure trust and confidence in thy fatherly care; through the
same Jesus Christ our Lord. *Canadian Prayer Book*

1018

Father of mercies and God of all comfort, look in thy tender love
and pity, we beseech thee, on thy sorrowing servants. Be thou to
them their refuge and strength, a very present help in trouble; make
them to know the love of Christ, which passeth knowledge; who by
death hath conquered death, and by rising again hath opened the
gates of everlasting life, even Jesus Christ our Lord.

Church of South India

1019

Have compassion, O Lord, upon all who are mourning for those
dear to them, and upon all who are lonely and desolate. Be thou
their comforter and friend; give them such earthly help and consolation as thou seest to be best for them; and grant them a fuller
knowledge and realization of thy love; for thy holy name's sake.

1020

O Eternal Father, who didst not spare thine only Son, but gave
him to be the Redeemer of mankind: Draw near, we beseech thee,
to those who mourn the loss of loved ones. Comfort them in their
loneliness; supply all their need; suffer them never to doubt thy
love, but draw them through their sorrow into closer fellowship
with thee; through the same Jesus Christ our Lord.

The burial of a child   1021

Almighty and merciful Father, who dost grant to children an
abundant entrance into thy kingdom: Grant us grace so to conform
our lives to their innocency and perfect faith that at length, united
with them, we may stand in thy presence in fullness of joy; through
Jesus Christ our Lord. *American Prayer Book*

1022

O God, whose most dear Son did take little children into his arms
and bless them: Give us grace, we beseech thee, to entrust the soul
of this child to thy never-failing care and love; and bring us all to
thy heavenly kingdom; through the same thy Son Jesus Christ our
Lord. *American Prayer Book*

1023

O most merciful Father, whose face the angels of thy little ones do
always behold in heaven: Grant us steadfastly to believe that this

thy child hath been taken into the safe keeping of thine eternal love; through Jesus Christ our Lord.   *American Prayer Book*
See also prayers for a Memorial Service, 849–68

PRAYERS WHICH MAY BE USED AT THE BURIAL OF ONE WHO HAS TAKEN HIS OWN LIFE

1024

Almighty God, who art ever ready to forgive, and to whom no prayer is made without hope of mercy: Speak to us thy word of consolation as we draw near to thee under the shadow of this great affliction. Deepen within our hearts the assurance of thy unfailing compassion; deliver us from all bitterness, despair, and doubt of thy love; and grant us to know the peace which passes all understanding, through Jesus Christ our Lord.   *Adapted*

1025

Holy and loving Father, who graciously showest mercy to thy children though they rebel against thee: Remember thy servant *N.* according to the favour that thou bearest unto thy people, and grant unto *him* forgiveness of all *his* sins and a place in the kingdom of thy Son, our Saviour Jesus Christ; who liveth and reigneth with thee in the unity of the Holy Spirit, one God, world without end.
Convocation of York

1026

Father of mercies and God of all comfort, who madest nothing in vain, and lovest all that thou hast made: Look in tender pity upon thy bereaved servants, that they may be enabled to find in thee their refuge and their strength, and may be delivered out of their distresses; through Jesus Christ our Lord.
Book of Common Order

1027

O Lord Jesus Christ, who didst weep at the grave of Lazarus thy friend: Have compassion upon thy servants who mourn this untimely death; and hasten the time when sin and sorrow shall be no more, and all shall rejoice in thee, the Resurrection and the Life; who with the Father and the Holy Spirit livest and reignest one God, world without end.
Convocation of York

1028

Eternal God, with whom there is mercy and plenteous redemption: We commend to thy love and keeping the soul of this our *brother*, and we commit *his* body to the ground, earth to earth, ashes to ashes, dust to dust. And we pray that by the most precious death and passion of thy dear Son, and sharing in the riches of his grace, both this our *brother* and we may at the last be found acceptable in thy sight; through Jesus Christ our only Saviour and Advocate.

IV
INTERCESSORY PRAYERS

GENERAL INTERCESSIONS

1029

Be mindful, O Lord, of thy people present here before thee, and of those who are absent through age, sickness, or infirmity. Care for the infants, guide the young, support the aged, encourage the faint-hearted, collect the scattered, and bring the wandering to thy fold. Travel with the voyagers, defend the widows, shield the orphans, deliver the captives, heal the sick. Succour all who are in tribulation, necessity, or distress. Remember for good all those that love us, and those that hate us; and those that have desired us, unworthy as we are, to pray for them. And those whom we have forgotten, do thou, O Lord, remember. For thou art the Helper of the helpless, the Saviour of the lost, the Refuge of the wanderer, the Healer of the sick. Thou, who knowest each man's need, and hast heard his prayer, grant unto each according to thy merciful loving-kindness and thy eternal love; through Jesus Christ our Lord. *A Prayer of the Eastern Church*

1030

O God of infinite mercy, who hast compassion on all men, hear the prayers of thy servants, who are unworthy to ask any petition for themselves, yet are in duty bound to pray for others.

Let thy mercy descend upon thy Church; preserve her in peace and truth, in unity and service; that her sacrifice of prayer and thanksgiving may ever ascend to thy throne.

In mercy remember the Queen; keep her perpetually in thy fear and favour; and grant that all who bear office under her may serve with a single eye to thy glory.

Remember our friends, all that have done us good; return all their kindness double unto their own bosom. Forgive our enemies; and help us to forgive, as we hope to be forgiven.

Comfort the afflicted; speak peace to troubled consciences; strengthen the weak; confirm the strong; instruct the ignorant; deliver the oppressed; relieve the needy; and bring us all by the waters of comfort and in the ways of righteousness to thy eternal kingdom; through Jesus Christ our Lord. *After Jeremy Taylor*

1031

Extend, O Lord, thy pity to the whole race of mankind. Enlighten the Gentiles with thy truth and bring into thy flock thy ancient people the Jews. Be gracious to thy Church, and grant that she may always preserve that doctrine and discipline which thou hast delivered to her. Let thy good hand be upon our nation, and guide us in the way of righteousness and peace. Bless our universities and schools, that they may be centres of true religion and useful learning. Be merciful to all that are in danger or distress; console all that are in pain or sorrow; and preserve those who travel. Give to all in error the light of thy truth, and bring sinners to repentance. O Lord, hear this our prayer through the merits of thy Son Jesus Christ; and to thy great name be all praise and glory, now and for evermore. *John Wesley's Prayers**

1032

Almighty God, who hast taught us to make prayers and intercessions for all men:

We pray for ministers of religion, and all who guide the thoughts of the people; for artists, authors, musicians, and journalists; that our common life may be crowned with truth and beauty;

For all who heal the body, guard the health of the people, and tend the sick; that they may follow in the footsteps of Christ, the great physician;

For all on whose labour we depend for the necessities of life; for those who carry on the commerce of the world, that they may seek no private gain which would hinder the good of all;

For parents and children; that purity, love, and honour may dwell in our homes, and duty and affection may be the bond of our family life;

For all who draw nigh unto death, that they may know thy presence with them through the valley of the shadow, and may wake to behold thy face; through Jesus Christ our Lord.

John Hunter

A bidding prayer   1033

Ye shall pray for Christ's holy catholic Church, that is, for the whole congregation of Christian people dispersed throughout the whole earth, and especially for the Church of England;

For our sovereign Lady, Queen Elizabeth, and all the royal family; for the ministers of God's holy Word and sacraments; for the High Court of Parliament; and for all the Magistrates of this realm: that all and every one of them, in their several callings, may serve truly to the glory of God, and the edifying and well governing of his people.

Also ye shall pray for all the people of this realm, that they may live in the true faith and fear of God, and in brotherly charity one to another.

And, that there may never be wanting a succession of persons duly qualified for the service of God in Church and State, ye shall implore his blessing on all schools, colleges and universities; that therein true religion and sound learning may for ever flourish.

To these your prayers ye shall add unfeigned praises for mercies already received; for our creation, preservation, and all the blessings of this life; but above all for the inestimable love of God in the redemption of the world by our Lord Jesus Christ, for the means of grace, and for the hope of glory.

Finally, let us praise God for all those who are departed this life in the faith of Christ, and pray unto God that we may have grace to direct our lives after their good example; that this life ended, we may be made partakers with them of the glorious resurrection in the life everlasting.

All these our prayers and praises let us humbly offer to our heavenly Father through Jesus Christ our blessed Lord and Saviour, saying as he taught us:

Our Father . . .   *After the 55th Canon of 1603*

THE COMING OF GOD'S KINGDOM

1034

O FATHER of men, who hast promised that all the kingdoms of this world are to become the kingdom of thy Son: Purge the nations of error and corruption; overthrow the power of sin, and establish the kingdom of grace in every land. Incline the hearts of rulers and peoples to open their gates to the King of glory. May he enter into their cities, churches, and homes, to dwell there, and govern all things by his word and spirit. So may justice, mercy, and peace prevail among the nations and thy name be glorified; through Jesus Christ our Lord. *George H. Russell*

1035

O Thou King eternal, immortal, invisible, thou only wise God our Saviour: Hasten, we beseech thee, the coming of thy kingdom upon earth, and draw the whole world of mankind into willing obedience to thy blessed reign. Overcome all the enemies of Christ, and bring low every power that is exalted against him; and let thy Holy Spirit rule the hearts of men in righteousness and love; through the victory of Christ our Lord. *Book of Common Order**

1036

O God, to whom we pray for the coming of thy kingdom: Let this be no vain repetition on our part. Give us the zeal that will not rest till it sees thy kingdom on earth. Make us to hate all evil things that are contrary to thy will and to fight against them in thy name. May we ever be found working for thee, hastening the time when the earth shall be filled with the knowledge of thy love; for the glory of Jesus Christ our Lord. *School Prayers**

1037

O God, who hast set before us the great hope that thy kingdom shall be established upon earth: So rule our lives by thy Spirit, that all our thoughts, desires, and acts being made obedient unto thee, thy power, thy glory, and the mightiness of thy kingdom may be made known unto men; grant this, O merciful Father, for Jesus Christ's sake thy Son our Lord. *The Kingdom, the Power, and the Glory*

1038

O Father of light and God of all truth, purge the whole world from all errors, abuses, corruptions and sins. Beat down the standard of Satan and set up everywhere the standard of Christ. Abolish the reign of sin and establish the kingdom of grace in all hearts. Let humility triumph over pride, charity over hatred, meekness over passion, generosity over covetousness; and let the gospel of Christ in faith and practice prevail throughout the world; through him who liveth and reigneth with thee and the Holy Spirit, one God, world without end. *Percy Dearmer**

1039

O Thou, whose kingdom is without territory yet covers all lands, whose realm is without boundaries yet crosses all frontiers: Extend thine empire over human hearts, and break down all adverse barriers which keep mankind asunder. Grant to the nations of the world the saving knowledge of thy love, so that there may be one kingdom of righteousness and truth in which all peoples may praise thy glorious name; through Jesus Christ our Lord.

In Watchings Often

1040

O Eternal God, the Father of all mankind, in whom we live and move and have our being: Have mercy on the whole human race. Pity their ignorance, their foolishness, their weakness, their sin. Set up an ensign for the nations, O Lord; hasten thy kingdom; and bring in everlasting righteousness; for the honour of thy Son, our Lord and Saviour Jesus Christ. *R. Ambrose Reeves*

1041

O Lord God Almighty, we pray thee in thy wisdom and mercy to overrule all the events of these days for the advancement of thy kingdom in the hearts of men. Let the nations hear thy voice, and the people acknowledge thy sovereign claims. Scatter the darkness of sin and unbelief. Break down every barrier that hinders the triumph of thy gospel. And speed the glad day when in the name of Jesus every knee shall bow and every tongue shall confess him Lord, to whom with thee and the Holy Spirit be all honour and glory, dominion and power, for ever and ever.

Frank Colquhoun

1042

O God, who by thy Son Jesus Christ hast set up on earth a kingdom of holiness, to measure its strength against all others:

Make faith to prevail over fear, and righteousness over force, and truth over the lie, and love and concord over all things; through the same Jesus Christ our Lord. *War Prayers, 1940*

1043

O Lord, who hast set before us the great hope that thy kingdom shall come on earth, and hast taught us to pray for its coming: Give us grace to discern the signs of its dawning, and to work for the perfect day when thy will shall be done on earth as it is in heaven; through Jesus Christ our Lord. *Percy Dearmer*

1044

Enlarge thy kingdom, O God, and deliver the world from the tyranny of Satan. Hasten the time, which thy Spirit hath foretold, when all nations whom thou hast made shall worship thee and glorify thy name. Bless the endeavours of those who strive to propagate thy holy gospel, and prepare the hearts of all men to receive it; to the honour and glory of thy Son Jesus Christ our Lord.

1045

Thy kingdom, O God, is an everlasting kingdom, and thy dominion endureth throughout all ages. Come to thy world and to us thy children by every means that love may choose; come and make all things new. O thou who art Lord of all and rich in mercy to all who call upon thee, hasten the coming of thy kingdom throughout the world, that among all nations and peoples thy reign of love may be established; through Jesus Christ our Lord. *Prayers of the World-wide Church**

1046

Almighty and everlasting God, who hast willed to restore all things in thy well-beloved Son, the King and Lord of all: Mercifully grant that all peoples and nations, divided and wounded by sin, may be brought under the gentle yoke of his most loving rule; who with thee and the Holy Spirit liveth and reigneth, ever one God, world without end.

The peace of the world 1047

ETERNAL God, in whose perfect kingdom no sword is drawn but the sword of righteousness, and no strength known but the strength of love: So guide and inspire, we pray thee, the labours of those who seek to establish righteousness and peace among the nations, that all peoples may find their security, not in force of arms, but in the perfect love that casteth out fear, and in the fellowship revealed to us in thy Son, Jesus Christ our Lord. *Adapted*

1048

O God, who wouldest fold both heaven and earth in a single peace: Let the design of thy great love lighten upon the waste of our wraths and sorrows; and give peace to thy Church, peace among nations, peace in our dwellings, and peace in our hearts; through thy Son our Saviour Jesus Christ. *After the Third Collect*

1049

O God, who makest men to be of one mind in an house and hast called us into the fellowship of thy dear Son: Draw into closer unity, we beseech thee, the people of all races in this and every land; that in fellowship with thee they may understand and help one another, and that, serving thee, they may find their perfect freedom; through the same thy Son Jesus Christ our Lord. *Joost de Blank*

1050

O God of love, look in thy mercy, we pray thee, upon the nations of the world and unite them in the bonds of peace. Strengthen the love of righteousness and freedom among all peoples, and bring the whole earth into obedience to thy reign; through Jesus Christ our Lord. *Adapted*

1051

Almighty God, our heavenly Father, guide, we beseech thee, the nations of the world into the ways of justice and truth. Establish among them that peace which is the fruit of righteousness; and grant that in every land thy kingdom may come and thy will be done; through Jesus Christ our Lord. *American Prayer Book**

1052

O Almighty God, the Father of all mankind, we pray thee to turn to thyself the hearts of all peoples and their rulers, that by the power of thy Holy Spirit peace may be established among the nations on the foundation of justice, righteousness, and truth; through him who was lifted up on the cross to draw all men unto himself, even thy Son Jesus Christ our Lord.   *William Temple*

1053

Inspire, we beseech thee, O Lord, the hearts of all men everywhere with the spirit of love and justice; and enlighten the leaders of the nations with the wisdom which is from above, that they may seek first the coming of thy kingdom. Deliver us thy people from faithlessness and fear, save us from the sins and cruelties of war, and guide our feet into thy way of peace; through Jesus Christ our Lord.

Frederick B. Macnutt

1054

O Thou Prince of Peace, shed abroad thy peace upon the world. By the might of thy Holy Spirit quench the pride and anger and greediness which cause man to strive against man, and people against people. Lead all nations in the ways of mutual help and goodwill, and hasten the time when the earth shall confess thee for its Saviour and King; for thy holy name's sake.

In time of international anxiety   **1055**

O God, who callest peace-makers thy children and hast declared that thou wilt scatter the nations that delight in war: We beseech thee that as thou didst send thy Son to be the Prince of Peace among men, so thou wilt keep our hearts and minds in his peace, and establish unity and concord among the nations, that all mankind may render to thee the fruits of righteousness; through the same Jesus Christ our Lord.   *E. W. Benson*

1056

Have mercy, O God, on our distracted and suffering world, on the nations perplexed and divided. Give to us and to all people a new spirit of repentance and amendment; direct the counsels of all who are working for the removal of the causes of strife and for the promotion of goodwill; and hasten the coming of thy kingdom of peace and love; through Jesus Christ our Lord.

Charles F. d'Arcy

1057

O Almighty God, the refuge of all them that put their trust in thee: We turn to thee in this time of trouble. Direct the course of this world, we humbly beseech thee, in accordance with thy holy will; take away whatever hinders the nations from unity and concord; and prosper all counsels which make for righteousness and peace; through Jesus Christ our Lord.

A Form of Prayer, August 1914

1058

O God, who hast made of one blood all the nations of the earth, and hast set the bounds of their habitation that they might seek after thee and find thee: Mercifully hear our supplications, and remove from us the menace of war. Guide the rulers with thy counsel and restrain the passions of the people, so that bloodshed may be averted and peace be preserved; through Jesus Christ our Lord. *W. E. Orchard**

1059

Almighty and eternal God, who madest thy light to shine in the darkness by the sending of thy Son Jesus Christ to deliver us from the dominion of evil: Visit us now, we pray thee, in the darkness of these times, and let thy truth and righteousness shine forth among us. Take from the world the fears which oppress mankind, that we may live in the power of justice and the freedom of thy truth; through the same Jesus Christ our Lord *New Every Morning**

1060

O God, who hast knit together in one family all the nations of the earth: Remove far from us, we beseech thee, the menace of war; pour out upon the rulers of the peoples thy spirit of peace; restrain the passions of such as plan aggression; and hasten the time when the kingdoms of this world shall become the kingdom of thy Son, our Saviour Jesus Christ.

Racial co-operation 1061

Loving Father, who hast made all men in thine own likeness, and lovest all whom thou hast made: Suffer not the world to separate itself from thee by building barriers of race and colour. As thy Son our Saviour was born of a Hebrew mother yet rejoiced in the faith of a Syrian woman and a Roman soldier, welcomed the Greeks who sought him and suffered an African to carry his cross, so teach us rightly to regard the members of all races as fellow-heirs of thy kingdom; through the same Jesus Christ our Lord.

Olive Warner

1062

O God, who hast made of one blood all nations to dwell upon the face of the earth, and who by thy Son Jesus Christ hast broken down the wall of partition between the races of men: Break down, we beseech thee, all that divides us one from another. Shame our jealousies and lay low our pride; do away all race-prejudice, that the bonds of fellowship and mutual service may unite all peoples, and we may live in peace together, to the glory of thy great name; through the same Jesus Christ our Lord.   *G. C. Binyon**

1063

Lord of the nations, who hast broken down in Christ the wall of partition between Jew and Gentile, bond and free: Unite the Christian people of different races in the bonds of true brotherhood; so that East and West, made one in Christ, may together labour for the bringing in of thy kingdom; through the same Jesus Christ our Lord.   *A Book of Prayers for Students**

1064

O Heavenly Father, whose love embraces all the nations upon earth: Deliver us, we pray thee, from racial prejudice and pride, from the desire to dominate, from injustice to others, and from the denial of their human dignity. Look with compassion on all who suffer on account of their colour; and by the saving grace of our Lord Jesus Christ draw together in true fellowship men of all races and languages, that sharing one another's burdens, and working together in brotherly concord, they may fulfil thy purpose and set forward thy everlasting kingdom; through the same Jesus Christ thy Son our Lord.   *Adapted*

Freedom

1065

Almighty God, who hast created man in thine own image: Grant us grace fearlessly to contend against evil, and to make no peace with oppression; and, that we may reverently use our freedom, help us to employ it in the maintaining of justice among men and nations, to the glory of thy holy name; through Jesus Christ our Lord.   *American Prayer Book*

1066

Grant, O Lord God, that laying aside the sins that hinder the coming of thy kingdom, the nations of the world may be assured of the right which thou hast given them to live in freedom; freedom from want and fear, freedom of thought and speech, and freedom to worship thee according to thy will; through Jesus Christ our Lord.   *Frederick B. Macnutt*

The right use of power   1067

Almighty and merciful God, without whom all things hasten to
destruction and fall into nothingness: Look, we beseech thee,
upon thy family of nations and men, to which thou hast committed
power in trust for their mutual health and comfort. Save us and
help us, O Lord, lest we abuse thy gift and make it our misery and
ruin; draw all men unto thee in thy kingdom of righteousness and
truth; and renew our faith in thine unchanging purpose of goodwill
and peace on earth; for the love of Jesus Christ our Lord.

Frederick B. Macnutt

1068

Almighty God, who hast given to men the capacity to search out
and use the wonderful powers of thy universe: Grant to us also
the sense of responsibility to use these powers not for destruction
but for the benefit of all mankind; for the sake of Jesus Christ our
Lord.   *Gladys E. Bretherton*

1069

Almighty and eternal God, who hast entrusted the minds of men
with the science and skill which can greatly bless or wholly destroy:
Grant them also a new stature of spirit to match thy trust; that they
may use their many inventions to thy glory and the benefit of mankind; through Jesus Christ our Lord.   *Peace Prayers, 1946*

Leaders of the nations 1070

MAY thy Holy Spirit, O God, rest upon all who bear great responsibilities for government among the nations, and teach them to seek thy will. When they turn to thee for guidance, let thy way be plain to them; and when they seek thee not, yet overrule their decisions for the good of thy children and the honour of thy kingdom; through Jesus Christ our Lord.

*New Every Morning**

1071

O God, the Lord of all kings and kingdoms, let thy strong hand control the nations and cause them to long for thy love to rule on the earth. Strengthen the hands of those who are working for righteousness and peace. Guide the hearts and minds of all rulers and statesmen, that they may seek first thy kingdom and the establishment of justice and freedom for all peoples, both small and great; through Jesus Christ our Lord. *Leslie S. Hunter*

1072

O God, by whose power alone men are enabled to live together as brethren: Look upon the broken body of humanity, and grant that wherever men meet in council for the ordering of the world, thy Holy Spirit may bring them into unity and lead them in the way of peace; through Jesus Christ our Lord.

*New Every Morning**

1073

Eternal God, wonderful in counsel, excellent in wisdom, we pray for the representatives of the nations who have been called to the difficult task of laying firm foundations for peace. Inspire their minds, enlarge their vision, direct their councils; that wisely and fearlessly they may stand for righteousness and truth, and set forward thy purposes for the welfare of mankind; through Jesus Christ our Lord. *George H. Russell**

1074

Almighty God, who alone givest wisdom and understanding: Inspire, we pray thee, the minds of all to whom thou hast committed the government of the nations of the world. Give them the vision of truth and justice, that by their counsels all races and classes may work together in true brotherhood, and thy Church throughout the world may serve thee in freedom and peace; through Jesus Christ our Lord.

The Kingdom, the Power, and the Glory*

An international conference 1075

O God, who art the lover of justice and concord: Direct, we beseech thee, the minds and wills of those who are called at this time to deliberate for the welfare of the nations of the world; that as faithful stewards of the things which belong unto righteousness, they may have regard to thy laws and the good of mankind, and set forth peace and mutual goodwill among all peoples: through Jesus Christ our Lord.

United Nations Organization 1076

Almighty God and most merciful Father, who wouldest have the kingdoms of the world become the kingdom of thy Son Jesus Christ: Bestow thy blessing, we beseech thee, upon the Assembly of the United Nations and all who are labouring for peace and righteousness among the peoples; that the day may be hastened when war shall be no more, and thy will only shall govern the nations upon earth; through the same Jesus Christ our Lord.

Armistice Day Prayers, 1931*

1077

Eternal God, we beseech thee for all who serve in the United Nations Organization. Grant thy blessing upon their endeavours to heal the wounds of the world and to minister to human need; and so guide their deliberations in council and assembly that all causes of strife may be removed, and peace and concord be secured among the nations of the world; through Jesus Christ our Lord.

OUR NATION AND GOVERNMENT

Our country and people   1078

O LORD, bless this kingdom and commonwealth, that there may be peace and prosperity in all its borders. In peace, so preserve it that it corrupt not; in trouble, so defend it that it suffer not; and so order it, whether in plenty or in want, that it may faithfully serve thee and patiently seek thy kingdom, the only sure foundation both of men and states; through Jesus Christ our Saviour and Redeemer.   *After William Laud*

1079

O God, who hast graciously preserved our nation through the years and hast led us in wondrous ways: Grant that we may be worthy of our high calling. Purge out from among us the sins that dishonour thee. Give us true religion; crown our faith with righteousness; and lift us up, a holy people, to thy praise and honour; through Jesus Christ our Lord.   *Adapted*

1080

Almighty and everlasting God, we praise thee for all that thou hast done for us as a nation. Deepen the root of our national life in thy everlasting righteousness, lest thy blessing be withdrawn. Make us equal to our high trusts, reverent in the use of freedom, just in the exercise of power, and generous in the protection of weakness. Inspire the men who direct the State, that they may guide it wisely and well; give insight and faithfulness to our legislators and judges; and may our deepest trust ever be in thee, the Lord of nations and the King of kings; through Jesus Christ our Lord.   *George H. Russell**

1081

Almighty God, who hast called our nation to a place of trust and responsibility among the nations of the world: We humbly thank thee for all the ways in which thou hast blessed and guided us unto this day. We confess before thee with shame all that has been evil in our history, and all that makes us unworthy to be called a Christian people. Take from us all pride and greed and injustice, and grant us the spirit of unselfish service which alone can make us great; through Jesus Christ our Lord.   *Adapted*

1082

Almighty God, who hast given us this good land for our heritage: We humbly beseech thee to bless us with honourable industry, sound learning, and unwavering faith. Defend our liberties, preserve our unity; endue with wisdom and grace all those to whom is entrusted the authority of government; and ever lead us in the paths of righteousness and peace, to the honour and glory of thy name; through Jesus Christ our Lord. *Adapted*

1083

Let thy mercy and blessing, O Lord of lords, rest upon our land and nation; upon all the powers which thou hast ordained over us; our Queen and those in authority under her, the ministers of state, and the great councils of the nation; that we may lead a quiet and peaceable life in all godliness and honesty. Rule the hearts of our people in thy faith and fear; rebuke the power of unbelief and superstition; and preserve to us thy pure Word in its liberty and glory even to the end of days; through Jesus Christ our Lord.

*Handley C. G. Moule**

1084

Almighty God, King of kings and Lord of lords, hear us as we pray to thee for the nation to which we belong. Guide with thy eternal wisdom our Queen and her counsellors; make us strong in faith and righteousness and in the love of freedom; and grant that we may still be counted worthy to do our part in leading the nations of the world into the paths of peace; for the honour of Jesus Christ our Lord. *Adapted*

1085

Bless, we beseech thee, merciful Lord, our nation and people. Give thine abundant grace to our Queen, and to all who bear office throughout the realm, that in all things we may be governed righteously and in thy fear. Grant us such outward prosperity as may please thee; but above all things grant us such faith and true religion that thy holy name may ever be glorified in our midst; through Jesus Christ our Lord. *William Bellars*

1086

O Lord our Governor, we humbly pray thee to look with thy favour upon our country and to visit us with thy salvation. Graciously bless thy servant our Queen and every member of the royal family. Give wisdom and courage to our leaders; prosper the work of thy Church in our land; and so turn the hearts of our people to thyself that thy name may be exalted among us as our mighty God and Saviour; for the glory of thy Son Jesus Christ our Lord.

1087

Bless, O Lord, we beseech thee, our Queen and parliament, our judges and magistrates, and all who bear any office or rule in the state. Save us from the sins that most easily beset us; bless every effort for the well-being of our people; and make us a nation fearing thee and doing righteousness, to the glory of thy holy name; through Jesus Christ our Lord. *W. E. Scudamore**

See also 844–5

The Queen's Majesty 1088

Almighty God, who rulest over all the kingdoms of the world, and dost order them according to thy good pleasure: We give thee hearty thanks for that thou hast set thy servant our sovereign lady, Queen Elizabeth, upon the throne of this realm. Let thy wisdom be her guide and thine arm strengthen her; let truth and justice, holiness and righteousness, peace and charity, abound in her days; and direct all her counsels and endeavours to thy glory, and the welfare of her subjects; through Jesus Christ our Lord.

From the Accession Service

1089

O God, who providest for thy people by thy power, and rulest over them in love: Vouchsafe so to bless thy servant Elizabeth our Queen, that under her this nation may be wisely governed, and thy Church may serve thee in all godly quietness; through Jesus Christ our Lord. *From the Accession Service*

1090

Almighty God our heavenly Father, we pray thee to multiply thy heavenly gifts upon thy servant Elizabeth our Queen. Establish her throne in righteousness, uphold her continually with thy strength and guidance, and make her a blessing to the peoples over whom thou hast called her to rule; for the honour of thy Son Jesus Christ our Lord. *Adapted*

The Government and those in authority 1091

Bless, O Lord, those whom thou hast set over us both in Church and State. Govern their hearts in thy fear, and guide their understanding to do those things which are acceptable to thee; that they may faithfully serve thy people and set forward thy everlasting kingdom; through Jesus Christ our Lord. *Gavin Hamilton**

1092

Guide, we beseech thee, O Lord, all those to whom is committed the government of this nation; and grant to them at this time special gifts of wisdom and understanding, of counsel and strength; that they may consider all questions calmly in their deliberations, and act wisely and promptly, upholding what is right, abhorring what is wrong, and performing that which is just, so that in all things thy will may be done; for the sake of Jesus Christ our Lord.

Adapted

1093

O Lord, thou God of righteousness and truth, grant to our Queen and her government, to members of parliament and all in positions of responsibility, the guidance of thy Spirit. May they never lead the nation wrongly through love of power, desire to please, or unworthy ideals, but always love righteousness and truth; so may thy kingdom be advanced and thy name be hallowed; through Jesus Christ our Lord. *Book of Prayers for Students*

1094

Righteous Lord, that lovest righteousness, may the spirit of wisdom be given to our rulers, to the Queen and all in authority under her. Grant that they may govern in thy faith and fear, striving to put down all that is evil and to encourage all that is good, to the advancement of the true welfare of thy people; through Jesus Christ our Lord. *Adapted from Thomas Arnold*

1095

O God, the Lord of men and nations, we remember before thee our Queen and all in authority under her who share the responsibility of government. Give them wisdom and insight, courage and high resolve, that truth and justice may inspire their counsels and govern their decisions, to the glory of thy name; through Jesus Christ our Lord. *Adapted*

Parliament **1096**

Almighty God, by whom alone kings reign and princes decree justice, and from whom alone cometh counsel and understanding: We humbly beseech thee to grant thy heavenly wisdom to those who have been called to serve in the parliament of this nation. Grant that, having thy fear always before their eyes, they may lay aside all private interests and partial affections, and take counsel together for the glory of thy name, the maintenance of true religion

and justice, and the welfare, peace and unity of the realm; through
Jesus Christ our Lord.

An adaptation of the House of Commons Prayer

1097

Most gracious God, we humbly beseech thee for the High Court
of Parliament, under our sovereign lady the Queen at this time
assembled; that thou wouldest be pleased to direct and prosper all
their consultations to the advancement of thy glory, the good of thy
Church, and the safety, honour, and welfare of this realm; to the
end that peace and happiness, truth and justice, religion and piety,
may be established among us for all generations; through Jesus
Christ our Lord. *Adapted from Book of Common Prayer*

1098

O Lord our God, who art the lover of justice and truth: Give
thy grace to our parliament and to all who direct the affairs of our
nation; and so guide them by thy Holy Spirit, we beseech thee, that
by word and deed they may promote the well-being of this people,
and set forward peace and goodwill among all men; through Jesus
Christ our Lord.

Leaders of the nation **1099**

O God, Almighty Father, King of kings and Lord of all our
rulers: Grant that the hearts and minds of all who go out before us,
the statesmen, the judges, the men of learning, and the men of
wealth, may be so filled with the love of thy laws, and of that which
is righteous and life-giving, that they may serve as a wholesome salt
unto the earth, and be worthy stewards of thy good and perfect
gifts; through Jesus Christ our Lord.

Prayer of the Order of the Garter

1100

We remember before thee, O God, those who bear rule among us
in Church and State, in industry and commerce; all who speak to
men through broadcasting and the press; and all who have power
over the lives of others. Grant them the humility to seek thy
guidance, and the courage to do thy will, so that our people may be
led to the knowledge of thee and to the service of thy kingdom;
through Jesus Christ our Lord. *New Every Morning*

1101

Raise up, we beseech thee, O Lord, to be leaders of our people,
able men and such as fear thee, men of truth and hating covetousness, neither regarding persons nor seeking rewards; and so

strengthen them by thy Spirit that in singleness of heart they may always endeavour to loose the bonds of wickedness, to undo the heavy burdens, and to let the oppressed go free, that the nation may be ordered in equity and righteousness according to thy will; through Jesus Christ our Lord.

1102

Graciously hear us, O heavenly Father, for those who guard the health of the nation, that they may preserve us from sickness and disease; for those who guide the thought of the nation, that they may inspire us with noble and worthy ideals; for those who mould the character of the nation, that they may fashion us into a people strong in faith and righteousness; to the glory of thy Son Jesus Christ our Lord. *Adapted*

Writers, artists, broadcasters   **1103**
Almighty God, who hast proclaimed thine eternal truth by the voice of prophets and evangelists: Direct and bless, we beseech thee, those who in this our generation speak where many listen and write what many read; that they may do their part in making the heart of the people wise, its mind sound, and its will righteous; to the honour of Jesus Christ our Lord. *The Boys' Prayer Book*

1104

O God, who by thy Spirit in our hearts dost lead men to desire thy perfection, to seek for truth, and to rejoice in beauty: Illuminate and inspire, we beseech thee, all thinkers, writers, artists, and craftsmen; that, in whatsoever is true and pure and lovely, thy name may be hallowed and thy kingdom come on earth; through Jesus Christ our Lord. *The Kingdom, the Power, and the Glory*

1105

O God our Father, who through thy Son Jesus Christ hast commanded us to preach the gospel to every creature: Mercifully grant unto all those who broadcast thy Word the light of thy Holy Spirit, and to those who listen the gift of understanding; so that thy praise may be in all the earth, who livest and reignest one God for evermore. *New Every Morning*

The armed forces   **1106**
O Lord our God, we commend to thy gracious care and keeping the men and women of the Royal Navy, the Army, and the Royal Air Force. We beseech thee to protect them from all dangers to body and soul; to give them a loyal, courageous, and disciplined spirit;

to instil in them the love of justice and liberty; and to grant that they may be called to serve only for the maintenance of order and peace throughout the world; for the sake of Jesus Christ our Lord.

A Book of Public Worship

1107

O Lord of hosts, stretch forth, we pray thee, thine almighty arm to strengthen and protect the forces of our Queen in every peril of sea and land and air. Shelter them in the day of battle, and in time of peace keep them safe from all evil; endue them with loyalty and courage; and grant that in all things they may serve as seeing thee who art invisible; through Jesus Christ our Lord.

A Form of Prayer, August 1918
See also prayers in time of war, 1196–1213

A general election
1108

Almighty God, who givest wisdom, and rulest the hearts of men: Guide and direct, we beseech thee, the minds of all those who are called to exercise the responsibility of electing fit persons to serve in the parliament of this nation; grant that the issue of their choice may promote thy glory and the welfare of this people; and to those who shall be elected give the spirit of understanding, courage, and true godliness; through Jesus Christ our Lord. *Adapted*

1109

O Lord, we beseech thee to govern the minds of all who are called at this time to choose faithful men into the great council of the nation; that they may exercise their choice as in thy sight, for the welfare of all our people; through Jesus Christ our Lord.

Charles Gore

Before an election, national or local
1110

O Lord most high, who alone rulest in the kingdoms of men: Guide and direct, we beseech thee, the minds of those who are about to exercise their responsibility in the election of fit persons to serve in the ——; and we pray thee in thy good providence to overrule all things for the promotion of thy glory and the welfare of this nation [*or* community]; through Jesus Christ our Lord.

Administration of justice
1111

O God, mighty and merciful, the Judge of all men: Grant to those who minister justice the spirit of wisdom and discernment; and that they may be strong and patient, upright and compassionate, fill them, we beseech thee, with the spirit of thy holy fear; through Jesus Christ our Lord. *J. Armitage Robinson*

1112

Almighty God, who sittest in the throne judging right: We humbly beseech thee to bless the courts of justice, and the magistrates, in all this land; and give unto them the spirit of wisdom and understanding, that they may discern the truth, and impartially administer the law in the fear of thee alone; through him who shall come to be our judge, thy Son our Saviour Jesus Christ.

American Prayer Book

National freedom
1113

O Eternal God, through whose mighty power our fathers won their liberties of old: Grant, we beseech thee, that we and all the people of this land may have grace to maintain these liberties in righteousness and peace; through Jesus Christ our Lord.

American Prayer Book

1114

O Lord God Almighty, who hast made for thy glory all nations over the face of the earth, that they may do thee service in the joy of freedom; give to this people of England the passion of righteousness, and the strength of self-control, that they may exercise their liberty with a serious and single desire to fulfil thy gracious will; through Jesus Christ, our Master, Redeemer, and King.

Henry Scott Holland

National unity
1115

O Lord Jesus Christ, who wast lifted up on the cross to draw all men unto thee: Look in mercy, we beseech thee, upon this nation. Send out thy light and thy truth that they may lead us into paths of fellowship and peace; break down all barriers of contention and strife; and grant that we may live together in brotherly unity and concord, to thy glory and the welfare of this realm; for thy holy name's sake.

F. T. Woods

Patriotism
1116

Lord, who hast given us this land for our abiding place: Help us to love it with a passion so strong and true that we may be jealous for its honour and instant in its service; and we pray thee so to work through us that it may become a land where men walk in the freedom of the truth and in the light of the knowledge of thy love, which thou hast manifested in thy Son our Saviour Jesus Christ.

1117

O God, by whose will we were born to be citizens of this land: Enable us to love our country, not in word only, but in deed and in truth. Let us never rejoice in any selfish pleasures, nor accept a life of idleness while others toil for our comfort; but rather let us who have received most be ready to give most, in the spirit of thy Son, Jesus Christ our Lord.

Strangers and immigrants 1118

O God, the Father of all men, who hast bidden thy people to show kindness to the stranger: We pray for those who come from other countries and make their home in this land. Help them to overcome the difficulties of custom, language, and race; surround them with companions who welcome and befriend them; and bless the societies which foster understanding and goodwill; that in thy great family we may live as members one of another; through Jesus Christ our Lord.

1119

We pray thee, O Lord our God, for Christians from other lands who come to these shores, and especially for those who make their home among us. May their faith not be shaken by the irreligion of so many in this country, but grant that they may live as faithful followers of Jesus Christ, and be loyal members of the Church which is his body; through the same Jesus Christ our Lord.

In time of national anxiety 1120

O God, who art the Father of all, and who alone makest men to be of one mind in a house: We beseech thee, at this time of strife and unrest, to grant to us by the inspiration of thy Holy Spirit a fuller realization of our brotherhood, man with man. Allay all anger and bitterness, and deepen in us a sense of truth and equity in our dealings one with another; for the sake of thy Son, our Lord Jesus Christ. *Randall T. Davidson*

1121

O God our Father, who hast led our nation wondrously in ages past: We thank thee for the guidance of thy overruling providence; and we pray thee to give us now and in the days to come sure confidence in thee, that in all perplexities we may see thy light, and in hours of weakness may know thy strength; through Jesus Christ our Lord. *William Temple*

1122

Almighty God, who hast ordained that men should serve thee in serving one another by their labours: Have regard, we pray thee, to this nation, oppressed at this time by many burdens. Grant to its citizens grace to work together with honest and faithful hearts, each caring for the good of all; that seeking first thy kingdom and its righteousness, they may have added to them all things needful for their daily sustenance and the common good; through Jesus Christ our Lord. *Geoffrey F. Fisher*

1123

O God, beyond all time and space, eternal, unchangeable: Have pity upon our ignorance and upon the confusion of our efforts. Help us to understand the anxieties of others and to know our own limitations. By thy Holy Spirit raise us above all strife and prejudice, scorn and bitterness, that in the calm light of thy manifold wisdom we may be drawn together in a common will to serve thee and set forward thy kingdom; through Jesus Christ our Lord.

Diocese of Rochester

1124

Grant, O God, that in this time of testing our people may know thy presence and obey thy will: that with integrity and courage we may accomplish that which thou givest us to do, and endure that which thou givest us to bear; through Jesus Christ our Lord.

In a time of disaster 1125

Grant, we beseech thee, merciful Lord, thy help and comfort to all who at this time are visited with tragedy and bereavement; and prosper with thy continual blessing those who labour to devise protection for mankind against disaster; through him who both healed and hallowed suffering, thy Son Jesus Christ our Lord.

The spirit of service 1126

Grant, O Lord, that the men and women of our nation may devote themselves heartily to the common cause, not seeking gain for themselves, but placing the needs of others above their own interests, giving much and taking little; that we may all know the joy of service and the discipline of self-denial, for the sake of him who died for us, our Saviour Jesus Christ.

The peril of prosperity 1127

O God, who in thy love hast bestowed upon us gifts such as our fathers never knew or dreamed of: Mercifully grant that we be not so occupied with material things that we forget the things which are spiritual; lest, having gained the whole world, we lose our own soul; for thy mercy's sake. *Daily Prayer*

Battle of Britain Sunday 1128

O Lord our God, who art the refuge and strength of all who put their trust in thee: We give thee our humble and hearty thanks for the deliverance granted to our nation in the Battle of Britain, and for those who by their sacrifice won that deliverance for us. Teach us, we pray thee, as we honour their memory and call to mind thy great mercy, to renew the dedication of our lives to thy service, and always to use our freedom for thy glory; through Jesus Christ our Lord.

THE COMMONWEALTH

1129

O GOD, who hast made us members of the British commonwealth of nations, and hast bound us together as one family under one Queen: Grant that we may ever live in remembrance of our great responsibilities and set before us that righteousness which exalteth a nation. Help us to seek to excel in the practice of faith, courage, duty, self-discipline, fair dealing and true sympathy; that as loyal patriots, good citizens, and a God-fearing people, we may glorify thee, the King of kings and Lord of lords; through Jesus Christ our Saviour.   *The Earl of Meath**

1130

Almighty God, our heavenly Father, bless our country and commonwealth, that we may be made a blessing to the world. Grant us sound government and just laws, good education and a clean press, simplicity and justice in our relations with one another, and, above all, a spirit of service which will abolish pride of place and inequality of opportunity; through Jesus Christ our Lord.
                         *Book of Prayers for Students**

1131

Almighty God, Father of all mankind, who hast given to our nation a place of responsibility in the earth: Help us ever to remember that we are stewards of thy gifts. Give to us the spirit of wisdom and understanding, and of the fear of the Lord; make us just and fair in our dealings with other peoples; and keep the nations of our commonwealth united in one bond of faith and fellowship; to the honour of thy Son, Jesus Christ our Lord.

1132

Eternal God, who rulest in the kingdoms of men: Grant, we most humbly beseech thee, honour and safety to our sovereign lady the Queen; peace throughout the commonwealth of her peoples; promotion to true religion; encouragement to learning and godly living; a patient service to the concord of the world; and, by all these, glory to thy holy name; for his sake to whom thou hast given all power in heaven and earth, even our Lord and Saviour Jesus Christ.   *Jeremy Taylor*

1133

O Lord God of our fathers, who in thy goodness hast led this people hitherto by wondrous ways, who makest the nations to praise thee, and knittest them together in the bonds of peace: We beseech thee to pour thy blessing on the commonwealth of nations over which thou hast called thy servant Elizabeth to be Queen. Grant that all, of whatever race or tongue, may, in prosperity and peace, be united in the bond of brotherhood, and in the fellowship of the one Faith, so that we may be found a people acceptable unto thee; through Jesus Christ our Lord.

*A Form of Prayer, August 1918**

1134

O King of kings, help us to become worthy citizens of our country and commonwealth. Give us such a sense of responsibility that, shunning all false pride and narrow prejudices, we may use the privileges we have inherited as a means of promoting justice and peace, health and happiness, among the nations of the earth, and may work for the unity of all men in the citizenship of thy heavenly kingdom; through Jesus Christ our Lord. *E. M. Venables**

1135

Almighty and everlasting God, who art King of kings and Lord of lords: Guide, we pray thee, the destinies of our commonwealth of nations. Direct the counsels of our Queen and all in authority under her. Strengthen the resolve of our people; deepen the sense of unity among the members of this great family; and grant us grace that we may strive manfully under thy banner for the establishment of righteousness and peace among the nations of the world; through Jesus Christ our Lord.

SOCIETY AND INDUSTRY

Social justice   **1136**

ALMIGHTY God, who hast created man in thine own image:
Grant us grace fearlessly to contend against evil, and to make no
peace with oppression; and, that we may reverently use our freedom
help us to employ it in the maintenance of justice among men and
nations, to the glory of thy holy name; through Jesus Christ our
Lord.   *American Prayer Book*

1137

O Almighty God, who hast entrusted this earth unto the children
of men, and through thy Son Jesus Christ hast called us unto a
heavenly citizenship: Grant us, we humbly beseech thee, such
shame and repentance for the disorder and injustice and cruelty
which are among us, that fleeing unto thee for pardon and for grace
we may henceforth set ourselves to establish that city which has
justice for its foundation and love for its law, whereof thou art the
architect and maker; through the same Lord Jesus Christ, thy Son,
our Saviour.   *William Temple*

1138

Almighty God, who fillest the earth with thy riches for the use of
all thy children: Have regard, we pray thee, to the impoverishment
of the nations; and on all who are in authority bestow thy gifts of
wisdom and goodwill, that, being lifted above self-regard, they may
establish a new order, wherein the needs of all men shall be supplied; through Jesus Christ our Lord.

1139

O Lord, we pray that thou wilt hasten the time when no man shall
live in contentment while he knows that his neighbour has need.
Inspire in us and in all men the consciousness that we are not our
own but thine and our neighbours'; for his sake who prayed that we
might all be one in him, thy Son Jesus Christ our Lord.

1140

O God, who providest for the creaturely needs of men and hast
given them in Jesus Christ the food of their souls: Forgive the
stupidity and sin whereby men have abused thy providence and

squandered thy gifts. Guide with thy just and peaceable wisdom those who take counsel for the nations and direct our industries; and inspire each of us to share more fairly the produce of thy world, and to be generous to feed the hungry and succour those in want; through Jesus Christ our Lord. *A Diocesan Service Book**

1141

O Jesus, Son of God, carpenter of Nazareth, grant sight to those blinded by luxury, and deliverance to those bound by want; that the rich may joyfully follow the simplicity of thy most holy life, and the poor may obtain their inheritance, and that the hearts of all may be set with one accord to discover the way of salvation; through thy mercy who for our sake didst become poor, our Saviour and our Lord.

1142

O God, our Father, increase in every nation the sense of human brotherhood, true respect for man and for woman, loyalty in service and charity, happiness in work, and justice in reward; that our homes may be kept safe and pure, our cities renewed in beauty and order, and all our world may reflect the radiance of thy kingdom; through Jesus Christ our Lord. *Book of Common Order*

Industry and human society

1143

O Blessed Saviour, who wast pleased thyself to be numbered among the craftsmen: We pray thee to guide and prosper all who labour with mind and hand, that their work may be done for thy honour, and rewarded with thy approval; who livest and reignest with the Father and the Holy Spirit, one God, world without end.

1144

Almighty Father, who art the wise Creator of the land and sea and all that is therein: We beseech thee to take from us the spirit of covetousness and to give us the spirit of brotherhood; that none may suffer want, but each according to his need may share thine abounding gifts; through Jesus Christ our Lord.

1145

O God, who hast given all men their work to do, help them to do it with all their might. Grant the spirit of wisdom and justice to all leaders of industry. Bless the men and women who work in offices and factories; strengthen those who labour at the docks or in the fields; take care of the miners and those whose work is dangerous; and help us all to follow in the steps of him who worked as a carpenter, even Jesus Christ our Lord. *Adapted*

For a blessing on local industries   1146

O Almighty Father, who through thy Son Jesus Christ hast consecrated labour to the blessing of mankind: Prosper, we pray thee, the industries of this place; defend those who are engaged therein from all perils, and grant that they may rejoice in the fruits of thy bounty, and bless thee for thy loving-kindness; through the same Jesus Christ our Lord.   *Irish Prayer Book*

For industrial peace and goodwill   1147

Let us pray that all men may learn to seek first the kingdom of God and his righteousness, caring for justice more than for gain, and for fellowship more than for domination.

Let us pray that all may have the courage and the energy to think for themselves strongly and clearly, and to seek for the truth and follow it whatever the cost.

Let us pray for deliverance from prejudice and for a desire to appreciate what is just and true in the opinions of those who differ from us.

Let us pray that all may have the faith to believe that whatever is right is always possible, and that what is according to the mind of Christ is upheld by the limitless resources of omnipotence.

Let us pray that in ourselves and in others suspicion may give place to trust, and bitterness to goodwill; and that we may all become trustworthy, whether we work with hand or brain.

Let us pray that God will grant peace in our time, and give us abundantly of his Holy Spirit, whose fruits are love and joy and peace.   *William Temple*

1148

O God, the King of righteousness, lead us, we pray thee, in ways of justice and peace; inspire us to break down all tyranny and oppression, to gain for every man his due reward, and from every man his due service; that each may live for all, and all may care for each, in the name of Jesus Christ our Lord.   *William Temple*

1149

O God, who hast taught us that we are members one of another: Remove, we beseech thee, from among us all distrust and bitterness in industrial disputes; and grant that, seeking what is just and equal, and caring for the needs of others, we may live and work together in unity and love; through Jesus Christ our Lord.
Acts of Devotion

For leaders of commerce 1150

O God, our heavenly Father, guide with thy Holy Spirit those who direct the commercial life of the nation. Grant them to look on their life's work as an opportunity of service rather than of gain; fill them with jealous care of their employees; and so bless them that the whole nation may be better for their labours; for the sake of Jesus Christ our Lord. *Peter Green*

Earning and spending 1151

O God, whose blessed Son Jesus Christ earned his bread at Nazareth by the labours of his hands, and taught us that our possessions are a trust from thee: Help us to be faithful stewards of what thou givest; that in earning we may be just and honest, and in spending we may seek not our own but thy glory, and the good of others; through the same our Lord Jesus Christ.

The unemployed 1152

O Lord, our Heavenly Father, we commend to thy care and compassion the men and women of our land now suffering distress through lack of work; support and strengthen them, we beseech thee; and so prosper the counsels of those who are engaged in the ordering of our industrial life, that thy people may be set free from want and fear, and be enabled to labour in security and peace, for the relief of their necessities and for the well-being of this realm; through Jesus Christ our Lord.

1153

O God, the Creator of all things, who hast made man in thine own image, so that he must ever seek his joy in creative work: Have mercy, we beseech thee, on all who are unemployed, or whose work is dull; and help us so to order our common life that every man may have work to do and find joy in doing it, to the good of this nation and to the glory of thy name; through Jesus Christ our Lord. *New Every Morning*

Housing 1154

O God, who wouldest not that any should live without comfort and hope: Have compassion on the multitudes in our day who have no homes, or who are overcrowded in wretched dwellings. Bless and inspire those who are labouring for their good. Stir the conscience of the whole nation, O Lord, and both break the bonds of covetousness and make plain the way of deliverance; for the sake of Jesus Christ our Saviour.

Village life 1155

O God, whose Son was content to share the life of his village at
Nazareth: Bless, we beseech thee, the life of this village with thy
continual presence. Grant that in every family thy name may
be hallowed, and thy will be done; that our children may learn to
love the faith of Jesus Christ, and that men and women may be
good neighbours and live godly lives; through Jesus Christ our Lord.

*D. L. Couper**

Local government 1156

O God, who dost gather thy children together, that they may
prepare a city for habitation and dwell together in unity: We pray
for all who bear authority in our cities, our towns, and our parishes;
for local government officers, and all who give their time and energy
in caring for the common good. Grant them to plan and work for
thy glory, and the delight of man. And continue to raise up, we
beseech thee, men and women who offer service to the community
as a vocation from thee; through Jesus Christ our Lord.

H. F. Leatherland

Agriculture 1157

Give, O Lord, to all who till the ground the wisdom to understand thy laws, and to co-operate with thy wise ordering of the
world. Give to farmers and labourers the desire to work together in
the spirit of justice and goodwill. And grant that the fruits of
thy bountiful earth may not be hoarded by selfish men or squandered by foolish men, but that all who work may share abundantly
in the harvest of thy soil, according to thy will, revealed to us in
Jesus Christ our Lord. *Harold Anson*

Fisheries 1158

O Almighty God, who hast made the seas, and all that moveth
therein: Bestow thy blessing on the harvest of the waters, that it
may be abundant in its season, and on our sailors and fishermen,
that they may be safe in every peril of the deep; so that all with
thankful heart may acknowledge thee, who art the Lord of the sea
and of the dry ground; through Jesus Christ our Lord.

Canadian Prayer Book

Those who work in mines 1159

Almighty God, who art present in the highest heaven and in the
deep places of the earth: Let thy protecting care be over all who work
in the mines of our land, that they may be preserved in safety and in
health; and grant that, knowing the dangers that beset them, they may

ever take thought one for another, and be sustained by a sure trust in thee; through Jesus Christ our Lord.   *Canadian Prayer Book*

Those who work by night   **1160**

Bless, O Lord, all those who, in the night, watch over our lives and homes, and guard all who through the hours of darkness carry on the unresting commerce of men by land and sea and air. Grant them rest and refreshment, and make us thankful for their service; through Jesus Christ our Lord.   *New Every Morning*

For a school 1161

ALMIGHTY God, in whom we live and move and have our being: Make this school as a field which the Lord has blessed; that whatsoever things are true and pure, lovely and of good report, may here abound and flourish. Preserve in it an unblemished name, enlarge it to a wider usefulness, and exalt it in the love of all its members as an instrument of thy glory; through Jesus Christ our Lord. *Henry Hayman*

1162

O God, by whose providence the duties of man are variously ordered: Grant to us all in this school such a spirit that we may labour heartily to do our work in our several stations. Teach us to put to good account whatever talents thou hast lent us, that as good and faithful servants we may enter into the joy of our Lord, even thy Son our Saviour Jesus Christ. *B. F. Westcott*

1163

O God, our heavenly Father, by whose Spirit man is taught knowledge, who givest wisdom to all that ask thee: Grant thy blessing, we beseech thee, upon this school, and help us in the work that thou hast given us to do. Enable us all to labour diligently, not with eye-service, but in singleness of heart, remembering that without thee we can do nothing, and that in thy fear is the beginning of wisdom; through Jesus Christ our Lord. *F. D. Maurice*

The beginning of term 1164

Heavenly Father, we praise thee for the holidays which are now over and for all the happiness we have enjoyed. At the beginning of this new term we present ourselves to thee for thy blessing. Give us courage and cheerfulness in facing the tasks before us; make us loyal and unselfish in our dealings with one another; and help us both in our work and in our games always to give of our best; for the sake of Jesus Christ our Lord. *Frank Colquhoun*

The end of term 1165

We give thee thanks, O God, for thy guidance, help and care during the term that is past. We commend to thee all that has been attempted and accomplished, and ask thee to forgive what has been unworthy or left undone. And grant, O heavenly Father, that in the holidays before us we may enjoy rest and renewal, health and happiness, and never forget thee, the giver of all good things; through Jesus Christ our Lord. *Frank Colquhoun*

Those leaving school 1166

We commend to thy fatherly care, O Lord, those who are about to leave this school. May thy goodness and mercy follow them throughout their life. Guard them in danger and keep them from evil; guide them continually in the right way; and assist them in every good work, for the glory of thy name; through Jesus Christ our Lord. *Adapted*

Teachers 1167

O Lord and Master, who thyself didst come into the world to bear witness to the truth, and didst say that the good and faithful teacher should be greatly accounted of in thy kingdom: Send, we beseech thee, thy blessing upon all who are engaged in the work of education. Give them clearness of vision and freshness of thought, and enable them so to train the hearts and minds of the children that they may take their appointed places in the work of this life, and may be ready for the service of the life to come. We ask it for thy honour and glory, who livest and reignest with the Father and the Holy Spirit, one God for ever and ever. *Arthur W. Robinson*

1168

Let thy Spirit, O God, rest upon all who teach in our schools. Enable them both by word and by example to lead their scholars to reverence truth, to desire goodness, and to delight in beauty; that, following after these things, both those who learn and those who teach may come to know and worship thee, the giver of all that is good; through Jesus Christ our Lord. *New Every Morning*

Teacher training colleges 1169

O Lord and heavenly Father, the only wise God our Saviour, we commend to thy grace those who in the training colleges are preparing for their work as teachers in our schools. Foster within them a sense of their vocation and a true dedication to thy service; and so deepen their trust in thee that, in time to come, they may be enabled not only to implant knowledge but to kindle the flame of faith in the lives of those committed to their care; for the honour of Jesus Christ our Lord. *Frank Colquhoun*

Students 1170

Grant, O Lord, to all students, to love that which is worth loving, to know that which is worth knowing, to praise that which pleaseth thee most, to esteem that which is most precious unto thee, and to dislike whatsoever is evil in thine eyes. Grant that with true judgment they may distinguish things that differ, and, above all, may search out and do what is well-pleasing unto thee; through Jesus Christ our Lord. *Thomas à Kempis*

Overseas students in Britain 1171

O God the Father of all mankind, we would remember before thee the men and women who come from many lands to study in our universities. Guide them and protect them in the difficulties and temptations which beset them in their new surroundings. Keep alive in their hearts the love of all that is good in their home life, and give them also insight to appreciate and share that which is good in ours. Pardon the faults of temper and manners by which we so often offend them; and grant us true humility, love and patience that we may welcome them in the spirit of the Master whom we desire to serve. *Student Christian Movement*

Those sitting for examinations 1172

O God, who knowest the secrets of the heart: Be with those now preparing [sitting] for examinations. Help them to face their task with calmness, confidence, and courage; with wisdom, faithfulness, and honesty; that they may do justice both to themselves and to their teachers, and set forth thy glory, who thyself art wisdom and truth, and the giver of knowledge, and of every virtue and good gift in Jesus Christ our Lord. *S. P. T. Prideaux*

The use of knowledge 1173

O Lord Jesus Christ, who by thy cross and resurrection hast overcome the powers of darkness: Guide all men who in seeking knowledge acquire power which can be used for good or evil purposes. Help them to recognize their stewardship and to fulfil their responsibility as in thy sight; who livest and reignest with the Father and the Holy Spirit, one God, world without end. *Student Prayer**

1174

Deliver us, O God, from following the fashions of the day in our thinking. Save us from the worship of power, whether power over nature or power over men. Save us from the worship of science, and grant that, giving thee thanks for the skill of the scientist, we may be preserved from the abuse of his discoveries. Help us never to confuse any creature with the Creator, or man with God. May we acknowledge man's reason as thy gift, and, being freed from all false hopes and misplaced trust, find in thee our hope and our salvation; through Jesus Christ our Lord. *Student Prayer*

1175

Heavenly Father, with whom are hid the treasures of wisdom and knowledge, and who hast permitted men of our day to learn things kept secret from the foundation of the world: In mercy save thy children from misusing these thy gifts for selfish and destructive ends; and grant them grace to use them only for thy glory and the good of mankind. *Book of Common Order*
See also prayers for Education Sunday, 702–20

A youth club 1176

Almighty Father, we pray thy blessing on all members of this club. Grant that we together may so work and play, and think and pray, that we may be more fitted to serve thee. Help us to look wide; fill us with high ideals; inspire us with love and good will to all men; that we may lead others in the paths of chivalry and honour, ourselves following in the steps of him who died in the service of men, thy Son, our Saviour Jesus Christ. *Toc H Prayers*

1177

Almighty Father, we pray that thy blessing may rest upon us in this club. Grant that all its members may follow Christ and be bound together in loyalty and love. Remove all selfishness and jealousy and rivalry which may prevent unity and fellowship. Make us kind and thoughtful for one another. Keep thou the door of our lips, that we may not sin against one another, nor against thee whose servants we desire to be; for Jesus Christ's sake.
Adapted

A youth club 1178

O God, our heavenly Father, we pray for all who are joined together in this fellowship of youth. Help us so to think and work and play together, that we may become one in purpose to seek thy will for our lives, and to serve thee faithfully in thy holy Church; through Jesus Christ our Lord.

Scouts 1179

O God, our Father, we thank thee for the brotherhood of Scouts throughout the world. Bless the troop in this parish and all its members. Give them grace to keep the threefold promise they have made; and make them strong to follow thee all along life's way, in the faith of thy Son Jesus Christ our Lord.

Guides   1180

Almighty Father, we pray thee to send thy blessing on those whom thou hast joined together in the fellowship of Guiding in this parish. Strengthen them to be loyal to their vows and to fulfil faithfully the daily calls of duty; fill them with high ideals; and inspire them with love and goodwill to all mankind, that they may follow in the footsteps of him who died in the service of men, thy Son our Saviour Jesus Christ.

Adapted from A Book of Guide Prayers

Any youth organization   1181

Help us, O Lord, who are united in the fellowship of Scouts [*or* Guides, the Boys' Brigade, *etc.*] throughout the world, to be worthy of our high calling. Give us grace to keep our vows and to fight manfully under thy banner, that in the end we may be found true citizens of thy heavenly kingdom; for the sake of Jesus Christ our Lord.

Young people   1182

O Lord Jesus Christ, who didst behold with love the young ruler who came to thee and didst call him to follow thee: We pray that young people everywhere may hear and obey thy call; and grant them such a vision of thy loving purpose for the world that they may surrender themselves gladly and unreservedly to thyself for the service of thy kingdom. We ask this for the honour of thy holy name. *Frank Colquhoun*

See also prayers for a Youth Festival, 782–92

Doctors and nurses   1183

O LORD Jesus Christ, who alone hast power over life and death, over health and sickness: Give skill, wisdom and gentleness to doctors and nurses and all who minister to the sick; that always bearing about thy presence with them, they may not only heal but bless, and shine as lamps of hope in the darkest hours of distress and fear; who with the Father and the Holy Spirit livest and reignest ever one God, world without end.

1184

O Heavenly Father, who by thy Son Jesus Christ hast taught us the glory of self-sacrifice and service: Bless all those who are called to care for the sick in mind and body; may they always remember that they are fellow-workers with thee; and give them such patience, skill and love that they may bring healing and comfort to those whom they serve; through the same Jesus Christ our Lord.

Adapted

1185

Almighty God, who didst send thy blessed Son to be the great physician of the souls and bodies of men: Look, we beseech thee, upon those who have dedicated their lives to the ministry of healing. Bless and strengthen them in thy service; use their skill and all such means as they shall employ for the relief of suffering and the restoration of health; and help them ever to remember that in ministering to others they minister to thee; through the same Jesus Christ our Lord.   *Adapted*

The ministry of healing   1186

Almighty and everlasting God, who didst send thy Son Jesus Christ to be the Saviour and Healer of men: We pray thee to bless the work of all hospitals and medical schools. Grant that all who are called to the ministry of healing may ever have present to their minds the example of our Lord, and his tenderness and sympathy for all human suffering. Give them grace and patience faithfully to fulfil their holy calling, and crown their work with good success; for the love of the same thy Son, Jesus Christ our Lord.

Adapted from a prayer at the London Hospital

1187

O God our Father, as we praise thee for thy goodness and mercy through the past years, so we beseech thee to continue thy work of healing among us. Grant to physicians, surgeons, nurses, and all who co-operate with them, wisdom and skill, patience, strength and tenderness, that by their endeavour many may be made whole in body and mind; through Jesus Christ our Lord.

A Diocesan Service Book

1188

O Lord Jesus Christ, who in thy life on earth didst heal both the bodies and souls of men: Guide, we pray thee, all who now minister to body or to soul; and grant that those who serve things spiritual may not despise the body, nor those who treat the body set at nought the soul; but that, patiently seeking to understand the unity of our human nature, they may work together for the cure of all sickness and disease, and for the recovery of that true health which is thy gift to those who wait upon thee. We ask it for thy name's sake.

1189

O Lord and Master Jesus Christ, Word of the everlasting Father, who hast borne our griefs and carried the burden of our infirmities: Renew by thy Holy Spirit in thy Church, we beseech thee, thy gifts of healing, and send forth thy disciples again to preach the gospel of thy kingdom, and to cure the sick and relieve thy suffering children, to the praise and glory of thy holy name. *Liturgy of St. Mark*
See also *981–1002*

Thanksgiving for health

1190

Lord of all power and might, we praise thee for thy good gifts of health and strength; for the sight of our eyes, the hearing of our ears, the strength of our limbs, the powers of our mind, and the energy which forges them into a fit instrument for thy service. Praise be to thee, O God of our health, through Jesus Christ our Lord. *With all our Strength*

Hospitals

1191

Most merciful Father, who hast taught us to love thee with all our strength and to glorify thee in our bodies: We commend to thee for thy continual blessing the hospitals of our land and those who serve in them. Prosper all that is being done for the healing of the sick, the conquest of disease, and the training of doctors and nurses; that thy will may be done in the relief of suffering and the making of lives whole; through Jesus Christ our Lord. *Frank Colquhoun*

British Red Cross Society 1192

O Merciful God, giver of life and health, whose will is made known to us in Jesus Christ our Lord: Send thy blessing, we beseech thee, upon all who are engaged in the ministry of healing. More especially we pray at this time for the British Red Cross Society and those who serve therein. Inspire all who wear the Red Cross with the spirit of Christian charity and self-sacrifice, that they may be compassionate in their care for the sick and afflicted, fearless in their efforts to promote the health and well-being of the people in this and other lands; for the sake of him whose cross is the pledge of victory over all the powers of evil, even thy Son our Saviour Jesus Christ.

Medical students 1193

O Lord, the Healer of all our diseases, who knowest how the sick have need of a physician: Bless all whom thou hast called to be sharers in thine own work of healing with health alike of body and soul; that they may learn their art in dependence upon thee, and exercise it always under thy sanction and to thy glory; who livest and reignest with the Father and the Holy Spirit, one God, world without end. *Sursum Corda*

1194

O Merciful Father, who hast made man's body to be a temple of thy Holy Spirit: Sanctify, we pray thee, all those whom thou hast called to study and practise the art of healing and the prevention of disease; strengthen them in body and soul, and bless their work, that they may themselves live as members and servants of Christ, and give comfort to those whom he lived and died to save; through the same Jesus Christ our Lord.

Medical research 1195

Almighty God, who art the Father of truth and understanding: Shed forth, we beseech thee, upon those engaged in medical and surgical research the light of thy heavenly guidance; grant to them the spirit of patient discernment, that they may be skilled to discover the way of health and healing; and strengthen them with the assurance that they are fellow-workers together with thee; through Jesus Christ our Lord. *Frederick B. Macnutt*

IN TIME OF WAR

Under threat of war   1196

O GOD, who hast made of one blood all the nations of the earth, and hast set the bounds of their habitation that they might seek after thee and find thee: Mercifully hear our supplications, and remove from us the menace of war. Guide the rulers with thy counsel and restrain the passions of the people. Quicken the sense of our common brotherhood, bind the nations into a new bond of fellowship, and hasten the time when the kingdoms of this world shall become the kingdom of thy Son, our Lord and Saviour Jesus Christ.   *W. E. Orchard**

In time of war   1197

Lord God Almighty, who hast brought thy judgments upon all the earth, that the inhabitants of the world may learn righteousness: We entreat thy divine Majesty so to turn the hearts of the people of this land, that sorrowing for our sins with true repentance, and trusting in the hope of thy salvation, we may be renewed to do thee service and show forth thy praise from one generation to another; through Jesus Christ our Lord.   *National Mission*, 1916

1198

O God, who hast taught us in thy holy Word that thou dost not willingly afflict the children of men: Grant that in the present time of warfare and distress of nations our people may know thy presence and obey thy will. Remove from us arrogance and feebleness; give us courage and loyalty, tranquillity and self-control, that we may accomplish that which thou givest us to do, and endure that which thou givest us to bear; for his sake who was lifted up on the cross to draw all men unto him, Jesus Christ our Lord.   *A Form of Prayer*, August 1914

1199

God of our fathers, on whom our confidence is set, who hast delivered us from of old, and wilt still deliver: Support with thy whole might this people in the day of their proving; that they fear not the threatenings and strokes of the enemy, but stand to maintain thy cause, in the faith of thy Son, our Saviour Jesus Christ.   *A Form of Prayer*, March 1941

1200

O Lord God, who in the day of danger knowest how many and stern are the tasks to which we are set: Help us to honour thee by a strenuous devotion to duty and work, and to the high cause which demands them; and strengthen and shield thy people in body and soul, by day and by night; through Jesus Christ our Lord.

A Form of Prayer, May 1940

1201

Look with thy compassion, O Lord, upon the earth that is full of darkness and cruelty. Break the power of the oppressor, and deliver his victims; and unite them together in a common submission to thy most holy will; through Jesus Christ our Lord.

1202

Heavenly Father, God both of righteousness and peace: Have mercy upon the nations now engaged in bitter war. Cleanse both us and our enemies of hatred and covetousness; and make us so worthy of our cause, so steadfast in thy strength, that no weakness may delay the victory of our arms, and no selfishness mar the righteousness of our peace; for Jesus Christ's sake.

William Temple

1203

O Lord God Almighty, who from thy throne dost behold all the dwellers upon earth: Look down with pity upon those on whom have fallen the miseries of war. Have compassion on the wounded and dying; comfort the broken-hearted; assuage the madness of the nations; guide our rulers; make war to cease; give peace in our time, O Lord. We ask it in the name of him who is the Prince of Peace, even thy Son Jesus Christ our Lord.

Leaflet of the Collegium, 1914

On active service
1204

O Almighty Lord God, the Father and Protector of all that trust in thee: We commend to thy fatherly goodness the men and women who through perils of war are serving this nation by land or sea or in the air; beseeching thee to take into thine own hand both them and the cause they serve. Be thou their strength when they are set in the midst of so many and great dangers. Make all bold through death or life to put their trust in thee, who art the only giver of victory and canst save by many or by few; through Jesus Christ our Lord. *A Form of Prayer*, October 1939

1205

Look in thy mercy, we beseech thee, O Lord, on those who are called to tasks of special peril in the air, or beneath the sea. Even there also shall thy hand lead them, and thy right hand shall hold them. Help them to do their duty with prudence and with fearlessness, confident that in life or in death the eternal God is their refuge, and underneath them are the everlasting arms; through Jesus Christ our Lord.   *J. Armitage Robinson*

1206

O Lord God, our Father, our Saviour, our might: We commend to thy keeping all those who are venturing their lives on our behalf; that, whether by life or by death, they may win for the whole world the fruits of their sacrifice, and a righteous and abiding peace; through Jesus Christ our Lord.

Chaplains   **1207**

Remember, O Lord, all whom thou hast called to minister to the souls of those engaged in warfare. Give them grace to enlighten the ignorant, to strengthen the weak-hearted, to comfort those who suffer, and to speak peace to the dying. So grant that in all their ministrations, in all their life and conversation, they may shepherd the men and women committed to their care, and advance the honour of our Saviour and his kingdom; through the same Jesus Christ our Lord.   *J. Taylor Smith**

Those who minister to the wounded   **1208**

O Merciful God, whose blessed Son went about doing good: Uphold with thy strength and grace those who do service to the wounded and the sick. Grant to the ministers of thy gospel faithfulness and love; to doctors and nurses, skill, sympathy and patience; and to those who labour in the place of danger, thy protection; through Jesus Christ our Lord.

A Form of Prayer, May 1940

War victims   **1209**

O God, who hast promised that they that wait upon thee shall renew their strength: We commend to thee all who suffer in this time of war; the wounded, the sick, and the prisoners; the homeless, the hungry, and the oppressed; the anxious, the frightened, and the bereaved. Strengthen them, O Lord, with thy Holy Spirit, and give them friends to help them; we ask it in his name, who bore for us the agony of the cross, thy Son, our Lord Jesus Christ.

Frederick B. Macnutt

1210

O Merciful Father, look with thy tender compassion upon all prisoners of war. Supply all their needs, and hasten the time of their release; let thy love protect them and thy presence cheer them, that day by day in weariness and hardship they may have strength to endure patiently, and may find peace in thee; through Jesus Christ our Lord. *A Form of Prayer, August 1918*

1211

O Lord God, whose compassions fail not: Support, we entreat thee, the peoples on whom the terrors of invasion have fallen; and if their liberty be lost to the oppressor, let not their spirit and hope be broken, but stayed upon thy strength till the day of deliverance; through Jesus Christ our Lord.

For our enemies
1212

Lord Jesus Christ, before whose judgment seat we all shall stand, we pray as thou hast taught us for our enemies; so turn their hearts to thee that they may truly repent; and grant that they and we and all the peoples of the earth, being cleansed from sin, may know and do thy will, who wast lifted up upon the cross to draw all men to thyself, our Saviour, our Lord and our God.

Form of National Prayer, 1942

For a righteous peace
1213

O Almighty God, who canst bring good out of evil, and makest even the wrath of man turn to thy praise: We beseech thee so to order and dispose the issue of this war that we may be brought through strife to lasting peace; and that the nations of the world may be united in a new fellowship for the promotion of thy glory and the good of all mankind; through Jesus Christ our Lord.

Form of National Prayer, May 1940

HOME AND FRIENDS

Family life **1214**

ALMIGHTY God and heavenly Father, whose Son Jesus Christ was subject to Mary and Joseph at Nazareth, and shared there the life of an earthly home: Send down thy blessing, we beseech thee, upon all Christian families. Grant to parents the spirit of understanding and wisdom, and to children the spirit of obedience and true reverence; and so bind each to each in thy love that every Christian family may be an image of the Holy Family, and every Christian home a school of heavenly knowledge and virtuous living; through the same Jesus Christ our Lord.   *E. C. Ratcliff**

1215

Almighty Father, from whom every family in heaven and on earth is named: We entreat thy mercy for the families of this and every land, for man and wife and child, and for all who have the care of children; that by thy hallowing our homes may be blessed and our children may grow up in the knowledge of thee and of thy Son, Jesus Christ our Lord.   *St. Paul's Cathedral*

1216

Almighty God, in whose house are many mansions, we pray thee to surround our dwellings with the unseen wall of thy protection; that we may be devoted to thy service and may serve one another in love; until we come at last to that home which thou hast prepared for them that love thee; through Jesus Christ our Lord.
Salisbury Book of Occasional Offices*

1217

O Holy Father, from whom every family in heaven and on earth is named: We commend to thy gracious keeping the homes and children of our people; beseeching thee so to dwell in our hearts that we may know in daily life, and show forth to all men, the power and depth of thy grace; through Jesus Christ our Lord.
New Every Morning

1218

Almighty Father, who art ever present with us in all the duties of our daily life: Be thyself, we beseech thee, the defender of our households and our constant guide; and as thy Son, Jesus Christ, abode on earth in his home at Nazareth, so let him now abide with us and we with him; that continuing ever in his love we may love one another in him; through the same Jesus Christ our Lord.

1219

Almighty God, our heavenly Father, whose blessed Son did share at Nazareth the life of an earthly home: We beseech thee to bless our homes, and our families, and to keep us in our going out and in our coming in. Grant us day by day thy strength and protection; watch over us in times of danger and necessity; and unite us with each other in thy steadfast fear and love; through the same Jesus Christ our Lord. *Adapted*

1220

Sanctify, O Lord, the homes of our people, that they may be places of prayer and purity and true religion. Knit together in constant love those whom thou hast made one in holy wedlock. Bestow upon children the dew of thy blessing, that they may grow up in the faith of thy name and in the spirit of love and service; for the glory of our Lord Jesus Christ.

1221

O God our Father, in whom all the families of the earth are blessed: We pray thee to regard with thy loving-kindness the homes of our country; that marriage may be held in due honour by the Church, by the State, and by society; and that husbands and wives may live faithfully together, in honour preferring one another. We pray that the members of every family may be rich in mutual understanding and forbearance, in courtesy and kindness, bearing one another's burdens, and so fulfilling the law of Christ, thy Son, our Lord. *New Every Morning*

1222

Almighty and eternal God, who didst send thy Holy Spirit from above to renew thine image in our souls: Inspire the heart of every husband and father and of every wife and mother in the land to love and serve thee. Awaken us all to a full sense of our responsibilities, and take possession of ourselves and of our homes; through Jesus Christ our Lord. *Mothers' Union*
See also *673–6, 717, 776–8*

Children 1223

Grant to our children, O God, this gift above all, that as they grow in knowledge they may grow also in grace, and enter into their heritage of faith in thee. So may they walk in thy world as children of their Father, giving thee thanks for all things; through Jesus Christ our Lord. *New Every Morning*

1224

O Lord Jesus Christ, who didst take little children in thine arms and bless them: Bless, we beseech thee, all children dear to us. Take them into the arms of thy everlasting mercy, keep them from all evil, and bring them into the company of those who ever behold the face of thy Father in heaven; to the glory of thy holy name.

Priest's Prayer Book

1225

O God our Father, we pray thee to bless all children, and to give to those who have the care of them wisdom, patience, and love; so that the home in which they grow up may be to them an image of thy kingdom, and the care of their parents a likeness of thy love; through Jesus Christ our Lord.
See also 715–16, 766–72

Marriage **1226**

Almighty God, who hast ordained that a man and a woman should leave their parents, cleave to one another and become one flesh; and hast taught us that what God has joined together no man should put asunder: Deliver our nation at this time from all corrupting influences. May marriage be held in honour among us all, and the gift of sex be acknowledged as a sacred trust from thee. Grant to both young and old the grace of self-control. Beautify our homes with thy presence, that husband and wife, parents and children, may love one another as thou hast loved us; through Jesus Christ our Lord. *J. R. W. Stott*
See also 952–69

Those we love **1227**

Almighty God, whose goodness loved us into life and whose mercies never fail: We commend to thee those who are joined to us by the ties of kindred, friendship and love; all children dear to us; all who help us to be faithful and whose goodness turns duties into love. Keep them both outwardly in their bodies and inwardly in their souls, and pour upon them the dew of thy blessing; through Jesus Christ our Lord. *John Hunter*

1228

We call to mind, O God, before thy throne of grace all those whom thou hast given to be near and dear to us, and all for whom we are specially bound to pray, beseeching thee to remember them all for good, and to fulfil as may be expedient for them all their desires and wants. We commend to thee any who may have wronged us, whether by word or deed, beseeching thee to forgive them and us all our sins, and to bring us to thy heavenly kingdom; through Jesus Christ our Lord. *Gavin Hamilton*

1229

O God, who by the grace of thy Holy Spirit hast shed thy love abroad in the hearts of thy faithful people: Mercifully grant to those whom we love health of body and soul; that they may serve thee with all their strength and gladly fulfil all thy good pleasure; through Jesus Christ our Lord. *Gregorian Sacramentary*

1230

O God our heavenly Father, who hast made pleasant and lovely the bonds of friendship: We thank thee for the many friends with whom thou hast enriched our lives; strengthen the bonds of love which unite us in thee, and in death divide us not; for the sake of Jesus Christ our Lord. *Adapted*

1231

O Loving Father, we commend to thy gracious keeping all who are near and dear to us. Have mercy upon those who are sick, and comfort all who are in pain, anxiety, or sorrow. Awaken all who are careless about eternal things. Bless those who are young and in health, that they may give the days of their strength unto thee. Comfort the aged and infirm, that thy peace may rest upon them. Hallow the ties of kindred, that we may help, and not hinder, one another in all such good works as thou hast prepared for us to walk in; through Jesus Christ our Lord. *Canadian Prayer Book*

1232

O God, our heavenly Father, from whom every family in heaven and on earth is named: We entrust to thy loving care the members of our families, both near and far. Supply their needs; guide their footsteps; keep them in safety of body and soul; and may thy peace rest upon our homes and upon our dear ones everywhere; for Jesus Christ our Saviour's sake. *Frank Colquhoun*

Absent friends **1233**

O Lord our God, who art in every place and from whom no space or distance can ever separate us: We thank thee that those who are absent from each other are present with thee. We therefore pray thee to have in thy holy keeping those dear ones from whom we are now separated; and grant that both they and we, by drawing nearer to thee, may be drawn nearer to each other, and be bound together in thy love; through Jesus Christ our Lord.

*William Martin**

1234

O Lord of love, who art not far from any of thy children: Watch with thy care those who are absent from us. Be thou about their path; be thou within their hearts; be thou their defence upon their right hand; give them unfailing trust in thee; grant them power against temptation; qualify them for whatever task thou givest them, and make it their joy to do thy will; for the sake of Jesus Christ our Lord.

*W. Boyd Carpenter**

1235

O God, whose fatherly care reacheth to the uttermost parts of the earth: We humbly beseech thee graciously to behold and bless those whom we love, now absent from us. Defend them from all dangers of soul and body; and grant that both they and we, drawing nearer to thee, may be bound together by thy love in the communion of thy Holy Spirit, and in the fellowship of thy saints; through Jesus Christ our Lord.

American Prayer Book

1236

O God, who art present in thy power in every place, mercifully hear our prayers for those we love who are now parted from us. Watch over them, we beseech thee, and protect them in all anxiety, danger and temptation; and teach us and them to feel and know that thou art always near, and that we are one in thee for ever; through Jesus Christ our Lord.

1237

O Heavenly Father, who hast bestowed upon us the comfort of earthly friends: Look in love upon those dear to us from whom we are separated. Protect them and keep them from all harm; prosper and bless them in all good things; suffer them never to be desolate or afraid, and let no shadow come between them and us to divide our hearts; but in thine own good time may we renew the fellowship of sight and hand; through Jesus Christ our Lord.

TRAVEL

Travellers 1238

O GOD, our heavenly Father, who art present in thy power in every place: Preserve, we beseech thee, all who travel by land, water, or air [*especially those for whom our prayers are desired*]; surround them with thy loving care; protect them from every danger; and bring them in safety to their journey's end; through Jesus Christ our Lord. *Canadian Prayer Book*

Before a journey 1239

O God of infinite mercy and might, whom no distance of place nor length of time can part from those who serve thee: Receive into thy protection those whom we now commend to thy care; and through all the way in which they are to go, be pleased to be their guide and companion; through Jesus Christ our Lord.
Adapted from Gelasian Sacramentary

Seafarers 1240

O Almighty God, whose way is in the sea and whose paths are in the great waters: Be present, we beseech thee, with our brethren in the manifold dangers of the deep; protect them from all perils, prosper them in their course, and bring them in safety to the haven where they would be, with a grateful sense of thy mercies; through Jesus Christ our Lord. *Scottish Prayer Book*

1241

Merciful God, who holdest the waters in the hollow of thy hand: Prosper, we pray thee, the voyages of our sailors and merchantmen as they go down to the sea in ships and do business in great waters; and as they see thy works in the deep, give them grace to acknowledge and trust in thee, who art the confidence of all the ends of the earth and of those that are far off upon the sea; for thy name's sake. *W. Charter Piggott*

Travellers on the roads 1242

Almighty God, giver of life and health: Guide, we pray thee, with thy wisdom all who are striving to save from injury and death the travellers on our roads. Grant to those who drive along the highways consideration for others, and to those who walk on them or play beside them thoughtful caution and care; that so without fear or disaster we may all come safely to our journey's end, by thy mercy who carest for us; through Jesus Christ our Lord.

Douglas Crick

1243

Almighty God, who dost sanctify with thy Spirit the common ways of life: Give to us and to all who use the roads the spirit of courtesy and goodwill, of carefulness and self-control; that by our thought for others we may all be preserved from needless danger and sudden death, and may live to glorify thee in our going out and our coming in; through Jesus Christ our Lord.

Those on holiday 1244

Almighty God, our heavenly Father, who didst rest from the work of creation on the seventh day: Grant us thy blessing not only in our labour but when we lay aside our toil; that so, returning to our duties with body rested, mind renewed and spirit refreshed, we may in all things seek thy glory and do thy will; through Jesus Christ thy Son our Saviour.

J. W. R. Stott

1245

O Heavenly Father, we commend to thee those who at this time are seeking rest and change. Grant them refreshment of spirit and renewal of strength, that they may return to the duties of their daily life better fitted for thy service; through Jesus Christ our Lord.

1246

Heavenly Father, who art the source of all refreshment: Be with us and all who are seeking rest and holiday at this time. Make us grateful for all thy good gifts which we enjoy; help us to see thee in the beauty and majesty of nature; and grant us on our return renewed strength of mind and body for the duties of our daily life; through Jesus Christ our Lord.

Adapted

1247

Almighty God, from whom all good things do come, protect and bless, we beseech thee, all who, released for a season from their daily tasks, are enjoying the rest and refreshment of their annual holidays; and grant that, renewed in body and spirit, they may return home better able to serve thee and their fellow men; through Jesus Christ our Lord.

Peter Green

Valedictory prayer 1248

O God, who art the refuge and strength of those who trust in thee: We commend to thy merciful care thy servants now departing from us. Prosper them, we pray thee, in all their undertakings; guide and protect them in the way that they go; and of thy great goodness bring them again to their homes and friends in peace; through Jesus Christ our Lord. *Adapted*

Life's journey 1249

Be thou, O Lord, our shield and defence as we travel along the perplexing path of life, with its many difficulties and dangers. So guide and protect us here on earth, that we may find eternal rest when our journey is finished and our work is done; through Jesus Christ our Lord.

THE SUFFERING

Those in need **1250**

O LORD God, our heavenly Father, regard, we beseech thee, with thy divine pity the pains of all thy children; and grant that the passion of our Lord and his infinite love may make fruitful for good the tribulations of the innocent, the sufferings of the sick, and the sufferings of the bereaved; through him who suffered in our flesh and died for our sake, the same thy Son our Saviour Jesus Christ.

1251

O Thou who art love, and who seest all the suffering, injustice and misery which reign in this world: Have pity, we implore thee, on the work of thy hands. Look mercifully upon the poor, the oppressed, the destitute and all who are heavy laden. Fill our hearts with deep compassion for those who suffer, and hasten the coming of thy kingdom of justice and truth; for the sake of Jesus Christ our Lord.   *Eugène Bersier**

1252

Almighty and most merciful Father, who hast taught us not to think of ourselves only, but also for the wants of others; we remember before thee all who are burdened and oppressed, those who are afflicted by poverty, or worn down by disease and illness, the weary and the heavy-laden, those also who are in darkness or despair, or who are suffering for righteousness' sake. Help them all to rest in thee; through Jesus Christ our Lord.   *William Knight*

1253

O God of love, whose compassions fail not: We bring before thee the sufferings of all mankind; the necessities of the homeless; the sighing of prisoners; the pains of the sick and injured; the sorrows of the bereaved; the helplessness of the aged and weak. Comfort and relieve them, O Father, according to their several needs, and thy great mercy; for the sake of thy Son our Saviour Jesus Christ.

After St. Anselm

1254

Blessed Lord, who thyself hast borne our griefs and carried our sorrows: Hear thou our prayer for all that are in trouble and distress. Draw them, we pray thee, to thyself, that they may find the comfort and strength which thou alone canst give; and grant to all of us the loving heart and ready hand to help, that serving the needs of others we may show forth our love and gratitude to thee, our Lord and Saviour Jesus Christ.

1255

Hear us, O Lord, as we remember before thee those who have special need of thee at this time; those who are handicapped in the race of life through no fault of their own; those who have lost the health and strength that once were theirs; all who lie in pain; the blind, the deaf, the dumb; the hungry and the homeless; all refugees and displaced persons; those who are in doubt or anguish of soul, and all who have wandered away from thee. Succour them, O Lord, and raise up helpers for them in their need, for the sake of Jesus Christ our Saviour.

1256

O God, Almighty and merciful, who healest those that are broken in heart, and turnest the sadness of the sorrowful to joy: Remember in pity such as are this day destitute, homeless, or forgotten of their fellow men. Uplift those that are cast down; cheer with hope all discouraged and unhappy people; and by thy heavenly grace preserve from falling those who are tempted to sin. Grant this, O Lord, for the love of him who for our sakes became poor, thy Son our Saviour Jesus Christ.   *American Prayer Book**

1257

O God, remember in thy mercy the poor and needy, the widow and the fatherless, the stranger and the friendless, the sick and the dying. Relieve their needs, sanctify their sufferings, uphold their faith, and in due time bring them out of all their trouble; for the sake of Jesus Christ our Lord.

1258

Lord Jesus, we beseech thee, by the loneliness of thy suffering on the cross, be near to all who are desolate, and in pain or sorrow, this day; and let thy presence transform their sorrow into comfort, and their loneliness into fellowship with thee; for thy tender mercy's sake.   *Sursum Corda*

1259

Almighty and most merciful God, let thy compassion be shown to all who suffer, and to all who are stricken with sorrow. Use us to comfort them as we are able, and what we cannot do for them, be

pleased thyself to do; that in the mystery of thy love they may find
peace and healing and faith; through Jesus Christ our Lord.

New Every Morning

1260

We commend to thy merciful care, O Lord, all who are passing
through suffering and distress; beseeching thee to grant them,
according to their need, peace of heart, strength of body, and
healing of the mind; for the sake of Jesus Christ our Saviour.

1261

O Heavenly Father, look in thy compassion on those in need,
especially on those for whom our prayers are desired. Grant them
the comfort of thy presence; let thy peace rule in their hearts; and
fulfil in them thy perfect will, for the glory of Jesus Christ our
Saviour.

1262

Almighty and everlasting God, the comfort of the sad, the
strength of them that suffer: Let the prayers of thy children who
cry out of any tribulation come unto thee; and unto every soul that
is distressed grant thou mercy, grant relief, grant refreshment;
through Jesus Christ our Lord.   *After Gelasian Sacramentary*

1263

We humbly beseech thee of thy goodness, O Lord, to comfort and
succour all those who are in trouble, sorrow, need, sickness, or any
other adversity; that by thy blessing upon them, and those who try
to help them, they may find encouragement and peace; through
Jesus Christ our Lord.

The sick in body   1264

O Lord, we beseech thee graciously to visit and relieve thy servants for whom our prayers are desired. Look upon them with the
eyes of thy mercy, give them comfort and sure confidence in thee,
and keep them in perpetual peace and safety; through Jesus Christ
our Lord.   *Adapted from Book of Common Prayer*

1265

O Lord of all compassion, whose hand is ever stretched out in
blessing and healing upon the sick: We pray for these thy servants
whom we have named before thee; that they may be set free from
the sickness which afflicts them, and healed by thy power, for the
honour and glory of thy name; through Jesus Christ our Lord.

Guild of Health★

1266

O God, whose compassions fail not, whose faithfulness is new every morning: Draw near, we pray thee, to those who are stricken with sickness and pain. Ease their discomfort, allay their fears, strengthen their faith, be thou their salvation and their peace; through Jesus Christ our Lord. *J. R. W. Stott*

1267

Almighty Father, we commend to thy loving care all who suffer, especially the sick in body and mind. Grant them patience in their suffering; cheer and uphold them with the knowledge of thy love; and if it be thy will restore them to health and strength; for the sake of Jesus Christ our Lord.

1268

O Almighty God, who art the giver of life and health and the aid of all who seek thy succour: Mercifully grant that thy help and goodness may be shown to the suffering and the sick; that being healed of their infirmities they may give thanks to thee in thy holy Church; through Jesus Christ our Lord.

1269

O Lord Jesus Christ, unto whom the sick were brought that they might be healed, and thou didst send none of them away without thy blessing: Look in pity upon all who come to thee for healing of body or mind, and grant them the blessing of thy saving health, both now and evermore. *Adapted*

1270

Grant, O Lord, to all those who are bearing pain, thy healing grace and power; thy spirit of peace and hope, of courage and endurance. Cast out from them the spirit of anxiety and fear; and grant them perfect confidence and trust in thee; through Jesus Christ our Lord. *Adapted*

1271

O God, who knowest the needs of all thy children, look with compassion upon *him* for whom our prayers are offered; give *him* courage and confidence; bless those who minister to *him* of thy healing gifts, and, if it be thy gracious will, restore *him* to that perfect health which is thine alone to give; through Jesus Christ our Lord. *Robert N. Rodenmeyer*

The sick in mind   1272

O Holy Spirit, who dost search out all things, even the deep things of God and of man: We pray thee so to penetrate into the springs of personality of all who are sick in mind as to bring them peace and unity and healing. Dispel all anxiety and cast out all fear, that they may be restored to health and glorify thee in lives made whole and free; for the sake of Jesus Christ our Saviour.

Adapted from George Appleton

1273

O Heavenly Father, who in thy love and wisdom knowest the anxieties and fears of thy children: Grant that this thy servant may be enabled to cast all *his* care upon thee, for thou carest for *him*. Give *him* quietness of mind and unshaken trust in thee, and guide his feet into the way of peace; through Jesus Christ our Lord.

Irish Prayer Book★

1274

O Thou who art the Mind of all creation, we remember to our comfort that thou hast in thy special care all broken, outworn and imperfect minds. Give to those who live with them the understanding and loving Spirit of Christ. Enlighten those who are tempted to laugh at such infirmity, or regard it with shame. To all who are separated in this life by barriers of mental infirmity, grant the comfort of thy Holy Spirit, who with thee and thy Christ ever liveth and reigneth, one God, world without end.

The handicapped   1275

O Loving Father, we pray for all who are handicapped in the race of life: the blind, the defective, the delicate, those worn with sickness, and all who are permanently injured. May they learn the mystery of the road of suffering which Christ has trodden and saints have followed, and bring thee this gift which angels cannot bring, a heart that trusts thee even in the dark; and this we ask in the name of him who himself took our infirmities upon him, even the same Jesus Christ, our Saviour.   *A. S. T. Fisher*

Children in need   1276

O God whose heart is as the heart of a child: Hear our prayer for children who are suffering through the sin, hatred, and stupidity of men and women. In thy mercy restore to them what has been taken from them. Raise up fathers to the fatherless, mothers to the motherless, friends to the friendless. Wipe out from their souls the stain of misery and fear; and give back to them the trustfulness and untroubled joy which should be theirs. To those who look after them and teach them, grant faith that thou art able to do this, and patient wisdom to co-operate with thee, for the sake of Jesus Christ, who, taking the children in his arms, blessed them, saying, Of such is the kingdom of heaven.

1277
O God, our Father, we remember before thee all orphaned, homeless and unwanted children, the children of loveless homes, and those who suffer from bodily defect and disease. Make our hearts burn within us for the children of our dark places, and teach us how to turn to good account the laws that protect them and the efforts of those who strive to succour them; through Jesus Christ our Lord. *Mothers' Union*

1278
We would remember before thee, O God, all those whose powers are hampered by affliction of mind or body, and especially children burdened by suffering and physical limitations. Give patience and hope to all who tend them, and amidst all the mysteries of life grant us such a vision and assurance of thy love that we may never doubt thee, though thy way is hidden from us; this we ask for Jesus' sake.

1279
O Heavenly Father, watch with us, we pray thee, over the sick child for whom our prayers are offered, and grant that *he* may be restored to that perfect health which is thine alone to give; through Jesus Christ our Lord. *American Prayer Book*

One facing an operation   1280
Father of compassion and mercy, who never failest to help and comfort those who cry to thee for succour: Give strength and courage to this thy *son* in *his* hour of need. Hold thou *him* up and *he* shall be safe; enable *him* to feel that thou art near, and to know that underneath are the everlasting arms; and grant that, resting on thy protection, *he* may fear no evil, since thou art with *him*; through Jesus Christ our Lord. *Irish Prayer Book*

Incurables   1281
O Heavenly Father, we pray thee for those suffering from diseases for which at present there is no cure. Give them the victory of trust and hope, that they may never lose their faith in thy loving purpose. Grant thy wisdom to all who are working to discover the causes of disease, and the realization that through thee all things are possible. We ask this in the name of him who went about doing

good and healing all manner of disease, even thy Son Jesus Christ
our Lord. *George Appleton*

The dying 1282

O Lord Jesus Christ, who in thy last agony didst commend thy
spirit into the hands of thy heavenly Father: Have mercy upon all
sick and dying persons; may death be unto them the gate of everlasting life; and give them the assurance of thy presence even in the
dark valley; for thy name's sake who art the resurrection and the
life, and to whom be glory for ever and ever.

Adapted from Sarum Primer

1283

O God, who hast appointed unto men once to die, but hast
hidden from them the time of their death: Help us so to live in this
world that we may be ready to leave it; and that, being thine in death
as in life, we may come to that rest that remaineth for thy people;
through him who died and rose again for us, Jesus Christ our Lord.

William Bright

The hungry 1284

O Merciful and loving Father, look in thy mercy, we pray thee,
on the many millions who are hungry in the world of to-day and
are at the mercy of disease. Grant that we who have lived so com-
fortably and gently all our lives may have true sympathy with them
and do all in our power, as individuals and as a nation, to help them
to that abundant life which is thy will for them; through Jesus
Christ our Lord. *George Appleton*

1285

O Christ, whose heart was moved with compassion for the hunger
of the multitude, and didst use thy disciples to minister to their
needs: Fill us with thine own love and concern for the hungry
peoples of the world of our day and make us the instruments of
thy purpose to relieve their sufferings; for thy tender mercy's
sake.

1286

O Heavenly Father, who by thy blessed Son hast taught us to ask
of thee our daily bread: Have compassion on those who have been
brought to poverty and hunger. Relieve their distress; make plain
the way of help; and grant thy grace unto us all, that we may bear
each other's burdens according to thy will; through Jesus Christ
our Lord. *George Appleton*

The homeless 1287

Have mercy, O Lord our God, on those whom war or oppression or famine has robbed of homes and friends, and prosper all who seek to help them. We commend also to thy care those whose homes are broken by conflict and lack of love; grant that where the love of man has failed, the divine compassion may heal; through Jesus Christ our Lord. *New Every Morning**

Refugees 1288

We remember before thee, O God, the multitudes of refugees throughout the world, and all who are without homes and without hope. Show thyself to them in thy great compassion; save them from despair and bitterness of spirit; and graciously bless all that is being done for their present relief and their future security; for the sake of him who had not where to lay his head, thy Son Jesus Christ our Lord.

1289

O God, who art the Father of all mankind, we ask thy mercy for the refugees of many nations who bear the mark of pain and suffering. We pray for the sick, the homeless, and the lonely, and for those separated from their families and friends; and we beseech thee to direct the minds of statesmen and the charity of all men to the relief of their sufferings and the healing of their sorrows; through Jesus Christ our Lord. *New Every Morning*

Alcoholics 1290

Most gracious God, the strength of all who put their trust in thee: We pray for those who are enslaved by intoxicants or by some other evil habit; give them the desire and the will to be free, and the grace to continue in the right way; and show us how we may serve and help them in their need; through Jesus Christ our Lord.

The aged and infirm 1291

Remember, O Lord, the aged and infirm, those who feel their life's work is done and can no longer lend a helping hand where once they did; all who are passing through the valley of the shadows, that they may find that the risen Christ is with them, and that there is light at evening time; through the same Jesus Christ our Lord. *When Two or Three*

The anxious and bereaved 1292

Almighty God, who art afflicted in the afflictions of thy people: Regard with thy tender compassion the anxious and bereaved.

Bear their sorrows and cares; give them comfort and peace in thee; and grant them evermore sure trust and confidence in thy fatherly care: through Jesus Christ our Lord.   *Adapted*

A Thanksgiving   1293

We thank thee, O Father, Lord of heaven and earth, for all who hallow pain by triumphing over it; for sufferers whose thought is always for others; for those whose faith brings light to the dark places of life; for those whose patience inspires others to endure. And grant, we beseech thee, O loving Father, to all who are bound together in the mysterious fellowship of suffering, the sense of comradeship with each other and with their crucified Saviour; granting them in this life the peace that passeth all understanding, which the world cannot give nor take away, and in the world to come life everlasting.   *Adapted*

See also prayers for Ministry to the Sick (981–1002) and for Health Services (1183–95)

THOSE IN SPIRITUAL NEED

The unconverted   1294

ALMIGHTY God, we beseech thee to hear our prayers for such as sin against thee or neglect to serve thee; that thou wouldest vouchsafe to bestow upon them true repentance and an earnest longing for thy service; through Jesus Christ our Lord.

Office of Sext

1295

Have compassion, O Lord, upon all who are careless ˏabout *and confused* eternal things and are living without thee and without hope. Send to them the light of thy Holy Spirit to teach them their great need, and in thy tender mercy bring them to the knowledge of thy love, through faith in Jesus Christ our Lord.   *Adapted*

The worldly minded   1296

O God, have mercy on all who live without faith, on all who forget thee amid their worldly business, and on all who are hardened by the deceitfulness of sin, and convert them to thy service, for the merits of Jesus Christ our Lord.   *William Bright*

Those who have erred   1297

Almighty God our heavenly Father, whose property is always to have mercy: We most humbly beseech thee to enlighten by thy Holy Spirit all who have gone astray from the truth of thy holy Word, and to bring them to a due sense of their error, that they may with hearty faith receive and hold fast thine unchangeable truth; through Jesus Christ our Lord.   *Lutheran Church*

1298

Almighty and everliving God, who hast given us the Catholic Faith of Christ for a light to our feet amid the darkness of this world: Have pity on all who, by doubting or denying it, are gone astray from the path of safety; bring home the truth to their hearts, and grant them to receive it as little children; through the same Jesus Christ our Lord.   *William Bright*

1299

O Most blessed Saviour, who art the Way, the Truth, and the Life: Bring back to the fold of thy Church all those who are in error, and subdue the pride of man to the obedience of thy holy laws; and grant that thy truth may be so publicly maintained, constantly taught, humbly believed, and zealously practised by all men in their several stations, that we may dwell together in faith and charity, to the glory of thy holy name, now and for evermore.

Adapted from Jeremy Taylor

The tempted

1300

Almighty God, who gavest thine only begotten Son Jesus Christ to die for the sins of the whole world: Have mercy on all who are in temptation and upon all who through weakness or wilfulness fall into sin; make known to them thy gracious love, and so teach them the evil of hatred and malice, of envy and contempt, of lust and greed, that, turning to thee for help, they may be led into fellowship with thee and obedience to thy will; through Jesus Christ our Lord.

William Temple

1301

Most merciful and faithful High Priest, who didst deign for us to be tempted of the devil: Make speed to aid thy servants who are assaulted by manifold temptations; and as thou knowest their several infirmities, let each one find thee mighty to save; who livest and reignest with the Father and the Holy Ghost, one God, world without end.

The despondent

1302

Comfort, we beseech thee, most gracious God, all who are cast down and faint of heart amidst the sorrows and difficulties of the world: and grant that by the quickening power of thy Holy Spirit they may be lifted up to thee with hope and courage, and be enabled to go upon their way rejoicing in thy love; through Jesus Christ our Lord.

R. M. Benson

The doubting and perplexed

1303

O Lord, our heavenly Father, almighty, everlasting God, who givest light to them that sit in darkness and in the shadow of death: Lift up, we beseech thee, the light of thy countenance upon those who are wandering uncertain and doubtful in the night of this world. Make known to them the way of truth and peace, and open the eyes of their understanding to acknowledge thee, the living God,

Father, Son, and Holy Spirit; to whom be praise and dominion for ever and ever. *South African Prayer Book**

1304

O Lord our God, whose blessed Son has promised that those who follow him shall not walk in darkness but shall have the light of life: Have pity upon all who are afflicted by doubt or perplexity, and grant that they may see thy light in Jesus, and learn, amid the mysteries of life, to walk humbly by faith in him. We ask it for his name's sake.

*

1305

REMEMBER, O Lord, thy Church, to deliver it from all evil and to make it perfect in thy love. Enlarge its borders through the preaching of the everlasting gospel, and gather the faithful from all the ends of the earth into the kingdom which thou hast prepared. For thine is the power and the glory for ever and ever.

Adapted from Didache

1306

O God of unchangeable power and eternal light, look favourably upon thy whole Church and make it the instrument of thy saving purpose for the world; that the life of mankind, redeemed in Christ, may everywhere be renewed, and all things may return into unity through him from whom they took their origin, even the same thy Son Jesus Christ our Lord.

An adaptation of the Gelasian prayer

1307

Almighty and everlasting God, who hast revealed thy glory in Christ to all nations: Protect, we beseech thee, what thy compassion has created, that thy Church which is spread abroad throughout the world may persevere with steadfast faith in the confession of thy name; through the same Jesus Christ our Lord.

Gelasian Sacramentary

1308

O God, Redeemer and Governor of mankind: We beseech thee to grant that thy Church may continually be enlarged by the gathering in of new children to thee, and perfected by the increasing devotion of those who have been regenerated; through Jesus Christ our Lord.

Gelasian Sacramentary

1309

We beseech thee, O Lord, to guide thy Church with thy perpetual governance; that it may walk warily in times of quiet, and boldly in times of trouble; through Jesus Christ our Lord.

Franciscan Breviary

1310

We pray thee, Lord, to guide and uphold thy Church with thy unfailing goodness; that in prosperity it lose not zeal, and in adversity have faith and patient endurance; through Jesus Christ our Lord.

1311

Remember, O Lord, according to the multitude of thy mercies, thy whole Church, all who join with us in prayer, and all our brethren, wherever they may be in thy vast kingdom, who stand in need of thy grace and succour. Pour down upon us all the riches of thy mercy, so that, preserved in soul and body, and steadfast in our faith, we may ever praise thy wonderful and holy name; through Jesus Christ our Lord.

From a prayer of the Eastern Church

1312

Most gracious Father, we most humbly beseech thee for thy holy catholic Church. Fill it with all truth; in all truth with all peace. Where it is corrupt, purge it; where it is in error, direct it; where anything is amiss, reform it; where it is right, strengthen and confirm it; where it is in want, furnish it; where it is divided, heal it, and unite it in thy love; through Jesus Christ our Lord.

William Laud*

1313

Preserve, O God, the catholic Church in holiness and truth, in unity and peace, free from persecution, or glorious under it; that she may advance the honour of her Lord Jesus, for ever represent his sacrifice, and glorify his person, and advance his religion, and be accepted of thee in her blessed Lord, that being filled with his Spirit she may partake of his glory.

Jeremy Taylor

1314

O God, let thy mercy descend upon thy whole Church; preserve her in truth and peace, in unity and safety, in all storms and against all enemies; that she, offering to thy glory the never-ceasing sacrifice of prayer and thanksgiving, may advance the honour of her Lord, and be filled with his Spirit, and partake of his glory; through the same Jesus Christ our Lord.

Jeremy Taylor

1315

O Lord God, we pray for thy whole Church throughout the world. May her witness be faithful and her worship sincere; may her divisions be healed and her life renewed; and may all her members be bound together in loving service to one another and in true devotion to thee; for the sake of Jesus Christ our Lord.

1316

O Lord, we beseech thee to maintain thy Church in truth and patience; that her pastors may be faithful, her watchmen vigilant, her flock loyal, her camp united, her war spiritual, her weapons heavenly, her lamp burning and shining; and as thy Son Jesus Christ hath given so great a price for us, let us not count it a hard thing to give up all for him, and to spend and be spent for the souls he hath redeemed; who liveth and reigneth with thee and the Holy Ghost, now and for evermore.   *Percy Dearmer*

1317

Remember in thy mercy, O Lord our God, thy holy Church throughout the world. Heal its divisions; restore its unity; quicken its life; empower its witness; that so it may become the instrument of thy purpose for the reconciliation of mankind and the healing of the nations; through our Saviour Jesus Christ.

Frank Colquhoun

1318

O Most Holy Spirit of God, from whom alone floweth the fullness of wisdom and life: Come in thine everlasting power and glory, we beseech thee, upon thy Church, and into the hearts of all men, to bring to the world a new birth of righteousness, new understanding of truth, and new unity in love; through Jesus Christ our Lord.

New Every Morning

The revival of the Church   1319

Almighty God, our heavenly Father, whose Son Jesus Christ came to cast fire upon the earth: Grant that by the prayers of thy faithful people a fire of burning zeal may be kindled, and pass from heart to heart, till all our hardness is melted in the warmth of thy love; through him who loved us and gave himself for us, Jesus Christ our Lord.   *G. C. Binyon*

1320

Almighty and most merciful God, remember, we beseech thee, thy holy Church throughout the world. Send down upon thy ministers, and upon the congregations committed to their charge, the quickening spirit of thy grace; unite all true followers of Christ in the bond of a holy faith as one body; and so fill us all with the power of thy Holy Spirit, that we may bring forth abundantly the fruits of truth and goodness; through Jesus Christ our Lord.

1321

O Lord Jesus Christ, we beseech thee to quicken and purify thy holy Church, against which thou hast promised that the powers of death shall never prevail; revive the ancient fires of devotion and zeal, and kindle in the hearts of all thy people a new spirit of prayer and adventure; for the glory of thy name, who livest and reignest with the Father and the Holy Spirit ever one God, world without end.

1322

O God, who from time to time dost send a gracious rain upon thine inheritance, refreshing it when it is weary: Hearken now, we beseech thee, to the supplications of thy people, who confess their need of thy quickening grace. Revive us by the Holy Ghost, the giver of life; that all men may see and know that thou art in the midst of us, who are called by thy name; through Jesus Christ our Lord.

1323

God, our Shepherd, give to the Church a new vision and a new charity, new wisdom and fresh understanding, the revival of her brightness and the renewal of her unity; that the eternal message of thy Son, undefiled by the traditions of men, may be hailed as the good news of the new age; through him who maketh all things new, Jesus Christ our Lord. *Percy Dearmer*

1324

Eternal and gracious God, who art slow to anger and of great kindness: Have mercy upon thy faithless and backsliding Church. We mourn, and confess to thee, our sins, the poverty of our devotion and the weakness of our testimony. Pardon, cleanse and restore us, we humbly beseech thee. Fill us with the power of thy Holy Spirit, that we thy people may be humbled and sanctified, and that the multitudes who are lost to thee may be convicted of their sins and converted to their Saviour; for the glory of his saving name. *J. R. W. Stott*

1325

Almighty and everlasting God, who didst form thy Church to be of one heart and one soul in the power of the resurrection and the fellowship of the Holy Spirit: Renew her evermore in her first love; and grant to thy people such a measure of thy grace that their life may be hallowed, their way directed, and their work made fruitful to the good of thy Church and the glory of thy holy name; through the same Jesus Christ our Lord. *Community of the Resurrection*

1326

O Heavenly Father, who saveth not by might, nor by power, but by thy Spirit: We humbly beseech thee to pour out thy Holy Spirit from on high and to revive thy work in the midst of the years. Grant to thy Church Universal a new vision of thy glory, a new experience of thy power, a new fidelity to thy Word, a new consecration to thy service; that through the witness of a renewed and dedicated people thy holy name may be glorified and thy blessed kingdom advanced in all the world; through Jesus Christ our Lord.

Frank Colquhoun

The unity of the Church   1327

Almighty God, who art one Lord, and hast called us to glorify thee as one body in Christ: We earnestly pray for the restoration of the visible unity of the catholic Church; that all who confess thy holy name may be reunited, as at the beginning, in the apostles' teaching and fellowship, in the breaking of bread and in prayers. Remove from us and from others all suspicions and prejudices and whatever may hinder thy purpose; and endue us with such love towards thee and towards one another that we may be one in thee; to whom be all praise and glory, now and for evermore.

Adapted

1328

We commend to thee, Almighty God, the whole Christian Church throughout the world. Bless all in every place who call on the name of our Lord Jesus Christ. May the grace and power of the Holy Spirit fill every member, so that all the company of thy faithful people may bear witness for thee on the earth. If it be good in thy sight, heal the outward divisions of thy people, disposing the wills of all to a true union of order in the truth, for the work of the one Lord. And above all we pray for the unity of the Spirit, through whom alone we are guided into all truth; through the same Jesus Christ our Lord.   *Handley C. G. Moule★*

1329

O God, the physician of men and of nations, the restorer of the years that have been destroyed: Look upon the distractions of the world and the divisions of thy Church, and be pleased to stretch forth thy healing hand. Draw all men unto thee and one to another by the bands of thy love; make thy Church one, and fill it with thy Holy Spirit, that by thy power it may unite the world in a sacred brotherhood of nations, wherein justice and mercy, truth and freedom, may flourish and thou mayest be for ever glorified; through Jesus Christ our Lord.   *William Temple*

1330

O God our Father, in whom is all quietness and concord: Teach us to overcome all dissensions within thy Church which divide us from one another and from thee; and by thy grace make us all one in thee by the uniting power of true faith and fervent charity, so that thy Church may patiently serve and glorify thee; through Jesus Christ our Lord. *Lambeth Conference, 1958*

1331

Almighty and everlasting God, who by thy holy apostle hast taught us to make prayers and supplications for all men: We humbly beseech thee to inspire continually the universal Church with the spirit of truth, unity, and concord; and grant that all they that do confess thy holy name may agree in the truth of thy holy Word, and live in unity and godly love; through Jesus Christ our Lord. *Adapted from Book of Common Prayer*

1332

O God, who art the Father of all, and who alone makest men to be of one mind in a house; We beseech thee to grant to us, by the inspiration of thy Holy Spirit, a fuller realization of our brotherhood in thee. Enlarge our sympathies; remove all prejudice and bitterness; and deepen our understanding one of another; for the sake of thy Son our Lord Jesus Christ.

1333

O God of peace, good beyond all that is good, in whom is calmness and concord: Do thou make up the dissensions which divide us from one another, and bring us into unity of love in thee; through Jesus Christ our Lord. *Liturgy of St. Dionysius*

1334

O Lord Jesus Christ, who on the night before thy passion didst pray for the unity of thy people: Touch the hearts of all who believe in thee, that we may love one another, as thou didst command, and may realize our oneness in thee. Illuminate by thy Spirit the minds of those who seek to overcome the differences which divide us, so that we, growing in knowledge of thy truth and thy purpose, may indeed be knit together in one communion and fellowship within thy holy Church; who livest and reignest with the Father and the same Spirit, ever one God, world without end.

See also Week of Prayer for Christian Unity, 656–67

The Church in persecution   1335

O God, our refuge and strength, who art a very present help in trouble: Have mercy upon thy Church in the midst of oppression and persecution. Deliver thy people by thy mighty aid from tyranny and wrong; keep them faithful in the hour of trial; and restore to them the blessings of freedom and peace; through Jesus Christ our Lord.   *Adapted*

1336

Blessed Lord, who thyself didst undergo the pain and suffering of the cross: Uphold, we beseech thee, with thy promised gift of strength all those of our brethren who are suffering for their faith in thee; that from their steadfastness thy Church may grow in grace, and we ourselves increase in perseverance, to the honour of thy holy name; who with the Father and the Holy Spirit art ever one God, world without end.

1337

Be merciful, O Father of all mercies, to thy Church universal dispersed throughout the whole world, that all thy faithful people may have grace to confess thy holy name; and especially be merciful to such as are under persecution for their testimony, and their profession of the gospel; that as they stand fast for thy holy Word, so they may be upheld by it; through thy Son our Saviour Jesus Christ.   *After Prayers of 1585*

1338

O God, we remember especially before thee those who are facing hardship, danger and persecution for thy name's sake. Uphold them in their need; give them strength to endure; and may their example inspire us to more courageous service, that we together with them may strive for the advancement of thy kingdom throughout the world; for Jesus Christ our Saviour's sake.
    Adapted

1339

Look with mercy, O God, upon our brethren who are witnesses for thee amidst the conflicts of faiths and peoples, and upon all who suffer for thy name and gospel. Give them patience, constancy and steadfast hope. Make them mediators in time of strife, turning the hearts of those at enmity, that thy kingdom may be advanced and thy Church strengthened by adversity; through Jesus Christ our Lord.

Church leaders 1340

O God, who of old didst give thy Holy Spirit to the elders of thy people: Grant, we beseech thee, wisdom and courage to the bishops and pastors of thy flock, that they may have a right judgment in all things, and be enabled to discern and to use what thy divine providence has ordained at this time for the good of thy people, and the extension of thy kingdom; through Jesus Christ our Lord.

1341

O Almighty God, who hast given to thy Church apostles, prophets, evangelists, pastors and teachers, for the perfecting of the saints, for the work of the ministry, for the edifying of the body of Christ: Grant that all those whom thou dost call to this thy service may labour faithfully and effectually in the same; till we all come in the unity of the faith, and of the knowledge of the Son of God, to the measure of the stature of the fullness of Christ; to whom be praise and glory, now and for evermore.

Based on Ephesians 4. 11–13

1342

Spirit of the living God, source of light and life, who in the days of old didst speak to men by prophets and guided them through apostles into the way of righteousness and truth: We beseech thee to raise up in these days an increasing number of wise and faithful men, filled with prophetic fire and apostolic zeal, by whose ministry the Church may be quickened and thy kingdom greatly advanced; for the glory of Jesus Christ our Lord.

A Book of Prayers for Students

The world-wide commission **1343**

O GOD, who didst choose for thyself a nation to be thy agent in
the world and when it failed thee didst recreate it in the Church
of thy Son: Grant that thy Church may be truly the body of Christ,
giving itself for the world as thou didst give thy Son and as he did
give his life. Let thy Church be a light to the nations, the messenger
of thy gospel, the agent of thy salvation. And to us who are members
of thy body, give faithfulness, obedience, zeal and love, that thy wise
and loving purpose may be accomplished and all men may know
thee as their God and Saviour, through Jesus Christ our Lord.

George Appleton

1344

O Saviour Christ, we pray thee for the millions who have never
heard thy name or known thy love. Make thyself known to them in
whatever state they be. Help us to proclaim thy gospel in urgency
and love, that men may not be left to live without thee or die without
thee, but may know with us the joy of sins forgiven, of overflowing
grace, of peace in life and death, and of good things prepared for
them that love thee. O Saviour of the world, fetch them home
that they may be saved for ever. *George Appleton*

1345

Remember for good, we beseech thee, O Lord, the missionary
work of thy Church throughout the world. Protect and provide
for thy servants in the mission fields, and bestow upon them all
things needful for their work. And give to the churches abroad
and to us at home such an increased spirit of faith, sacrifice and
service, that the work of the gospel may not be hindered, but that
in every land thy kingdom may be advanced; through Jesus Christ
our Lord. *C. C. B. Bardsley**

1346

Make thyself known, O Christ, throughout the world which thou
didst die to save. Reveal thyself among all nations, amid all people, and
across all barriers. Renew thy Church with love and power, that the
kingdoms of this world may become thine own; who with the Father
and the Holy Spirit livest and reignest one God, for ever and ever.

1347

O God, who by thy Son Jesus Christ didst command thine apostles to preach the gospel to every creature: Prosper, we pray thee all missions of thy Church. Send forth labourers into thy harvest, and grant such success to their labours that thy kingdom may be extended among the nations, till the whole earth be filled with the knowledge of thy love; through the same Jesus Christ our Lord. *Adapted*

1348

O God, our heavenly Father, as we thank thee for thy love to us and above all for the gift of thy dear Son to die for us, we pray thee for all who do not know thy love and have never heard of our Saviour Jesus Christ. Bless all who work in other lands as messengers of thy truth; and help us here at home by our prayers and offerings to hasten the coming of the kingdom of thy love; through Jesus Christ our Lord.

1349

O Christ, our Lord, whose resurrection did turn thy timid disciples into men of courage and daring: Let thy risen power come upon thy Church that she may be bold to proclaim thy saving truth to the world. Grant her such a love of the souls of men that she may draw all men into thy family and so into union with thee, who with the Father and the Holy Spirit art our God for ever and ever.
George Appleton

Missionaries 1350

Bestow, O Lord, thy heavenly grace upon all who are called to be fellow-workers with thee, that by them Christ may be lifted up in every land and all men be drawn to him. In times of loneliness and weariness cheer them with thy presence; in disappointment give them patience; in failure give them strength to persevere; and at all times deepen in them the sense of dependence upon thee, and give them peace in thy service; through Jesus Christ our Lord.

1351

O Blessed Lord, who hast commanded thy Church to bear witness to thee among all nations: We beseech thee to give the assurance of thy presence to those who have gone forth as thy ambassadors in distant lands. Sanctify them, we beseech thee, with the Holy Spirit; teach them to endure hardship; gird them with thy truth; make their hearts burn with thy love; and use them in thy service for the furtherance of the gospel, and for the honour and glory of thy holy name.

1352

Almighty God, who hast called the Church out of the world that she might bring the world to thee: Make her faithful, we beseech thee, in the work thou hast entrusted to her hands. Bless and uphold thy servants who are gone forth in her name to preach the gospel in distant lands; be with them in weariness and painfulness, in discouragement and persecution; endue them with power from on high; and so prosper their labours by thy Holy Spirit that the time may be hastened when all the kindreds of the nations shall worship before thee; through Jesus Christ our Lord.

Book of Common Order

Our part   1353

O Most merciful Father, we confess that we have done little to forward thy kingdom in the world and to advance thy glory. Pardon, we pray thee, our shortcomings; give us greater zeal for thy glory; and make us more ready and diligent by our prayers, our gifts and our example to spread abroad the knowledge of thy truth and to enlarge the boundaries of thy kingdom; through Jesus Christ our Lord.   *W. Walsham How**

1354

Lord of all power and might, who hast commanded thy Church to preach the Word and make disciples of all nations: Inflame us with the fire of thy love, that we may give ourselves, our time and our money, as faithful stewards of the gospel, to the honour and glory of thy holy name; who livest and reignest with the Father and the Holy Spirit, one God, world without end.

1355

O Saviour of the world, who by thy cross didst finish thy great work for the redemption of mankind: Bless the witness of thy Church, and help us to finish the work which thou hast given us to do in making thy love known in all the world; for thy name's sake.

1356

Almighty God, our heavenly Father, who didst send thine only Son to redeem the world: Vouchsafe to thy Church at this time we beseech thee, a new responsiveness to thy call to proclaim to all men the everlasting gospel of thy grace. Forgive us for our past negligence in thy service, our lack of zeal, our little faith; and help us so to dedicate ourselves to thee that thy work may prosper in our hands, and thy name be hallowed in all the world; through Jesus Christ our Lord.

1357

O Lord Christ, to whom all authority has been given in heaven and on earth, and who hast charged thy Church to make disciples of all nations: Kindle within us, we pray thee, such a spirit of devotion and zeal that we may ever obey thy Word, and serve thy purpose, and advance thy kingdom in the world; for the glory of thy name. *Frank Colquhoun*

1358

O God, we thank thee that thou hast called us into the fellowship of thy world-wide Church. Unite us, and all its members everywhere, in love and loyalty to carry out thy purpose of love in the world, that we fail thee not in this day of opportunity; through Jesus Christ our Lord.

Missionary recruits **1359**

Almighty God, who by thy Son Jesus Christ didst give commandment to the apostles that they should go into all the world, and preach the gospel to every creature: Raise up, we beseech thee, true and faithful men to continue that work in this our day, that they may seek and find thy sheep dispersed and lost, and bring them home to thy flock; and grant us grace to labour with them by our prayers and offerings for the furtherance of thy kingdom among men; through the same Jesus Christ our Lord.

*Canadian Prayer Book**

1360

O Lord Jesus Christ, who callest to thee whom thou willest and sendest them whither thou dost choose: We give thanks to thee for those who were first sent to preach thy gospel in our own land; and we humbly pray thee to raise up among us those who shall be heralds and evangelists of thy kingdom in our own day, and shall build up thy Church in every land; who livest and reignest with the Father and the Holy Spirit, one God world without end.

1361

O Christ, Teacher and Saviour of men, who didst train thy disciples to do thy work in thy way: Call into the service of thy Church, we pray thee, men and women of thine own heart and choice. And that they may truly serve thee, pour upon them thy Holy Spirit that they may be humble and wise, understanding and kind; for the true serving of thy will and the showing forth of thy way among men, to thy honour and glory.

The sending forth of missionaries 1362

Blessed be thou, O Lord our God, because thou dost call thy servants to be witnesses to thy Son in every land, even unto the uttermost parts of the earth, that through them he may establish and strengthen his kingdom, for the salvation of the world. Graciously behold those who now set forth in thy name, to whom thou hast given this great honour; that they, holding fast to thee, may faithfully accomplish the work which thou wouldest have done; through the same Jesus Christ our Lord.

Praying for the Church Overseas

Returning missionaries 1363

We commend to thy mercy, O Lord our God, thy servants who are about to return to the work to which thou hast called them. As they go forth again in obedience to thy call, so may they go in thy strength and under thy care. Guard and guide them in all their work for thee; keep them in health of body and peace of mind; and use them abundantly for the furtherance of the gospel and the glory of thy name; through Jesus Christ our Lord.

Frank Colquhoun

A missionary diocese 1364

O God our Father, from whom cometh every good and perfect gift: Send thy blessing, we pray thee, upon the diocese of ——, upon thy servant *N.*, its bishop, his clergy, and all his fellow workers; that by their teaching and example they may strengthen their brethren, promote the unity of the Church, and commend the gospel to all who have not known thy redeeming love; through thy Son Jesus Christ our Lord.

1365

O Lord God, who willest that all men should be saved and come to the knowledge of thy Son, our Saviour: Give thy Holy Spirit to all in thy Church in the diocese of ——; that by the setting forth of Christ as Saviour many may find new life, and thy Church be extended and united in her true work of bringing men to thee; in the name and power of Jesus Christ our Lord.

Diocese of Uganda

Those young in the faith 1366

O Lord Jesus Christ, who art the Way, the Truth and the Life: Bless and build up in the fellowship of thy Church all who are young in the faith. Deliver them from idolatry, superstition and fear; instruct them in the truth of thy holy gospel; endue them with constancy, and establish them in holiness and righteousness; for the honour and glory of thy name.

Our countrymen abroad   1367

O God, who art in every place: We pray for our fellow country-men abroad, that as they move among men, busy with affairs of government and commerce, they may uphold the honour of Christ's kingdom and bear witness to his name; through the same Jesus Christ our Lord.

The Jews   1368

O God, who didst choose Israel to be thine inheritance: Look, we beseech thee, upon thy chosen people; take away the blindness which is fallen upon them; grant that they may see and confess the Lord Jesus to be thy Son and their true Messiah, and that, believing, they may have life through his name; through the merits of the same Jesus Christ our Lord.   *Canadian Prayer Book**

1369

O God, of all the nations of the earth, remember thine own people the Jews, who though the heirs of thine everlasting covenant are ignorant of thy saving love in Christ. Take away their blindness and open their eyes to the fullness of thy truth. Write thy law upon their hearts and make them wise unto salvation, that they may know thee the only true God, and Jesus Christ whom thou hast sent; through the same Jesus Christ our Lord.

Church's Ministry among the Jews

The Moslem world   1370

Almighty God, our heavenly Father, have mercy upon the Mus-lims and all others who are strangers to thy redeeming love; and grant that thy Church may so powerfully exhibit to them the saving truth of the gospel that they may be brought to confess thy Son Jesus Christ as their Prophet, Priest and King, and to share with us the fellowship of the Spirit, to the glory of thy name; through the merits of the death and passion of the same thy Son, Jesus Christ our Lord.

Followers of the religions of the East   1371

O God, who willest that all men should come to the knowledge of the truth, and hast not left thyself without witness anywhere in the world: We pray for Hindus, Buddhists and all others who are seeking after thee through the good that is known to them. We beseech thee to illuminate their hearts and minds with the knowledge of thy glory in the face of Jesus Christ, that henceforth they may walk in thy light and in thy love; through the same Jesus Christ our Lord. *Adapted*

Christian literature 1372
O Almighty God, who hast hallowed words to be an instrument of thy Word: We beseech thee to direct and use the labours of all Christian writers and translators, and of those who distribute Christian literature, to the advancement of the knowledge of thy love among the nations of the world, and the building up of thy Church in every land; through Jesus Christ our Lord.
Adapted from a prayer of S.P.C.K.

1373
Almighty and everlasting God, whose Word alone is truth: Hear us as we pray now for those millions who have lately learned to read, or who will shortly become literate. Protect them, we beseech thee, from the poison of evil literature, and grant thy help to those who strive to provide them with Christian books; that thy saving truth may be made available to all mankind, and thy light may shine in earth's darkest places; through Jesus Christ our Lord.

1374
Almighty God, who hast taught us that man shall not live by bread alone but by every word that proceedeth out of thy mouth: We remember before thee the spiritual hunger of the world. Give grace to those who are teaching the multitudes to read. Raise up gifted authors to expound thy truth with clarity and power. Prosper the work of all who are engaged in the production and distribution of Christian literature; and grant that everywhere the entrance of thy words may give light and understanding; through Jesus Christ our Lord. *J. R. W. Stott*

1375
O God, our Father, grant to the seeking millions of mankind the experience of thy redeeming love in Jesus Christ. Give guidance to all who attempt to widen the outreach of the gospel through the use of Christian literature. Where no man may enter, nor human voice be heard, may the written word call to penitence, faith and discipleship, by the power of thy Holy Spirit, through Jesus Christ our Lord. *United Society for Christian Literature*

Bible translators 1376
Almighty God, who dost reveal thyself to us through the written Word: We thank thee for all who have worked so that we may

know that Word in our own tongue. We pray thee to inspire with thy Holy Spirit all who are now translating the Scriptures into other languages, that by thy blessing upon their work the Word of the Lord may have free course and be glorified; through Jesus Christ our Saviour.

The Bible in the world   1377

O God, who hast given thy Word to be a lamp unto our feet and a light upon our path: Prosper, we beseech thee, the work of the British and Foreign Bible Society, and increase the support it receives from all who love thy Word. Guide with thy wisdom those who translate the Scriptures; remember in thy goodness those who distribute them; and grant success to all who teach others to read. May the witness of thy Church and the inward testimony of thy Spirit bring all who study the Bible to the knowledge and love of Christ, our Lord and only Saviour.   *James M. Todd*

Medical missions   1378

O Lord Jesus Christ, physician of men and nations, who didst show thy love by healing all manner of sickness and disease: Bless, we beseech thee, all doctors and nurses who are serving in missionary hospitals and dispensaries, and all who are preparing for this service. Give to them the joy of dedicated lives which reveal thy power and thy love; for thy name's sake.

1379

Almighty God, who in thy great love towards mankind didst send thy Son to be the physician both of the body and of the soul: Bless, we pray thee, the ministry of thy servants now working in mission hospitals and dispensaries of countries overseas; and so prosper them that thy way may be known upon earth, thy saving health among all nations; through the same Jesus Christ our Lord.

A parish missionary campaign   1380

Almighty and most merciful Father, who didst give thine only Son for the sins of the whole world, and didst send thy Holy Spirit that the Church should be his witness in all the earth: Pour out thy blessing upon those taking part in this campaign, and open the hearts of the hearers to receive thy message delivered by them; so that a deeper interest in missionary work may be aroused at home, and thy kingdom be advanced overseas; for the honour of Jesus Christ our Lord.   *A Book of Prayers for Students**

A missionary sale   1381

Almighty God, our heavenly Father, bless, we pray thee, our work which we now present and dedicate to thee for the extension of thy kingdom in the world; and make us so thankful for the precious gift to us of thy beloved Son, that we may pray fervently, labour diligently, and give liberally to make him known to all nations as their Saviour and King; through the same Jesus Christ our Lord.   *Francis J. Moore**

See also prayers for a Missionary Festival, 753–65

THE CHURCH AT HOME

Church and nation **1382**

ALMIGHTY and merciful God, who in days of old didst give to
this land the benediction of thy holy Church: Withdraw not,
we pray thee, thy favour from us, but so correct what is amiss, and
supply what is lacking, that we may more and more bring forth
fruit to thy glory; through Jesus Christ our Lord.

Irish Prayer Book

1383

Almighty God, who dost from age to age revive and inspire thy
Church: Look graciously upon that branch of it which thou hast
planted in this land; and grant that we and all thy people, being
mindful of thy great goodness, may be worthy of the rich heritage
which thou hast given to us, and with zeal and courage, faithfulness
and love, may show forth our gratitude in service of our nation and
the world; through Jesus Christ our Lord. *Adapted*

1384

We give thee thanks, Almighty Father, for thy gifts to this
nation in times past through thy Church; and we pray thee so to
quicken the life of the Church in this our day that, bearing faithful
witness to the gospel of thy love, it may draw the people of our
land to thyself and unite them in a sacred brotherhood wherein
justice and mercy, truth and freedom, may flourish and abound, to
the glory of thy name; through Jesus Christ our Lord. *Adapted*

1385

O Lord, we beseech thee to visit with thy grace and heavenly
benediction thy Church in this land. Give to our bishops and
pastors wisdom and holiness and unwearied zeal for souls; bestow
upon thy people the increase of faith, and hope, and love; and grant
us to be of one heart and mind, that we may diligently do thy will
and show forth thy glory before the world; through Jesus Christ
our Lord. *W. Bellars**

1386

Bestow thy blessing, we beseech thee, O Lord, upon thy Church
and thy ministers everywhere. May increasing multitudes hear thy

Word, receive it, and live by it. May its power be seen more and more in the lives of them that believe. So work thy great work Almighty God, in this our country, and in this our generation, that the doubter may be convinced, the wavering established, the sinful converted and the gainsayer silenced; and grant that at the last, according to thy blessed Word of prophecy, the Lord may be king over all the earth, one Lord and his name one; through Jesus Christ our Lord.   *C. J. Vaughan*

1387

O Lord Jesus Christ, who didst charge thine apostles to preach the gospel to every creature: Prosper, we pray thee, the work of thy Church in this land. Give vision and courage to our bishops and all who exercise spiritual leadership; and so inflame the hearts of thy people with burning love that they may be moved to share with others the blessings of thy redeeming love; who livest and reignest with the Father and the Holy Spirit, one God, for ever and ever.

1388

Almighty God, whose mercy reaches unto the heavens and thy faithfulness unto the clouds: We bless thee for thy gracious providence towards our nation in the creation, preservation and reformation of thy Church within its borders; and we beseech thee to stretch forth thy mighty hand in this our day to purge us from sin, to establish us in truth, to unite us in love, and to inspire us with zeal for the extension of thy kingdom; through Jesus Christ our Lord.   *J. R. W. Stott*

1389

Continue, O Lord, thy most holy Word and gospel in this realm of England, and grant that we may truly and thankfully embrace it. Give peace to thy Church from external troubles and persecutions, and from domestic discord and dissension; that all who profess thy Word and gospel may have the same as well in heart as in mouth; for thy name's sake and for thy Christ's sake.
From an ancient prayer

A diocese 1390

O Merciful Father, who wouldest not that any should perish, but that all should come to repentance: Strengthen, we humbly beseech thee, the hands of those who are labouring for the extension of thy kingdom in this diocese. Endow the bishops and all the clergy with the needful grace, wisdom and health for their work; give to them, and to all who work in our parishes, courage and faithfulness to persevere amidst all difficulties. Stir up the zeal and love of many, that they may offer themselves for some work in thy service; and grant that all, both clergy and laity, may labour with a single eye to thy glory, and in the spirit of love and self-sacrifice; through Jesus Christ our Lord. *Southwark Diocese*

1391

O Lord God, our ruler and guide, who from generation to generation dost grant to thy people the direction of thy wise and loving Spirit: Be present, we pray thee, with us to whom thou hast given in trust the welfare of this diocese. Unite us ever more closely in the fellowship of faith and devotion; and so lead us in all our works and ways that thy people may faithfully serve thee, to the glory of thy name, the extension of thy Church, and the coming of thy kingdom; through Jesus Christ our Lord.

Adapted from a prayer of A. E. Daldy

1392

O God, who hast called us to be members together of thy Church, which is the body of thy Son: Pour out, we beseech thee, thy Spirit on this diocese. Endue with strength and love and wisdom all who bear authority therein. Accept our gifts, our labours, and our love, and use them for the advancement of thy kingdom and the glory of thy name. Lead us in all our work for thee, and unite us in the joyful service of thy Son, our Saviour Jesus Christ. *C. M. Blagden*

1393

O God, who hast graciously united us in a goodly fellowship: We pray for thy Church in this diocese and for thy people in our parishes, that comeliness of worship, preaching of the faith, and holiness of living may always abound and everywhere be spread abroad among us; through Jesus Christ our Lord.

After A. J. Mason

The bishops 1394

Almighty God, who by thy Son Jesus Christ didst give to thy holy apostles many excellent gifts, and didst charge them to feed thy flock: Give thy grace, we beseech thee, to all bishops, the pastors of thy Church, that they may diligently preach thy Word, and duly administer the godly discipline thereof; and grant to the people that they may obediently follow the same; that all may receive the crown of everlasting glory; through Jesus Christ our Lord.

Adapted from Book of Common Prayer

A diocesan bishop 1395

O God, the Pastor and Ruler of thy Church, look down in mercy on thy servant *N.*, our bishop, to whom thou hast given charge over this diocese; and so direct and defend him by thy grace that he may, by word and good example, lead the flock committed to him into the ways of truth and love, holiness and peace; through him who is the good Shepherd, thy Son Jesus Christ our Lord.

Adapted

A cathedral 1396

O God, the King of glory, who art ever adored by thy holy angels, yet delightest in the praises of the sons of men: Prosper with thy blessing, we beseech thee, the work of our cathedral church; that they who minister or worship therein may offer unto thee true and laudable service, for thy honour and glory; through Jesus Christ our Lord.

The parishes of our land 1397

O Lord Jesus Christ, who didst go, as thy custom was, into the synagogue on the sabbath day: Quicken with thy abiding presence the life of thy Church in the parishes; and grant that every parish church in our land may be as a city set on a hill, a witness to thy claims upon our worship and service, a power-house of prayer, and a joy and comfort to thy servants. Hear us from thy throne in heaven, where with the Father and the Holy Ghost thou livest and reignest, one God, world without end. *Peter Green*

Convocation or Church Assembly 1398

Eternal Father, who wouldest make the Church of thy dear Son a city great and fair, the joy of the whole earth: We beseech thee, by the sending of thy Holy Spirit, to direct its counsels in all manner of wisdom, love, and might. Remove perplexity, establish concord, kindle flame; and gather a people single and strong of faith, to the praise of him who with thee and the same Spirit liveth and reigneth, one God, world without end. *Lambeth Conference, 1930*

1399

O Lord God, our heavenly Father, we humbly beseech thee to look with thy favour upon the bishops, clergy and laity who take counsel together at this time in the Church Assembly. Mercifully grant that thy Holy Spirit may rest upon them, to enlighten and guide them; that all their consultations may be prospered to the advancement of thy glory and the welfare of thy Church; through Jesus Christ our Lord.

The Anglican Communion 1400

O Almighty God, our heavenly Father, who hast called us to be members of the Anglican Communion and to a partnership of churches in all parts of the world: Grant, we beseech thee, that we may understand the mission which thou hast entrusted to us, and our duty to those who are separated from us; that penitently recognizing our failings in the past, we may go forward in unity and love to the fulfilment of our common work; through Jesus Christ our Lord.

Based on a prayer of the Pan-Anglican Congress, 1908

1401

Almighty God, our heavenly Father, who in thy providence hast made us members of a great family of churches: We pray thee to pour out thy blessing upon the Anglican Communion throughout the world. Grant that we and all its members may be faithful to the trust which thou hast committed to us, and advance thy honour in the cause of Christian unity and mission; through Jesus Christ our Lord.

Religious communities 1402

O Lord, who for our sakes didst become poor, that we through thy poverty might be made rich: Strengthen and sanctify, we pray thee, all religious communities, that they may enrich thy Church by their gifts of prayer and service; and grant that all their members, living before thee with a single eye to thy glory, may accomplish the work of their vocation; who livest and reignest with the Father, in the unity of the Holy Spirit, ever one God, world without end. *South African Prayer Book*

1403

We beseech thee, O Lord, to bless all those who, at thy call, have left possessions, parents, hope of house and children, and their own wills also, that they might take up the cross and follow thee in holy poverty, obedience, and chastity. Give them plentifully of thy grace, that, through the consecration of their lives and the power of their prayers, they may strengthen the Church and draw many to love and worship thee; through our Lord Jesus Christ.

EVANGELISM

Home missions **1404**

O LORD Jesus Christ, thou good Shepherd of the sheep, we beseech thee to be present in thy power with the missions of thy Church in this our land. Show forth thy compassion to all who are out of the way, and bring them home in safety to thy fold; who livest and reignest with the Father and the Holy Spirit, one God, world without end. *Adapted from Irish Prayer Book*

1405

O Lord Jesus Christ, great Shepherd of the sheep, who seekest those that are gone astray, bindest up those that are broken, and healest those that are sick: Bless, we beseech thee, all efforts that are made to convert souls unto thee. Open the deaf ears of the wandering, that they may hear the words which belong unto their peace; and grant that those whom thou dost raise to newness of life may through thy grace persevere unto the end, of thy mercy, blessed Lord, who livest and reignest with the Father and the Holy Spirit, one God, world without end. *R. M. Benson*

1406

Merciful and gracious Father, who wouldest have all men to be saved and to come to the knowledge of the truth: Stir in the hearts of the clergy a desire to do the work of an evangelist and to make full proof of their ministry; that so those who are as yet unconverted may hear thy summons to choose whom they will serve and may own thee Lord of all; for Jesus Christ's sake. *Peter Green*

1407

Lord Jesus, our Master, who at thy first coming didst send out messengers into every village and town before thee, to announce the good news of thy coming and to call to repentance of sin: We pray thee to go forth with those whom thou sendest now in England, as then in Galilee; that all may hear thy voice and obey thy call, and may make themselves ready for the coming of thy kingdom; to the glory of thy name, who ever livest and reignest, Jesus Christ our Lord. *National Mission, 1916*

1408

Almighty God, to forget whom is to stumble and fall, to remember whom is to rise again: We pray thee to draw the people of this country to thyself; prosper all efforts to make known to them the truth of thy gospel; that many may learn their need of thee and thy love for them, and that so thy Church and kingdom may be established to the glory of thy name; through Jesus Christ our Lord.

A parish mission *Church May in this benefice* **1409**

O God, send thy blessing upon the ~~mission to be held in this place;~~ and grant that Jesus Christ may be so presented in the power of the Holy Spirit that many may come to put their trust in thee through him, to accept him as their Saviour and serve him as their King in the fellowship of his Church; for the honour of thy holy name.

1410

O God, our heavenly Father, we pray thee to bless the mission to this parish. Prepare the hearts of the people for thy message, and fill the missioners and those taking part with thy Holy Spirit, that many souls may be won for him who is the Way, the Truth and the Life, thy Son Jesus Christ our Lord.   *Church Army*

1411

O God, our heavenly Father, we humbly pray thee to bless abundantly the efforts that are now being made (*or*, about to be made) to turn the people of this parish to thyself in sincere repentance and living faith. Prepare all hearts to receive the seed of thy Word, and grant that it may take deep root and bring forth fruit to thy glory; through Jesus Christ our Lord.

Adapted from Irish Prayer Book

1412

O God, our heavenly Father, we humbly pray thee to pour out thy Holy Spirit upon the mission in this parish. Give power to the preaching of the gospel, that it may be good news indeed to those who hear it. Arouse the careless, convict the sinful, humble the self-righteous, restore the backsliding. Get glory to thy holy name, and visit us with thy salvation; through Jesus Christ our Lord.

Frank Colquhoun

1413

Almighty Father, whose blessed Son came to seek and to save that which was lost: We pray thee to use for thine own glory the

mission to be held in this parish. Prepare and empower thy servant
the missioner; revive and sanctify thy people; and bring many
souls to a knowledge of thyself; through Jesus Christ our Lord.

1414

O Heavenly Father, prosper with thy blessing, we pray thee, the
mission to be held in this parish, and use it for the winning of many
souls to Christ and his Church. Prepare the hearts of all to hear
thy Word; give thy grace to the missioner and to those who work
with him; and show us each one what thou wouldest have us to do;
for the sake of Jesus Christ our Saviour.   *Frank Colquhoun*
See also 1437–8

Commissioning of missioners   **1415**
God the Father, God the Son, God the Holy Ghost, bless, pre-
serve and keep you. The love of God the Father encompass you.
The presence of God the Son uphold you. The power of God the
Spirit rest upon you. Go forth in the name of God, as ambassadors
of Christ and servants of his holy Church. And may the Lord bless
your labours abundantly, for the glory of the same our Saviour
Jesus Christ.

After a mission   **1416**
Heavenly Father, we commend to thee and to the word of thy
grace those who in the mission have found new life in Christ.
Deepen within them, we pray thee, the good work which thou hast
begun; strengthen them in their daily life and witness; and keep
them ever faithful to thee in the fellowship of thy Church; through
the same Jesus Christ our Lord.   *Frank Colquhoun*

Our Christian witness   **1417**
Show us, O Lord and Master, in this new day in which we are
called to witness for thee, how we may effectively present thy claims
to those who are outside thy Church. May thy Holy Spirit fill us
with love for them and deepen our understanding of their needs;
and grant that our lives as well as our lips may so commend thee to
them that they may come to find in thee the Way to the Father, the
Truth that sets them free, and the Life that is life indeed; for the
glory of thy name.   *Frank Colquhoun*

1418

O Lord our God, who through the preaching of the gospel didst
call our fathers into the fellowship of thy true religion, and dost
summon us their children to return to thee: Give us grace to hear
and obey thy call. Release us from the bondage of ignorance and fear;
restore unto us the joy of thy salvation; and so inspire and strengthen

us by thy Holy Spirit that by word and good example we may devote ourselves wholly to thy service, for the glory of thy name; through Jesus Christ our Lord. *Frederick B. Macnutt*

1419

O Lord Jesus Christ, who hast called those who believe on thee to be evangelists of thy kingdom and to carry thy gospel to the souls of men: Renew in us the spirit of faith and service; enlighten our minds to understand thy message; and inflame our hearts with such love toward thee that thy word upon our lips may be mighty to overthrow the powers of darkness, and to turn the feet of many into thy way of light and peace; to the glory of thy name. *Frederick B. Macnutt*

1420

Lord Jesus, who didst stretch out thine arms of love on the hard wood of the cross, that all men might come within the reach of thy saving embrace: Clothe us in thy Spirit, that we, stretching forth our hands in loving labour for others, may bring those who know thee not to the knowledge and love of thee; who with the Father and the Holy Ghost livest and reignest one God for ever and ever. *Charles H. Brent*

1421

O Lord, who hast called us to be thy witnesses to all the nations: Have mercy upon us, who have known thy will but have failed to do it. Cleanse us from sloth and unbelief, and fill us with zeal and love, that we may do thy work with hope and courage, and set forth thy glory; who with the Father and the Holy Spirit art one God, world without end. *Adapted*

THE PARISH

1422

ALMIGHTY and everlasting God, who dost govern all things in heaven and earth: Mercifully hear our prayers and grant to this parish all things needful for its spiritual welfare. Give grace to those who minister thy holy Word and sacraments; strengthen and increase the faithful; protect and guide the children; comfort and relieve the sick; arouse the careless, recover the fallen, restore the penitent. Remove all hindrances to the advancement of thy truth, and bring us all to be of one heart and mind in the fellowship of thy holy Church; through Jesus Christ our Lord.   *W. J. Butler**

1423

Most merciful Father, we beseech thee to send down thy heavenly blessing upon thy Church in this parish, that all its members may dwell together in unity and brotherly love. Endue thy ministers with righteousness, and enable them faithfully to dispense thy holy Word and sacraments, and to seek the lost. And grant to us so to receive their ministrations, and to use thy means of grace, that in all our words and deeds we may set forward thy glory and the advancement of thy kingdom; through Jesus Christ our Lord.

Canadian Prayer Book*

1424

Most gracious God, who hast called the Church out of the world to bring the world unto thee: We pray for thy Church in this parish and for all who serve thee therein. Confirm us in the faith once delivered to the saints; preserve us in the liberty wherewith Christ has made us free; and enable us with courage and assurance to bear our witness before men; through the same Jesus Christ our Lord.   *A Book of Public Worship*

1425

O Lord Jesus Christ, who didst build thy Church upon the rock, that even the gates of hell might not prevail against it: Have mercy on the churches of this land, and especially upon our own church of ——. Make the worship of thy people acceptable in thy sight; sweeten our fellowship with brotherly love; and unite us in a continuous, bold and effective witness to our parish, for the spread of thy kingdom and the glory of thy name. *J. R. W. Stott*

1426

Most merciful Father, who hast called us to thy service in the fellowship of the gospel: We beseech thee to bless and prosper thy work in this parish. Unite us one with another in brotherly love; teach us to worship thee in spirit and in truth; be pleased to use our endeavours to extend thy kingdom in the hearts and homes of our people, and so visit us with thy salvation; through Jesus Christ our Lord. *Frank Colquhoun*

1427

Almighty Father, who in thy redeeming love hast drawn us together as members of thy Church in this parish: Deepen our love for thee, we pray thee, and strengthen our fellowship one with another; and grant that by the witness of our corporate life others within this place may be brought to the knowledge of thee, and thy blessed kingdom may be enlarged; for the glory of Jesus Christ our Lord.

A parish church 1428

O Holy Spirit of the living God, proceeding from the Father and the Son, Spirit of truth and love, the Lord and Giver of life: Sanctify with thy presence this place of prayer.

Here may the people be drawn into thy fellowship and conquered by thy love; here may the ignorant learn the way of truth, the sinful find pardon, and the weary rest; here may the members of thy holy Church be strengthened in the bond of peace and righteousness of life, manfully to confess the faith of Christ crucified.

Fulfil the prayers of those who worship here, hallow their praises and enrich their lives; unite them in the service of the kingdom which hath no end, that in all things and by all men thy name may be adored; who with the Father and the Son livest and reignest, one God, world without end. *A Diocesan Service Book*

An incumbent 1429

Almighty God, our heavenly Father, who makest us both to will and to do of thy good pleasure: Give thy grace, we pray thee, to thy servant N. whom thou hast called to have the oversight of the Church in this parish. Grant that he may be a faithful dispenser of thy holy Word and sacraments, and a godly example to the people committed to his charge; so that, this life ended, they with him may be partakers of thy heavenly kingdom; through Jesus Christ our Lord. *Adapted*

Clergy of the parish 1430
Bless, we beseech thee, O Lord, the clergy of this parish, and strengthen them with thy heavenly grace. May they be diligent in prayer and in the study of thy holy Word, that by wise counsel and good example they may guide thy people committed to their charge, and labour with unwearied zeal for the extension of thy kingdom; through Jesus Christ our Lord.

During an interregnum 1431
Almighty God, our heavenly Father, giver of every good gift: Be pleased to hear the prayers of thy people, and send to us as the *vicar* of this parish a man after thine own heart who shall faithfully and wisely exercise the cure of souls, to the good of thy Church and the glory of thy name; through Jesus Christ our Lord.

1432
O God, who knowest the needs of thy Church in every place: Look graciously at this time upon the people of this parish, and give to them a faithful pastor who may serve before thee in all diligence and lowliness of heart, and, by thy blessing, bring many souls to the joys of thine eternal kingdom; through Jesus Christ our Lord.

Canadian Prayer Book

For church workers 1433
Almighty God, we beseech thee to bless all who are working for the Church in this parish. Give them courage, strength and vision. May they set thy holy will ever before them, and seek to do that which is righteous in thy sight; through Jesus Christ our Lord.

1434
O Most Holy Trinity of perfect love, come in thy power upon thy whole Church, and especially upon those who serve thee in this parish; that in all their life and labour for thy kingdom they may always be guided, strengthened and upheld by thy peace and thy presence; who livest and reignest one God, world without end.

1435
O Lord, without whom our labour is but lost, and with whom thy little ones go forth as the mighty: Be present to all works in thy Church which are undertaken according to thy will; and grant

341

to thy labourers a pure intention, patient faith, sufficient success upon earth, and the bliss of serving thee in heaven; through Jesus Christ our Lord. *William Bright*

1436

O Thou true Light that lightest every man, coming into the world: Do thou in thy mercy touch the hearts and enlighten the understanding of all whom thou dost call to the service of thy Church; that they may cheerfully acknowledge and readily obey thy claims upon their lives, to the benefit of thy people and the glory of thy holy name, who with the Father and the Holy Spirit livest and reignest, world without end.

The Kingdom, the Power, and the Glory

Parochial evangelism

1437

O Heavenly Father, whose blessed Son Jesus Christ came to seek and to save that which was lost: Have compassion, we beseech thee, on the multitudes scattered abroad as sheep having no shepherd, especially here in this parish; and enable us so to minister to their needs that they may be brought to thyself and become one flock under one Shepherd, the same thy Son Jesus Christ our Lord.

1438

Almighty God, who in thy great love for the world didst send thy Son to die for us men and for our salvation: Grant that in the work of this parish the claims of thy love may be so fully and faithfully presented to young and old in the power of the Holy Spirit that the company of Christ's faithful people may continually be increased, and his kingdom extended in the hearts and lives of men; through the same Jesus Christ our Lord.

Worship and witness

1439

Heavenly Father, who hast called thy Church to worship thee and to bear witness for thee in the world: Make us faithful to our calling; that offering to thee the spiritual sacrifice of our praise and thanksgiving, we may preach the faith of Christ crucified, in the power of the Holy Spirit; through the same Jesus Christ thy Son, our Saviour. *J. R. W. Stott*

Open air services

1440

O Lord Jesus Christ, who by thy example hast taught us that the Father's love can be proclaimed under the vault of heaven no less than in temples made with hands, and hast bidden us in our love for souls to go out into the highways and hedges and compel them to come in: Prosper and bless every effort to carry the message of the gospel to those that are without; that as of old the common people may hear thee gladly, O blessed Lord and Saviour, who now livest and reignest with the Father and the Holy Spirit, one God, world without end.   *Peter Green*

See also prayers for a Dedication Festival, 739–52

VARIOUS

Sunday observance 1441

ALMIGHTY God, who by thy Spirit hast taught thy Church to sanctify the first day of the week as a perpetual memorial to the glorious resurrection of thy Son our Lord: Teach us to use this gift for the worship of thy holy name, and the refreshment of our souls and bodies; and prosper, we pray thee, every endeavour to preserve the sanctity of thy day in our national life; through Jesus Christ our Lord.

1442

O Lord Jesu Christ, who as on this day didst rise from the dead; Teach us to reverence this thy holy day, and give us grace so to use it that we may rise to newness of life; to thy honour and glory, who livest and reignest with the Father and the Holy Ghost, one God world without end. *Irish Prayer Book*

1443

O Lord Jesus Christ, who on the first day of the week didst rise again: Raise up our souls to serve the living God; and as thou didst also on this day send down on thy apostles thy most Holy Spirit, so take not the same Spirit from us, but grant that we may be daily renewed and plentifully enriched by his power; for thine own mercy's sake, who livest and reignest with the Father and the Holy Spirit, ever one God, world without end. *Lancelot Andrewes*

Moral welfare workers 1444

O Lord, our heavenly Father, whose blessed Son came not to be ministered unto but to minister: We beseech thee to bless all who, following in his steps, give themselves to the service of their fellow men; that being inspired by thy love, they may worthily minister in thy name to the fallen, the friendless, and the needy; for the sake of the same thy Son our Saviour Jesus Christ.

*American Prayer Book**

Social workers 1445

O God, our heavenly Father, who knowest our needs and dost care for us all: We pray for those who give counsel and help to their fellow men; for probation officers and all other social workers;

344

for all who by their skill and training ease the burden of the aged, the lonely, and the perplexed, and guide those who have missed the right way; that they may have both wisdom and sympathy, and see men through the eyes of Christ, who beheld the multitudes distressed and scattered, as sheep not having a shepherd; grant this for his sake, our Lord and Saviour. *H. F. Leatherland*

Temperance work 1446

O God, who didst give thy blessed Son for the redemption of the whole life of man: Prosper, we beseech thee, the efforts of all who labour to free the land from the curse of intemperance, and to establish our people in holiness and self-control. Put it into the hearts of many to give themselves to this service, and grant them abundantly the spirit of wisdom and love, of zeal and patience; through Jesus Christ our Lord.

1447

Almighty God, who dost require of all men that they should be faithful stewards of thy gifts: Deliver us, we beseech thee, from the selfishness that seeks gain without labour, or excitement without care for its cost to others. Set free those who are possessed by the gambling spirit, and break the power of those who exploit their weakness; and lead all men to seek in thee their true joy and to find in thy service the fullness of life; through Jesus Christ our Lord.

Animals 1448

We beseech thee, O Lord, to hear our supplications on behalf of the dumb creation, who after their kind bless, praise and magnify thee. Grant that all cruelty to animals may cease in our land; and deepen our thankfulness to thee for the faithful companionship of those whom we delight to call our friends; for Jesus Christ's sake.

1449

O God, who hast made all the earth and every creature that dwells therein: Help us, we pray thee, to treat with compassion the living creatures entrusted to our care, that they may not suffer from our neglect nor become the victims of any cruelty; and grant that in caring for them we may find a deeper understanding of thy love for all creation; through Jesus Christ our Lord.

For rain or favourable weather 1450

O Lord our heavenly Father, who by thy blessed Son hast taught us not to be anxious for our daily life: Mercifully hear our prayers and send rain upon the earth [*or*, send us favourable weather]; that our land may yield its increase and our hearts may rejoice in thee, who art the giver of all good things; through the same Jesus Christ our Lord.   *Frank Colquhoun*

1451

O Almighty Lord God, our heavenly Father: Look, we beseech thee, in thy loving-kindness upon us thine unworthy servants, and grant us such weather as may relieve our present distress, to our comfort and to the glory of thy holy name; through Jesus Christ, our Mediator and Advocate.   *Irish Prayer Book*

V
DEVOTIONAL PRAYERS

OPENING PRAYERS

The presence of God
1452

LET us remember the presence of God with us now, and lift up our hearts to:
God the Father, to whom we pray;
God the Son, through whom we pray;
God the Holy Spirit, in whom we pray.

1453

Lift up our souls, O Lord, to the pure, serene light of thy presence; that there we may breathe freely, there repose in thy love, there may be at rest from ourselves, and from thence return, arrayed in thy peace, to do and bear what shall please thee; for thy holy name's sake.
E. B. Pusey

1454

O God of peace, who hast taught us that in returning and rest we shall be saved, in quietness and confidence shall be our strength: By the might of thy Spirit lift us, we pray thee, to thy presence, where we may be still and know that thou art God; through Jesus Christ our Lord.
American Prayer Book

The spirit of prayer
1455

O Almighty God, from whom every good prayer cometh, and who pourest out on all who desire it the spirit of grace and supplication: Deliver us, when we draw near to thee, from coldness of heart and wanderings of mind; that with steadfast thoughts and kindled affection we may worship thee in spirit and in truth; through Jesus Christ our Lord.
William Bright

1456

O God, who art Spirit, and willest to be worshipped in spirit and in truth: Grant to us that, loving thee in all things and above all things, we may please thee by our prayers and by our lives; through Jesus Christ our Lord.
William Bright

1457

O Lord God, who never failest both to hear and to answer the prayer that is sincere: Let not our hearts be upon the world when our hands are lifted up to pray, nor our prayers end upon our lips, but go forth with power to work thy will in the world; through Jesus Christ our Lord. *Daily Prayer*

1458

O Holy Father, to whom we draw near with boldness through our Lord Jesus Christ: Look, we beseech thee, on his merits and not on our unworthiness; and grant that our prayers, being asked in his name, may be accepted for his sake; to whom with thee and the Holy Spirit be all praise and glory, now and for evermore.

Frank Colquhoun

1459

O God, the glory of thy saints, who being above all, and through all, and in all, dost yet accept the prayer of the contrite: Grant that we, being hallowed in mind, fervent in spirit, and chaste in body, may offer to thee the pure sacrifice of hearts uplifted in thy praise, and lives devoted to thy service; through Jesus Christ our Lord.

From the Gothic

Before worship 1460

Eternal God, of whom the whole family in heaven and earth is named; Unite us, as we worship thee here, with all who in far-off places are lifting up their hands and hearts to thee; that thy Church throughout the world, with the Church in heaven, may offer up one sacrifice of thanksgiving; to the praise and honour of thy holy name. *Daily Prayer*

1461

O Thou high and lofty one that inhabitest eternity, whose name is holy, who hast promised to dwell with those that are of a contrite and humble spirit: Cleanse our hearts, we pray thee, from every stain of pride and vainglory; that though the heaven of heavens cannot contain thee, yet thou wouldest consent to abide with us for ever; through Jesus Christ our Lord.

1462

Eternal God, whose majesty is revealed in mercy: Grant that as we draw near to thee thy truth may set us free from the bondage of our own thoughts and desires, and that as we abide in thee our prayers may be an instrument of thy righteous will; through Jesus Christ our Lord. *Leslie S. Hunter*

1463

Almighty God, our heavenly Father, in whom alone our hearts find rest and peace: We beseech thee to reveal thyself to us in this hour of worship; pour down upon us thy spiritual gifts; and grant that this season of holy quiet may be profitable to us in holy things, and refresh and strengthen us to finish that which thou hast given us to do; through Jesus Christ our Lord.   *Book of Common Order*

1464

O Loving Lord, be near us in this time of worship. Open our ears to hear thy voice; open our eyes to behold thy glory; open our hearts to receive thy grace; open our lips to show forth thy praise; for the sake of Jesus Christ our Saviour.   *Frank Colquhoun*

1465

O God our heavenly Father, who hast taught us by thy Son Jesus Christ that the true worshippers are those who worship thee in spirit and truth: Grant that we may not draw near to thee with our lips while our hearts are far from thee, but that all that is within us may magnify thy holy name; through the same Jesus Christ our Lord.   *Based on John 4. 23; Isaiah 29. 13; Psalm 103. 1*

1466

O Eternal Light, illuminate us; O eternal Power, strengthen us; O eternal Wisdom, instruct us; O eternal Mercy, have pity upon us; and grant us with all our hearts and minds to seek thy face, and to love thy name; through Jesus Christ our Lord.
     William Bright

1467

O Holy Father, give us grace to praise thee not only with our lips but also with our hearts and minds; and grant that when our worship is ended we may continue to glorify thee in our lives, to the honour of Jesus Christ our Lord.

1468

Grant, O Lord, that we may come before thee with clean hands and pure hearts; that, serving thee with reverence and godly fear, we may now and always be acceptable in thy sight; through Jesus Christ our Lord.

See also prayers for a Prayer Meeting, 1724–9

CONCLUDING PRAYERS

After prayer   **1469**

O GOD, who hast given us the desire to pray: Grant us whatever is needful for us, and help us to live as mindful of what we have prayed for; through Jesus Christ our Lord.

William Bright

1470

Let these our prayers, O Lord, find access to the throne of grace, through the Son of thy love, Jesus Christ the righteous; to whom with thee, O Father, in the unity of the Spirit, be all love and obedience, now and for ever.   *John Wesley's Prayers*

1471

O God our Father, have regard to our intercessions, answer them according to thy will, and make us the channels of thine infinite pity and helpfulness; through Jesus Christ our Lord.

1472

Mercifully incline thine ear, O Lord, to these our prayers, and fill our hearts with thy grace; that, loving thee with an unfeigned love, we may evermore be defended under thy most gracious protection, and be accepted in our prayers and services; through Jesus Christ our Lord.

1473

O God, mercifully receive these our prayers which we have offered to thee through our Lord Jesus Christ; and with our prayers accept also our lives, which we present to thee anew for thy service and for the glory of thy holy name.

1474

Eternal God, whose ear is open to the prayers of thy children: Be pleased to accept these our petitions, and answer them, not according to the littleness of our faith, nor yet according to the greatness of our need, but according to the riches of thy grace, and for the glory of thy name; through Jesus Christ our Lord.

1475

O Almighty God, receive these our supplications and prayers which we now offer unto thee. Let thy fatherly hand ever be over us; let thy Holy Spirit ever be with us; and so lead us in the knowledge of thy Word, that in the end we may obtain everlasting life; through Jesus Christ our Lord.

Adapted from Book of Common Prayer

1476

Almighty Lord and everlasting God, dismiss us now with thy blessing; and help us to glorify thee henceforth in all the thoughts of our hearts, in all the words of our lips, and in all the works of our hands, as becomes those whom thou hast redeemed in Jesus Christ our Lord. *Adapted*

1477

And now, O loving Father, we go forth to do the work that thou hast taught us, to use the strength that thou hast given us. Be thou with us henceforth in all thy love and power, through Jesus Christ our Lord.

General **1478**

Remember, O Lord, what thou hast wrought in us, and not what we deserve; and, as thou hast called us to thy service, make us worthy of our calling; through Jesus Christ our Lord.

Leonine Sacramentary

1479

Grant to thy servants, O God, to be set on fire with thy love, to be strengthened by thy power, to be illuminated by thy Spirit, to be filled with thy grace, and to go forward by thine aid; through Jesus Christ our Lord. *Gallican Sacramentary*

1480

The Lord enrich us with his grace, and further us with his heavenly blessing; the Lord defend us in adversity and keep us from all evil; the Lord receive our prayers, and graciously absolve us from our offences; for the sake of Jesus Christ our Saviour.

Gregorian Sacramentary

1481

Grant, O Lord, that we may cleave to thee without parting, worship thee without wearying, serve thee without failing; faithfully seek thee, happily find thee, and for ever possess thee, the one only God, blessed, world without end. *St. Anselm*

1482

Grant, O Lord, that we may live in thy fear, die in thy favour, rest in thy peace, rise in thy power, reign in thy glory; for thine own beloved Son's sake, Jesus Christ our Lord. *William Laud*

1483

Let thy mighty outstretched arm, O Lord God, be our defence; thy mercy and lovingkindness in Jesus Christ, thy dear Son, our salvation; thy all true word our instruction; the grace of thy life-giving Spirit our comfort and consolation, unto the end and in the end; through the same Jesus Christ our Lord.

Knox's Book of Common Order, 1564

1484

O God, mercifully grant that the fire of thy love may burn up in us all things that displease thee, and make us meet for thy heavenly kingdom; for the sake of Jesus Christ our Lord.

The Kingdom, the Power, and the Glory

1485

O Lord, forgive, we pray thee, what we have been; sanctify what we are; and order what we shall be. What we know not, teach us; what we have not, give us; what we are not, make us; for Jesus Christ's sake.

1486

Defend, O Lord, us and all thy children with thy heavenly grace, that we may continue thine for ever, and daily increase in thy Holy Spirit more and more, until we come unto thy everlasting kingdom; through Christ our Lord.

Adapted from Book of Common Prayer

1487

Thou hast shown us, O Lord, what is good: Enable us, we beseech thee, to perform what thou requirest, even to do justly, to love mercy, and to walk humbly with our God; through Jesus Christ our Lord. *Adapted from Micah 6. 8*

1488

Enlarge our hearts, O God, that we may love thee more and more; kindle our souls that we may praise thee aright; and so order our thoughts, words, and deeds that we may serve thee and glorify thee for evermore; through Jesus Christ our Lord.

1489

Teach us, O God, to walk trustfully to-day in thy presence, that thy voice may encourage us, thine arm defend us, and thy love surround us; through Jesus Christ our Lord.

New Every Morning

See also General Prayers (1533–42) and Benedictions and Doxologies (1683–99)

IN THE MORNING

1490

INTO thy hands, O Lord, we commend ourselves this day. Let thy presence be with us to its close. Strengthen us to remember that in whatsoever good work we do we are serving thee. Give us a diligent and watchful spirit, that we may seek in all things to know thy will, and knowing it, gladly to perform it, to the honour and glory of thy name; through Jesus Christ our Lord.

*Gelasian Sacramentary**

1491

We give thee hearty thanks, O heavenly Father, for the rest of the past night, and for the gift of a new day, with its opportunities of pleasing thee. Grant that we may so pass its hours in the perfect freedom of thy service, that at eventide we may again give thanks unto thee; through Jesus Christ our Lord.

Daybreak Office of the Eastern Church

1492

O Lord our God, who hast bidden the light to shine out of darkness, and hast again awakened us to praise thee for thy goodness and to ask for thy grace: Accept now in thy endless mercy the sacrifice of our worship and thanksgiving, and grant unto us all such requests as may be acceptable to thy holy will. Make us to be children of the light and of the day, and heirs of thy everlasting kingdom; that redeemed in soul and body, and steadfast in faith, we may ever praise thy holy and wonderful name; through Jesus Christ our Lord.

From a prayer of the Eastern Church

1493

Grant us, O Lord, to pass this day in gladness and peace, without stumbling and without stain; that reaching the eventide victorious over all temptation, we may praise thee, the eternal God, who art blessed, and dost govern all things, world without end.

Mozarabic Liturgy

1494

O Lord, who hast brought us through the darkness of night to the light of the morning, and who by thy Holy Spirit dost illumine

356

the darkness of ignorance and sin: We beseech thee, of thy loving-kindness, to pour thy holy light into our souls; that we may ever be devoted to thee, by whose wisdom we were created, by whose mercy we were redeemed, and by whose providence we are governed; to the honour and glory of thy great name.   *Book of Hours, 1864*

1495

O God, the King eternal, who dividest the day from the darkness and turnest the shadow of death into the morning: Drive far from us all wrong desires, incline our hearts to keep thy law, and guide our feet into the way of peace; that, having done thy will with cheerfulness while it was day, we may when the night cometh rejoice to give thee thanks; through Jesus Christ our Lord.

American Prayer Book

1496

O God of love, who art the true sun of the world, evermore risen and never going down: We beseech thee mercifully to shine into our hearts, that the night of sin and the mists of error being driven away, we may this day and all our life long walk without stumbling in the road which thou hast prepared for us; through thy Son our Saviour Jesus Christ.   *Erasmus**

1497

O Thou who sendest forth the light, createst the morning, and makest the sun to rise on the good and the evil: Enlighten the blindness of our minds with the knowledge of the truth; lift up the light of thy countenance upon us, that in thy light we may see light, and, at the last, in the light of grace the light of glory; through Jesus Christ our Lord.   *Lancelot Andrewes*

1498

Into thy hands, O Lord, we commend ourselves and all who are dear to us this day. Be with us in our going out and in our coming in. Strengthen us for the work which thou hast given us to do. And grant that, filled with thy Holy Spirit, we may walk worthy of our high calling, and cheerfully accomplish those things that thou wouldest have done; through Jesus Christ our Lord.

F. T. Woods

1499

Into thy hands, O Lord, we commit ourselves this day. Give to each one of us a watchful, humble, and diligent spirit, that we may seek in all things to know thy will; and when we know it may gladly perform it, to the honour and glory of thy name.

357

1500

O Heavenly Father, in whom we live and move and have our being: We humbly pray thee so to guide and govern us by thy Holy Spirit, that in all the cares and occupations of our daily life we may never forget thee, but remember that we are ever walking in thy sight; through Jesus Christ our Lord.

1501

O God, who knowest that we are not sufficient of ourselves to think anything as of ourselves, but that all our sufficiency is of thee: Assist us with thy grace in all the work which we are to undertake this day. Direct us in it by thy wisdom, support us by thy power; that doing our duty diligently, we may bring it to a good end, so that it may tend to the greater glory of thy name; through Jesus Christ our Lord.

1502

God Almighty bless us with his Holy Spirit this day; guard us in our going out and coming in; keep us ever steadfast in his faith, free from sin and safe from danger; through Jesus Christ our Lord.

AT EVENING

BE present, O merciful God, and protect us through the silent hours of this night, so that we who are wearied by the changes and chances of this fleeting world may repose upon thy eternal changelessness; through Jesus Christ our Lord.

Leonine Sacramentary

1504

Look down, O Lord, from thy heavenly throne, illuminate the darkness of this night with thy celestial brightness, and from the sons of light banish the deeds of darkness; through Jesus Christ our Lord. *Order of Compline*

1505

Thine, O Lord, is the day, thine also is the night; cover our sins with thy mercy as thou dost cover the earth with darkness; and grant that the Sun of Righteousness may ever shine in our hearts, to chase away the darkness of all evil thoughts; through Jesus Christ our Lord.

1506

Into thy hands, O Lord, we commend ourselves, our souls and bodies, beseeching thee to keep us this night under thy protection, and to strengthen us for thy service on the morrow; for the sake of Jesus Christ our Lord. *William Laud**

1507

O God, with whom there is no darkness, but the night shineth as the day: Keep and defend us and all thy children, we beseech thee, throughout the coming night. Renew our hearts with thy forgiveness, and our bodies with untroubled sleep, that we may wake to use more faithfully thy gift of life; through Jesus Christ our Lord. *Adapted*

1508

Merciful Lord, who of thine abundant goodness hast made the day to travail in, and ordained the night wherein to take our rest: Grant us such rest of body that we may continually have a waking soul, and may rise up again with cheerful strength and gladness, to serve thee in all good works; through Jesus Christ our Lord.

*John Cosin**

1509

Into thy hands, O Lord, we commend ourselves and all whom we love, beseeching thee to keep us under the shadow of thy wings. Drive from us every evil thing; give thine angels charge over us; guard us ever, in life or death, that whether we wake or sleep, we may live together with thee; through Jesus Christ our Lord.

Book of Common Order

1510

O Lord, who hast pity for all our weakness, put away from us worry and every anxious fear; that having ended the labours of the day as in thy sight, and committing our tasks, ourselves, and all we love into thy keeping, we may, now that night cometh, receive as from thee thy priceless gift of sleep; through Jesus Christ our Lord.

Canadian Prayer Book

1511

Holy Father, we beseech thee, keep us and ours this night through the hours of darkness, and bring us in safety to the morning light, that thou mayest receive our praise at all times; through Jesus Christ our Lord.

1512

Watch thou, dear Lord, with those who wake, or watch, or weep to-night, and give thine angels charge over those who sleep. Tend thy sick ones, O Lord Christ. Rest thy weary ones. Bless thy dying ones. Soothe thy suffering ones. Pity thine afflicted ones. And all for thy love's sake.

St. Augustine

1513

O Lord Jesus Christ, to whom the sick were brought that they might be healed, and who didst send none of them away without thy blessing: Look in thy pity on all who come to thee this night for healing of body or mind or spirit, and grant them thy comfort and help; for thy tender mercies' sake.

1514

O God, the strength of them that labour and the rest of the weary: Grant us when we are tired with our work to be recreated by thy Spirit; that being renewed for the service of thy kingdom, we may serve thee gladly in freshness of body and mind; through Jesus Christ our Lord.   *The Kingdom, the Power, and the Glory*

1515

Abide with us, Lord, for it is toward evening and the day is far spent. Abide with us and with thy whole Church. Abide with us in the end of the day, in the end of our life, in the end of the world. Abide with us in thy grace and bounty, with thy holy Word and sacrament, with thy comfort and blessing. Abide with us when cometh the night of affliction and fear, the night of doubt and temptation, the night of bitter death. Abide with us and with all thy faithful ones, O Lord, in time and in eternity.

Lutheran Church

1516

O Lord, support us all the day long of this troublous life, until the shades lengthen, and the evening comes, and the busy world is hushed, the fever of life is over, and our work is done. Then, Lord, in thy mercy, grant us safe lodging, a holy rest, and peace at the last; through Jesus Christ our Lord.   *After J. H. Newman*

Adoration   **1517**

WORTHY of praise from every mouth, of confession from every
tongue, of worship from every creature, is thy glorious name,
O Father, Son, and Holy Spirit, who didst create the world by the
word of thy power, and in love didst wonderfully redeem it. Where-
fore with angels, and archangels, and all the company of heaven,
we adore and magnify thy holy name, evermore praising thee, and
saying:

> Holy, Holy, Holy, Lord God of Hosts,
> Heaven and earth are full of thy glory:
> Glory to be thee, O Lord, most High.

1518

> Blessing and honour, and thanksgiving and praise,
>> more than we can utter,
>> more than we can conceive,
> be unto thee, O holy and glorious Trinity,
>> Father, Son, and Holy Spirit,
> by all angels, all men, all creatures,
>> for ever and ever.   *Lancelot Andrewes*

1519

O Thou in whom all things live, who commandest us to seek thee,
and art ever ready to be found: To know thee is life, to serve thee
is freedom, to praise thee is our souls' joy. We bless thee and adore
thee, we worship thee and magnify thee, we give thanks to thee for
thy great glory; through Jesus Christ our Lord.   *St. Augustine*

1520

O God, whose love we cannot measure, nor even number thy
blessings: We bless and praise thee for all thy goodness, who in our
weakness art our strength, in our darkness, light, in our sorrows,
comfort and peace, and from everlasting to everlasting art our God,
Father, Son, and Holy Spirit, world without end.

Daily Prayer

1521

O Lord God, most high, most holy, to whom angels and archangels and all the host of heaven ascribe unceasing praise: Accept

the homage and adoration of us thy humble servants who are not worthy to draw near to thee but for the infinite merits of thy Son, our Lord and Saviour Jesus Christ.

Thanksgiving: general   1522

Glory be to God in the highest, the Creator and Lord of heaven and earth, the preserver of all things, the Father of mercies, who so loved mankind as to send his only begotten Son into the world, to redeem us from sin and misery, and to obtain for us everlasting life. Accept, O gracious God, our praise and thanksgiving for thine infinite mercies towards us; and teach us to love thee more and to serve thee better; through Jesus Christ our Lord.

Gavin Hamilton

1523

We give thee humble and hearty thanks, O most merciful Father, for all thy goodness and loving-kindness to us and to all men, for the blessings of this life and for the promise of everlasting happiness. And as we are bound, we especially thank thee for the mercies which we have received: for health and strength and the manifold enjoyments of our daily life; for the opportunities of learning, for the knowledge of thy will, for the means of serving thee in thy Church, and for the love thou hast revealed to us in thy Son, our Saviour; to whom with thee and the Holy Spirit be praise and glory for ever and ever.   *B. F. Westcott**

1524

O God of love, we yield thee hearty thanks for whatsoever thou hast given us richly to enjoy; for health of mind and body, for the love and care of home, for the joys of friendship, and for every good gift of happiness and strength. We praise thee for thy servants who by their example and encouragement have helped us on our way, and for every vision of thyself which thou hast given us in sacrament or prayer; and we humbly beseech thee that all these thy benefits we may use in thy service, and to the glory of thy holy name; through Jesus Christ thy Son our Lord.

1525

We thank thee, Lord, for all thy goodness to us.
> for the world which thou hast made, and for strength to serve thee in it;
> for daily revelations of thyself, in nature, in art, and in the lives of men;
> for the Bible, through which thy Word is spoken to men;
> for all other writings which reveal thy truth;

for the tasks to which thou art calling us.

But above all we thank thee for thy Son our Saviour Jesus Christ, through whom we see thee, who art our Father.

May his Spirit dwell within us, making us to serve thee with gladness all the days of our life; through Jesus Christ our Lord.

The Splendour of God

1526

O Lord, our heavenly Father, we thank thee for all thy gifts so freely bestowed upon us. For life and health, for home and friends, for power to work and leisure to rest; for all that enriches thought, or ennobles character; for all that is beautiful in creation, or in the lives of men; we praise and magnify thy holy name. But above all, we thank thee for our spiritual mercies in Christ Jesus our Lord; for the gift of the Holy Spirit, for the means of grace, and for the hope of glory. Fill our hearts with all joy and peace in believing, and help us to show forth thy praise not only with our lips but in our lives; through Jesus Christ our Lord.

For the Church   1527

O God, most gracious, most bountiful, accept, we humbly beseech thee, our thanksgiving for thy holy Catholic Church; for the light of faith which it hath handed on to us, and for the mercies by which it has enlarged and comforted the souls of men; for the virtues which it has established upon earth, and for the holy lives in which it has revealed thee to mankind. To thee, O blessed Trinity, be ascribed all honour, might, majesty, and dominion, now and for evermore.   *Adapted*

1528

Almighty God, whose mercy is over all thy works: We praise thee for the blessings which have been brought to mankind by thy holy Church throughout all the world. We bless thee for the grace of the sacraments; for our fellowship in Christ with thee and with one another; for the teaching of the Scriptures and for the preaching of thy Word. We thank thee for the holy example of thy saints in all ages; for thy servants departed this life in thy faith and fear, and for the memory and example of all that has been true and good in their lives. And we humbly beseech thee that we may be numbered with them in the great company of the redeemed in heaven; through Jesus Christ our Lord.   *Irish Prayer Book*

For all saints   1529

Here, O Lord, do we give thee most high praise and hearty thanks for the wonderful grace and virtue declared in all thy saints from the beginning of the world; and particularly in the ever-blessed Virgin Mary, mother of thy Son Jesus Christ, our Lord and our God; and in the holy patriarchs, apostles, martyrs, and confessors; whose examples, O Lord, and steadfastness in thy faith, and keeping of thy holy commandments, grant us to follow, for the honour and glory of thy name. *Non-Jurors' Prayer Book*

For the faithful departed   1530

O God of the spirits of all flesh, we praise and magnify thy holy name for thy saints and martyrs of every age, for the whole multitude of the redeemed, and for all thy servants dear to us, who, having finished their course, have entered into the joy of thy heavenly presence . ✻.; and we beseech thee that we, being encouraged by their example and strengthened by their fellowship, may in the end have part with them in the inheritance of the saints in light; through the merits of thy Son Jesus Christ our Lord.

Book of Common Order

For the sacrament of the Lord's Supper   1531

O Lord, most glorious Lamb of God, most tender priest of man, we praise and glorify thee for the blessed sacrament of thy Body and Blood, wherein thy servants celebrate the mystery of thy redeeming love and partake of thy spotless and immortal life; and we beseech thee that by these holy gifts we may be made holy, and have our portion and inheritance among the blessed who have pleased thee from the beginning of the world; to whom with the Father and the Holy Spirit be glory and dominion world without end. *After the Third Collect*

For our spiritual mercies   1532

O God, who hast given us life and all good things in this world: Thou hast created us for thy service, and when we have forsaken thee in our wanderings thou hast sought us out; thou hast vouchsafed to us the precious treasure of thy gospel; thou hast ordained that we should be born in the bosom of thy Church; thou hast revealed to us thy exceeding great riches in Jesus Christ our Lord. For all these gifts of thy grace, and for thy benefits which we remember not, we thine unworthy servants do give thee thanks, and bless thy holy name for ever and ever. *Eugène Bersier*

GENERAL PRAYERS

1533

O THOU, from whom to be turned is to fall, to whom to be turned is to rise, and in whom to stand is to abide for ever: Grant us in all our duties thy help, in all our perplexities thy guidance, in all our dangers thy protection, and in all our sorrows thy peace; through Jesus Christ our Lord. *St. Augustine*

1534

May the strength of God pilot us.

May the power of God preserve us.

May the wisdom of God instruct us.

May the hand of God protect us.

May the way of God direct us.

May the shield of God defend us.

May the host of God guard us against the snares of evil and the temptations of the world.

May Christ be with us, Christ before us, Christ in us, Christ over us.

May thy salvation, O Lord, be always ours this day and for evermore. *St. Patrick's Breastplate*

1535

O gracious and holy Father, give us wisdom to perceive thee, diligence to seek thee, patience to wait for thee, eyes to behold thee, a heart to meditate upon thee, and a life to proclaim thee; through the power of the Spirit of Jesus Christ our Lord. *St. Benedict*

1536

Eternal Light, shine into our hearts;

Eternal Goodness, deliver us from evil;

Eternal Power, be our support;

Eternal Wisdom, scatter the darkness of our ignorance;

Eternal Pity, have mercy upon us;

that with all our heart and mind and soul and strength we may seek thy face and be brought by thine infinite mercy to thy holy presence; through Jesus Christ our Lord. *Alcuin*

1537

Merciful God, to thee we commend ourselves and all those who need thy help and correction.

Where there is hatred, give love;
Where there is injury, pardon;
Where there is doubt, faith;
Where there is despair, hope;
Where there is sadness, joy;
Where there is darkness, light.

Grant that we may not seek so much to be consoled, as to console;
to be understood, as to understand;
to be loved, as to love;

For in giving we receive, in pardoning we are pardoned, and dying we are born into eternal life. *St. Francis of Assisi*

1538

Give us, O Lord, a steadfast heart, which no unworthy affection may drag downwards; give us an unconquered heart, which no tribulation can wear out; give us an upright heart, which no unworthy purpose may tempt aside. Bestow upon us also, O Lord our God, understanding to know thee, diligence to seek thee, wisdom to find thee, and a faithfulness that may finally embrace thee; through Jesus Christ our Lord. *St. Thomas Aquinas*

1539

Lord God Almighty, shaper and ruler of all thy creatures: We pray thee of thy great mercy to guide us to thy will, to make our minds steadfast, to strengthen us against temptation, to put far from us all unrighteousness. Shield us against our foes, seen and unseen; teach us that we may inwardly love thee before all things with a clean mind and a clean body. For thou art our Maker and Redeemer, our help and our comfort, our trust and our hope, now and for evermore. *King Alfred*

1540

O Lord our God, grant us grace to desire thee with our whole heart; that so desiring thee we may seek and find thee; and so finding thee may love thee, and loving thee may hate those sins from which thou hast redeemed us; through Jesus Christ our Lord.

St. Anselm

1541

O God, who hast created man after thine own image and made him capable of discerning and striving after truth and goodness, honour and loyalty, unselfishness and purity: Grant that by the power of thy indwelling Spirit we may learn to prize these above all else, knowing that in them we truly live; through Jesus Christ our Lord. *A Devotional Diary*

1542

Almighty and most merciful Father, whose dearly beloved Son Jesus Christ died that we might live: Grant to us thy children grace to follow in his most holy steps. Fill us with the spirit of reverence and godly fear; make us swift to obey thy holy will; and so turn our weakness into strength by the presence of thy Holy Spirit, that we may fight faithfully against selfishness, impurity, and pride, and ever be true to thy calling in Jesus Christ our Lord.

PENITENCE AND PARDON

1543

WE confess to thee, O heavenly Father, as thy children, our hardness, indifference, and impenitence; our grievous failures in pure and holy living; our trust in self, and misuse of thy gifts; our timorousness as thy witnesses before the world; and the sin and bitterness that every man knoweth in his own heart. Give us, O Father, contrition and meekness of soul; grace to amend our sinful life; and the holy comfort of thy Spirit to overcome and heal all our evils; through Jesus Christ our Lord.

*E. W. Benson**

1544

O God, our Judge and Saviour, set before us the vision of thy purity, and let us see our sins in the light of thy holiness. Pierce our self-contentment with the shafts of thy burning love, and let that love consume in us all that hinders us from perfect service of thy cause; for as thy holiness is our judgment, so are thy wounds our salvation.   *William Temple*

1545

O Lord God, our Father most loving, we would not, even if we could, conceal anything from thee, but rejoice rather that thou knowest us as we are and seest every desire and every motive of our hearts. Help us, O Lord, to strip off every mask and veil when we come into thy presence, and to spread before thee every thought and every secret of our being, that they may be forgiven, purified, amended and blessed by thee; through Jesus Christ our Lord.

C. J. Vaughan

1546

Almighty and merciful God, the fountain of all goodness, who knowest the thoughts of our hearts: We confess that we have sinned against thee, and done evil in thy sight. Wash us, we beseech thee, from the stains of our past sins, and give us grace and power to put away all hurtful things; that, being delivered from the bondage of sin, we may bring forth fruits worthy of repentance, and at last enter into thy promised joy; through the mercy of thy blessed Son Jesus Christ our Lord.   *Alcuin*

1547

Almighty and most merciful God, we acknowledge and confess that we have sinned against thee in thought, word, and deed; that we have not loved thee with all our heart and soul, with all our mind and strength; and that we have not loved our neighbour as ourselves. We beseech thee, O God, to be forgiving to what we have been, to help us to amend what we are, and of thy mercy to direct what we shall be; so that we may henceforth walk in the way of thy commandments, and do those things which are pleasing in thy sight; through Jesus Christ our Lord. *John Hunter*

1548

Forgive us our sins, O Lord; the sins of our present and the sins of our past, the sins of our souls and the sins of our bodies, the sins which we have done to please ourselves and the sins which we have done to please others. Forgive us our casual sins and our deliberate sins, and those which we have laboured so to hide that we have hidden them even from ourselves. Forgive us, O Lord, forgive us all our sins, for the sake of thy Son our Saviour Jesus Christ.
Thomas Wilson*

1549

Blessed Lord, grant us thy Holy Spirit to work in us daily a true and lasting repentance, and keep us ever, as contrite Christian people, willing to acknowledge and lament our sins; yet also keep us ever, O Lord, steadfast and strong in our faith in the forgiveness of our sins, and in our purpose to amend our lives; through Jesus Christ our Lord. *Christian von Bunsen*

1550

We are not worthy, O Lord, to enter into thy presence, for thou art of purer eyes than to behold iniquity. But thou, Lord, art merciful and full of compassion; forgive us therefore all the sins and offences whereby we have grieved or dishonoured thee, and receive us again into thy favour, that we may worthily magnify thy holy name; through Jesus Christ our Lord.

1551

Almighty God, long-suffering and of great goodness, we confess to thee with our whole heart our neglect and forgetfulness of thy commandments, our wrong doing, speaking and thinking, the harm we have done to others, and the good we have left undone. O God, forgive thy people who have sinned against thee, and raise us to newness of life; through Jesus Christ our Lord.

1552

Lord, for thy tender mercies' sake, lay not our sins to our charge, but forgive us all that is past; and give us grace to amend our lives, to decline from sin and incline to virtue, that we may walk with a perfect heart before thee, now and evermore.

LOVE

1553

O GOD of love, who hast given us a new commandment through thine only begotten Son, that we should love one another even as thou didst love us, the unworthy and the wandering, and gavest him for our life and salvation: We pray thee to give to us thy servants, in all time of our life on earth, a mind forgetful of past ill-will, a pure conscience, and a heart to love our brethren; for the sake of Jesus Christ our Lord. *Coptic Liturgy of St. Cyril*

1554

Almighty and most merciful God, who hast given us a new commandment that we should love one another: Give us also grace that we may fulfil it. Make us gentle, courteous, and forbearing. Direct our lives so that we may look to the good of others in word and deed. And hallow all our friendships by the blessing of thy Spirit; for his sake who loved us and gave himself for us, Jesus Christ our Lord. *B. F. Westcott*

1555

O God, who hast taught us to keep all thy commandments by loving thee and our neighbour: Grant us the grace of thy Holy Spirit, that we may both be devoted to thee with our whole heart, and united to each other with a pure affection; through Jesus Christ our Lord. *Leonine Sacramentary*

1556

O God of patience and consolation, grant we beseech thee that with free hearts we may love and serve thee and our brethren; and, having thus the mind of Christ, may begin heaven on earth, and exercise ourselves therein till that day when heaven, where love abideth, shall seem no strange habitation to us; for Jesus Christ's sake. *Christina Rossetti*

1557

Almighty God, whose Son, our Lord and Saviour Jesus Christ, was moved with compassion for all who had gone astray, with indignation for all who had suffered wrong: Inflame our hearts with the burning fire of thy love, that we may seek out the lost, have mercy on the fallen, and stand fast for truth and righteousness; through the same Jesus Christ our Lord. *Daily Prayer**

1558

O God, fountain of love, pour thy love into our souls, that we may love those whom thou lovest with the love thou givest us, and think and speak of them tenderly, meekly, lovingly; and so loving our brethren and sisters for thy sake, may grow in thy love, and dwelling in love may dwell in thee; for Jesus Christ's sake. *E. B. Pusey*

1559

O God, our heavenly Father, who so loved the world that thou didst give thine only Son to die upon the cross: Pour thy love into our hearts, we humbly beseech thee; that we loving thee above all things, may give up ourselves, our time, our money, our talents, to thy service; for the sake of him who loved us and gave himself for us, Jesus Christ thy Son our Lord. *J. R. W. Stott*

1560

O Jesus, Master and Lord, pour into our hearts thine own heroic love; that being filled with love we may know the love which passeth knowledge, and live in the unknown power of love to win men to trust in love, to the glory of God who is love.
William Temple

1561

O God, who hast taught us that love is the fulfilling of the law: Help us by thy Holy Spirit so to love thee that we may evermore seek to do thy holy will; and so to love our neighbour that we may in all things do to others as we would that they should do unto us; for the sake of him who loved us and gave himself for us, thy Son Jesus Christ our Lord. *W. Walsham How*

FAITH

ALMIGHTY God, who in thy wisdom hast so ordered our earthly life that we should walk by faith and not by sight: Grant us such faith in thee, that, amid all the things that pass our understanding, we may believe in thy fatherly care, and be ever led and strengthened by the assurance that underneath are the everlasting arms, and that thy mercy endureth for ever; through Jesus Christ our Lord.

1563

O God, who, calling Abraham to go forth to a country which thou wouldest show him, didst promise that in him all the families of the earth would be blessed: Fulfil thy promise in us, we pray thee, giving us such faith in thee as thou shalt count unto us for righteousness; that in us and through us thy purpose may be fulfilled; through Jesus Christ our Lord.   *Church of South India*

1564

Almighty and eternal God, who art able to do exceeding abundantly above all that we ask or think: Give us grace to believe that the things which are impossible with men are possible with thee; save us from all doubt of thy goodness and questioning of thy love; and help us to trust in thy wisdom and mercy, that we may be calm and unafraid; through Jesus Christ our Lord.   *James M. Todd*

1565

Lord, increase our faith. Grant us to know in daily life something more of the faith that pleases thee; the faith that removes mountains; the faith that overcomes the world; the faith that works through love; the faith that makes all things possible. So may we prove more fully thine own faithfulness and receive the blessedness which thou hast promised to those who trust in thee; through Jesus Christ our Lord.   *Frank Colquhoun*

1566

O God our Father, who in the gospel of thy Son hast manifested thy love to us and given us exceeding great and precious promises: Lift us, we pray thee, above all our doubts and fears, and grant us the full assurance of faith; that trusting to thy grace alone, and holding fast by thy word, we may evermore rejoice in thy salvation; through the merits of him who died for us, and rose again victorious, the same Jesus Christ our Saviour. *Frank Colquhoun*

1567

Almighty God, whose we are and whom we serve: Keep us ever in thy faith and fear, and in obedience to thy commandments; confident that, being thine, none can pluck us out of thine hand; and, fearing thee, none can make us afraid; through Jesus Christ our Lord. *Daily Prayer*

1568

Lord, increase our faith; that relying on thee as thy children, we may trust where we cannot see, and hope where all seems doubtful, ever looking unto thee as our Father who ordereth all things well; according to the word of thy Son Jesus Christ our Lord.
George Dawson*

1569

Enable us, O heavenly Father, to walk with thee this day and every day in sure and simple trust; ever remembering that our little things are all big to thy love, and our big things are all small to thy power; through Jesus Christ our Lord.

1570

O Lord God, who dost call thy servants to ventures of which we cannot see the ending, by paths as yet untrodden, through perils unknown: Give us faith to go out with good courage, not knowing whither we go, but only that thy hand is leading us, and thy love supporting us; to the glory of thy name.

GROWTH IN GRACE

1571

WE beseech thee, O Lord, to perfect within us the work of grace which thou hast begun; grant us always to think, speak and do what is pleasing to thee; and keep us from falling back into the sins we have repented of; that we may live as in thy presence, and finish our lives in thy fear; through Jesus Christ our Lord.

William Bright

1572

O Christ, to whom all authority is given both in heaven and earth: Transform our wills, cleanse our hearts, and enlighten our minds; that all our thoughts and desires being made obedient to thy pure and holy law, we may grow up in all things unto thee, and present ourselves a living sacrifice, to the praise and glory of thy name; who livest and reignest with the Father and the Holy Spirit, now and ever.

The Kingdom, the Power, and the Glory

1573

God our Father, who hast created us in thine own image, with a mind to understand thy works, a heart to love thee, and a will to serve thee: Increase in us that knowledge, that love and that obedience, that we may grow daily in thy likeness; through Jesus Christ our Lord.

The Daily Service

1574

We beseech thee, O Lord, to give us more love to thee, more joy in our worship, more peace at all times, more longsuffering, more kindness of heart and manner. Grant us the grace of meekness and the power of self-control. May we know something of what it is to be filled with the Holy Ghost; for the sake of Jesus Christ our Lord.

1575

O Lord Jesus Christ, who didst deign to be made like unto men, the sharer of our sorrows, the companion of our journeys, the light of our ignorance, the remedy of our infirmity: So fill us with thy Spirit and endue us with thy grace that, as thou hast been made like unto us, we may grow more like unto thee; for thy tender mercies' sake.

Daily Prayer

1576

Almighty God, who by the washing of water and the Word hast made us members of the mystical body of thy dear Son: Grant us grace, we beseech thee, to continue steadfastly in the apostles' teaching and fellowship, in the breaking of bread and the prayers; that united in love one to another we may with one mind and one mouth glorify thee, the God and Father of our Lord Jesus Christ.

INWARD PEACE

1577

O GOD, who art peace everlasting, whose chosen reward is the gift of peace, and who hast taught us that the peacemakers are thy children: Pour thy peace into our hearts, that everything discordant may utterly vanish, and all that makes for peace be loved and sought by us always; through Jesus Christ our Lord.

Mozarabic Sacramentary

1578

Most loving Father, who willest us to give thanks for all things, to dread nothing but the loss of thee, and to cast all our care on thee who carest for us: Preserve us from faithless fears and worldly anxieties, and grant that no clouds of this mortal life may hide us from the light of thy love which is immortal, and which thou hast manifested to us in thy Son, Jesus Christ our Lord.

William Bright

1579

O Lord God, in whom we live and move and have our being, open our eyes that we may behold thy fatherly presence ever about us. Draw our hearts to thee by the power of thy love. Teach us to be anxious for nothing, and when we have done what thou hast given us to do, help us, O God our Saviour, to leave the issue to thy wisdom. Take from us all doubt and mistrust. Lift our thoughts up to thee in heaven; and make us to know that all things are possible to us through thy Son, our Redeemer Jesus Christ.

B. F. Westcott

1580

Set free, O God, our souls from all restlessness and anxiety; give us that peace and power which flow from thee; keep us in all perplexities and distresses, in all fears and faithlessness; that so, upheld by thy power, and stayed on the rock of thy faithfulness, we may through storm and stress abide in thee; through Jesus Christ our Lord.

1581

Lord, who alone art God, the gracious and merciful; who commandest them that love thy name to cast away all fear and care, and to lay their burden upon thee: Receive us under thy protection, and give us now and evermore that everlasting rest which thou hast promised to them that obey thy Word; through Jesus Christ our Lord.   *From Primer of 1555*

1582

O Lord, whose way is perfect: Help us, we pray thee, always to trust in thy goodness; that walking with thee in faith, and following thee in all simplicity, we may possess quiet and contented minds, and cast all our care on thee, because thou carest for us; for the sake of Jesus Christ our Lord.   *Christina Rossetti*

1583

Heavenly Father, who hast taught us to be anxious for nothing, but to cast all our care upon thee: Increase our faith, we beseech thee, and strengthen our resolve; that with a calm and courageous spirit we may meet all life's duties and demands, and know in daily experience thy peace which passes all understanding; through Jesus Christ our Lord.   *Frank Colquhoun*

1584

O God, whose grace is sufficient for all our need: Lift us, we pray thee, above our doubts and anxieties into the calm of thy presence; that guarded by thy peace we may serve thee without fear all the days of our life; through Jesus Christ our Lord.

GUIDANCE

O GOD, by whom the meek are guided in judgment, and light riseth up in darkness for the godly: Grant us, in all our doubts and uncertainties, the grace to ask what thou wouldest have us to do; that the Spirit of wisdom may save us from all false choices, and that in thy light we may see light, and in thy straight path may not stumble; through Jesus Christ our Lord. *William Bright*

1586

We beseech thee, O Lord, to enlighten our minds and to strengthen our wills, that we may know what we ought to do, and be enabled to do it, through the grace of thy most Holy Spirit, and for the merits of thy Son, Jesus Christ our Lord.

William Bright

1587

O Eternal God, the fountain of all wisdom and the giver of all grace, who didst send thy Spirit to dwell with our fathers and to lead them into the way of truth: Grant to us that in all our difficulties and dangers we also may be enabled, by the light and power of the same Spirit, to know thy mind and to do thy will, for the glory of thy name and the benefit of thy Church; through Jesus Christ our Lord. *Arthur W. Robinson*

1588

Guide us, O Lord, in all the changes and varieties of the world, and grant us evenness and tranquillity of spirit; that we may not murmur in adversity, nor in prosperity wax proud, but in serene faith resign our souls to thy will; through Jesus Christ our Lord.

After Jeremy Taylor

1589

Almighty God, in whom is no darkness at all: Grant us thy light perpetually, and when we cannot see the way before us, may we continue to put our trust in thee; that so, being guided and guarded by thy love, we may be kept from falling, this day and all our days; through Jesus Christ our Lord. *William Knight*

1590

Almighty Father, in whom is no darkness at all: Shine upon our path, we pray thee, that we may walk in thy light. Lift from our hearts all anxiety and fear, and teach us to trust thee both for that which we see and for that which is hidden from us. So evermore lead us in thy way and keep us in thy peace; through Jesus Christ our Lord.   *Adapted*

1591

Lord, lift thou up the light of thy countenance upon us, that in thy light we may see light: the light of thy grace to-day, and the light of thy glory hereafter; through Jesus Christ our Lord.

Lancelot Andrewes

The knowledge of God 1592

ETERNAL God, who art the light of the minds that know thee, the joy of the hearts that love thee, and the strength of the wills that serve thee: Grant us so to know thee that we may truly love thee, and so to love thee that we may fully serve thee, whom to serve is perfect freedom, in Jesus Christ our Lord.

After St. Augustine

1593

O Almighty God, eternal, righteous, and merciful, give us poor sinners to do for thy sake all that we know of thy will, and to will always what pleases thee; so that inwardly purified, enlightened, and kindled by the fire of thy Holy Spirit, we may follow in the steps of thy well-beloved Son, our Lord Jesus Christ.

St. Francis of Assisi

1594

O Living God, in whom is the fountain of life: So teach us to know thee through Jesus Christ that we may share the power of that eternal life which is in him, and that all our lives may be brought into obedience to thy holy will; through the same Jesus Christ our Lord. *Eric Fenn*

1595

O God of our Lord Jesus Christ, the Father of glory, give unto us, we pray thee, the spirit of wisdom and revelation in the knowledge of him. Enlighten the eyes of our understanding, that we may know what is the hope of his calling, what the riches of the glory of his inheritance in the saints, and what the exceeding greatness of his power towards us who believe; according to the working of thy mighty power who raised him from the dead to set him at thine own right hand in heavenly places; to whom be glory and dominion for ever and ever. *Based on Ephesians 1. 17–21*

The truth 1596

Almighty God, who hast sent the Spirit of truth unto us to guide us into all truth: We beseech thee so to rule our lives by thy power that we may be truthful in word and deed and thought. Keep us, most merciful Father, with thy gracious protection, that no fear or hope may ever make us false in act or speech. Cast out from us whatsoever loveth or maketh a lie, and bring us all into the perfect freedom of thy truth; through Jesus Christ thy Son our Lord.

B. F. Westcott

1597

We beseech thee, O God, the God of truth, that what we know not of the things we ought to know, thou wilt teach us; that what we know, thou wilt keep us therein; that in what we are mistaken, thou wilt correct us; that at whatsoever truths we stumble, thou wilt stablish us; and that from all that is false, and all knowledge that would be hurtful, thou wilt evermore defend us; through Jesus Christ our Lord.   *After St. Fulgentius*

1598

We thank thee, O God, that thou hast given us powers of mind to search into thy laws and to understand thy truth; and we pray that our reverence may increase with our knowledge, so that we may be led to worship thee in deepening humility, and may devote ourselves to the fulfilment of thy great purposes for mankind; for the glory of Jesus Christ our Lord.

1599

O God, who hast taught us something of thy truth: Teach us more, we pray thee. When our minds are confused, direct them; when they are obstinate, win them; when they are filled with thoughts of self, fill them with thoughts of thee; and at all times give us a humble and teachable spirit; for Jesus Christ's sake.

The Splendour of God ★

1600

O God, in whose holy kingdom there is nothing that worketh evil or maketh a lie: Help us, we pray thee, to guard our words, to keep our promises, and to speak the truth in love; through Jesus Christ our Lord.

DEDICATION

1601

LOOK upon our lives, O Lord our God, and make them thine in the power of thy Holy Spirit; that we may walk in thy way, faithfully believing thy Word, and faithfully doing thy commandments; faithfully worshipping thee, and faithfully serving our neighbour; to the furtherance of thy glorious kingdom, through Jesus Christ our Lord.   *York Diocese*

1602

Almighty God, in whom we live and move and have our being, who hast made us for thyself, so that our hearts are restless till they rest in thee: Grant us purity of heart and strength of purpose, that no selfish passion may hinder us from knowing thy will, no weakness from doing it; but that in thy light we may see light clearly, and in thy service find our perfect freedom; through Jesus Christ our Lord.   *St. Augustine*

1603

O Almighty God, who by thy holy apostle hast called upon us to present our bodies to thee a living sacrifice, holy and acceptable, which is our reasonable service: Graciously hear us, we beseech thee, O Lord, and grant that we may so dedicate ourselves wholly to thy service that henceforth we may live only to thy glory; through Jesus Christ our Lord.

Liturgy of the Catholic Apostolic Church*

1604

Come, Lord, and reign over us as our rightful King. Rule in our hearts and fill them with thy love; rule in our minds and bring every thought into captivity to thyself; rule in our lives and make them holy like thine own; for thine is the kingdom and the power and the glory, for ever and ever.

1605

O God our Father, who in thy great wisdom hast prepared for each one of us our task to do for thee: Grant that we may seek to know thy will, and may dedicate ourselves to serve thee wherever we are needed. May we never from love of ease or from any fear

turn from the path which thou dost appoint, but steadfastly walk in
thy way, through the grace of thy Holy Spirit; for the glory of Jesus
Christ our Lord. *Adapted*

1606

Almighty and eternal God, so draw our hearts to thee, so guide
our minds, so fill our imaginations, so control our wills, that we may
be wholly thine, utterly dedicated unto thee; and then use us, we
pray thee, as thou wilt, but always to thy glory and the welfare of
thy people; through our Lord and Saviour Jesus Christ.
William Temple

1607

O Thou who sittest on the throne, making all things new: Renew
our faith, and hope, and love. Renew our wills, that we may serve
thee more gladly and watchfully than ever; renew our delight in
thy Word and thy worship; renew our joy in thee; renew our longing that all may know thee; renew our desires and labours to serve
others; that so we may walk in the light of thy love and in the power
of thy Spirit, now and for evermore.

1608

O God, who didst make us for thy service: Help us to train ourselves to be good servants by ready obedience, punctual fulfilment of
duty, and strict honour in our dealings with one another; so that
whenever the time shall come, thou shalt deem us worthy to do the
work to which thou hast called us. Grant this for Jesus Christ's
sake.

1609

O Lord, take thou full possession of my heart, raise there thy
throne, and command there as thou dost in heaven. Being created
by thee, let me live to thee. Being created for thee, let me ever act
for thy glory. Being redeemed by thee, let me render to thee what
is thine, and let my spirit ever cleave to thee alone; for thy name's
sake. *John Wesley's Prayers*

1610

Set our hearts, O God, at liberty from ourselves, and let it be our
meat and drink to do thy will; through Jesus Christ our Lord.

1611

Almighty God, who hast highly exalted thy Son Jesus Christ
and given him the name which is above every name: Grant that we
may ever acknowledge him to be the Lord, and offer to him both

the homage of our hearts and the service of our lives; to the glory
of thy holy name, who art our God and Father, now and for evermore.   *Based on Philippians 2. 9–11*

1612

O Lord God, we acknowledge thee as our Father, ourselves as
thy children, our neighbours as our brethren; and we dedicate to
thine obedience and to their service our hearts and minds, our wills
and works; resolved to stand fast in thy faith, to tell of thy salvation,
and to do battle for thy glorious kingdom; in the name of Jesus
Christ our Lord.

1613

Lord Jesus, my Saviour, let me now come to thee:
  My heart is cold; O Lord, warm it with thy selfless love.
  My heart is sinful; cleanse it by thy precious blood.
  My heart is weak; strengthen it by thy joyous Spirit.
  My heart is empty; fill it with thy divine presence.
Lord Jesus, my heart is thine; possess it always and only for thyself.
                              M. A. P. Wood (after St. Augustine)

COURAGE AND PERSEVERANCE

1614

O LORD God, when thou givest to thy servants to endeavour any great matter, grant us also to know that it is not the beginning, but the continuing of the same, until it be thoroughly finished, which yieldeth the true glory; through him who for the finishing of thy work laid down his life for us, our Redeemer, Jesus Christ.

After Sir Francis Drake

1615

Give us, O Lord, a steadfast heart, which no unworthy thought can drag downwards; an unconquered heart, which no tribulation can wear out; an upright heart, which no unworthy purpose may tempt aside. Bestow upon us also, O Lord our God, understanding to know thee, diligence to seek thee, wisdom to find thee, and a faithfulness that may finally embrace thee; through Jesus Christ our Lord.

After St. Thomas Aquinas

1616

O God, give us courage: courage to make experiments, and not to be afraid of making mistakes; courage to get up when we are down and to go on again; courage to work with all our might for the coming of thy kingdom on earth; through Jesus Christ our Lord.

1617

Give unto us, O Lord our God, the spirit of courage. Let no shadow oppress our spirit, lest our gloom should darken the light by which others have to live. Remove from our inmost souls all fear and distrust, and fill us daily more completely with thy love and power; through our Lord and Saviour Jesus Christ. *Adapted*

1618

Teach us, O gracious Lord, to begin our works with fear, to go on with obedience, and to finish them in love, and then to wait patiently in hope, and with cheerful confidence to look up to thee, whose promises are faithful and rewards infinite; through Jesus Christ our Lord.

George Hickes

1619

O God, who hast commanded us to be perfect, as thou our Father in heaven art perfect: Put into our hearts, we pray thee, a continual desire to obey thy holy will. Teach us day by day what thou wouldest have us to do, and give us courage and strength to fulfil the same. May we never, from love of ease, decline the path which thou pointest out, nor, for fear of shame, turn away from it. We ask it for the honour of Jesus Christ our Saviour.

Henry Alford

1620

Almighty and everlasting God, who hast received us into the fold of thy Church, and hast given us thy Holy Spirit to abide with us for ever: Keep us, we beseech thee, under thy fatherly care and protection; enrich us abundantly with thy heavenly grace; and lead us to witness a good confession, and to persevere therein to the end; through Jesus Christ our Lord. *Adapted*

1621

O Lord Jesus Christ, who when on earth wast ever about thy Father's business: Grant that we may not grow weary in well-doing. Give us grace to do all in thy name. Be thou the beginning and the end of all: the pattern whom we follow, the redeemer in whom we trust, the master whom we serve, the friend to whom we look for sympathy. May we never shrink from our duty from any fear of man. Make us faithful unto death; and bring us at last into thy eternal presence, where with the Father and the Holy Ghost thou livest and reignest for ever. *E. B. Pusey*

1622

O God, who hast willed that the gate of mercy should stand open to the faithful: Look on us, and have mercy upon us, we beseech thee; that we who by thy grace are following the path of thy will may continue in the same all the days of our life; through Jesus Christ our Lord. *Leonine Sacramentary*

1623

O God, give us strength to change those things that we can change, the patience to accept those that we cannot change, and the wisdom to know the difference, always; for Jesus Christ's sake.

THE SPIRIT OF SERVICE

1624

O LORD, who though thou wast rich yet for our sakes didst become poor, and hast promised in thy holy gospel that whatsoever is done to the least of thy brethren thou wilt receive as done to thee: Give us grace, we humbly beseech thee, to be ever willing and ready to minister, as thou enablest us, to the needs of others, and to extend the blessings of thy kingdom over all the world; to thy praise and glory, who art God over all, blessed for ever.

St. Augustine

1625

O Son of Man, who hast taught us that in ministering to the needs of others we are ministering to thee: Fill our hearts, we beseech thee, with thine own spirit of love and self-sacrifice, and teach us so to see thee in all our suffering brethren that we may serve them gladly for thy sake; who livest and reignest with the Father and the Holy Spirit, one God, world without end.

1626

Almighty God, the giver of all good things, without whose help all labour is ineffectual, and without whose grace all wisdom is folly: Grant, we beseech thee, that in our undertakings thy Holy Spirit may not be withheld from us, but that we may promote thy glory, and the coming of thy kingdom; through Jesus Christ our Lord.

Samuel Johnson

1627

Blessed Lord, who for our sakes wast content to bear sorrow and want and death: Grant to us such a measure of thy Spirit that we may follow thee in all self-denial and tenderness of soul. Help us by thy great love to succour the afflicted, to relieve the needy, to share the burdens of the heavy laden, and ever to see thee in all that are poor and destitute; for thy great mercy's sake.

B. F. Westcott

1628

Almighty God, give us grace to do the work to which thou hast called us with reverence and godly fear; not with eye-service as pleasers of men, but with singleness of heart as in thy sight; and do thou so direct all our thoughts, words and deeds by thy Holy Spirit, that we may set thy will ever before us, and give ourselves to thee, to spend and be spent in thy service; through our Lord and Saviour Jesus Christ.

1629

Heavenly Father, whose blessed Son Jesus Christ has shown us that the secret of happiness is a heart set free from selfish desires: Help us to look not only on our own things, but also on the things of others; and inspire in us such fair dealing and fellow-feeling as may show our brotherhood in thee; through the same Jesus Christ our Lord.

1630

O Heavenly Father, whose blessed Son declared to his disciples, I am among you as he that serveth: Take from us, we pray thee, the spirit of selfishness, and deepen within us the spirit of service; that we may think less of our own interests and more of the needs of others, after the perfect example of the same thy Son, Jesus Christ our Lord. *Frank Colquhoun*

1631

O Everlasting God, who from all eternity dost behold and order all things, and hast called us to serve in this our generation, doing the work of God after the manner of men: Enable us to use the talents entrusted to us, to thy glory and the service of others, that at the last we may hear that most joyful voice, Well done, thou good and faithful servant, enter thou into the joy of thy Lord; through the same our Saviour Jesus Christ. *After Jeremy Taylor*

1632

O Son of God, who by thy lowly life hast made manifest the royalty of service: Teach us that it is better to give than to receive, better to minister than to be ministered unto, after thine own example, who now livest and reignest in the glory of the eternal Trinity, world without end.

1633

O Lord God, who dost by thy Holy Spirit endow thy servants with manifold gifts of knowledge and skill: Grant us grace to use the same always to thy glory and for the service of men; through Jesus Christ our Lord. *Artists' Prayer Guild**

OUR DAILY WORK

1634

O ALMIGHTY God and Heavenly Father, who by thy divine providence has appointed for each of us our work in life, and hast commanded us that we should not be slothful in business, but fervent in spirit, serving thee; help us always to remember that our work is thy appointment, and to do it heartily as unto thee. Preserve us from slothfulness, and make us to live with loins girded and lamps burning, that whensoever our Lord may come, we may be found striving earnestly to finish the work that thou hast given us to do; through the same Jesus Christ our Saviour.

E. M. Goulburn

1635

O Lord, our heavenly Father, by whose providence the duties of men are variously ordered: Grant to us all such a spirit that we may labour heartily to do our work in our several stations, as serving one Master and looking for one reward. Teach us to put to good account whatever talents thou hast lent to us, and enable us to redeem our time by patience and zeal; through Jesus Christ our Lord.

B. F. Westcott

1636

O Lord, renew our spirits and draw our hearts to thyself, that our work may not be to us a burden but a delight; and give us such a mighty love to thee, who thyself didst work as a craftsman in wood, as may sweeten all our obedience. O let us not serve thee in a spirit of bondage, as slaves, but with cheerfulness and willingness, cooperating with thee in thy work of creation; for the glory of thy holy name.

*Benjamin Jenks**

1637

We offer to thee, O Lord our God, the work which thou hast appointed for us. Help us to do it heartily and faithfully, as in thy sight and for thy glory, that so we may be drawn nearer to thee and confirmed in thy service, which alone is true freedom; in the name of our Master and Saviour, Jesus Christ.

William Bright

1638

O God of love, who dost give to each of us our appointed work: Help us steadfastly, and as in thy sight, to fulfil the duties of our calling; so that when our Lord shall take account of us, we may be found his good and faithful servants and enter into his eternal joy; through the same Jesus Christ our Lord. *Westminster Prayers**

1639

O Lord Jesus Christ, who at the carpenter's bench didst manifest the dignity of honest labour, and dost give to each of us our tasks to perform: Help us to do our daily work with readiness of mind and singleness of heart, not with eye-service as menpleasers, but as thy servants, labouring heartily as unto thee and not unto men, so that whatever we do, great or small, may be to the glory of thy holy name. *J. R. W. Stott*

1640

O Master Workman, who in the carpenter's shop at Nazareth spent thy days from youth to manhood in making and mending things: We thank thee that thou hast ever sanctified all labour by thyself making it an offering of service in thy Father's world. Increase in us the spirit of service, of joy in work well done, of loyalty and devotion, so that with all our strength we may do the tasks that fall to our share, for thy sake who did all things well, Jesus Christ our Lord. *With all our Strength*

1641

Almighty God, who didst ordain that thy Son, Jesus Christ, should labour with his hands to supply his own needs, and the needs of others: Teach us, we beseech thee, that no labour is mean, and all labour is divine, to which thou dost call us; to the glory of thy holy name.

1642

O GOD, our Father, we are exceedingly frail, and indisposed to every virtuous and gallant undertaking: Strengthen our weakness, we beseech thee, that we may do valiantly in this spiritual war; help us against our own negligence and cowardice, and defend us from the treachery of our unfaithful hearts; for the sake of Jesus Christ our Lord.   *St. Augustine*

1643

O Lord God, keep ever in our remembrance the life and death of our Saviour Jesus Christ. Make the thought of his love powerful to win us from evil. As he toiled and sorrowed and suffered for us, in fighting against sin, so may we endure constantly and labour diligently, as his soldiers and servants, looking ever unto him and counting it all joy to be partakers with him in his conflict, his cross and his victory; through the same Jesus Christ our Lord.
                                                        C. J. Vaughan

1644

O Lord Christ, thou Prince of peace, the faithful and true: Grant to us all, we beseech thee, that putting on the whole armour of God, we may follow thee as thou goest forth conquering and to conquer; and, fighting manfully under thy banner against sin, the world, and the devil, may be found more than conquerors, and at the last may be refreshed with the multitude of peace in the holy city of our God; whose is the greatness and the power, the victory and the majesty, world without end.   *A Form of Prayer, May 1940*

1645

Almighty God, in whose presence is fullness of joy, and whose power is made perfect in our weakness: Grant us so to dwell in thy presence, that we may ever be glad of heart; and so to rest on thy strength, that we may have victory over evil; through Jesus Christ our Lord.   *New Every Morning*

1646

O God our Father, who hast sent thy Son to be our Saviour: Renew in us day by day the power of thy Holy Spirit, that with

393

knowledge and zeal, with courage and hope, we may strive manfully in thy service, and ever live as faithful soldiers and servants of thy Son, our Lord and Saviour Jesus Christ. *Adapted*

1647

O Lord God, who hast called us to be thy soldiers and to fight manfully under Christ's banner: Enable us constantly to contend for truth, goodness, and justice without fear or favour; and relentlessly to oppose evil wherever it is found, and whatever form it takes; in the name and strength of Jesus Christ our Saviour.

Frank Colquhoun

Contending for the faith 1648

Heavenly Father, the Father of all wisdom, understanding, and true strength: We beseech thee look mercifully upon thy servants, and send thy Holy Spirit into their hearts, that when they must join to fight in the field for the glory of thy holy name, then they, strengthened with the defence of thy right hand, may manfully stand in the confession of thy faith, and continue in the same unto their lives' end; through Jesus Christ our Lord. *Nicholas Ridley*

1649

Eternal God, who hast taught us that the weapons of our warfare are not carnal, but mighty to the pulling down of strongholds: Help thy soldiers to fight the good fight of faith, refusing the weapons of the devil and the world, and overcoming hatred with love, evil with goodness, falsehood with truth, and so extending the victory of the cross; through him who triumphed thereon, even thy Son, our Saviour Jesus Christ. *Adapted*

1650

O Lord, who lovest not the strife of men, and yet wouldest have thy servants strive earnestly for the faith of the gospel; grant us so to seek thy truth that we may never forget to obey it, so to contend for it that we may never cause our brethren to stumble, and so to hold the form of godliness that we lose not at last the life and substance of it; through Jesus Christ our Lord.

Trinity College, Dublin

VARIOUS

For purity

M OST merciful Lord, who hast taught us that the pure in heart shall see God: Cleanse our hearts from all impurity; give us such hatred of all that is evil, and such love of all that is beautiful and good, that we may be delivered from temptation, and become a strength to others who are tempted; for the glory of thy name.

A Book of Prayers for Students*

1652

Almighty and everlasting God, in whom we live and move and have our being: Grant unto us such purity of heart and strength of purpose that no selfish passion may hinder us from knowing thy will, and no weakness from doing it; but in thy light may we see light, and in thy service find perfect freedom; through Jesus Christ our Lord. *Uppingham School Prayers*

1653

Cleanse our hearts, O God, we beseech thee, by the fire of thy Holy Spirit, that we may henceforth serve thee with chaste bodies and pure minds, to the glory of thy name; through Jesus Christ our Lord. *Adapted*

1654

O Lord, help us to be masters of ourselves, that we may be the servants of others; in obedience to thy Son, our Lord and Saviour Jesus Christ.

For humility

1655

O Lord God, we pray thee to keep us from all self-confidence and vainglory, and to bestow upon us thy great grace of humility and self-forgetfulness. To thee may we look, in all that we do, both for the will and for the power; and to thee may we ascribe with a sincere heart all the praise; through Jesus Christ our Lord.

C. J. Vaughan

1656

Almighty and everlasting God, who resisteth the proud and givest grace to the humble: Grant, we beseech thee, that we may not exalt

ourselves and provoke thy indignation, but bow down to receive
the gifts of thy mercy; through Jesus Christ our Lord.

William Temple

1657

O God our Father, who hast taught us never to think of ourselves
more highly than we ought to think: Help us to attain to that greatness of spirit that is ready for humble tasks, and ever to be servants
of others because we are servants of thine; through Jesus Christ
our Lord.   *Adapted*

For sincerity   1658

Lift up our hearts, we beseech thee, O Christ, above the false
show of things, above fear, above laziness, above selfishness and
covetousness, above custom and fashion, up to the everlasting truth
and order that thou art; that so we may live joyfully and freely, in
faithful trust that thou art our Saviour, our example, and our
friend, both now and for evermore.   *Charles Kingsley*

1659

Lord Jesus Christ, who hast called us to be thy disciples: Defend
us by thy power from all self-deception and hypocrisy, that our
eyes may never be blind to thy truth, nor our ears deaf to thy call,
nor our wills slow to thy bidding; but that in all the tasks of life
we may seek thy kingdom and serve thy cause; for the glory of thy
holy name.   *New Every Morning*

1660

Uphold us, O Lord of life, with thy free Spirit. Save us from un-
reality, from praising what is lofty while practising what is base,
from thinking high thoughts while living a poor life. Keep us from
ignoble fears, and send us on our way with hope; through Jesus
Christ our Lord.

For freedom   1661

O thou who hast taught us that we are most truly free when we
lose our wills in thine: Help us to attain to this liberty by continual
surrender unto thee; that walking in the way which thou hast prepared for us, we may find our life in doing thy will; through Jesus
Christ our Lord.   *Gelasian Sacramentary*

1662

O God our Father, whose perfect law is a law of liberty: Give us
wisdom to use aright the freedom which thou hast given to us by

surrendering ourselves to thy service; knowing that, when we are
thy willing bondsmen, then only are we truly free; through Jesus
Christ our Lord.

1663

Set us free, O Lord God, from the bondage of sin and the fear of
man; that in thy service we may find our freedom, and in thy will
our peace; through Jesus Christ our Lord.

For joy 1664

O God, who hast made the heaven and the earth and all that is
good and lovely therein, and hast shown us through Jesus our Lord
that the secret of joy is a heart free from selfish desires: Help us to
find delight in simple things, and ever to rejoice in the riches of thy
bounty; through Jesus Christ our Lord.

The Kingdom, the Power, and the Glory

1665

O God, who by the lowliness of thy Son hast raised a fallen world:
Grant to thy faithful people perpetual gladness; and as thou hast
delivered them from eternal death, so do thou make them partakers
of everlasting joys; through the same Jesus Christ our Lord.

Roman Breviary

1666

O Thou who art the sun of righteousness, the eternal source of
light and life: Shine upon us, we beseech thee, with the beams of
thy mercy, that we may rejoice and be glad in thee all the days of
our life; for the praise and glory of thy holy name.

Adapted from an ancient collect

For a forgiving spirit 1667

Grant, O Lord, that as thy Son our Saviour Jesus Christ prayed
for his enemies on the cross, so we may have grace to forgive those
that wrongfully or scornfully use us, that we ourselves may be
able to receive thy forgiveness; through the same Jesus Christ our
Lord.

For contentment 1668

Teach us, O Father, in whatsoever state we are, therewith to be
content, that we may know both how to be abased and how to
abound; that in prosperity we may bless thee who givest us richly
all things to enjoy, and in adversity may not suffer our faith in thy
love to fail; through Jesus Christ our Lord.

For grace 1669

O God our Father, let us find grace in thy sight so as to have grace to serve thee acceptably with reverence and godly fear; and further grace not to receive thy grace in vain, nor to neglect it and fall from it, but to stir it up and grow in it, and to persevere in it unto the end of our lives; through Jesus Christ our Lord.

Lancelot Andrewes

For reverence 1670

O God, most holy, most loving, infinite in wisdom and power: Teach us to reverence thee in all the works of thy hands, and to hallow thy name both in our lives and in our worship; through Jesus Christ our Lord.

For heavenly mindedness 1671

Grant us, O Lord, not to mind earthly things, but to love things heavenly; and even now, while we are placed among things that are passing away, to cleave to those that shall abide; through Jesus Christ our Lord. *Leonine Sacramentary*

Reconciliation 1672

Heavenly Father, who hast reconciled us to thyself through the cross of thy Son, and hast committed to us the ministry of reconciliation: Grant that we who bear witness to thy reconciling word with our lips may also demonstrate thy reconciling power in our lives; through the same thy Son Jesus Christ our Lord.

Frank Colquhoun

Think on these things 1673

O God our Father, whose will is our sanctification: Grant that thy Holy Spirit may so fill and possess our souls that we may be delivered from all unclean thoughts and imaginations, and may have grace to direct our minds to whatsoever things are true and honourable, just and pure, lovely and of good report, as revealed to us in thy Son Jesus Christ our Lord. *Frank Colquhoun*

Jesus Master Carpenter 1674

O Jesus, Master Carpenter of Nazareth, who on the cross through wood and nails didst work man's whole salvation: Wield well thy tools in this thy workshop; that we who come to thee rough hewn may by thy hand be fashioned to a truer beauty and a greater usefulness; for the honour of thy holy name.

An act of faith, hope, and love   1675

My God, I believe in thee, and all that thy Church doth teach, because thou hast said it and thy Word is true.

My God, I hope in thee, for grace and for glory, because of thy promises, thy mercy, and thy power.

My God, I love thee, because thou art good; and for thy sake I love my neighbour as myself.

The beauty of the world   1676

O Heavenly Father, who hast filled the world with beauty: Open our eyes, we beseech thee, to behold thy gracious hand in all thy works; that rejoicing in thy whole creation, we may learn to serve thee with gladness; for the sake of him by whom all things were made, thy Son, Jesus Christ our Lord.   *American Prayer Book*

1677

O God, who hast made the earth so fair, and written thy glory in the heavens: Help us inwardly to respond to all that is outwardly true and beautiful, so that as we pass through things temporal we may never lose the vision of the things eternal; through Jesus Christ our Lord.

Health of body   1678

O God, the Father of lights, from whom cometh every good and perfect gift: We beseech thee to grant us such health of body as thou knowest to be needful for us; that both in our bodies and our souls we may evermore serve thee with all our strength and might; through Jesus Christ our Lord.   *John Cosin*

1679

O Lord our God, who hast taught us to love thee not only with all our heart and soul and mind but also with all our strength: Grant us, we pray thee, the blessing of good health, and also wisdom to guard the health that thou dost give; that we may devote the whole of our powers to thy service and evermore glorify thee in our bodies, which are thine; through Jesus Christ our Lord.

Frank Colquhoun

In time of adversity   1680

Almighty God, whose sovereign power none can make void: Give us faith to stand calm and undismayed amid the tumults of the world, knowing that all things work together for good to them that love thee; through thy beloved Son our Saviour Jesus Christ.

A Form of Prayer, May 1940

1681

Be thou unto us at this time, O Lord, a tower of strength, a place of refuge, and a defence in our day of trouble. Keep us calm and brave, because our trust is in thee. Let thy comfort support us, thy mercy pardon us, and thy wisdom guide us; and give us, if it please thee, deliverance from all adversity; through Jesus Christ our Lord.

1682

Grant us, O Lord our God, ever to find in thee a very present help in trouble.

When we are in the darkness of doubt or perplexity, shed thy light upon our way.

When we are burdened with the affairs of our daily life, lift us to the calm of thy presence.

When we are battling with temptation and the flesh is weak, by the might of thy Spirit make us strong to overcome.

We ask these things through him in whom we are more than conquerors, thy Son Jesus Christ our Lord.   *Frank Colquhoun*

BENEDICTIONS AND DOXOLOGIES

Benedictions **1683**

BLESS us, O God the Father, who hast created us.
Bless us, O God the Son, who hast redeemed us.
Bless us, O God the Holy Spirit, who sanctifieth us.
O Blessed Trinity, keep us in body, soul, and spirit unto ever-
lasting life.

1684

May the blessing of God Almighty, the Father, the Son, and the
Holy Spirit, rest upon us and upon all our work and worship done
in his name. May he give us light to guide us, courage to support us,
and love to unite us, now and for evermore.

1685

God grant to the living, grace; to the departed, rest; to the
Church, the Queen, the commonwealth, and all mankind, peace
and concord; and to us and all his servants, life everlasting; and the
blessing of God Almighty, the Father, the Son, and the Holy
Ghost, be with you and abide with you always.

Based on a sixteenth century prayer

1686

May the love of the Lord Jesus draw us to himself;
may the power of the Lord Jesus strengthen us in his service;
may the joy of the Lord Jesus fill our souls;
and may the blessing of God Almighty, the Father, the Son, and
the Holy Ghost, be with you and abide with you always.

William Temple

1687

Unto God's gracious mercy and protection we commit you.
The Lord bless you and keep you.
The Lord make his face to shine upon you, and be gracious unto
you.
The Lord lift up his countenance upon you, and give you peace,
both now and for evermore. *Based on Numbers 6. 24–26*

1688

May the love of the Father enfold us, the wisdom of the Son enlighten us, the fire of the Spirit inflame us; and may the blessing of the triune God rest upon us, and abide with us, now and evermore.

1689

God the Father, Maker of men; God the Son, born amongst men; God the Holy Spirit, sanctifying men; bless, preserve, and keep us, and all for whom we pray, now and for evermore.

1690

Go in peace; and may the blessing of God the Father, the Son, and the Holy Spirit rest upon you and remain with you, this day (*night*) and for evermore.

1691

May the Lord of his great mercy bless you, and give you understanding of his wisdom and grace;

May he nourish you with the riches of the Catholic Faith, and make you to persevere in all good works;

May he keep your steps from wandering, and direct you into the paths of love and peace;

And the blessing of God Almighty, the Father, the Son, and the Holy Spirit, be upon you and remain with you always.

Southwark Diocese

Doxologies
1692

To God the Father, who first loved us, and made us accepted in the Beloved; to God the Son, who loved us, and washed us from our sins in his own blood; to God the Holy Ghost, who sheds the love of God abroad in our hearts; to the one true God be all love and all glory, for time and for eternity. *Thomas Ken*

1693

Blessing and honour, thanksgiving and praise, more than we can utter, be unto thee, O most adorable Trinity, Father, Son, and Holy Ghost, by all angels, all men, all creatures, for ever and ever.

Thomas Ken

1694

To God the Father, who has made us and all the world; to God the Son, who has redeemed us and all mankind; to God the Holy Spirit, who sanctifies us and all the elect people of God; to the one living and true God be all glory for ever and ever.

1695

Now unto him that is able to do exceeding abundantly above all that we ask or think, according to the power that worketh in us; unto him be glory in the Church and in Christ Jesus, throughout all ages, world without end.   *Ephesians 3. 20, 21*

1696

Now the God of peace, that brought again from the dead our Lord Jesus Christ, that great shepherd of the sheep, through the blood of the everlasting covenant, make you perfect in every good work to do his will, working in you that which is well-pleasing in his sight; to whom be glory for ever and ever.

Hebrews 13. 20, 21

1697

Now unto him that is able to keep you from falling, and to present you faultless before the presence of his glory with exceeding joy, to the only wise God our Saviour be glory and majesty, dominion and power, both now and ever.   *Jude 24, 25*

1698

May the God of all grace, who hath called us unto his eternal glory by Christ Jesus, make us perfect, stablish, strengthen, settle us; to whom be glory and dominion for ever and ever.

I Peter 5. 10, 11

1699

Unto him that loveth us, and loosed us from our sins by his own blood, and hath made us kings and priests unto his God and Father, to him be glory and dominion for ever and ever.

Revelation 1. 5, 6

VI
SUPPLEMENTARY PRAYERS

A parochial church council   **1700**

O LORD God, the Father of lights and the fountain of all wisdom, who hast promised through thy Son Jesus Christ to be with thy Church to the end of the world: We humbly beseech thee with thy favour to behold us thy servants who are now assembled in thy name to take counsel together for this parish. Mercifully grant that thy Holy Spirit may rest upon us, enlighten, and guide us; that all our consultations may be prospered to the advancement of thy honour and glory, and the welfare of thy Church; through Jesus Christ our Lord.

Adapted from a prayer for the General Synod in the Irish Prayer Book

1701

Almighty God, who in thy great mercy hast called us into the fellowship of thy Church and the service of thy kingdom: Hear us as we lift up our hearts to thee to seek thy blessing upon the work of this council. So guide and empower us by thy Holy Spirit that we may be enabled both to know and to do thy will; unite us in brotherly love one towards another; and fill us with zeal to work together for the benefit of thy Church in this place, and for the advancement of thy kingdom throughout the world. We ask these things in the name of Jesus Christ thy Son our Lord.

1702

O Lord and heavenly Father, who hast united us as members of one body in the work of thy Church in this parish: Give us grace faithfully and wisely to discharge our duties as in thy sight. Guide us by thy Holy Spirit in all our deliberations, and bring our minds into accordance with thy perfect will. Keep our vision clear, our sympathies broad, our resolution firm, our zeal unabating; and grant that whatever we do, in word or deed, we may do all for thy glory, and in the name of thy Son Jesus Christ our Lord.

Frank Colquhoun

1703

Almighty God, give us grace to do the work to which thou hast called us with reverence and godly fear; not with eye-service as pleasers of men, but with singleness of heart as in thy sight; and do thou so direct all our thoughts, words and deeds by the power of thy Holy Spirit, that we may set thy will ever before us, and give ourselves wholly to thee, to spend and be spent in thy service; through our Lord and Saviour Jesus Christ.   *Adapted*

1704

O Eternal God, the fountain of all wisdom, who didst send thy Holy Spirit to lead thy disciples into all truth: Vouchsafe his gracious presence, we beseech thee, to thy servants here assembled; and grant that he may so rule our hearts and guide our counsels that in all things we may seek only thy glory and the good of thy holy Church; through Jesus Christ our Lord.

Adapted from Scottish Prayer Book

1705

Almighty and everlasting God, from whom cometh wisdom and understanding: Be present, we humbly beseech thee, with thy servants assembled to deliberate in council upon those things that make for the maintenance, well-being, and extension of thy holy Church; and grant that they, seeking only thine honour and glory, may be guided in all their consultations to perceive the more excellent way, and may have grace and strength to follow the same; through Jesus Christ our Lord.   *Scottish Prayer Book*

An annual church meeting   1706

We praise thee, O God, that thou hast made us members of the Church of Jesus Christ ~~which he purchased with his own blood~~, and hast called us into a worldwide fellowship of love and service; and now, meeting in his name, we pray that thou wilt preside over this gathering in the power of thy Holy Spirit. So direct our thoughts and our words that all our decisions may be pleasing to thee; enable us to elect to the various offices in our church men and women endowed with the gifts that their service requires; keep us from all misunderstanding, from all dissension, and from every breach of the law of love; and prosper every effort to make Christ known throughout this parish. Thus, O Lord, may thy name be glorified and thy kingdom extended, through Jesus Christ our Saviour.   *Frank Houghton*

1707

O God our heavenly Father, who hast called us to be members of thy Church which is the body of thy Son: Grant, we beseech thee, that thy Holy Spirit may direct us now in all our concerns and deliberations for the welfare of this parish. We give thanks to thee

for all the blessings of the past year, and for the opportunities of
the present time; and we pray thee so to lead us forward into the
work that lies before us that we may advance from strength to
strength in the service of thy kingdom, and ever magnify thy holy
name; through Jesus Christ our Lord.

1708

Almighty God, our heavenly Father, who by thy wise and loving
Spirit dost guide thy Church into the way of truth and holiness:
We beseech thee to direct the counsels of us thy servants at this
time, that we may be enabled to do those things that are pleasing in
thy sight, and may wisely plan for the furtherance of thy Church
in this place. Remove from us all that hinders thy purposes;
establish among us peace and love, unity and concord; and grant
that thy blessing may continually rest upon our worship, our
work, and our witness; for the glory of thy Son Jesus Christ our
Lord.

A committee meeting 1709

Almighty and everlasting God, from whom alone cometh wisdom
and understanding: Be present, we pray thee, with thy servants
here assembled; that seeking only thy honour and glory, we may
wisely take counsel together for the good of thy Church and the
advancement of thy kingdom; through Jesus Christ our Lord.

1710

Grant us, O God, the light of thy Holy Spirit, and ~~declare~~ unto
us thy will; that in the business before us we may be guided to make
right decisions, for the edifying of thy Church and the glory of
thy name; through Jesus Christ our Lord.

1711

Mercifully look upon us, O Lord, as we meet together at this
time in thy name and in thy service; save us from all pride and self-
assertion, from all desire for the praise of men; and grant that whatever we do for thy Church may be done for his sake alone, who
loved us and gave himself for us, thy Son our Saviour Jesus Christ.

Adapted

1712

O Lord, who hast taught us that the way of man is not in himself,
and hast mercifully promised to keep the way of thy saints: Direct
our thoughts and inspire our actions, we humbly pray thee, to the
good of thy Church and the fulfilment of thy eternal purpose;
through Jesus Christ our Lord. *J. Armitage Robinson*

A missionary committee 1713

Lord of the nations and God of love, who through thy Son Jesus Christ hast bidden us to lift up our eyes and look on the fields, white unto harvest: Mercifully enlarge our vision of the world's great need, and of thy yet greater love. May thy Holy Spirit assist us now as we think and speak and plan together for the furtherance of the gospel and the work of the Church overseas. Show us, O Lord, what thou wouldest have us to do, and fill us with such burning love and zeal that we may not fail to fulfil whatever purpose thou hast for us. We ask it that thy power, thy glory, and the mightiness of thy kingdom might be known unto men, in the name of Jesus Christ our Lord. *Frank Colquhoun*

A finance committee 1714

Almighty Father, who hast taught us in thy holy Word that the silver and the gold are thine, and that we are but stewards of thy bounty: Graciously assist us, we pray thee, as we meet together at this time to care for the financial interests of thy Church in this parish. Give us heavenly wisdom in handling these earthly things; enable us faithfully to fulfil our responsibility as in thy sight; and grant that, seeking first thy kingdom and righteousness, we may prove thy sufficiency in all things, according to the promise of thy Son Jesus Christ our Lord. *Frank Colquhoun*

A school managers' meeting 1715

O Lord and heavenly Father, who hast called us to serve thee in the administration of this school, and hast committed to us a solemn trust: Prosper, we beseech thee, the work of our hands and accept the service we now seek to render. Give us understanding of thy will in all matters that lie before us, and also grace faithfully to discharge our duties; that in all things we may seek the true well-being of those who are in our care; through Jesus Christ our Lord.

A men's meeting 1716

O God, who in thy Son Jesus Christ our Lord has given us an example of perfect manhood: Give us strength to follow in his footsteps; give us courage ever to stand for the hard right against the easy wrong; give us compassion for weakness, and chivalry towards womanhood; and grant us ever to walk before men as the devoted servants of him who sacrificed his life for the cause of good, and went to the cross for our salvation, even the same Jesus Christ our Lord. *W. L. Anderson*

1717

Almighty Father, whose blessed Son for thirty years shared our human life and showed forth the glory of our manhood: We pray that the mind that was in him may also be in us, that we may be conformed to his image. Save us from the fear of man, from the bondage of self, from indifference to the claims of others; and grant that, following his steps, we may dedicate our life, our strength, our time, and all that we have, to the service of mankind and the advancement of thy kingdom; through the same Jesus Christ our Lord.   *Adapted*

Church of England Men's Society Prayer   **1718**

O Almighty God, who hast called us to thy service in the fellowship of thy holy Church: Bless, we beseech thee, the Church of England Men's Society in all its branches, both in this place and throughout the world. Make all our members sound in faith and holy in life; bestow upon us the spirit of prayer and supplication; grant us by love to serve one another; and perfect in us that good work which thou hast begun; through Jesus Christ our Lord.

A women's meeting   **1719**

O Blessed Lord, who by thy holy incarnation didst consecrate womanhood to thy glory: Make us pure, we beseech thee, by the vision of thy purity; make us lowly by the example of thy lowliness; make us holy by the indwelling of thy Holy Spirit. Strengthen us, we beseech thee, that we may strengthen each other in courage and in faith; and show us how to use all our gifts in thy service; for thy tender mercy's sake.

1720

O God our heavenly Father, whose blessed Son grew up at Nazareth in his mother's care, and in his earthly ministry revealed to us the true honour of womanhood: Grant us, we pray thee, the blessing of thy Holy Spirit, that as Christian women we may walk worthy of our calling, and may faithfully serve our church, our homes, and our neighbours; for the honour of the same thy Son Jesus Christ our Lord.

1721

Gracious Lord, who wast born of a woman, look in mercy, we beseech thee, on the women of thy Church. Grant that they may know and enjoy the honour that thou didst purpose for women, and that as in old time women brought good tidings of thy resurrection, so in these days they may be the bearers of thy light and heavenly benediction; for thy name's sake, to whom with the Father and the Holy Spirit be honour and glory, world without end.

1722

O Merciful Jesus, who when thou tookest upon thee to deliver man didst not abhor the Virgin's womb: Vouchsafe evermore to dwell in the hearts of us thy servants; inspire us with thy purity; strengthen us with thy might; make us perfect in thy ways; guide us into thy truth; that we may be wholly devoted to thy service and conformed to thy will, to the glory of God the Father.

The Mothers' Union Prayer 1723

O Lord, fill us with thy Holy Spirit, that we may firmly believe in Jesus Christ, and love him with all our hearts. Wash our souls in his precious blood. Make us to hate sin, and to be holy in thought, word, and deed. Help us to be faithful wives and loving mothers. Bless us and all who belong to the Mothers' Union, unite us together in love and prayer, and teach us to train our children for heaven. Pour out thy Holy Spirit on our husbands and children. Make our homes homes of peace and love, and may we so live on earth, that we may live with thee for ever in heaven; for Jesus Christ's sake.

A PRAYER MEETING

1724

HEAVENLY Father, this is the hour of prayer, and we come to this place where prayer is wont to be made. We come to thee, who hearest prayer. We thank thee for the prayers thou hast answered; for thou hast heard our cry, and hast met our deepest need. We thank thee for the prayers thou hast denied, for often we have asked amiss. Grant us now thy Holy Spirit to help our infirmity, that we may pray as we ought, and our prayers may be acceptable in thy sight; through Jesus Christ our Lord.

A Book of Services and Prayers

1725

Eternal and holy God, we ask that thou wilt meet with us in this hour of prayer. As we remember thy love to us, may thanksgiving rise from our hearts. As we remember our failures and sins, may we become contrite and humbly beseech thy forgiveness. As we remember the needs of mankind, may we become more sure that Jesus is the Light of the world, the Bread of life, and the Saviour of all men. As we remember our own need, deepen our trust in thee, renew our faith in thy purpose, and grant us some word from thyself for our comfort and help; through Jesus Christ our Lord.

A Book of Services and Prayers

1726

O Lord Jesus Christ, who hast promised that where two or three are gathered together in thy name, there thou art in the midst of them: Fulfil to us now thy gracious word as we unite our hearts in this fellowship of prayer. Make us to know the joy of thy presence; teach us how to pray aright; and grant that all that we say and do may be acceptable in thy sight, O Lord our strength and our redeemer. *Frank Colquhoun*

1727

Heavenly Father, who through thy Son Jesus Christ hast taught us, saying, Ask, and it shall be given you; seek, and you shall find; knock, and it shall be opened to you: Give us grace now to ask in faith, according to thy Word; to seek only what is agreeable to thy holy will; and to knock with patience at the door of thy mercy, until our petition is granted and prayer is turned to praise; for the glory of thy holy name. *Frank Colquhoun*

1728

This is the hour of prayer. Draw near to us, O Lord, in the fullness of thy blessing as we wait upon thee. May we know that thou art in our midst, according to thy word. As thou hast given a place for prayer, so also give us hearts to pray; and grant that in the fellowship of intercession we may be drawn nearer to thee and to those for whom we pray; for thy honour and glory. *Adapted*

1729

O Almighty God, we believe that thou art here present; help us to remember thy presence. Thou knowest all things; there is nothing in us but thou, O Lord, knowest it altogether. Help us in the prayers we are about to offer for thy Church, for the world, and for ourselves, that what we ask may be according to thy will and for the enlargement of thy kingdom; through Jesus Christ our Lord.

Concluding prayer 1730

Lord, it has been good for us to be here, for thou hast been here with us. We thank thee for thy presence, and for the fellowship we have enjoyed one with another in this act of intercession. And now, O Lord, we ask thee to accept our petitions, to answer them as seems best in thy sight, and to bless all those for whom we have prayed. So send us now upon our way refreshed in spirit, and with thy peace in our hearts; and to thy name be praise and honour both now and for evermore. *Frank Colquhoun*

BEFORE BIBLE STUDY

1731

O LORD Jesus Christ, who art the truth incarnate and the teacher of the faithful: Let thy Spirit overshadow us in reading thy Word, and conform our hearts to thy revelation; that learning of thee with honest hearts, we may be rooted and built up in thee, who livest and reignest with the Father and the Holy Ghost, ever one God, world without end. *William Bright*

1732

O Lord, thy holy Word is before us; open to us its sacred truths, and enable us to receive it, not as the word of men, but as the Word of God which liveth and abideth for ever. Be thou, O blessed Spirit, our teacher. Enlighten our minds and prepare our hearts. Bring home some portion to our souls, and thus make us wise unto salvation; through Jesus Christ our Lord. *Ashton Oxenden**

1733

O Almighty God, who hast taught us that thy Word is a lantern unto our feet and a light unto our path: Grant that we, with all who devoutly read the holy Scriptures, may realize our fellowship one with another in thee, and may learn thereby to know thee more fully, to love thee more truly, and to follow more faithfully in the steps of thy Son Jesus Christ our Lord; who liveth and reigneth with thee and the Holy Spirit, one God blessed for evermore. *Bible Reading Fellowship*

1734

O Lord, heavenly Father, in whom is the fullness of light and wisdom: Enlighten our minds by thy Holy Spirit, and give us grace to receive thy Word with reverence and humility, without which no man can understand thy truth; for the sake of Jesus Christ our Lord. *John Calvin*

1735

O God, eternal light, in whom is no darkness at all: Illuminate our hearts and minds, we pray thee, in this time of corporate Bible study; and grant that thy Holy Spirit, who is the inspirer of all holy Scripture, may be to us its interpreter, and may lead us through the written word to him who is the living Word and the Truth incarnate, even thy Son our Lord and Saviour Jesus Christ.

Frank Colquhoun

1736

O Heavenly Father, by whose inspiration all holy Scripture has been written: Grant that thy Word may be profitable to us for teaching, for reproof, for correction, and for training in righteousness; that thereby we may be made wise unto salvation and equipped for every good work; through Jesus Christ our Lord.

Based on 2 Timothy 3. 15–17

1737

O Lord, who hast given us thy Word for a light to shine upon our path: Grant us so to meditate upon that Word and to follow its teaching, that we may find in it the light that shineth more and more unto the perfect day; through Jesus Christ our Lord.

After St. Jerome

1738

O God, whose Word is a lamp to our feet and a light to our path: Open our eyes, we pray thee, that we may behold wondrous things out of that Word, and rejoice as one who finds great spoil; through Jesus Christ our Lord.   *Based on Psalm 119. 105, 18, 162*

VESTRY PRAYERS

Before divine service **1739**

CLEANSE us, O Lord, and keep us undefiled, that we may be numbered among those blessed ones, who, having washed their robes and made them white in the blood of the Lamb, shall stand before thy throne, and serve thee day and night in thy holy temple; through the same Jesus Christ our Lord.

1740

Sanctify, O Lord, our hearts and minds, and inspire our praise; and give us grace to glorify thee alike in our worship and in our work; through Jesus Christ our Saviour.

1741

O Lord our God, we humbly beseech thee to purify our hearts from all vain and sinful thoughts, and so to prepare us to worship thee acceptably, with reverence and godly fear; for the glory of Jesus Christ our Lord.

1742

O Heavenly Father, who hast called us to thy service in the ministry of praise: Grant us grace to serve thee faithfully, that both in our hearts and with our lips we may magnify thy holy name; through Jesus Christ our Lord.

1743

Cleanse our consciences, we beseech thee, O Lord, by thy visitation; that with pure hearts and minds we may worship thee, the only God; through Jesus Christ our Lord.

1744

Deliver us, we beseech thee, O Lord, as we enter thy house from all vain and wandering thoughts; and grant that with pure hearts and hallowed lives we may show forth thy praise; through Jesus Christ our Lord.

1745

O Lord, open thou our lips, and purify our hearts, that we may worthily praise and magnify thy holy name; through Jesus Christ our Lord.

1746

O God, who hast given us minds to know thee, hearts to love thee, and voices to show forth thy praise: Help us to worship thee with understanding, with reverence, and with joy; for the glory of thy Son Jesus Christ our Lord.

After divine service   **1747**

Grant, we beseech thee, merciful Lord, that the words we have said and sung with our lips we may believe in our hearts and show forth in our lives, to thy honour and glory; through Jesus Christ our Lord.

1748

Accept, O Lord, the praise we bring to thee; pardon the imperfections of our worship; write upon our hearts thy holy Word; and give us grace to love and serve and praise thee all our days; through Jesus Christ our Lord.

1749

Sanctify, O Lord, both our coming in and our going out; and grant that when we leave thy house we may not leave thy presence, but may abide evermore in thy love; through our Lord and Saviour Jesus Christ.

1750

O Thou who art the high and holy one that inhabitest eternity, yet dwellest with the humble in heart: Be pleased to accept the worship which we have now offered in thy house, and prepare us for the service of thy heavenly kingdom; through Jesus Christ our Lord.

1751

Heavenly Father, be pleased to accept and bless all that we have offered to thee in this act of worship; and give us grace to show forth thy praise not only with our lips, but in our lives; through Jesus Christ our Lord.

1752

Accept, O Lord, these our prayers and praises, to the glory of thy great name and the benefit of thy holy Church; through Jesus Christ our Lord.

For the Holy Communion   1753

O Lord, who in this wonderful sacrament hast left unto us a memorial of thy passion: Grant us so to venerate the sacred mysteries of thy Body and Blood that we may ever perceive within ourselves the fruit of thy redemption; who livest and reignest with the Father and the Holy Ghost, one God, world without end.

Gelasian Sacramentary

1754

Visit, O Lord, we pray thee, and cleanse our consciences; that thy Son our Lord Jesus Christ may find in us a dwelling prepared for himself; who liveth and reigneth with thee in the unity of the Holy Spirit, one God, world without end.   *Roman Missal*

1755

O God, of whom and through whom and unto whom are all things: Let our participation in these holy mysteries be unto us both a foretaste of that heavenly city which thou hast prepared for us, and also a quickening of our zeal to walk worthy of our vocation; through Jesus Christ our Lord.

1756

Most gracious God, incline thy merciful ears to our prayers, and enlighten our hearts by the grace of thy Holy Spirit; that we may worthily approach thy holy mysteries, and love thee with an everlasting love; through Jesus Christ our Lord.

1757

As watchmen look for the morning, so do we look for thee, O Christ; come with the dawning of the day, and make thyself known to us in the breaking of the bread; for thou art our God for ever and ever.

Before a choir practice   1758

O God, whose glory the countless hosts of heaven so ceaselessly proclaim: Graciously aid us, we beseech thee, as we seek worthily to fulfil our service and ministry in thy house; that in psalms and hymns and spiritual songs we may sing and make melody to thee with our whole heart; through Jesus Christ our Lord.

Book of Common Order

1759

O God, who hast given us minds to know thee, hearts to love thee, and voices to show forth thy praise: Give us grace, we beseech thee, to dedicate ourselves freely to thy service, that we may reverently fulfil the worship of thy sanctuary, and beautify the praises of thy house; through Jesus Christ our Lord.

Book of Common Order

PULPIT PRAYERS

1760

O GOD, the Father of lights, who by the entrance of thy Word giveth light unto the soul: Grant to us the spirit of wisdom and understanding; that, being taught of thee in holy Scripture, we may receive with faith the words of eternal life, and be made wise unto salvation; through Jesus Christ our Lord.

Book of Common Order

1761

O God, whose truth is hidden from the wise and prudent, and revealed to babes: Grant us pure and childlike hearts, that being taught of thy Spirit we may know the things which belong to our peace and to our salvation; through Jesus Christ our Lord.

1762

O God, who hast so made us that we live not by bread alone but by every Word of thine: Cause us to hunger after the heavenly food, and to find in it our daily provision on the way to eternal life; through Jesus Christ our Lord.

1763

O God, who didst command the light to shine out of darkness: We pray thee to shine into our hearts, to give the light of the knowledge of thy glory in the face of Jesus Christ; to whom be praise and honour for evermore.   *Based on 2 Corinthians 4. 6*

1764

Heavenly Father, we pray that thy Holy Spirit may rest upon us now, as we approach the study of thy holy Word, and that he may make that Word a living message to our souls; through Jesus Christ our Lord.

1765

O Lord, uphold me, that I may uplift thee; and may the words of my mouth, and the meditation of our hearts, be acceptable in thy sight, O Lord, our strength and our redeemer.

1766

Give us grace, O Lord, not only to hear thy Word with our ears, but also to receive it into our hearts and to show it forth in our lives; for the glory of thy great name.

1767

O Lord, open to us thy Word, and our hearts to thy Word, that we may know thee better and love thee more; for thy mercy and for thy truth's sake.

1768

Heavenly Father, sanctify us by thy truth, and grant that the Spirit of truth may guide us into all truth, through him who is the truth incarnate, thy Son Jesus Christ our Lord.

OFFERTORY PRAYERS

1769

ALL things come of thee, and of thine own do we give thee. Accept and bless, O God our Father, these our gifts, and pour out upon us the spirit of thine own abundant giving; that as we have freely received, so we may freely give, to the glory of thy name; through Jesus Christ our Lord.

1770

Almighty God, from whom all good things do come: Mercifully accept these our gifts as a token of our love and gratitude; and teach us to bring to thee also that which thou most desirest, the offering of ourselves for thy service; through Jesus Christ our Lord.

1771

O God, the fountain of all good, we bring to thee our gifts, according as thou hast prospered us; and we pray thee to enable us, with our earthly things, to give thee the love of our hearts and the service of our lives; through Jesus Christ our Lord.

1772

O Lord our God, the author of all good things, who lovest the cheerful giver: We beseech thee to receive and bless these our offerings which we here present to thee, and with them ourselves, our souls and bodies, a living sacrifice, holy and acceptable; through Jesus Christ our Lord.

1773

O God of love, who didst not spare thine only Son, and with him dost freely give us all things: Mercifully accept and bless the offerings which we here present to thee with thankful hearts; and grant us grace this day, with our gifts, to dedicate our lives anew to thy service; through the same Jesus Christ our Lord.

1774

O Lord our God, send down upon us, we beseech thee, thy Holy Spirit, to cleanse our hearts, to hallow our gifts, and to perfect the offering of ourselves to thee; for the glory of thy Son Jesus Christ our Lord.

1775

Accept, O Lord God, these our gifts which we here present to thee, and grant that they may be wisely used for the extension of thy kingdom and the greater glory of thy name; through Jesus Christ our Lord.

1776

Grant, we beseech thee, Almighty God, that these our gifts, being dedicated to thy service, may be used for thy glory and the good of thy Church and people; through Jesus Christ our Lord.

A retreat or quiet day 1777

O LORD Jesus Christ, who didst say to thy disciples, Come ye apart into a desert place and rest awhile: Grant, we beseech thee, to thy servants now gathered together, so to seek thee whom our souls desire to love, that we may both find thee and be found of thee; and grant such love and such wisdom to accompany the words which shall be spoken in thy name, that they may not fall to the ground, but may be helpful in leading us onward through the toils of our pilgrimage to that rest which remaineth to the people of God; where, nevertheless, they rest not day nor night from thy perfect service; who with the Father and the Holy Spirit livest and reignest ever one God, world without end. *R. M. Benson*

1778

O Almighty God, whose blessed Son held communion with thee in the retirement of solitary places: Look mercifully, we beseech thee, upon thy servants who, following his example, do seek in solitude and silence refreshment for our souls and strength for thy service, and grant that we may be abundantly blessed; through the same thy Son Jesus Christ our Lord. *James Wareham*

A parish convention 1779

O Lord and Saviour Jesus Christ, who didst gather round thee thy holy apostles and didst teach them the things concerning the kingdom of God: Grant that all those who come together in this convention may desire to be taught of thee, and to learn those things which thou dost desire to impart to us. Give us the open ear and the willing mind; clear our thoughts of all prejudice; remove all hindrances to the glad acceptance of thy holy will; and train us in all godliness of life, that we may be further equipped to serve thee and glorify thy holy name; who art with the Father and the Holy Spirit one God, world without end.

A parish conference 1780

We thank thee, heavenly Father, for the conference which lies before us and which we now begin in thy name. Give us quiet in our minds, seriousness in the depth of our hearts, and the restful spirit which comes from faith in thee. Bless those who are to instruct us, that their words may possess clarity and power. Bless our listening, and give us grace both to understand and to take to heart all that thou wouldest teach us. Bless our fellowship one with another and make us to realize the unity of the Spirit. So come, Lord, and visit us; manifest thy presence, fulfil thine own purpose, and glorify thy holy name. *Adapted from Student Prayer*

1781

O Lord and Master, who didst take thy disciples apart with thyself, that they might more perfectly learn thy holy will: We pray thee to draw near to us who at this time would draw near to thee. Deepen our fellowship one with another; make us sensitive to the guidance of thy Holy Spirit; and so direct our thoughts and words that thy purpose for our lives and for this parish may be advanced; for the honour and glory of thy name. *Frank Colquhoun*

A parish fellowship 1782

O Lord Christ, who on the night before thy passion didst have a last supper with thine apostles and prayed that they might be one family, united in loyalty to thee and in the service of mankind: Inspire, we pray thee, our fellowship with the spirit of love and sacrifice, that we may be true to thee and to one another, and serve thee gladly in thy Church all the days of our life; to the glory of God the Father. *The Kingdom, the Power, and the Glory**

A mission of teaching 1783

O God of truth and charity, be pleased to use these days of teaching, learning, and discussion to furnish thy Church with men and women committed unto thee. Direct what is said and done in thy name, that it may have success beyond our endeavour; and grant to all so to learn of thee that our faith in thy kingdom, our hope in thy promises, our love towards all men, may be renewed and enlarged; through our Lord and Saviour Jesus Christ. *A Diocesan Service Book*

Parish visitors 1784

O Lord Jesus Christ, who didst bless thy home at Nazareth with love and understanding and with the labour of thy hands: Let thy blessing, we beseech thee, rest upon all the homes in this parish; open their doors to those who come in thy name, and make all who live in them swift to hear and ready to answer thy call. We ask it in thy name, to whom be glory for ever and ever.

1785

Blessed Lord, who didst send thy disciples into every place whither thou thyself wouldest come: Pour out thy Holy Spirit upon these thy servants as they go forth in thy name, that they may humbly prepare the way before thee as messengers of thy peace; for the praise of thy holy name.

Bell ringers
1786

Grant, O Lord, we pray thee, that those who are appointed to ring the bells of this house of prayer may do it worthily and to thy glory; and that those who shall be called by the ringing of these bells to worship thee may enter into thy gates with thanksgiving, and into thy courts with praise; through Jesus Christ our Lord.

Music and worship
1787

O God, who hast bidden us to worship thee with the sound of the trumpet, with psaltery and harp, with stringed instruments and organs, and also to be glad in thee and to shout for joy: Help us to contrive by all means to set forth thy most worthy praise, that the art of man may be tuned to the glory of God; for the sake of him whose voice is as the sound of many waters, Jesus Christ thy Son our Lord.
J. R. W. Stott

Before a recital of music
1788

O Holy and eternal God, Father, Son, and Holy Spirit, whom all the companies of heaven laud and adore: Graciously vouchsafe to receive the offering we are about to make; and so bless us, as we magnify thee upon earth with music and the voice of melody, that hereafter we may sing the new song in the heavenly city; where thou reignest, almighty, all glorious, world without end.
King's College Chapel, Cambridge

1789

Almighty God, who hast given unto men power to invent for themselves instruments of music, and skill to use them in sounding forth thy praise: Grant that the music heard in this thy house may kindle a spirit of devotion in us thy servants; that we, taking our part in prayer and praise to thee here on earth, may hereafter be admitted to thy heavenly temple, and join in the everlasting songs of the redeemed around thy throne; through Jesus Christ our Lord.
Salisbury Cathedral

1790

O Lord Jesus Christ, who art adored by the holy angels in heaven, yet dost deign to receive the praises of thy Church on earth: We beseech thee to bless and accept this our offering of music; and grant that the hearts of all who hear may be refreshed, and uplifted to thy throne in heaven; who livest and reignest with the Father and the Holy Spirit, ever one God, world without end.

Religious drama: before rehearsal — 1791

Almighty God, Creator and Sustainer of all things, who art pleased to receive the gifts thy children bring of thine own bounty: Regard us, we beseech thee, with thy favour who purpose to present this play in thy name; grant us the help of thy Holy Spirit, that we may be enabled to create the characters we are to play; and make us one body, working together in love to thy glory; through Jesus Christ our Lord. *Religious Drama Society*

Religious drama: before performance — 1792

Before our play begins we offer it to thee, O Lord, beseeching thee to accept our good intention, for our desire is to do thee service. Assist our art, we pray thee, that by thy grace we may offer our best to thee; and grant that in fellowship with our audience we may rejoice in thy goodness and make manifest thy praise; through Jesus Christ our Lord. *Religious Drama Society*

A sale of work — 1793

O Gracious God, be pleased, we pray thee, to accept the offerings of us thine unworthy servants to-day; and grant that as we work together in Christian fellowship, thy name may be hallowed, thy kingdom be extended, and thy will be done; through Jesus Christ our Lord. *J. R. W. Stott*

Laying of a foundation stone — 1794

O Eternal Lord God, mighty in power, of infinite majesty, whom the heaven of heavens cannot contain, much less the walls of temples made with hands; yet who hast promised to be present wherever two or three are gathered in thy name: Direct and bless, we pray thee, our efforts to build this house for thy worship and service, and grant us such success as may tend to thy glory and the salvation of thy people; through Jesus Christ our Lord.

Canadian Prayer Book

1795

O Lord Jesus Christ, who art the one foundation of thy Church and its chief corner-stone: Bless the laying of this stone in thy name, we humbly beseech thee; and be thou the beginning, the increase, and the consummation of this work which is undertaken to thy glory; who livest and reignest with the Father and the Holy Spirit, one God, world without end.

Dedication of a house 1796

O Merciful Saviour, who with thy presence didst hallow an earthly home at Nazareth: Send thy blessing, we beseech thee, on all who dwell in this house; that, being preserved both in body and soul, they may offer to thee a faithful and willing service; who livest and reignest with the Father and the Holy Spirit, one God, world without end.

1797

O Heavenly Father, whose blessed Son was a welcome guest in the house of his friends at Bethany: Visit, we beseech thee, this home with thy blessing; and grant that all who dwell herein may be of one heart and soul, and remain in true love and peace together, according to thy laws; through the same our Lord and Saviour Jesus Christ.

Before a borough council meeting 1798

O Eternal Lord God, from whom alone cometh wisdom and understanding: We beseech thee to direct aright the minds of those who are about to take counsel together on matters pertaining to the common life of this borough; that in all their deliberations and decisions they may faithfully discharge the duties of their office, and ever promote the health, the safety, and the well-being of those whom they seek to serve; for the honour and glory of thy holy name.

Frank Colquhoun

ACKNOWLEDGMENTS

THE Editor wishes to express his thanks to the following for granting him permission to reproduce material of which they are the publishers, authors, or copyright owners:

The British Broadcasting Corporation for prayers from *New Every Morning*.

The Committee on Public Worship and Aids to Devotion of the Church of Scotland for prayers from *The Book of Common Order of the Church of Scotland*; *Prayers for the Christian Year (Revised Edition)*; *Let Us Pray*; and *Service Book for the Young*.

The Publications Committee of the Episcopal Church in Scotland for prayers from the Scottish Prayer Book.

The Standing Committee of the General Synod of the Church of Ireland for prayers from the Irish Prayer Book.

The General Synod of the Anglican Church of Canada and the Cambridge University Press for prayers from the Canadian Prayer Book.

The General Convention of the Protestant Episcopal Church in the U.S.A. for prayers from the American Prayer Book.

The Synod of Bishops of the Church of the Province of South Africa for prayers from the South African Prayer Book.

His Grace the Metropolitan of the Church of India, Pakistan, Burma, and Ceylon for a prayer from the C.I.P.B.C. Prayer Book.

The Synod of the Church of South India for prayers from *The Book of Common Worship of the Church of South India*.

Oxford University Press for prayers from *A Diocesan Service Book*, edited and ordered by Bishop Leslie Stannard Hunter; *Daily Prayer*, compiled by Eric Milner-White and G. W. Briggs; *The Daily Service (Revised Edition)*; *A Book of Public Worship*; *Divine Service* by W. E. Orchard; *A New Prayer Book*; and *The Kingdom, the Power, and the Glory*.

The Society for Promoting Christian Knowledge for prayers from *A Procession of Passion Prayers* by Eric Milner-White; *Euchologium Anglicanum* by John Wallis and Leslie Styler; *Black Letter Saints' Days* by W. H. Frere; *The Children's Service* by C. S. Woodward; *The Splendour of God*; and *Acts of Devotion*.

Messrs. A. R. Mowbray for prayers from *The Prayer Manual*, compiled by Frederick B. Macnutt (used by permission of Mrs.

Macnutt); *After the Third Collect,* edited by Eric Milner-White; *Sursum Corda;* and *The Priest's Book of Private Devotion.*

Student Christian Movement Press for prayers from *Student Prayer; A Book of Prayers for Students; A Devotional Diary,* arranged by J. H. Oldham; and *A Prayer Book for Juniors* by Margaret Cropper.

Independent Press for prayers from *A Book of Services and Prayers.*

Messrs. Allenson for prayers from *Prayers for Common Worship,* edited by James Ferguson.

Messrs. Rivingtons for prayers from *The Sanctuary.*

Scripture Union and C.S.S.M. for prayers from *Windylow Prayer Book* by Ruby Cleeve.

United Society for the Propagation of the Gospel for prayers from *Prayers of the World-wide Church.*

Church Missionary Society for prayers from *With all our Strength.*

The Epworth Press for a prayer from the *Book of Offices* of the Methodist Church.

The Faith Press for a prayer from *The Unfolding Year,* compiled by Francis W. Wheeler.

Iliffe Books for prayers from *Country Services* by D. L. Couper.

The Most Rev. George Appleton for prayers from *Daily Prayer and Praise* (by permission of Lutterworth Press) and *In His Name* (by permission of Edinburgh House Press).

The Most Rev. A. E. Morris for prayers from *Anglican Altar Services, 1941.*

The Right Rev. Leslie S. Hunter for prayers from *A Diocesan Service Book* and other sources; and for prayers by the Rev. Dr. John Hunter from *Devotional Services.*

The Bishop of Oxford for prayers from the *Oxford Diocesan Service Book.*

The Bishop of Salisbury for prayers from *The Salisbury Book of Occasional Offices.*

The Bishop of Southwark for prayers in use in the Southwark Diocese.

Mrs. Frances Temple for prayers by Archbishop William Temple.

Mrs. Beatrice Robinson for prayers by Canon Arthur W. Robinson.

Mrs. L. A. Anson for prayers by Canon Harold Anson.

The Rev. Harold Riley for prayers from *A Book of Daily Prayer* (S.P.C.K.).

The Rev. Dr. Leslie D. Weatherhead for prayers from *A Private House of Prayer* (Hodder and Stoughton).

The Rev. James M. Todd and the Rev. Dr. H. F. Leatherland for prayers from *A Book of Services and Prayers* (Independent Press).

ACKNOWLEDGMENTS

The Dean of St. Paul's for a prayer in use at St. Paul's Cathedral. The Dean of King's for prayers in use at King's College, Cambridge. The Most Rev. Archbishop Lord Fisher of Lambeth; The Rt. Rev. W. L. Anderson; the Rt. Rev. Douglas H. Crick; The Rt. Rev. Joost de Blank; The Rt. Rev. R. Ambrose Reeves; The Rev. A. S. T. Fisher; The Rev. Preb. P. N. Gilliat; The Rev. O. K. de Berry; The Rev. M. A. P. Wood; The Registrar of the Convocation of York.

Advisory Council for the Church's Ministry; The Central Board of Finance of the Church of England; The National Society; The Mothers' Union; Church of England Men's Society; The Church Army; The Royal School of Church Music; The Church's Ministry among the Jews; The Bible Reading Fellowship; Student Christian Movement; Inter-Varsity Fellowship; The Girl Guides Association; Radius (Religious Drama Society of Great Britain); The Guild of Health; The Guild of St. Raphael; Industrial Christian Fellowship.

The text of the 1662 Book of Common Prayer is Crown copyright, and the extracts used herein are reproduced by permission.

INDEX OF SOURCES

References are to the numbers prefixed to the prayers

BIBLE REFERENCES

INDEX OF SUBJECTS